Ingredient Equivalents

	Amount	Equivalent
Apple	1 medium (6 ounces)	1 cup sliced or chopped
Apricots	dried, 5 ounces	1 cup
Asparagus	1 pound	16 to 20 stalks
Beans	dried, 1 pound	2 1/4 cups dried; 5 to 6 cups cooked
Beans	green, 1 pound	3 cups cut-up
Bread	1 1/2 slices	1 cup soft crumbs
Broccoli	3/4 pound	4 cups florets
Butter	1 pound	4 sticks or two cups
Cabbage	1 pound	4 cups shredded
Carrots	1 1/2 medium	1 cup shredded
Cauliflower	1 pound	3 cups florets
Celery	2 med. stalks	1 cup thinly sliced or chopped
Cheese	hard, 1/4 pound	1 cup shredded
Coconut	3 ounces	1 1/3 cups shredded
Corn	2 ears	1 cup kernels
Cucumber	1 medium	1 1/3 cup chopped
Cranberries	1 pound	4 cups
Eggplant	1 pound	2 1/2 cups chopped
Egg, large	1	1/4 cup cholesterol-free egg product
Flour, all-purpose	1 pound	3 1/2 to 4 cups
Lemon	1 medium	2 to 3 tablespoons juice; 1/2 to 1 tablespoon grated peel

	Amount	Equivalent
Lettuce	1 pound	6 cups torn leaves
Meat	6 ounces	1 cup chopped pieces
Mushrooms	1 pound	6 cups sliced
Nuts	1 pound	3 to 4 cups whole; 4 cups chopped
Onion, yellow	1 average	1 cup chopped
Orange	1 medium	1/3 to 1/2 cup juice; 1 to 2 tablespoons grated rind
Parsnips	1 1/4 pound	3 cups sliced
Pasta	uncooked, 8 ounces	4 cups cooked (average)
Peas	in pod, 1 pound	1 cup shelled
Pepper, bell	1 average	1 cup chopped
Pineapple	fresh, 3 pounds	4 cups cubes
Potatoes	1 1/2 pounds	4 large; 10 to 12 small
Pumpkin	1 pound	1 cup mashed
Rice	1 cup uncooked	3 to 4 cups cooked
Spinach	6 ounces	4 cups uncooked
Squash	winter, 1 pound	1 cup mashed
Strawberries	1 quart	4 cups sliced
Sugar	white, 1 pound	2 cups
	brown, 1 pound	2 1/4 cups packed
	10X (confectioners,) sifted, 1 pound	3 1/2 to 4 cups
Tomato	1 large	1 cup chopped
Zucchini	1 medium	2 cups sliced, chopped, or shredded

Vegetables
for *Vitality*

240 delicious recipes to add vegetables to every meal

Reader's Digest

The Reader's Digest Association, Inc.
Pleasantville, New York/Montreal

READER'S DIGEST PROJECT STAFF

Senior Editor *Nancy Shuker*
Senior Design Director *Elizabeth Tunnicliffe*
Production Technology Manager *Douglas A. Croll*
Manufacturing Manager *John L. Cassidy*
Production Coordinator *Leslie Ann Caraballo*

READER'S DIGEST HEALTH PUBLISHING

Editor in Chief and
Publishing Director *Neil Wertheimer*
Managing Editor *Suzanne G. Beason*
Art Director *Michele Laseau*
Marketing Director *Dawn Nelson*
Vice President and General Manager *Keira Krausz*

READER'S DIGEST ASSOCIATION, INC.

President, North America
Global Editor-in-Chief *Eric W. Schrier*

CONTRIBUTORS

Project Editor *Susan McQuillan*
Recipe Developers/Retesters *Elaine Khosrova, Michael Krondl, Anton Li, Wendye Pardue, Michele Peters*
Nutrition Analysis *Patty Santelli*
Recipe Editor *David Ricketts*
Copy Editors *Jeanette Gingold, Steven Frankl*
Indexer *Nan Badgett*
Design *Susan Bacchetti*
Production *Kate Frattarola*
Photographers *Sang An, Elizabeth Watt, Andrew McCul, Gus Filgate, William Lingwood, Martin Brigdale, Sean Myers, Alan Richardson, David Murray, Jules Selmes, Mark Ferri, Beatric daCosta, Lisa Koenig, Steven Mark Needham, Steven Mays; Christine Bronico, Photodisc/Getty Images, BrandX Pictures, Getty Images*

Library of Congress Cataloging-in-Publication Data

Vegetables for vitality / Reader's Digest ; editor, Nancy Shuker.— 1st ed.
p. cm.
Includes index.
ISBN 0-7621-0487-2 (hardcover)
1. Cookery (Vegetables) I. Shuker, Nancy. II. Reader's Digest Association.
TX801.V434 2004
641.6'5—dc22
2003027463

Address any comments about *Vegetables for Vitality* to:
The Reader's Digest Association, Inc.
Managing Editor, Home & Health Books
Reader's Digest Road
Pleasantville, NY 10570-7000

To order copies of *Vegetables for Vitality*, call 1-800-846-2100

Visit our website at **rd.com**

Printed in China

1 3 5 7 9 10 8 6 4 2
US3905/IC

contents

Introduction

Ask someone "What's for dinner?" and typically, the answer is chicken, hamburger, pork chops, or some other meat entrée. The reason is obvious: So many of us consider meat the heart of dinner, the part that's most special, most satisfying.

The follow-up question—"What's for dessert?"— is also obvious. After all, most everyone loves the sinful sweetness and richness of a good cake or ice cream. Who can resist?

With *Vegetables for Vitality,* we intend to introduce a new food question to your daily life: "What's for vegetable?" Give it a try. Don't be embarrassed.

Why this question? Is it that vegetables are incredibly healthy, the perfect foods for energy, weight loss, and disease prevention? Not really, even though all that's true. No, the reason you should ask "What's for vegetable?" with each meal is that when prepared well, vegetables are absolutely delicious! Vegetables have crunch and color and personality. They pair well with each other, with meats, with pastas. They are the perfect recipient for herbs, spices, sauces, and other flavorings. They are inexpensive, easy to prepare, and delightful on the plate. Best of all, you can eat an almost unlimited amount of them, thanks to their low-calorie, high-fiber, high-nutrient makeup!

Vegetables for Vitality is a complete guide to getting more vegetables into your diet. It is rich with meat, seafood, and pasta dishes made tastier and healthier with vegetables. Indeed, you'll find an extraordinary collection of breakfast dishes, appetizers, main dishes for lunch or dinner, side dishes, and rich desserts, all made with at least one vegetable. Some recipes are classics, using traditional ingredients and cooking methods. Others are modern spin-offs of old favorites that use surprising ingredients or more healthful cooking techniques but don't sacrifice the slightest bit of flavor.

Of course, you'll also find some pretty amazing vegetable-only recipes too. And along the way, you'll learn the extraordinary health benefits of vegetables, and loads of tips for how to buy, store, and prepare them to best advantage. In particular, the last portion of this book is a complete A–Z guide to vegetables that we think you'll find invaluable.

We created this book for all types of eaters, all types of health levels, all levels of cooking expertise. We urge you to take the step toward more vegetable-rich cooking, both for your pleasure and your health. And someday soon, talking with your loved one on a weekday afternoon, you'll find yourself asking, "What's for vegetable tonight?"

—*The Editors*

recipe ICONS

When appropriate, recipes in this book are flagged with icons:

QUICK
The recipe can be prepared in 30 minutes or less, from start to finish.

LOW-FAT
Less than 30 percent of the recipe's calories come from fat.

MAKE AHEAD
The dish can be made in advance and reheated. Or there is just one small step needed before serving, such as adding a last-minute ingredient or a garnish.

How to Use Nutrition Information *Compare the nutrition analysis at the end of each recipe with the following guidelines established by health experts to design daily menus that are within healthful limits.*

DAILY NUTRITION INFORMATION						
	Calories	Protein	*Fat	Cholesterol	**Sodium	**Fiber
WOMEN	2,000	50 grams	66 grams	300 mg	2,400 mg	20-35 mg
MEN	2,700	63 grams	90 grams	300 mg	2,400 mg	20-35 mg

*Limit to 30% of total calories   **American Heart Association recommended limit for healthy people.

THE JOYS OF
vegetables

A BOUNTY OF
choices

If you cook or shop for food, then you most certainly have noticed the quiet revolution that has taken place in the world of vegetables over the past two decades. Never before have there been so many choices, so many variations, so great a year-round bounty. Even the most mundane grocery chain outlet may carry as many as four kinds of cabbage, five different potatoes, and six types of lettuce. How about the tomato bin, with its cherry-, grape-, and plum-shaped varieties and vine-ripened, greenhouse, and heirloom choices? Or the mushroom section, with its mix of shapes, colors, and sizes?

Then there are the newcomers to many grocers' shelves: baby bok choy and other Chinese cabbages; okra and cooking greens; broccoli rabe and broccolini; shockingly colored beans and squashes and carrots. For the open-minded cook, it is a paradise of choices.

Many forces are driving this explosion in vegetable choices. Among the biggest, of course, is our growing knowledge of the health benefits of vegetables. As a basic nutrient, we now know, nothing beats a vegetable. It provides outstanding fuel, fiber, vitamins, and nutrients in a truly low-calorie form. Then there are the health benefits beyond daily nutrition. One of the most exciting areas of health research is in phytochemicals— the natural chemicals in vegetables that have surprising healing powers. In recent years, we've discovered that vegetables have nutrients that bolster immunity, battle cancer, improve your skin, reduce stress, and much more. We'll cover all this in a few pages.

Thanks to this new evidence, the medical world—as well as the government—began campaigning in the 1980s to get people to eat "5 a day" servings of fruits and vegetables. Enter the world of economics. Business has figured out that people want vegetables year-round; thanks to our new appreciation for vegetables, we don't accept empty produce bins in February anymore. So whereas we once drew our vegetables primarily from the warmer parts of the United States— California, Arizona, Texas, and Florida—enterprising food distributors now reach for produce from around the world, and in particular, Central and South America.

Don't want produce that's shipped from thousands of miles away? The consolidation of farmlands into large agribusiness conglomerates, designed to supply giant food processors as well as grocery chain produce departments, has caused an unpredicted benefit for food lovers: a steady and welcome growth in farmers' markets across the country. From New York City's Union Square to Seattle's Pike Place, individual concessionaires bring in their own freshly picked, vine-ripened produce to sell directly to consumers. This has breathed new life into many small farms.

And as anyone in business knows, the modern marketplace is always interested in the next new item. So suddenly the shelves are full of interesting new varieties of vegetables. Whereas broccoli rabe was hardly heard of a few years ago, today it is a common staple. Same goes for arugula, baby spinach, grape tomatoes, and napa cabbage.

The result: A tantalizing mix of vegetables, traditional and new, is widely available.

SOME FARMERS rely on cutting-edge science; others have gone natural. Never before has there been so much debate about how vegetables are grown.

OUR SOURCES FOR
vegetables

Most vegetables in North America are raised on large farms that specialize in one or two varieties of a particular plant. The varieties destined for market rather than a food processing plant have been bred to withstand long trips to market and to have a lengthy shelf life without losing their looks. A University of California study suggests that produce grown in the United States averages 1,300 miles of travel to market.

The farms that raise these vegetables are remarkably efficient operations that skillfully use large machinery, irrigation systems, chemical pesticides, herbicides, and fertilizers to ensure bumper crops. The result is beautiful, nutritious vegetables with very little flavor.

The Organic Alternative

Many people prefer to buy organic vegetables that are grown under more environmentally friendly conditions than on traditional commercial farms; that is, without the use of chemical pesticides, herbicides, and fertilizers.

In the United States, organic foods are now regulated and certified by the U.S. Department of Agriculture (USDA). A USDA organic seal may appear on foods and food products that are classified as "100 percent organic" (made with 100 percent organic ingredients) or "organic" (at least 95 percent organic by weight). Food products that contain between 70 percent and 95 percent organic ingredients cannot bear the USDA label but can display the statement "made with organic ingredients" on the front of the package. Foods that contain less than 70 percent organic ingredients cannot bear the USDA label or make a claim. They can simply list certified organic ingredients with other ingredients. Before any food product can be labeled "organic," a government inspector visits the farm to make sure it meets USDA standards for producing organic food.

Some small organic farmers, however, find the cost of government certification prohibitive and the required paperwork too overwhelming, so they may not participate in the certification program. As a result, it is possible for foods to be organic but not carry a government certification seal. These noncertified foods are often sold by small growers at farmers' markets. They may label their foods as organic or you can discuss farming methods with them.

Until recently, organic vegetables could only be found in health food stores, small natural food markets, and private farm stands. Slowly but surely, as farmers' markets and food cooperatives have proliferated, organic foods have worked their way into the mainstream. In fact, a new breed of supermarket has sprouted up around the country that specializes in so-called natural foods, which are mostly organic.

Biotechnology and the Food Supply

The business of agriculture, like most other businesses, entered a new age of technology in the twentieth century. Biology, biochemistry, chemical engineering, genetics, and computer science merged to form the science of food biotechnology, which helps create new forms of plant and animal life, as well as new means of enhancing the quality and quantity of agricultural products that are commercially produced.

Genetically engineered foods, sometimes referred to as genetically modified organisms (GMOs) or genetically modified foods (GMFs), are a controversial result of this science. Genetic engineering is the transfer of genes among plants and animals, allowing scientists to copy a gene for a desirable trait in one organism and implant it in another. Genetic engineering has produced corn that is resistant to insects, dairy cows that produce more milk, rice that is rich in beta-carotene, and tomatoes that can ripen more fully on the vine before they are shipped. While these all sound like positive advancements in agriculture, many consumer groups have concerns about the safety of "transgenic" foods.

A major concern is the possibility that introducing a gene from one organism into another may cause unexpected allergic reactions in susceptible people. Another concern is that genetic engineering will disrupt the natural ecological balance of the planet. Some critics fear what they call "gene pollution," or the escape of genetically engineered genes into the wild through natural cross-pollination. Although genetic engineering can be used to increase the nutritional value of some foods, there is also concern that it will diminish the healthfulness of others.

In the United States, where 70 percent of the world's genetically engineered food is grown, the government has concluded that, overall, genetically engineered foods are just as safe as other foods and therefore don't require special labeling.

There are actually very few whole genetically engineered foods on the market, but many processed foods, such as vegetable oils and breakfast cereals made with soy and corn products, contain genetically modified ingredients. Consumer groups around the world support mandatory labeling of genetically

community
supported agriculture

One of the healthiest trends in farming these days is the Community Supported Agriculture (CSA) arrangement. With a CSA, you are in effect buying shares in a farm's crops. Typically, you pay $400 to $600 in advance, which allows the farmer to buy seed and equipment and pay wages to his helpers to get the planting done. Come late spring, you will start reaping a weekly allotment of locally grown, seasonal produce from the farm.

Some CSAs also require 6 to 12 hours of work, either on the farm or helping with administration or distribution. If the farm is nearby, chances are that you will have to pick up your own share of bounty each week, but you may also get an opportunity to pick some unexpected bonus crops for yourself—from raspberries to zinnias. On the downside, if it was a bad year for broccoli, you just won't get any.

Although paying hundreds of dollars for a six-month supply of produce may sound expensive, research at the University of Massachusetts suggests that it is about half what you would spend in a supermarket for the same types of produce, not nearly so fresh or nutritious. A typical share for a week in June in the Northeast might include a bunch of baby beets, a bunch of spinach, a quart of sugar snap peas, three heads of lettuce, a quarter-pound of baby arugula, a bunch of red Russian kale, a bunch of baby Oriental turnips, and a quart of strawberries.

There are many forms of CSA; food co-ops, for example, qualify. All, however, are devoted to keeping small farmers going and the food supply diverse, nutritious, and plentiful.

engineered foods to allow those with preferences to avoid these products, if they wish.

Food Irradiation

Irradiation is a method of food preservation that uses ionizing radiation to destroy disease-causing bacteria and other pathogens on food. Also known as *cold pasteurization*, irradiation can be used to make fresh and dried foods such as meat, poultry, fruits, vegetables, herbs, and spices safer for consumers. Radiation extends the shelf life of fresh vegetables by delaying ripening in tomatoes and inhibiting sprouting in onions and potatoes.

All irradiated products carry a green, flowerlike symbol called a radura on their labels. This is an international symbol for identifying foods that have been irradiated. Food products that contain a minor irradiated ingredient, such as an herb or a spice, are not required to carry a logo.

Foods that can be irradiated in the United States include spices, domestically grown fruits and vegetables, and fruits imported from tropical areas. Because of consumer concern, the actual use of food irradiation in the United States is limited.

Hydroponic Farming

Hydroponics is a method of growing plants in nutrient-enriched (fertilized) water, rather than in soil. This technique is most popular in Europe, but commercial hydroponic greenhouses can be found all over the world. Most of the hydroponic farms in the United States are small, family operations that do business with local markets.

The most popular and widely cultivated hydroponic crops are tomatoes, cucumbers, lettuces, and herbs, because they are the most cost effective. Hydroponic farming is expensive, especially when crops are grown in greenhouses that must be heated or cooled. The nutrient mix given to hydroponic crops can be twice as expensive as field fertilizer. It is also a time-consuming growing technique that requires constant attention and special skills.

But the rewards are many to farmers who choose soil-less crops. Hydroponically grown plants are larger and grow faster than those grown in soil because they routinely receive high-grade nutrients and their growing conditions are so well controlled. The growing season is extended because the plants are often grown indoors, where temperature,

VEGETABLES FOR VITALITY

humidity, and light are constantly monitored and adjusted. Hydroponic crops can be farmed in places where there is no suitable soil for growing similar crops. Since they grow in water, hydroponic crops use much less extra water than crops grown in fields. Perhaps the greatest commercial advantage is that, with a hydroponic setup, significantly more crops can be grown in less space. A hydroponic farm can yield up to 30 times more tomatoes per acre than a conventional farm because the plants can be grown much closer together.

Pick Your Own

Short of growing your own, there's no better way to get the freshest fruits and vegetables than by visiting a pick-your-own farm. These farms give everyone an opportunity to connect with local farmers and their land, while learning firsthand about where food comes from and how it grows. They also offer small farmers a way to stay in business.

Harvests generally run from May through October, but some farms are open year-round. At one farm, you may pick carrots and cauliflower at the end of May, berries in June and July, corn or tomatoes in August. You can visit a farm in September to pluck potatoes from the ground and apples from the tree, and in October, the perfect pumpkin from the patch.

Larger farms offer hayrides, corn mazes, and other family events to round out your visit. Expect to pay an admission fee there. In general, though, you pay on a price-per-pound basis. To find a pick-your-own farm near you, check the phone book, do an Internet search for "pick-your-own farms" and the state you live in, or contact your state Department of Agriculture or Cooperative Extension Service. Here are some tips to help you get the most out of your visit:

- Always contact growers a day or two before going, and then again on the excursion day, for up-to-date information on picking hours, what's picking that day, the field conditions, and the current prices.
- Many pick-your-own farms do not provide bushels or containers. Ask in advance, and be prepared to bring your own buckets.
- It's a farm out there. Be prepared for lots of sunshine, bugs, mud, and animals. That means rugged clothing and shoes you don't mind getting filthy, suntan lotion, bug repellent, and bottles of water.

- Remember: This is probably a small family farm, eking out a modest income. Treat it with the respect it deserves: Follow the rules, don't be wasteful of the produce, pick up your garbage, and keep the kids from going too wild.
- Don't expect picture-perfect, pristine produce. This is not a conglomerate farm that uses chemicals and genetic engineering to create perfectly round tomatoes. What the goods lack in appearance, they will more than make up for in flavor.
- Don't bring pets. The cows and chickens will appreciate that.

All vegetables should be cleaned before eating, especially when the skin will be eaten. Some vegetables, like mushrooms, spinach, and potatoes, hold on to the dirt they were grown in and require more careful cleaning than others.

to clean

- **leafy greens:** Soak them in a sink filled with cold water, swirling the leaves around a few times to be sure all grit and sand is removed. Remove the greens from the water with your hands and then let the water drain. Inspect the greens, both visually and by touch. If still dirty, repeat. Greens straight from the farm may require multiple cleanings.

- **mushrooms:** Wipe them with a dry paper towel or use a soft-bristled brush designed for the purpose to remove surface dirt. Avoid using water to clean mushrooms or they will become soggy.

- **root vegetables** such as potatoes, sweet potatoes, and carrots: Scrub well with a vegetable brush to remove all pockets of dirt. Cut out any moldy, soggy, or soft parts with a knife. You should not have to peel carrots unless the outside is dried out or unusually filthy.

- **smooth vegetables** such as zucchini, tomatoes, eggplant, and peppers: Hold under cool water and rub the surface gently to remove residual dirt and chemicals. No matter how clean they look, always do a thorough cleaning. You cannot see all the dirt or fertilizers that may be there.

NOT ONLY has the way vegetables are grown undergone major changes; so has the way they are sold. No longer are you reliant on the chain grocery store for produce.

FARMERS'
markets

>> TO FIND A FARMERS' MARKET NEAR YOU, check the U.S. Department of Agriculture's National Directory of Farmers Markets, online at **http://www.ams.usda.gov/farmersmarkets/map.htm.**

Today suburbanites and city dwellers alike can enjoy—in an unprecedented way—the benefits of truly fresh and varied produce from the many small farmers who are willing to load up their trucks in the wee hours of the morning and drive to urban or suburban green-markets to sell their own vegetables, fruits, and other agricultural products.

In fact, one of the largest farmers' market programs in the United States is in New York City. Started in 1976, the Big Apple's Greenmarket program attracts some 200 farmers from New York State, Connecticut, New Jersey, and Pennsylvania to 42 locations in the city's five boroughs. These farmers, who truck in their produce on a regular schedule, serve as many as 250,000 customers—including 105 restaurateurs—a week. Over the course of a season, New York's greenmarket shoppers can pick from as many as 47 varieties of peas and beans, 120 varieties of tomatoes, and 350 varieties of peppers.

The market management rents space to farmers at its various sites and, with a council of participating farmers and consumers, makes sure that all the products brought into the market are homegrown.

A Friendly Way to Shop

Wandering through farmers' markets is not only a great way to ferret out fresh, local foods; it is also a wonderful opportunity to get to know the men and women who grow them. They can tell you about the different varieties of produce that they grow and the best ways to serve their vegetables and fruits or use them in recipes. They will also alert you to the crops that will be coming in the next week. It's no wonder that greenmarkets have become so popular that they rank as top tourist attractions in many cities.

Farmers, consumers, and the community at large all benefit from farmers' markets. Many small farmers are in business only because of the popularity of urban open-air markets. With no middlemen, farmers are able to charge low prices and still make a profit because they keep the money that would otherwise be lost to shipping, distribution, and marketing through supermarkets. As a result, city residents enjoy such culinary pleasures as corn picked the same day, vine-ripened tomatoes, tree-ripened peaches, and richly flavored honey, straight from the hive, all at fair prices.

A Boost to Nutrition

There are many ways vendors at farmers' markets help promote good health besides selling fresh, seasonal food. Small farmers often offer unusual varieties of

how to shop at the farmers' market

- Go early in the day. The market is likely to be less crowded and you will have the "pick of the crop."

- Browse before you buy. Wander around the market to see everything that is offered and to compare quality and prices.

- Talk to the vendors. Many market stands are manned by the farmers or producers themselves. They can provide ideas, tips, and sometimes even recipes for using their products.

- Plan your meals around what's available. Farmers' markets sell seasonal, locally grown vegetables and fruits. Whatever is there is at its peak, so it's best to see what's available rather than shop with a set menu in mind.

- Bring a large shopping bag or cart.

fruits and vegetables that can't be found in regular supermarkets, because they aren't grown on the larger commercial farms.

Local elementary schools often take field trips to farmers' markets, so the children can learn more about food and farming directly from the people who raise the crops. Where else will they see Brussels sprouts attached to their stem? Or eight kinds of potatoes at a single stand? Or carrots in four different colors—yellow, white, red, and orange?

Farmers' markets do more than provide fresh food and preserve a tradition of small family farms. They help bring excitement and pride to the areas where they are located. A food market can revitalize a failing neighborhood by filling it with people and making it safer. In many cities, the presence of a farmers' market has brought about neighborhood improvements and stimulated further commercial development in the area. Farmers' markets have also benefited many communities by donating impressive amounts of food to shelters and programs for feeding the poor.

VEGETABLES AS HEALTH
superstars

When visiting a grocery store, it's hard to avoid the "Five a Day" campaign. But are you ready for nine a day? The health world is beginning to recommend an even larger number of produce servings in our diet, based on the growing depth of research showing the benefits of eating a produce-rich diet. Here are seven of the most compelling health reasons to eat more vegetables, based on what we know today:

vegetables ❶ PROVIDE GREAT FUEL

Your body needs a very wide range of nutrients for health and daily function. But it only needs one for energy: glucose, commonly known as blood sugar. Your body is equipped to digest most any food into glucose, including fats and protein. But without question, the best source of fuel for your body is the carbohydrates found in vegetables.

The rise of high-protein weight-loss programs has contributed to a lot of confusion over whether starches or carbohydrates are as good for you as once thought. Rest easy. While there is truth that eating too many simple carbohydrates (foods easily converted to glucose, such as white flour, sugar, and white rice) causes blood sugar spurts and can contribute to weight gain, that doesn't hold true for most vegetables. The carbohydrates in vegetables are usually complex, meaning they need to be broken down substantially before they can be available to the cells for fuel. And last we heard, virtually no doctor has a problem with a diet rich in complex carbs.

In fact, nutrition experts continue to recommend getting up to 60 percent of your daily calories from carbohydrates, particularly the complex carbohydrates found in grains, beans, and such starchy vegetables as corn, peas, winter squash, and potatoes.

vegetables ❷ ARE RICH IN FIBER

Fiber, simply defined, is the stuff in a plant that your body cannot digest. On the surface, it would seem that fiber would provide little benefit, as it passes undigested through your body. But the opposite is true. There are two types of fiber—soluble and insoluble—and each has unique benefits.

"Soluble" refers to something that dissolves in water. Soluble fiber mixes with water and food in the digestive tract to form a gooey gel that slows digestion and makes blood sugar enter the bloodstream more gradually—a particularly good benefit for people with type 2 diabetes. This gel also binds with fats and cholesterol, making it beneficial for the heart.

Insoluble fiber has many benefits as well. It creates a feeling of fullness, making it important for weight loss; it helps bulk up stools, preventing constipation; it cleans the digestive tract as it passes through, which doctors believe may help prevent gastrointestinal diseases such as diverticulosis and colon cancer.

As you would surmise, vegetables and grains are a great source of fiber. In particular, cauliflower, green beans, and potatoes are rich in the fiber you need.

vegetables ❸ PROVIDE QUALITY PROTEIN

Although the proteins supplied by vegetables and other plant foods are considered "incomplete" when compared to animal sources, they find each other in the body, hook up, and form complete proteins that are equal in quality to protein from meat. A diet that includes a wide variety of vegetables, grains, and beans supplies the nine essential amino acids necessary to stock the pool. That's why a vegetarian diet can provide all the protein a person needs.

vegetables ④ ARE VIRTUALLY FAT-FREE

Reducing your total fat intake reduces your risk of developing heart disease, certain cancers, and other chronic diseases. Interestingly, some of the dietary fats that are considered most healthful are oils that come from vegetable sources such as olives and corn. These fats help keep blood cholesterol down, while fats from animal sources tend to raise cholesterol and total fat in the blood.

vegetables ⑤ HELP WITH WEIGHT LOSS

For the reasons listed above and more, vegetables are the perfect food for weight loss. Most vegetables—particularly leafy green ones—are low in calories, and can be eaten in large quantities without adding up very high. Indeed, some diets permit you to eat unlimited green vegetables, since they have so few calories and provide so much nutrition.

Then there's the fiber in vegetables, which makes you feel full more quickly, and which binds with fats as it passes through the digestive tract. Vegetable carbohydrates are mostly complex, meaning they provide great fuel, but in healthy, steady ways.

Even starchy plant foods—such as grains, legumes, sweet potatoes, corn, and winter squash—have their place in a weight-loss program. While they aren't especially low in calories, they are high in fiber and nutrients, and can be very filling in small amounts.

Still not convinced? Then try to find any weight-loss program that doesn't include a hearty level of vegetables. Even the most extreme protein diets call for green vegetables as a major part of your food selection!

vegetables ⑥ SUPPLY CRUCIAL NUTRIENTS

For everyday function, your body needs proteins, fats, and carbohydrates for fuel and cellular growth. Your body also needs vitamins, minerals, and other substances for the chemistry of life—the manufacturing of hormones, the creation of immune cells, the functioning of the brain and nervous system. Your body also needs ingredients like calcium and magnesium for bones and teeth, and iron and potassium for blood.

It's no surprise that vegetables are an outstanding source for all these nutrients. Plants are dense with the minerals, vitamins, and natural ingredients of life. While meats, dairy products, and seafood are a great source of some minerals, such as iron and calcium, they can't touch vegetables when it comes to offering the full menu of important chemicals you need to function.

vegetables ⑦ HELP PREVENT AND CURE DISEASE

For untold centuries, most every human culture has used food as part of the healing process. But only in the past 20 years or so have scientists dived deeply into the science of phytochemicals and the healing power of vegetables, fruits, and grains.

Phytochemicals are natural chemicals in plants that are beneficial to human health. Technically, vitamins and minerals in vegetables are phytochemicals, but the term is used for a whole group of ingredients that have complicated names and very specific usages. For example, broccoli, cabbage, and other green vegetables are rich in chemicals called glucosinolates that research reveals can be used to battle cancer. Garlic and onions are rich in sulfur compounds like allicin that also battle cancer and cholesterol. Peppers are rich in bioflavonoids, which help to neutralize free radicals in the bloodstream.

A single plant food can contain hundreds of these disease-fighting nutrients. These chemicals give vegetables their brilliant colors, distinct flavors, and healthy aromas. They protect the plants from insects, bacteria, viruses, UV light, and other environmental threats. In the human body, their benefits are similarly broad. They help the body dispose of hazardous substances, such as carcinogens and free radicals. They stimulate the body's immune cells and infection-fighting enzymes. They balance hormones, reducing the risk of hormone-related conditions and cancers.

Because phytochemical research is in its infancy, no one has set optimal levels of intake, let alone safety levels. Indeed, many phytochemicals have yet to be identified, named, or studied. While an increasing number of these plant chemicals are being sold in supplement form, doctors maintain that the best thing to do is to eat a diversity of fresh produce, spanning a wide range of colors and sources.

1 Broccoli is not only one of the most popular green vegetables; it is among the healthiest as well. It is a prime source of calcium; vitamins A and C; antioxidant beta-carotene; folate, which helps reduce the chances for cancer and heart disease; insoluble fiber; and potassium. That's a good start. But its super status is based on its many other phytochemicals. They include dithiolethiones, which are anticancer agents; indoles, which fight hormone-related cancers; isothiocyanates, which stimulate cancer-fighting enzymes and neutralize cancer-causing substances, including smoke; lutein, which fights colon cancer and eye diseases; and sulforaphane, which reduces tumor formation and stimulates cancer-fighting enzymes.

2 Brussels sprouts are in the same family as broccoli (a group called cruciferous vegetables) and so contain many of the same vitamins and disease-fighting phytochemicals, including isothiocyanates, indoles, and sulforaphane.

3 Cabbage a third member of the phytochemical-rich cruciferous vegetable family, is thought to reduce hormone-related cancers as well as colon and rectal cancer. Cabbage is also a great source of vitamin C, folate, and carotenoids.

4 Carrots are super sources of beta-carotene, an antioxidant and a precursor to vitamin A, which maintains proper eyesight, normal cell growth, and healthy healthy skin and hair. Carrots are also rich with calcium pectate, which helps remove cholesterol from the body, and insoluble fiber, which prevents constipation.

5 Cauliflower is yet another crucifer that is rich in vitamin C and folate and also provides such phyto-chemicals as indoles and isothiocyanates. In scientific studies, indoles have been shown to interfere with hormones that fuel the growth of breast cancer tumors. Isothiocyanates also protect against cancer by stimulating protective enzymes.

6 Dark leafy greens such as kale, collards, Swiss chard, and spinach contain a host of disease-fighting phytochemicals in addition to rich amounts of vitamin C, bone-building and anticlotting vitamin K, beta-carotene, and fiber. The chlorophyll in these greens may help block the damaging changes that convert healthy cells to precancerous cells. Their indoles may protect against hormone-related cancers. Their isothiocyanates are also thought to protect against some cancers and to inhibit environmental carcinogens. Their sulforaphane may help prevent harmful carcinogens from initiating cancer. Kale and collard greens are also rich sources of lutein and zeaxanthin, which are linked to the prevention of macular degeneration and some types of cancer.

7 Peppers of all types are good sources of vitamin C. Red peppers also contain lutein and zeaxanthin, carotenoids that may lower the risk of age-related blindness due to macular degeneration and cataracts, as

THE BIG TEN

All vegetables are good for you, but some do more than others to keep you healthy. And certain vegetables, like those listed here, are virtual superstars in the world of good nutrition. These are the vegetables to add first and most to your diet, and are the mainstays of the recipes in this book. They contain the macronutrients needed for fuel, the micronutrients needed for daily chemistry, and phytochemicals needed for long-term health.

well as certain forms of cancer. Hot peppers contain concentrated amounts of capsaicin, which is used topically to treat pain and inflammation and can also help inhibit cholesterol formation. Chlorophyll in peppers may protect against environmental carcinogens.

8 Sweet potatoes are very high in beta-carotene, which helps prevent certain cancers (stomach, pancreas, mouth, and gums); potassium, which is associated with lower blood pressure; vitamin B_6, which may help prevent heart disease; vitamin C, which bolsters immunity; and, if eaten with the skin on, insoluble fiber, which prevents constipation and diverticulosis. Sweet potatoes also contain caffeic acid, which may fight cancer and the AIDS virus; cancer-fighting chlorogenic acid; lutein and zeaxanthin to protect against cancer and eye diseases; and cholesterol-lowering plant sterols.

9 Tomatoes and tomato products, such as sauce, paste, puree, and juice, are rich sources of cancer-fighting beta-carotene and immunity-boosting vitamin C. In addition, tomatoes contain lycopene, a carotenoid that suppresses the damage caused by free radicals in the body and is associated with reduced risks of heart attack and prostate cancer; caffeic and ferulic acids, which enhance the body's production of cancer-fighting enzymes; and cancer-protective chlorogenic acid.

10 Winter squash like sweet potatoes, are super-rich in beta-carotene, potassium, vitamin B_6, vitamin C, and lutein. Winter squash has lots of soluble fiber, which helps lower cholesterol, and also contains brain-boosting thiamine and magnesium, a valuable mineral that may help control allergies, heart disease, and kidney stones.

TOP TEN vitamins & minerals

VITAMIN/MINERAL	MAY BE HELPFUL FOR	WHERE TO FIND IT
CALCIUM	osteoporosis, anxiety & stress, high blood pressure, hyperthyroidism, overweight, peri-menopause & menopause, PMS, pregnancy	broccoli, dairy products, salmon or sardines with bones, tofu
FOLATE	anemia, cancer, depression, heart disease, infertility & impotence, insomnia, osteoporosis, pregnancy, rheumatoid arthritis	asparagus, avocados, beans, beets, broccoli, cabbage family, citrus fruit, cooking greens, corn, lentils, peas, rice, spinach
IRON	anemia, immune deficiency, memory loss, pregnancy	apricots, fatty fish, figs, lentils, meat, peas, poultry, shellfish
MAGNESIUM	allergies & asthma, anxiety & stress, chronic fatigue syndrome, constipation, diabetes, high blood pressure, kidney stones, migraine, PMS	avocados, grains, nuts, rice, seeds, shellfish, spinach, winter squash
SELENIUM	allergies & asthma, cancer, hypothyroidism, infertility & impotence, macular degeneration, prostate problems	meats, mushrooms, nuts, poultry, rice, seeds, shellfish, whole grains
VITAMIN B$_6$	acne, anemia, anxiety & stress, depression, heart disease, hypothyroidism, insomnia, memory loss, PMS, pregnancy	asparagus, bananas, fatty fish, figs, mushrooms, peas, potatoes, poultry, rice, sweet potatoes, winter squash
VITAMIN B$_{12}$	anemia, depression, heart disease, infertility & impotence	dairy products, fatty fish, meat, poultry, shellfish
VITAMIN C	allergies & asthma, anemia, bronchitis, cancer, cataracts, chronic fatigue syndrome, cold sores, colds & flu, diabetes, eczema, heart disease, hemorrhoids, infertility & impotence, high blood pressure, hyperthyroidism, immune deficiency, macular degeneration, osteoarthritis, osteoporosis, rheumatoid arthritis, sinusitis, sprains & strains	berries, cabbage family, citrus fruits, kiwifruit, melons, peas, peppers, pineapple, potatoes, salad greens, spinach, sweet potatoes, tomatoes, turnips, winter squash
VITAMIN E	bronchitis, cancer, cataracts, eczema, hyperthyroidism, immune deficiency, infertility & impotence, memory loss, macular degeneration, osteoarthritis, prostate problems, rheumatoid arthritis	avocados, grains, nuts, olive oil, salad greens, seeds
ZINC	acne, bronchitis, chronic fatigue syndrome, colds & flu, cold sores, eczema, hemorrhoids, hypothyroidism, immunity, infertility & impotence, macular degeneration, rosacea, sinusitis	beans, grains, meat, poultry, seeds, shellfish

THE vegetable arsenal

Researchers are discovering that phytonutrients can help heal many medical conditions. Here is a sampling of vegetables that contain healing agents for 16 common health conditions or concerns.

CONDITION	VEGETABLES	HEALING NUTRIENT
ALLERGIES & ASTHMA	Red onions	Quercetin
	Broccoli	Vitamin C
	Peppers	Vitamin C
CANCER PREVENTION	Garlic	Allium compounds
	Onions	Allium compounds
	Carrots	Beta-carotene
	Sweet potatoes	Beta-carotene
	Broccoli	Flavonoids, glucosinolates
	Asparagus	Folate
	Beets	Folate
	Spinach	Folate
	Brussels sprouts	Glucosinolates
	Cabbage	Glucosinolates
	Tomatoes	Lycopene
	Mushrooms	Selenium
	Bell peppers	Vitamin C
DIABETES	Asparagus	Fiber
	Canola oil	Monounsaturated fat
	Olive oil	Monounsaturated fat
	Bell peppers	Vitamin C
	Broccoli	Vitamin C
HEART DISEASE	Carrots	Soluble fiber
	Asparagus	Folate
	Spinach	Folate
	Soy foods	Soy protein
HIGH BLOOD PRESSURE	Broccoli	Calcium
	Cooking greens	Calcium
	Asparagus	Dietary fiber
	Potatoes	Potassium
	Peppers	Vitamin C
HIGH CHOLESTEROL	Onions	Flavonoids
	Tomatoes	Lycopene
	Carrots	Soluble fiber
	Garlic	Sulfur compounds
IMMUNE DEFICIENCY	Carrots	Carotenoids
	Sweet potatoes	Carotenoids
	Tomatoes	Carotenoids
	Onions	Flavonoids
	Peppers	Vitamin C
MACULAR DEGENERATION	Carrots	Beta-carotene
	Spinach	Beta-carotene

CONDITION	VEGETABLES	HEALING NUTRIENT
MACULAR DEGENERATION (cont.)	Winter squash	Beta-carotene
	Collard greens	Lutein & zeaxanthin
	Peppers	Lutein & zeaxanthin
	Spinach	Lutein & zeaxanthin
	Sweet potatoes	Lutein & zeaxanthin
	Tomatoes	Lycopene
	Broccoli	Vitamin C
OSTEOARTHRITIS	Peppers	Vitamin C
	Sweet potatoes	Folate
OSTEOPOROSIS	Cooking greens	Calcium
	Peppers	Vitamin C
	Kale	Vitamin K
	Spinach	Vitamin K
OVERWEIGHT	Broccoli	Calcium
	Cooking greens	Calcium
	Asparagus	Dietary fiber
	Beets	Dietary fiber
SKIN PROBLEMS	Asparagus	Beta-carotene
	Sweet potatoes	Beta-carotene
	Winter squash	Beta-carotene
	Potatoes	Vitamin B_6
	Broccoli	Antioxidants
	Carrots	Antioxidants
	Tomatoes	Antioxidants
STRESS	Broccoli	Calcium
	Cooking greens	Calcium
	Potatoes	Vitamin B_6
	Peas	Tryptophan
	Turnips	Tryptophan
	Asparagus	Folate
	Peas	Folate
	Salad greens	Folate
STROKE	Broccoli	Calcium
	Asparagus	Dietary fiber
	Beets	Dietary fiber
	Onions	Flavonoids
	Potatoes	Potassium
	Peppers	Vitamin C
TOOTH/MOUTH CONDITIONS	Broccoli	Calcium
	Cooking greens	Calcium
	Celery	Insoluble fiber
	Salad greens	Insoluble fiber
	Peppers	Vitamin C
YEAST INFECTIONS	Garlic	Allicin
	Artichokes	Fructooligosaccharides
	Onions	Fructooligosaccharides

TEN WAYS TO GET MORE
vegetables
INTO YOUR DIET

Your goal is to get more vegetables into your diet. New recipes will help
you considerably. But there are many simple ways to add vegetables to your meals.
Here are ten that we particularly like:

1 Serve them straight up. Every dinner, put a plate of raw vegetables on the table. Good choices are cucumbers, tomatoes, carrots, celery, and green peppers. Consider offering a different dip each evening: salsas, herb dips, vinaigrettes, blue cheese and milk put through the blender. We guarantee: A plate of raw vegetables almost always gets eaten. Everyone enjoys the crunchiness and freshness.

2 Have a nightly salad. A fistful of mixed salad greens from a bag, a few cherry tomatoes, a few slices of cucumber or apple, and you have a delicious, healthy salad in barely a minute's time. It's a great way to start any dinner.

3 Roast them. Most vegetables taste great when roasted in the oven with olive oil, vinegar, salt, pepper, and garlic. In winter, use root vegetables like parsnips, turnips, beets, carrots, and potatoes. In summer, use mushrooms, zucchini, tomatoes, onions, and peppers. In general, cut the vegetables into large chunks before cooking, toss them with the oil, vinegar, and seasonings, and cook in a roasting pan at a medium heat for 20 to 40 minutes, depending on their thickness. Try to limit your mix to vegetables with similar textures and piece sizes to ensure that all cook evenly.

4 Puree into soup. Potatoes, carrots, winter squash, cauliflower, and broccoli—just about any cooked (or leftover) vegetable can be made into a creamy, comforting soup. The recipe for "any-vegetable soup" is simple: In a medium saucepan, sauté 1 cup finely chopped onion in a tablespoon of vegetable oil until tender. Combine the onion in a blender or food processor with cooked vegetables and puree until smooth. Return puree to saucepan and thin with broth or low-fat milk. Simmer and season to taste. (Check the vegetable seasoning guide on page 21 to match vegetables with complementary herbs and spices.)

5 Do a fast sauté. Many vegetables taste terrific with a simple, fast sautéing. Pick a favorite—and cut into bite-size pieces. Heat a skillet or small wok to a high temperature. Add a swirl of olive oil and then the vegetables. Constantly turn the vegetables until cooked through. Toss on your favorite seasonings (we like salt, pepper, and thyme; alternatively, we like soy sauce and a little sesame oil), give a final stir, and voilà! They're ready for the table.

6 Make into sauce. Wonderful cooked and uncooked sauces or salsas can be made with tomatoes, onions, peppers, mushrooms, and cooking greens, alone or in combination with other vegetables. Put them on chicken, pork, pasta, or most any other entrée.

7 Fill an omelet. There are few vegetables that can't go into an omelet, especially when combined with a little grated or crumbled cheese. Vegetables that make especially good omelet fillings include onions, peppers, tomatoes, mushrooms, and potatoes.

8 Grate into ground meat. Enhance the flavor and nutritional value of ground-meat mixtures for burgers and meat loaves by adding up to a cup of finely chopped or grated raw vegetables before shaping and cooking: carrots, zucchini, sweet peppers, mushrooms, spinach and other greens, and, of course, onions.

9 Ovens are great for vegetables. Stuff them in poultry; surround briskets and tenderloins with large chunks; put them inside rolled-up fillets of port, beef, or chicken.

10 Try a recipe makeover. Add chopped cooked spinach or grated carrot to the sauce you use to make lasagna. Increase the amount of vegetables and decrease the amount of meat you use to make homemade soups, stews, and casseroles. Add cooked vegetables and beans to baked ziti, stuffed manicotti, and other pasta dishes.

VEGETABLE SEASONING guide

Sometimes all you need is the right herb or spice to turn a plain vegetable into a spectacular side dish. And sometimes the best way to season a vegetable is by cooking it with another vegetable or with fruit or fruit juice. Here are some different ideas for adding great flavor to plain cooked vegetables:

Vegetable	Seasonings
ARTICHOKE	lemon, butter, garlic, oregano
ASPARAGUS	lemon, mustard, dill, Parmesan cheese, soy sauce, dark sesame oil, capers
AVOCADO	chili powder, cumin, grapefruit, lemon, lime, orange, oregano
BEANS	olive oil, parsley, lemon, sesame seeds, soy sauce, Asian black beans
BEETS	balsamic vinegar, dill, lemon, rosemary, apple, pecans
BELL PEPPERS	balsamic vinegar, garlic, cured olives, capers, thyme, soy sauce and ginger, chili powder, cumin
BROCCOLI	grapefruit, orange, garlic, soy sauce, dark sesame oil, mustard/mayonnaise combination
BROCCOLI RABE	olive oil, garlic, pepper flakes, soy sauce, hot sauce
BRUSSELS SPROUTS	chives, green onions, mustard
CABBAGE	caraway seeds, garlic, sugar and vinegar (sweet and sour), soy sauce, dark sesame oil, ginger, apple
CARROTS	citrus, curry powder, honey, ginger, lemon, dill, raspberry vinegar
CAULIFLOWER	basil, curry powder, a mustard/mayonnaise blend
CELERY (cooked)	garlic, oregano, soy sauce, dark sesame oil
CORN	basil, butter, chili powder,
CUCUMBER	dill, sugar and vinegar (sweet and sour), sesame seeds, soy sauce
EGGPLANT	basil, garlic, tomato, Asian black beans, hot sauce, sesame oil
FENNEL	bay leaf, tomato, Parmesan cheese
GREEN BEANS	garlic, soy sauce, sesame seeds
GREENS (such as spinach, kale, Swiss chard)	citrus, dill, garlic, green onions, pine nuts, raisins, sesame seeds
MUSHROOMS	balsamic vinegar, chives, green onion, parsley, thyme
OKRA	lemon, marjoram, tomato, thyme
PARSNIPS	Parmesan cheese, thyme
PEAS	mint, dark sesame oil, sesame seeds
POTATOES	chives, curry powder, garlic, yogurt, roast peppers, rosemary
SPINACH	raisins, garlic, cracked pepper, sea salt, soy sauce
SUMMER SQUASH	garlic, lemon, rosemary, tomato
SWEET POTATOES	maple syrup, butter, citrus, ginger, cinnamon, cranberries, dried fruit
TOMATO	balsamic vinegar, basil, garlic, Parmesan or Romano cheese, oregano
TURNIPS	honey, apples, pears, lemon, walnuts
WINTER SQUASH	maple syrup, nuts, citrus, ginger, cinnamon, apples, pears, cranberries, dried fruit

herbs & SPICES

One of the tastiest and healthiest ways to enhance the flavor of foods is to cook with herbs and spices. Fresh herbs are easy to find at the market, particularly in summer, and not too hard to grow in your own garden. Choose fresh-looking herbs with no wilted leaves or brown spots. Fresh herbs should always be fragrant. Store fresh herbs, loosely wrapped in a damp paper towel and then in plastic, in the crisper drawer of the refrigerator. They will last only a few days. Basil and mint do best standing upright in a jar of water in the refrigerator, loosely covered with a paper towel and then plastic.

Clean and chop fresh herbs and crush dried herbs just before using. Add herbs to cooked dishes within the last 30 minutes of cooking time or they will lose flavor. Add herbs to uncooked dishes at least an hour before serving, if possible, so that the flavors of the herb have time to marry with other foods.

Spices, on the other hand, are always sold dried; your choice in some cases is whether to grind your own for a fresher taste or buy the already-ground powdered version. Replace jars of dried herbs and spices after a year to assure good flavor.

Allspice is just what its name implies: a single spice that tastes like a mixture of cinnamon, nutmeg, ginger, and pepper, which adds a spiciness to all dishes.

Anise has a licorice flavor, making its seed popular in cakes and cookies. Ground anise seed is used with fruit or cabbage. Star anise is a similar spice from the Far East.

Basil has a distinctive warm, minty flavor and is most frequently used for pesto sauces and tomato dishes. It goes well with most Mediterranean-style dishes.

Bay leaf has a pungent woodsy flavor and aroma that complements meats,

soups, and stews. Add the dry, brittle leaf at the beginning of cooking to allow time for it to release its flavor. Remove leaf before serving.

Black peppercorns are sharp and aromatic. Freshly ground black pepper from a pepper mill gives the most flavor.

Caraway seeds, small and aromatic, have an anise-like flavor. They add that flavor and a nutty texture to breads, cakes, cheeses, vegetables, and meats.

Cardamom comes from the ground seed of an Indian plant in the ginger family. It is a spice used mainly in curries and baking.

Cayenne, ground dried red chile peppers and their seeds, is hot and peppery in sauces and stews.

Celery seeds, tiny as they are, can give a strong celery flavor to sauces, dips, stews, or soups.

Chervil is an anise-tasting herb that enhances egg, chicken, shrimp and salad dishes.

Chili powder, which comes in hot or mild versions, is a mixture of ground dried chiles, and other herbs, such as garlic, oregano, cumin, coriander, and cloves.

Chives add a sweet onion flavor to salads, sauces, and dips. They are an easy perennial to grow, but also can be bought fresh, frozen, or freeze-dried at grocery stores.

Cilantro, and **coriander,** refer to the same plant. Its fresh green leaves are very aromatic and distinct in their flavor, and are popular in Mexican and Southwest American dishes, as well as Oriental cooking. The ground seeds are used in curries and spice cakes.

Cinnamon comes in stick form (good for spicing up hot ciders) or ground (mix with sugar for cinnamon toast). Cinnamon flavors sweet rolls, spice cakes, and puddings. It is also used in Moroccan and Greek entrees and pilafs.

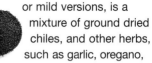

Cloves are used to stud hams before baking or spike apples for a cider punch. Use ground cloves for spice cakes or puddings.

Cumin seeds and ground cumin have an earthy flavor that adds richness to Mexican, bean, and shellfish recipes.

Dill, either freshly chopped or dried dill weed, gives a fresh flavor to beets, carrots, cucumbers, pickled vegetables, potatoes, and seafood. Dill seed is used in pickling.

Fennel seeds, have an anise flavor that goes well with fish and pork.

Gingerroot has a sharp, lemony flavor. Fresh gingerroot is peeled and grated or diced and added to stir-fries or spicy stews. Store fresh ginger, well wrapped, in the freezer. Ground dried ginger is used in cakes and cookies, as well as some curries.

Mace is the external covering, or aril, of the nutmeg seed that is also and ground for use as a spice. It is hotter and less subtle than nutmeg and a classic spice for pound cake.

Marjoram has a spicy, fresh flavor that goes with most vegetables, especially those used in Mexican, Greek, and Italian recipes.

Mint has a light, fresh taste that enlivens fruit drinks like lemonade and fruit salads; it also enhances the taste of lamb and fish.

Mustard seed is used to make many popular commercial spreads from Dijon to hot dog mustard. Ground mustard seed, hot and pungent, is also an important ingredient in homemade mayonnaise, and many sauces and gravies served with fish, poultry, and meat.

Nutmeg has a warm, sweet, nutty flavor that complements spinach, pumpkin, and cheese dishes, as well as puddings.

Oregano, like a stronger version of marjoram, enhances tomato, cabbage, poultry, beef, veal, and lamb recipes.

Paprika, like cayenne, is ground dried red peppers but in a combination that is milder and sweeter. Hungarian paprika is among the best, aromatic and delicious. Some paprika sold in the United States is so mild that it is used as decoration only.

Parsley comes in two versions, curly-leaf and flat-leaf. The two kinds can be used interchangeably to add a fresh taste to potatoes, grains, mushrooms, and meat. Chewing fresh parsley is said to freshen the breath.

Red pepper flakes are made from crushed dried chile peppers and are very hot; use to add hotness to chilies and stews.

Rosemary has an intense, earthy flavor that makes it especially good for marinades and grilled foods, such as lamb. Used sparingly (because it is strong), it complements beans, legumes, mushrooms, peas, summer squash, and zucchini.

Saffron, the most expensive of all spices, is obtained from the stamens of a single variety of fall crocus. It is used to flavor—and color—rice, vegetable soups, fish dishes, and sweet rolls.

Sage has a woodsy, aromatic flavor that is often used in Italian cooking, blending well with garlic and tomatoes. It also goes well with onions, legumes, pork, poultry, and stuffing.

Sea salt, such as *fleur de sel* from France and *alaea* from Hawaii, is literally taken from the sea; it's what's left when the water is evaporated. Depending on its source, sea salt has subtle flavors from trace minerals. It is coarse and should be sprinkled on food after cooking.

Summer savory is a slightly peppery herb that spices up green beans, dried beans, cabbage, Brussels sprouts, and potatoes, as well as fish, poultry, and pork.

Tarragon, a popular French herb, has an anise-like flavor that complements carrots, greens, chicken, seafood, and egg dishes.

Thyme has a light, spicy flavor that marries well with carrots, mushrooms, and salad greens, as well as beef, pork, lamb, poultry, and oil-rich fish. It is especially tasty in soups, and stews.

A WORLD OF flavors

There are so many popular herbs and spices, you could spend a lifetime exploring them. But if you really want to add some flair and personality to your cooking, you need to explore the world of ethnic cuisines.

Don't consider ethnic-style cooking exotic. Chances are, several people on your street will be using nontraditional vegetables and flavors in their kitchen this very evening. Not only do everyday grocery stores now carry new and interesting ethnic ingredients; ethnic markets are also on the rise, a result of people emigrating from different countries and bringing with them the foods and cooking styles of their culture.

In an American city with a large Asian population, for instance, it's easy to find the ingredients necessary to make authentic Chinese, Japanese, Vietnamese, or Thai food. Italian food markets abound in cities and towns where Italian families have settled. Even in areas where the population is more homogeneous,

ethnic foods may be available at farmers' markets or specialty food shops.

People from different cultures sometimes cook with different fruits and vegetables and these certainly help lend authenticity to a dish. But what really defines a cuisine, and sets one apart from another, is the unique blend of seasonings and spices used to create traditional, distinctly flavored dishes.

Following are some of the basic seasonings and condiments that help give each cuisine its own distinct flavor that you will find in an ethnic market.

chinese ˅

Chili paste: A peppery condiment served at the table that will spice up any food.

Five-spice powder: A blend of cinnamon, fennel, cloves, star anise, and Szechuan peppercorns, which is often used in marinades or as a seasoning for soups, stews, and stir-fries.

Hoisin sauce: A thick, sweet spicy sauce made from soybeans and used in stir-fries and as a condiment, like ketchup.

Hot mustard: A very sharp, vinegary mustard used as a dipping sauce.

Sesame oil: Light sesame oil has a slightly nutty flavor and is used for cooking and frying. Dark sesame oil, sometimes called Oriental sesame oil, is a dark

brown, fragrant and deeply flavored oil used sparingly and only as a seasoning.

Soy sauce: The most important and commonly used seasoning throughout China and all of Asia, this salty sauce made from fermented soybeans comes in several varieties. Light soy sauce is thinner and saltier (although, in America, "light" usually means less salt). Dark soy sauce is thicker and less salty. Chinese black soy sauce and Japanese tamari are very dark and sweeter than other soy sauces.

Star anise: A pretty, star-shaped spice that comes from a Chinese evergreen tree. Similar to anise seed but stronger in flavor, star anise is used to flavor soups, stews, and other cooked dishes.

french ˅

Chestnut puree: This is used to add rich, nutty flavor to gravies, sauces, baked goods, and vegetable side dishes.

Mustard: The most popular mustard, from the Dijon region, is sharp and moderately hot. It is served at the table and used to flavor sauces and salad dressings.

Nut oils: These are richly flavored seasoning oils made from hazelnuts, walnuts, or almonds. Nut oils are never used in cooking, because heat destroys their flavor. They are used in vinaigrettes for all types of salads or drizzled over cooked vegetables.

Peppercorns: Green and pink peppercorns are often used in more delicate dishes where a milder pepper flavor is desired.

greek

Kalamata olive spread: A puree of olives, olive oil, capers, and herbs used as a spread on toast or sandwiches.

Olive oil: Extra-virgin olive oil with strong, fruity flavor is a basic condiment in Greek cuisine. It is always used in vinaigrettes and drizzled over vegetables.

Pomegranate syrup: A tangy fruit sauce used in vinaigrettes, sauces, and marinades.

indian

Chutney: A spicy, often sweet, condiment used as a bread spread, a dip for appetizers, and a relish to go with rice dishes and other simple foods. Chutneys are made from a variety of ingredients. Some of the more popular varieties include mango, lemon, coriander, mint, and date.

Curry powder: An aromatic blend of many seeds and spices used to flavor curries, lentils, meat and poultry dishes, salad dressings, sauces, and cooked vegetables. Hot curry powder is seasoned with extra "hot" spices, such as ginger and red pepper.

Garam masala: A spicy blend of cinnamon, cumin, black pepper, coriander, cloves, and cardamom that is used to flavor curries, rice, beans, potatoes, eggplant, and meat dishes.

italian

Balsamic vinegar: Made from concentrated grape juice that is aged in wooden barrels. The barrels contribute their own distinctive flavor to the vinegar, so each brand has a somewhat unique flavor, depending on the type of barrel used. Balsamic vinegar is widely used as a simple flavoring sauce for fish, meats,

green salads, vegetables, and even citrus fruits and berries.

Extra-virgin olive oil: Deep green, intensely flavored and fragrant, high-grade olive oil is used to flavor pastas, salads, and cooked vegetables.

Olive paste (pate): An intensely flavored puree of black or green olives and olive oils that is added to pasta sauces and salad dressing. Olive paste can also be used as a spread on toast and sandwiches.

Sweet pepper paste or spread: A puree of roasted peppers, olive oil, vinegar, and cheese used as a spread on toast or sandwiches.

japanese

Miso: Fermented soybean paste used in soups, salad dressings, and marinades.

Tamari soy sauce: Darker and more flavorful than regular soy sauce.

Wasabi: A hot and spicy, somewhat bitter powder or paste used in dips, dressings, and sauces.

korean

Chili sauce: A garlicky sauce used on salads and also as a marinade or sauce.

Korean barbecue sauce: A sweet soy-based sauce used as a glaze for grilling or as a condiment to pass at the table.

latin american

Adobo: A seasoning salt flavored with garlic, pepper, oregano, and turmeric or cumin. The blend may vary, depending on the region it comes from.

Annatto (achiote): A deep red seed that is usually mixed into a paste with vinegar, garlic, and other seasonings, and used to flavor and color vegetables, soups, and meats.

Chili powder: A blend of seasonings that usually includes dried chiles, cumin, oregano, and garlic. Chili powders vary greatly in flavor from brand to brand, depending on the type of chile pepper used and the proportion of other ingredients.

Picante sauce: A flavorful hot sauce used as a table condiment and to flavor soups, salads, salsas, and other dishes.

Recaito: A blend of cilantro, peppers, onion, garlic, and olive oil used to season beans, rice, soups, and stews.

Sofrito: A blend of annatto seeds, onions, peppers, garlic, and other seasonings.

Tomatillos: Small, green tomato-like fruits with a fruity, sharp, and somewhat sour flavor used in salsas, salads, and guacamole.

thai

Chili paste: Thai chili paste is flavored with sweet basil and used to flavor stir-fries, curries, sauces, and marinades.

Lemongrass: A seasoning with sour-lemon flavor used in soups, stews, stir-fries, teas, and curries, which is commonly found in Thai and Vietnamese dishes.

Tamarind paste: Adds sweet-and-sour flavor to soups, stews, and other cooked dishes.

vietnamese

Fish sauce: A salty, fermented anchovy sauce used in small amounts to flavor soups, stews, stir-fries, and dipping sauces.

Sweet soy sauce: A thick, sweet, molasses-like sauce that is used extensively in Vietnamese and Thai cooking as a marinade or dipping sauce.

HOW MANY TOOLS do you need to cook with vegetables? Not so many, really. You can start with a few sharp knives:

kitchen
ESSENTIALS

SMALL PARING KNIFE

Has a 3½-inch blade for scraping carrots, paring asparagus stalks, peeling avocados, and "de-stringing" celery, among other jobs.

MEDIUM-SIZE SERRATED KNIFE

Slices tomatoes and other soft, juicy vegetables and fruits. It can also be used for slicing bread.

LARGE CHEF'S KNIFE

Has an 8-, 9-, or 10-inch blade for quick and easy slicing, dicing, and chopping.

Life in the kitchen is generally easier if you add just a few small appliances and utensils. The following are especially useful for preparing vegetables.

blender

Not as versatile as a food processor, but can be used for chopping, pureeing, or liquefying. A blender may be preferable to a food processor when only a small amount of food is involved. A hand blender is a narrow, handheld appliance that is excellent for making sauces and purees. This type of blender can be immersed right into the cooking pot to puree a soup or a batch of tomato sauce. It can also be immersed into a tall glass to blend a smoothie or shake.

colander

Made of plastic or metal with large holes to allow liquids to drain quickly. A metal colander can also be inserted into a large saucepan and used as a steamer.

cutting board

Made of wood, hard rubber, acrylic, or plastic. There is no evidence that one type is better, or safer, than another. Experts however, recommend using separate cutting boards for animal foods and plant foods to eliminate the risk of cross-contamination from raw meat, poultry, or seafood to uncooked vegetables or fruit.

food processor

Handy for shredding, chopping, grating, slicing, or pureeing large quantities of vegetables. Compact or "mini" food processors can be used to chop or grind smaller amounts of food or herbs. For chopping or grating very small quantities, it is usually more efficient (and less messy) to use a knife or grater.

grater

Comes in a variety of sizes and "grates." A four-sided box grater is good for grating, shredding, and slicing vegetables and cheese.

mandoline

For perfect slices. It is also faster than a knife for julienne or baton cuts. Keep a mandoline's guard in place to prevent injury.

potato masher

Also used to mash cooked carrots, beets, winter squash, and other vegetables.

salad spinner

Helps dry salad greens and fresh herbs quickly and evenly.

shears

Useful for quickly snipping fresh parsley and other herbs. A set of kitchen shears comes in handy for many other culinary tasks, such as trimming pastry and cutting through bones.

steamer

Consists of an upper pot with a mesh or perforated bottom that fits into a larger pot, which holds water or other liquid. Stackable bamboo or metal steamers that hold two or three layers of food can be placed over a skillet or saucepan. For small amounts of food, use a metal, collapsible steamer that fits inside a large or medium saucepan. Plastic, collapsible steamers are available for use in a microwave oven. To improvise a steamer, place a metal colander or wire mesh strainer in a large saucepan that can be tightly covered.

strainers

Come in different sizes and are made of different gauges of wire mesh attached to a ring frame. Strainers are generally used over a bowl to drain liquids from solids. They are also used for sifting and separating out fine particles.

swivel-bladed vegetable peeler

Easier to use than a knife to pare vegetables. Peelers are inexpensive tools that should be discarded and replaced when they grow dull.

what's in a serving?

Health and nutrition experts recommend eating a minimum of five to nine servings of vegetables every day. A serving of vegetables is the equivalent of:

- 1 cup raw, leafy greens such as lettuce, spinach, or cabbage
- 1 small baked potato
- ¾ cup vegetable juice
- ½ cup cut-up, raw, nonleafy vegetables, such as carrot sticks or cucumber rounds
- ½ cup cooked vegetables
- ½ cup legumes such as white beans, black beans, kidney beans, peas, or lentils

cooking to preserve nutrients

Cooking fresh vegetables helps release certain nutrients and phytochemicals, making them more available to your body. But at the same time, improper handling and cooking can destroy many of the essential nutrients provided by vegetables, especially vitamin C and folate. To preserve these vital nutrients:

- Store vegetables properly. The crisper section of the refrigerator, where many vegetables are stored, is designed to be several degrees cooler and more humid than the upper part of the refrigerator. (*See storage instructions under individual vegetable headings in the A–Z Guide to Vegetables, page 285.*)
- Leave skins on vegetables such as carrots, potatoes, and sweet potatoes when cooking. Vitamins and minerals are often concentrated in and near the skin. Remember to clean vegetables especially well when the skins are left on.
- Chop and slice vegetables into larger pieces to reduce the surface area exposed and thereby reduce nutrient loss. Whenever possible, cook vegetables whole. For instance, boil potatoes whole in their skins to retain nutrients, then slice or chop them after cooking.
- Cook vegetables in a minimum amount of water. Water-soluble vitamins leach out into cooking water and end up going down the drain when the water is discarded.
- Cook vegetables only as long as necessary. Long cooking times destroy vitamins that are susceptible to heat.
- Reheat leftover vegetables quickly to avoid further loss of nutrients.

VEGETABLE COOKING
techniques

For the sake of preserving their natural taste, texture, and nutritional value, most vegetables are best blanched, steamed, microwaved, or stir-fried. There are, however, many other methods for cooking vegetables that offer a variety of delicious tastes and textures. These include roasting, boiling, sautéing, frying, braising, and broiling or grilling.

Blanching

Cooking vegetables in a large amount of boiling water for a brief period of time. The food can then be immersed in cold water to stop the cooking process. Tomatoes are often blanched for a minute or two to help remove their skins. Other vegetables may be blanched to enhance their color and remove their raw flavor before being used as crudités on an appetizer relish platter or in a salad.

Boiling

Cooking vegetables in a pot of rapidly bubbling water to cover. Boiling is a suitable method for hard vegetables such as green beans, broccoli spears, and carrots. The secret is to cook the vegetable just long enough to brighten its color and soften its texture but not so long that it gets dull or mushy. Bring the water to a boil first, then add the vegetable and cook it uncovered or partially covered.

Braising

Sautéing vegetables briefly in fat before adding liquid to finish the cooking. Braising works well with fibrous vegetables such as celery hearts, leeks, and fennel. Root vegetables and leafy greens also lend themselves to braising.

Broiling

Browning the tops of vegetables with intense dry heat while cooking the inside through. Food is generally placed 4 to 6 inches from the broiler element for complete cooking; precooked foods may be placed closer to the heat for quick browning. Tomatoes, eggplant, zucchini, peppers, mushrooms, and onions are often broiled. Most vegetables need to be marinated or brushed with oil before broiling. Fibrous vegetables such as leeks, fennel, and celery should be blanched before broiling. The broiler should always be preheated before using.

Frying

Cooking vegetables in very hot fat. Pan-frying uses up to an inch of fat in a pan to cook larger pieces of food such as crumb-coated slices of eggplant. Deep-fat frying, where food is completely immersed in hot fat, is necessary for batter-coated vegetables, such as those cooked in Japanese tempura style. Sautéing and stir-frying are forms of frying that use a minimal amount of fat to cook small pieces of food for a short period of time.

Microwaving

Microwaving is a fast and convenient way to cook many vegetables and keep their nutrients, crispness, and color intact. Place vegetables in a microwave-safe dish with a vented cover and add a small amount of water. The greater the volume of vegetables, the longer it will take to cook them.

Parboiling

Partially cooking vegetables that require further preparation, by boiling for a brief period of time. Dense vegetables such as carrots and potatoes might be parboiled before they are sautéed with other vegetables so that all of the vegetables are done at the same time.

Roasting

Cooking vegetables slowly in an oven with dry heat. When vegetables are roasted, they are usually tossed first in oil or melted butter. High-temperature roasting (400°F to 450°F) results in well-browned food.

Sautéing

Cooking vegetables quickly in a small amount of fat over relatively high heat. Chefs constantly shake sauté pans during cooking to keep the food from sticking. Naturally tender vegetables, such as onions, peppers, mushrooms, and zucchini, can be cut up and sautéed very quickly. Hard vegetables such as carrots, broccoli, and cauliflower, may benefit from a blanching to soften them slightly before sautéing.

Steaming

Cooking food on a rack above, not in, boiling or simmering liquid, usually water. Cooking vegetables in the oven en papillote, or encased in parchment paper or foil packets with a bit of liquid, is also a form of steaming.

Stir-frying

Cooking small pieces of food quickly in a wok or skillet in a small amount of oil over high heat, stirring constantly. Most vegetables are stir-fried just until tender-crisp. Organized preparation is essential for successful stir-frying. All chopping and slicing of meat and vegetables must be done ahead of time. Seasoning ingredients must be measured out and mixed, where necessary, before heating the wok.

grilling
VEGETABLES

Outdoor cooking is no longer limited to burgers and hot dogs. Just about everything goes on the grill these days, including whatever vegetables are being served alongside the meat. There is an art to grilling vegetables, and it's easy to master if you follow these simple guidelines:

- Be sure the grill is at the right temperature. Set grill to medium-hot or allow hot coals to die down for about 30 minutes before placing vegetables on the grill rack.
- Rub all vegetables with cooking oil or toss them in an oil-based marinade or vinaigrette before grilling.
- Arrange long, thin vegetable pieces crosswise on the grill so they don't fall through.
- Use a long-handled brush to baste vegetables with marinade or vinaigrette while grilling to add flavor and preserve moisture.
- Use long-handled tongs to turn vegetables once, halfway through cooking time, or when they are lightly charred and almost tender.
- Cooking times vary greatly, depending on the type and size of the vegetables and the type of grill you are using. Test individual vegetables often and grill until lightly charred and easily pierced with a fork or skewer.
- If cooking in batches, transfer the finished vegetables to a platter and tent it with foil to keep them warm while you grill the remaining vegetables.
- Garnish platters of grilled vegetables with fresh herbs and lemon wedges.

HERE'S HOW TO PREPARE INDIVIDUAL VEGETABLES FOR GRILLING:

ASPARAGUS: Blanch trimmed asparagus spears in boiling water for a minute or two before grilling.

CARROTS: Grill slender, evenly shaped carrots whole. Cut tapered carrots in half and then slice the thick top half in half again lengthwise for even cooking.

EGGPLANT: Cut eggplant crosswise or diagonally into 1/2-inch-thick slices, or "steaks."

MUSHROOMS: Large mushrooms, such as portobellos, can be cooked directly on the grill. Thread smaller mushrooms onto skewers before grilling.

ONIONS: Cut large red, yellow, or white onions into very thick slices. Push a skewer though the slices to prevent the rings from separating and falling into the grill.

POTATOES: Cook whole, halved, or cut into thick slices or wedges. Whole baking potatoes can be nestled directly in the coals. To reduce cooking time for cut-up potatoes, blanch 5 to 10 minutes before grilling.

SWEET PEPPERS: Grill whole peppers, turning occasionally, until the skin is blackened and blistered on all sides. Wrap in foil or place in paper bag to cool for 15 minutes. When peppers are cool enough to handle, peel, cut, and discard stems and seeds.

TOMATOES: Grill tomatoes whole or halved. Thread cherry or grape tomatoes onto skewers before grilling.

ZUCCHINI AND OTHER SUMMER SQUASH: Cut into thick, lengthwise slices, or cut into chunks and thread onto skewers before grilling.

TAKING
stock

Homemade vegetable broth is easy to prepare and provides a healthful and flavorful base for soups, stews, and sauces. The combination of vegetables you use to make stock is up to you, but avoid strongly flavored vegetables such as asparagus, broccoli, Brussels sprouts, and cauliflower.

You can keep vegetable stocks in the refrigerator for up to a week, or freeze. To freeze, pour stock into one-pint freezer containers, leaving a half-inch space at the top. Seal containers, label with date and contents, and freeze for up to six months. Since some flavor is usually lost in freezing, you may want to add additional herbs and seasonings when reheating. Use either of the following vegetable broths as the base for a vegetable or fish soup.

Basic Vegetable Stock

ABOUT 4 CUPS

> 2 large carrots, coarsely chopped
> 1 large onion, coarsely chopped
> 2 stalks celery, coarsely chopped
> 1 large tomato, cut into 1-inch chunks
> 1 medium turnip, coarsely chopped
> 1 small parsnip, coarsely chopped
> 1 cup shredded Romaine lettuce
> 6 sprigs parsley
> 1 clove garlic
> 1 bay leaf
> ¾ teaspoon dried thyme
> 7 cups water

1 In large stockpot, combine carrots, onion, celery, tomato, turnip, parsnip, lettuce, parsley, garlic, bay leaf, and thyme. Add water. Bring to a boil over medium heat, skimming foam from surface as necessary. Reduce heat to low, partially cover, and simmer 1 hour.

2 Line strainer with two layers of dampened cheesecloth. Strain stock into large bowl. Discard vegetables and herbs. Cool stock completely.

TIPS FOR MAKING YOUR OWN VEGETABLE BROTH

> Be sure the vegetables are very clean before using, even if they are to be peeled.

> Simmer the vegetables for just about one hour or the broth may become bitter. For richer broth, continue cooking the strained broth for up to 30 minutes to reduce the liquid and concentrate the flavor.

Roasted Vegetable Broth

Roasting brings out the naturally rich flavor of vegetables and makes a more flavorful broth.

6 CUPS

> 2 tablespoons olive oil
> 3 large carrots
> 2 medium parsnips, peeled
> 2 onions, cut into eighths
> 2 stalks celery, with leaves, halved
> 4 cloves garlic, unpeeled
> 3 plum tomatoes, halved
> 8 cups water
> 6 sprigs parsley
> 3 thin slices ginger, unpeeled
> 1 teaspoon salt
> ¾ teaspoon dried rosemary, crumbled

1 Preheat oven to 400°F. Pour oil into 13 x 9 x 2-inch roasting pan. Add carrots, parsnips, onions, celery, and garlic. Stir to coat vegetables.

2 Roast until vegetables are lightly colored, 30 minutes. Scrape up any browned bits from the bottom of the pan.

3 Transfer vegetables to five-quart Dutch oven or stockpot. Add tomatoes, water, parsley, ginger, salt, and rosemary. Bring to a boil over high heat. Reduce heat to low, partially cover, and simmer until vegetables are very tender and broth is richly flavored, about 1 hour.

4 Line strainer with two layers of dampened cheesecloth. Strain stock into large bowl. Discard vegetables and herbs. Cool stock completely.

VEGETABLE-RICH
recipes

EGGS &
breakfast
DISHES

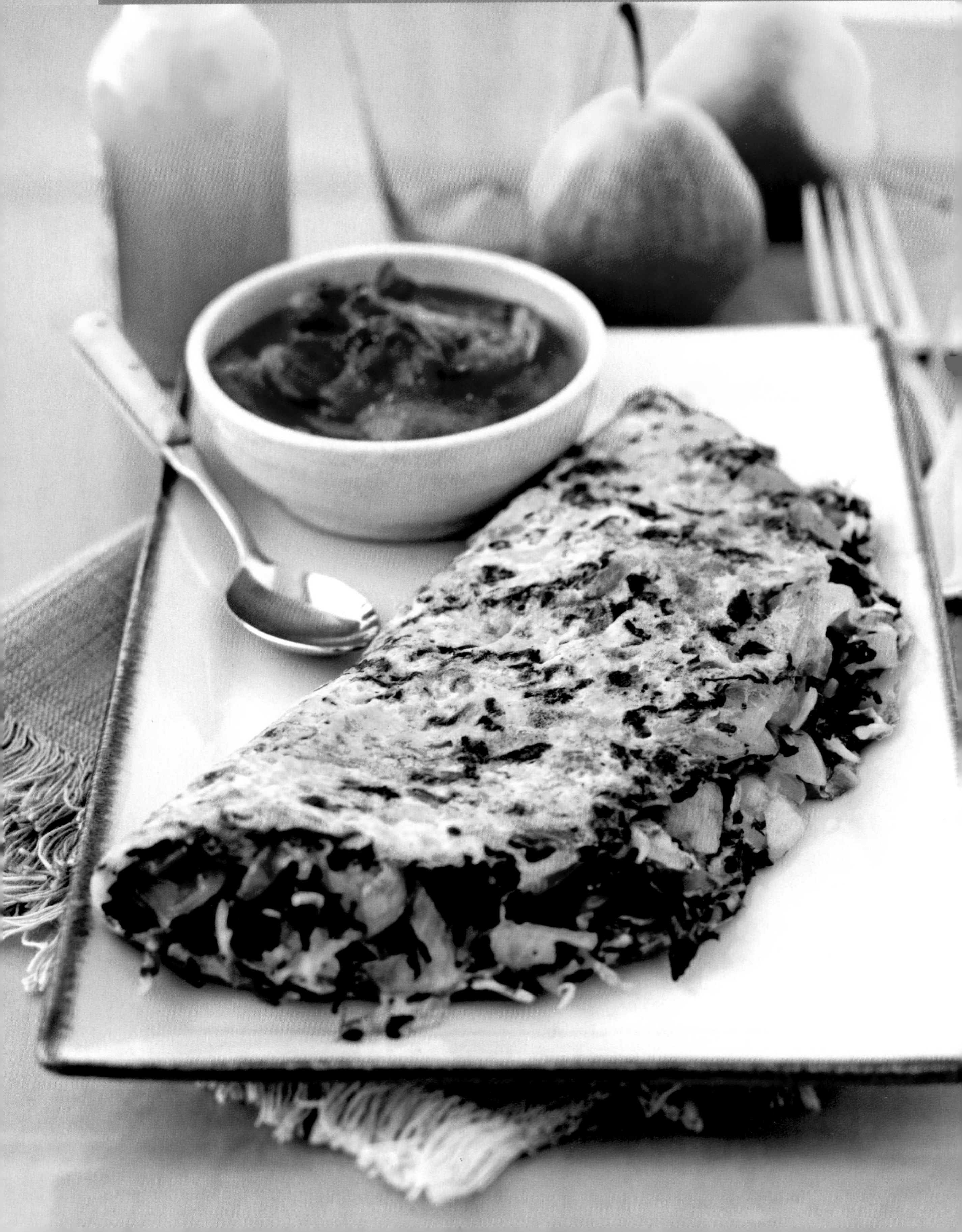

VEGETABLES FOR VITALITY

"Mostly Whites" Spinach Omelet with Tomato-Mushroom Sauce

A phytochemical in spinach known as lutein helps keep your eyes bright and healthy.

2 SERVINGS

Prep 10 min ◆ **Cook** 25 min

- 1½ teaspoons olive oil
- 4 ounces mushrooms, sliced (about ¾ cup)
- 1 can (8 ounces) seasoned tomato sauce
- 4 large egg whites
- 1 large egg
- ¼ teaspoon black pepper
- 1 small onion, chopped
- ½ cup packed cooked chopped spinach (about 5 ounces)
- ¼ teaspoon salt
- 2 teaspoons grated Parmesan cheese

1 In small nonstick saucepan over medium-high heat, heat ½ teaspoon oil. Add mushrooms. Cook until softened, 4 minutes, stirring once. Add tomato sauce. Simmer until thickened, about 5 minutes. Remove from heat. Cover.

2 In small bowl, beat egg whites, egg, and pepper until blended.

3 In large nonstick skillet over medium heat, heat remaining teaspoon oil. Add onion. Sauté until softened, 4 minutes. Stir in spinach and salt. Cook until heated through. Stir half of spinach mixture into egg mixture. Reserve remaining spinach mixture.

4 Coat same skillet with nonstick cooking spray. Heat over medium heat. Pour spinach-egg mixture into skillet, spreading evenly. Cook, without stirring, until eggs begin to thicken slightly around edge of skillet, about 1 minute. Run thin spatula around edge of skillet, lifting eggs so uncooked portion flows under cooked portion. Repeat until center of omelet is still moist but no longer runny, about 3 minutes total.

5 Spread reserved spinach mixture over half of omelet. Sprinkle with cheese. Fold omelet to cover filling. Reduce heat to low. Cover and cook until eggs are set but still soft, 3 to 4 minutes. Slide omelet onto serving plate. Top with mushroom sauce.

Per serving: 205 calories, 17 g protein, 22 g carbohydrates, 7 g fat, 2 g saturated fat, 108 mg cholesterol, 6 g fiber, 1,144 mg sodium

Broccoli, Tomato & Swiss Cheese Omelet

Two power vegetables turn this hearty omelet into a nutritional superstar.

2 SERVINGS

Prep 10 min ◆ **Cook** 8 min

- 3 large eggs
- 1 large egg white
- 1 tablespoon milk
- ⅛ teaspoon salt
- 1 cup cooked chopped broccoli
- 1 large plum tomato, sliced
- ½ cup shredded reduced-fat Swiss cheese

1 Coat 10-inch nonstick skillet with nonstick cooking spray. Heat over medium heat. Beat eggs, egg white, milk, and salt in medium bowl until blended. Stir in broccoli. Pour mixture into skillet, spreading evenly. Cook, without stirring, until eggs begin to thicken slightly around edge of skillet, about 1 minute. Run thin spatula around edge of skillet, lifting eggs so uncooked portion flows under cooked portion. Repeat until center of omelet is still moist but no longer runny, about 3 minutes total.

2 Arrange tomato slices over one half of omelet. Top with cheese. Fold omelet over to cover filling. Reduce heat to low. Cover and cook until eggs are set but still soft, 3 to 4 minutes. Slide omelet onto serving plate.

Per serving: 225 calories, 22 g protein, 8 g carbohydrates, 11 g fat, 4 g saturated fat, 329 mg cholesterol, 3 g fiber, 365 mg sodium

Bell Pepper & Ham Quiche

All bell peppers are bursting with vitamin C, but red peppers are an especially good source.

6 SERVINGS

Prep 10 min • **Cook** 1 hour 5 minutes

- 1 unbaked, 9-inch, deep-dish pastry crust
- 1 tablespoon vegetable oil
- 1 onion, finely chopped
- 1 red bell pepper, seeded and finely chopped
- 2 ounces lean sliced deli ham, finely chopped
- 1 cup part-skim ricotta cheese
- 1 cup plain low-fat yogurt
- 3 large eggs
- ¼ teaspoon salt
- ⅛ teaspoon black pepper

1 Preheat oven to 425°F. Prick bottom of crust with fork. Bake 8 minutes. Remove crust from oven. Reduce oven temperature to 325°F.

2 Meanwhile, in large nonstick skillet over medium heat, heat oil. Add onion. Sauté until softened, about 5 minutes. Add bell pepper. Sauté 2 minutes. Stir in ham. Spoon mixture into crust.

3 In blender or food processor, whirl ricotta, yogurt, eggs, salt, and pepper until very smooth, 2 minutes. Pour over mixture in crust, stirring gently.

4 Bake until set but still jiggly in center, 45 to 55 minutes. Remove to rack to cool slightly. Serve warm or at room temperature.

Per serving: 275 calories, 13 g protein, 20 g carbohydrates, 16 g fat, 6 g saturated fat, 126 mg cholesterol, 1 g fiber, 472 mg sodium

Spanish Omelet

Potatoes, tomato, and bell peppers add a whopping supply of vitamin C to this traditional egg dish.

4 SERVINGS

Prep 10 min • **Cook** 22 min

- 1 tablespoon olive oil
- 1 medium onion, coarsely chopped
- 2 cloves garlic, chopped
- 1 small green bell pepper, seeded and coarsely chopped
- 1 small tomato, seeded and coarsely chopped
- 1 roasted red bell pepper *(see page 295)*, seeded and coarsely chopped
- 2 small cooked potatoes, cut into ½-inch dice
- ½ teaspoon salt
- 4 large eggs, lightly beaten

1 In large nonstick skillet over medium heat, heat 2 teaspoons oil. Add onion and garlic. Sauté 5 minutes. Add green pepper and tomato. Sauté 3 minutes. Add roasted pepper, potatoes, and salt. Cover and cook, stirring often, until all vegetables are tender, 10 minutes. If vegetables begin to stick, add a little water.

2 Coat large nonstick skillet with nonstick cooking spray. Heat over medium heat. Swirl in remaining teaspoon oil. Add eggs. Cook, without stirring, until eggs start to thicken slightly around edges, about 1 minute. Run thin spatula around edge of skillet, lifting eggs so uncooked portion flows under cooked portion. Repeat until center of omelet is still moist but no longer runny, about 3 minutes total. Slide omelet onto plate. Top with vegetable mixture. Cut into 4 equal wedges.

Per serving: 163 calories, 8 g protein, 9 g carbohydrates, 11 g fat, 2 g saturated fat, 213 mg cholesterol, 2 g fiber, 74 mg sodium

HINT **helpful HINT** HINT HINT HINT HINT HINT HINT

To make a crustless quiche that's much lower in fat and calories, coat the bottom and side of a 9-inch pie plate with nonstick cooking spray. Combine the sautéed vegetables and the blended ricotta mixture together before pouring into the pan. Bake as directed, but start checking quiche for doneness after 30 minutes.

FRESH IDEAS

A traditional Spanish omelet, also called tortilla española, *is open-faced and topped with a simple combination of potatoes and onions. We've added tomatoes and bell peppers to liven up the mix. Other additions: zucchini and ham or marinated artichokes and olives. With a flat omelet such as this, the topping possibilities are endless. Use your imagination!*

Summer Greens Scramble

Leafy green vegetables like kale contain calcium, folic acid, and fiber, key nutrients for heart health.

4 SERVINGS

Prep 10 min ◆ **Cook** 10 min

- 2 **cups shredded, stemmed fresh kale**
- 5 **large eggs**
- 5 **large egg whites**
- ¼ **teaspoon ground cumin**
- ¼ **teaspoon salt**
- ¼ **cup chopped lean ham from the deli**
- 2 **scallions, trimmed and thinly sliced**

1 In large saucepan of boiling salted water, cook fresh kale until tender, 3 to 5 minutes. Drain. Rinse under cold water. Drain well.

2 In large bowl, whisk together eggs, egg whites, cumin, and salt.

3 Coat large nonstick skillet with nonstick cooking spray. Heat over medium heat. Add egg mixture. Stir until eggs start to thicken slightly, 2 to 3 minutes. Stir in kale, ham, and scallions. Cook, stirring occasionally, until eggs are soft-scrambled, 2 to 3 minutes.

Per serving: 145 calories, 15 g protein, 5 g carbohydrates, 7 g fat, 2 g saturated fat, 270 mg cholesterol, 1g fiber, 385 mg sodium

FRESH IDEAS

> *You can substitute other leafy green vegetables in the scrambled-egg dish. Try mustard greens, collards, or spinach for the kale, or use a combination.*

helpful HINT

Commercially prepared egg substitute products made from egg whites can replace all or some of the whole eggs in almost any recipe where the eggs are beaten. You can also make your own egg substitute. For every dozen egg whites, mix 1 tablespoon olive oil or vegetable oil. Substitute ⅓ cup of this mixture for each whole egg to be replaced in the recipe. Or you can simply replace each whole egg with 1½ to 2 egg whites.

Mushroom & Bell Pepper Frittata

Mushrooms contain niacin, a B vitamin that helps your body produce energy.

4 SERVINGS

Prep 10 min ◆ **Cook** 26 min

- 2 **tablespoons olive oil**
- 1 **red or orange bell pepper, seeded and cut into ¼-inch-thick slices**
- 1 **yellow bell pepper, seeded and cut into ¼-inch-thick slices**
- 2 **cups sliced mushrooms**
- 8 **large eggs**
- ¼ **teaspoon salt**
- ¼ **teaspoon black pepper**
- ⅓ **cup grated Parmesan cheese**
- 10 **fresh basil leaves, torn in small pieces**

1 In large nonstick skillet over medium-high heat, heat oil. Add red and yellow peppers. Sauté until softened, about 4 minutes. Add mushrooms. Sauté until vegetables are lightly browned, about 5 minutes. Reduce heat to medium.

2 In medium bowl, stir together eggs, salt, and pepper. Pour eggs into skillet, spreading evenly. Cook, stirring frequently, until soft-scrambled, 3 to 4 minutes. Reduce heat to medium-low. Stir in cheese and basil. Smooth top. Cook 5 minutes. Cover and cook until eggs are firm and bottom is browned, about 8 minutes.

3 To serve, loosen frittata around edge with spatula. Invert onto large plate. Cut into 4 equal wedges. Serve warm or at room temperature.

Per serving: 269 calories, 17 g protein, 8 g carbohydrates, 19 g fat, 5 g saturated fat, 430 mg cholesterol, 2 g fiber, 397 mg sodium

on the menu

A hearty strata makes a strong centerpiece for a brunch menu. You can start with orange juice or mimosas and plenty of strong fresh coffee. On the side, you might offer slices of cantaloupe with big fresh strawberries.

Tomato & Bacon Strata

The soluble fiber found in oat-bran bread helps lower cholesterol.

8 SERVINGS

Prep 10 min ◆ **Cook** 50 min

- 4 **large eggs**
- 4 **large egg whites**
- 1½ **cups 1% milk**
- 1½ **teaspoons curry powder**
- ½ **teaspoon salt**
- ⅛ **teaspoon black pepper**
- 2 **teaspoons vegetable oil**
- 10 **slices oat-bran bread**
- 2 **tomatoes, thinly sliced**
- 1 **cup shredded sharp cheddar cheese (4 ounces)**
- 4 **strips turkey bacon**

1 In large bowl, whisk together eggs, egg whites, milk, curry powder, salt, and pepper.

2 Grease 13 x 9 x 2-inch baking dish with oil. Arrange 5 slices of bread in single layer in bottom of baking dish, cutting 1 slice to fit, if necessary. Layer tomato slices over bread. Scatter ½ cup cheese over top. Repeat layering. Pour egg mixture over bread. Gently push down bread into liquid. Liquid should come almost to top of bread. Cover and let stand 1 hour or refrigerate overnight.

3 Preheat oven to 350°F. Uncover strata. Bake for 45 to 50 minutes or until puffed and golden. For last 10 minutes of cooking, arrange bacon on top. Let stand 10 minutes before serving.

Per serving: 244 calories, 15 g protein, 19 g carbohydrates, 12 g fat, 5 g saturated fat, 129 mg cholesterol, 2 g fiber, 562 mg sodium

HINT **helpful HINT** HINT HINT HINT HINT HINT HINT

If you are planning a breakfast for guests or a family special occasion, Eggs Baked in Tomato Cups (right) offers an easy but delicious solution. You can prepare the tomatoes and filling hours ahead, then fill the tomatoes and top with eggs right before mealtime. While they bake, you can broil bacon or sausage and make hash-brown potatoes to complete the menu.

Eggs Baked in Tomato Cups

Tomatoes are rich in cancer-fighting lycopene and vitamin C.

6 SERVINGS

Prep 35 min ◆ **Cook** 30 min

- 6 **large beefsteak tomatoes**
- 1½ **teaspoons salt**
- 10 **ounces spinach, stems removed**
- 1 **tablespoon olive oil**
- ¼ **cup finely chopped onion**
- 10 **ounces mushrooms, finely chopped**
- ⅓ **cup fresh bread crumbs**
- 2 **tablespoons grated Parmesan cheese**
- ¼ **teaspoon black pepper**
- 6 **large eggs**

1 Cut ⅛-inch-thick slice off top of each tomato. Core and seed. Sprinkle inside of tomatoes with 1 teaspoon of the salt, dividing evenly. Place, upside down, on paper towels to drain.

2 Meanwhile, wash spinach, letting water cling to leaves. Place in very large skillet. Cover and cook over medium heat until leaves are wilted, 1 to 2 minutes.

3 Preheat oven to 350°F. Lightly coat 13 x 9 x 2-inch baking pan with nonstick cooking spray. In large skillet over medium heat, heat oil. Add onion. Sauté until softened, about 3 minutes. Add mushrooms. Sauté until dry, about 5 minutes. Stir in spinach, bread crumbs, cheese, remaining ½ teaspoon salt, and pepper.

4 Pat tomato insides dry with paper towels. Stuff each tomato with spinach mixture. Arrange in baking pan. Crack egg on top of each. Cover loosely with foil. Bake until egg are set, 20 to 25 minutes.

Per serving: 163 calories, 11 g protein, 13 g carbohydrates, 9 g fat, 2 g saturated fat, 214 mg cholesterol, 4 g fiber, 739 mg sodium

Egg Burritos with Roasted Bell Peppers

The vitamin C in sweet bell peppers and the protein in eggs are essential for healthy skin.

4 SERVINGS

Prep 5 min ◆ **Cook** 5 min

- **4 flour tortillas (8 inches), warmed** *(see Hint)*
- **1 tablespoon vegetable oil**
- **8 large eggs, lightly beaten**
- **¼ teaspoon salt**
- **¼ teaspoon black pepper**
- **1 cup roasted red bell pepper pieces** *(see page 295)*, **seeded and cut into ½-inch slices**
- **2 tablespoons chopped cilantro**
- **¼ cup bottled salsa, at room temperature**

1 In medium nonstick skillet over medium heat, heat oil . Add eggs, salt, and pepper. Stir until eggs start to thicken slightly, 1 to 2 minutes. Stir in peppers and cilantro. Cook, stirring occasionally, until eggs are soft-scrambled, 2 to 3 minutes.

2 Spoon quarter of egg mixture in middle of each tortilla. Top each with 1 tablespoon salsa. Fold edges of tortilla over, then roll to enclose filling.

Per serving: 364 calories, 17 g protein, 36 g carbohydrates, 17 g fat, 4 g saturated fat, 425 mg cholesterol, 2 g fiber, 688 mg sodium

Huevos Rancheros

Sweet peppers, chiles, tomatoes, and avocado make this classic dish a hothouse of vitamins.

6 SERVINGS

Prep 15 min ◆ **Cook** 15 min

- **1 tablespoon olive oil**
- **1 medium red or yellow bell pepper** seeded and cut into ¼-inch pieces
- **2 medium tomatoes, seeded and cut into** ½-inch pieces
- **1 cup bottled salsa**
- **1 can (4½ ounces) green chiles, drained**
- **½ teaspoon ground cumin**
- **6 large eggs**
- **¼ cup shredded reduced-fat cheddar cheese**
- **6 flour tortillas (8 inches), warmed** *(see Hint)*
- **2 tablespoons chopped cilantro**
- **1 avocado, pitted, peeled, and chopped**

1 In medium skillet over medium heat, heat oil. Add bell pepper. Sauté until slightly softened, 3 minutes. Add tomatoes, salsa, chiles, and cumin. Simmer until thickened, 7 to 10 minutes.

2 Crack eggs onto sauce without breaking yolks. Top with cheese. Cover skillet. Cook until whites are set, 3 to 5 minutes.

3 To serve, place one egg with sauce on top of each tortilla. Sprinkle with cilantro and avocado.

Per serving: 294 calories, 13 g protein, 34 g carbohydrates, 12 g fat, 3 g saturated fat, 215 mg cholesterol, 4 g fiber, 595 mg sodium

HINT helpful HINT HINT HINT HINT HINT HINT HINT

To warm tortillas, preheat oven to 350°F. Stack up to six tortillas at a time and wrap loosely in aluminum foil. Warm in oven for 8 to 10 minutes. Leave wrapped until ready to serve.

DID YOU KNOW ● ● ●

. . .that corn tortillas are made from only cornmeal and water, but flour tortillas have wheat flour, vegetable shortening or lard, water, and salt?

on the menu

Serve this warm, homey chicken hash—a savory second act for a roasted chicken—with a crisp green salad and some hot corn bread. For dessert, consider some seasonal fresh fruit and a wedge of your favorite cheese.

Chicken Hash with Potatoes & Peppers

Combining red and green peppers boosts the beta-carotene and vitamin C content of this heart-healthy hash.

4 SERVINGS

Prep 10 min ◆ **Cook** 38 min

- ¾ **pound small red potatoes**
- 2 **tablespoons olive oil**
- 1 **medium onion, chopped**
- 1 **small green bell pepper, seeded and cut into ½-inch pieces**
- 1 **small red bell pepper, seeded and cut into ½-inch pieces**
- 1 **cup cooked chicken, cut into ½-inch dice**
- 1 **large clove garlic, finely chopped**
- 1 **teaspoon paprika**
- ½ **teaspoon dried thyme, crumbled**
- ½ **teaspoon salt**
- ½ **teaspoon black pepper**

1 In small saucepan of boiling water, cook potatoes until tender, about 25 minutes. Drain. Let cool. Cut into ½-inch dice.

2 In large nonstick skillet over medium-high heat, heat oil. Add onion. Sauté until lightly softened, 4 minutes. Add red and green bell peppers. Sauté until softened, about 4 minutes.

3 Stir in potatoes, chicken, garlic, paprika, thyme, salt, and pepper. With flat side of spoon, press hash into even layer over bottom of skillet. Cook, without stirring, until bottom is well browned, about 5 minutes.

Per serving: 202 calories, 13 g protein, 16 g carbohydrates, 10 g fat, 2 g saturated fat, 31 mg cholesterol, 3 g fiber, 325 mg sodium

DID YOU KNOW ● ● ●

...that the capsicum peppers used to make the best Hungarian paprika contain six to nine times the amount of vitamin C as tomatoes by weight? The redder the paprika, the milder the taste; the more yellow in the color, the hotter the bite.

Asparagus & Eggs on Toast with Tomatoes & Ham

The folic acid, vitamin C, and beta-carotene in asparagus help protect you from heart disease.

4 SERVINGS

Prep 15 min ◆ **Cook** 6 min

- 24 **thin stalks asparagus or 12 thick stalks, trimmed**
- 4 **slices seven-grain bread**
- 4 **teaspoons Dijon mustard**
- 8 **slices 97% fat-free ham**
- 2 **hard-cooked eggs, peeled and sliced**
- 8 **thin slices tomatoes**
- 2 **slices provolone cheese, cut into thin strips**

1 Preheat broiler.

2 In skillet of simmering water, cook asparagus until crisp-tender, 3 to 4 minutes. Drain well.

3 Place bread slices on baking sheet. Broil 3 to 4 inches from heat until bread is toasted, about 1 minute each side.

4 On each bread slice, spread 1 teaspoon mustard, then arrange 2 slices of ham, 6 thin or 3 thick asparagus spears, half of 1 sliced hard-cooked egg, 2 tomato slices, and a quarter of the provolone strips.

5 Broil sandwiches until cheese is melted and golden brown and sandwich is heated through, 1 to 2 minutes.

Per serving: 199 calories, 15 g protein, 17 g carbohydrates, 9 g fat, 4 g saturated fat, 128 mg cholesterol, 3 g fiber, 738 mg sodium

Winter Squash Waffles

The deep orange squash puree in these delicious breakfast treats packs each bite with beta-carotene and fiber.

12 (FOUR-INCH) WAFFLES

Prep 10 min ◆ **Cook** 20 min

- 3 cups sifted cake flour
- 1½ teaspoons baking soda
- 1 teaspoon cinnamon
- ½ teaspoon salt
- 4 large eggs
- ⅓ cup packed light-brown sugar
- 1 package (12 ounces) frozen pureed squash, thawed
- ¾ cup low-fat buttermilk
- ¼ cup vegetable oil
- 1½ teaspoons grated orange zest
- 1 teaspoon vanilla extract

1 Preheat oven to 200°F. Preheat waffle iron.

2 In medium bowl stir together flour, baking soda, cinnamon, and salt. In large bowl stir together eggs and sugar. Stir in squash, buttermilk, oil, zest, and vanilla. Whisk in flour mixture just until smooth.

3 Lightly coat waffle iron with nonstick cooking spray. Pour batter, about ½ cup for each 4-inch square waffle, onto iron, spreading quickly. Cook according to manufacturer's instructions. Place finished waffle on baking sheet in oven to keep warm. Make remaining waffles, coating waffle iron with cooking spray as needed. Serve hot with fresh fruit or hot maple syrup.

Per waffle: 211 calories, 5 g protein, 32 g carbohydrates, 7 g fat, 1g saturated fat, 71 mg cholesterol, 1g fiber, 295 mg sodium

Pumpkin Griddle Cakes

Whether it's fresh, frozen, or canned, pumpkin meat is high in fiber and an unbeatable source of beta-carotene.

18 GRIDDLE CAKES

Prep 14 min ◆ **Cook** 20 min

- 2 cups all-purpose flour
- 1½ teaspoons baking powder
- ½ teaspoon baking soda
- 1 teaspoon pumpkin pie spice
- ¼ teaspoon salt
- 3 large eggs
- ⅓ cup packed light-brown sugar
- 1¼ cups milk
- 1¼ cups fresh or canned solid-pack pumpkin puree
- 3 tablespoons vegetable oil

1 Preheat oven to 200°F.

2 In medium bowl, stir together flour, baking powder, baking soda, pie spice, and salt. In large bowl, stir together eggs and sugar. Stir in milk, pumpkin, and oil. Add flour mixture and stir just until smooth.

3 Heat griddle or large nonstick skillet over medium heat. Lightly coat with nonstick cooking spray. Working in batches, drop batter, ¼ cup at a time, onto hot griddle. Cook pancakes until bubbles form on top and bottoms are golden brown, about 2½ minutes. Turn pancakes over. Cook until bottoms are golden brown, about 2 minutes. Place on baking sheet in oven to keep warm. Make remaining pancakes, coating griddle with cooking spray as needed.

4 Top with dried cranberries or raisins softened in a pot of warm maple syrup, and a sprinkling of toasted walnuts.

Per cake: 115 calories, 3 g protein, 17 g carbohydrates, 4 g fat, 1 g saturated fat, 38 mg cholesterol, 1 g fiber, 120 mg sodium

HINT **helpful HINT** HINT HINT HINT HINT HINT HINT

Freeze leftover waffles and pancakes in plastic bags for another time when you need a quick breakfast. To reheat, place frozen waffles or pancakes in a pop-up toaster or toaster oven at 300°F for 3 to 5 minutes.

VEGETABLES FOR VITALITY

Potato Pancakes with Apple Rings

Adding carrot to these old-fashioned grated potato cakes gives them a big beta-carotene boost. The apples and potatoes already supply plenty of vitamins C and B$_6$—both good for fighting arthritis— and the onion offers some folate for healthy tissue growth.

12 (THREE-INCH) PANCAKES

Prep 20 min   **Cook** 45 min

- **2 teaspoons unsalted butter**
- **2 apples, cored and sliced into ¼-inch-thick rings**
- **1 pound russet potatoes, grated and blotted dry**
- **1 medium carrot, peeled, grated, and blotted dry**
- **⅓ cup grated onion**
- **2 large eggs, lightly beaten**
- **2 tablespoons all-purpose flour**
- **¾ teaspoon salt**
- **¼ cup vegetable oil**

1 Preheat oven to 200°F. In large nonstick skillet over medium heat, melt butter. Add apples. Cook, turning slices over occasionally, until tender, 10 to 12 minutes. Place in oven to keep warm.

2 In large bowl, combine potatoes, carrot, onion, and eggs. Stir in flour and salt until well combined.

3 In large nonstick skillet over medium heat, heat 2 tablespoons oil. Measuring ¼ cup batter, well packed, for each pancake, cook 4 pancakes at a time until well browned and crisp on bottom, about 4 minutes. Turn pancakes over and press down on each with back of metal spatula to flatten slightly. Cook until browned, crisp, and cooked through, another 4 minutes. Drain on paper towels. Place on baking sheet in oven to keep warm. Repeat to make another 8 pancakes, using remaining oil as needed. Top pancakes with apple rings.

Per pancake: 123 calories, 2 g protein, 15 g carbohydrates, 6 g fat, 1 g saturated fat, 37 mg cholesterol, 2 g fiber, 162 mg sodium

DID YOU KNOW ● ● ●

...that because they are fibrous and juicy and not at all sticky, raw apples are good at cleaning teeth and stimulating gums when you have no toothbrush handy?

HINT helpful HINT HINT HINT HINT HINT HINT HINT

You can keep both the apple rings and the potato pancakes from drying out in the oven while you finish up the last batches by covering them loosely with aluminum foil.

SIPS, snacks and STARTERS

VEGETABLES FOR VITALITY

Raspberry-Beet-Berry Smoothie

According to psychologists, food appeals to us through our eyes as well as our palates. The vibrant color and luxurious texture of this vitamin C-packed blend of beets, raspberries, and cranberry juice should make it irresistible.

4 SERVINGS

Prep 10 min

- 2 cooked beets (4½ ounces), cooled and coarsely chopped
- 2 ounces fresh or frozen raspberries
- 1 cup cranberry juice, chilled
- 1 cup lowfat plain yogurt
- Chilled raspberries for garnish *(optional)*

1 In food processor or blender, puree beets, raspberries, and cranberry juice until smooth.

2 Pour puree through a strainer into a large pitcher. Whisk in most of the yogurt.

3 Pour into 4 glasses and top with remaining yogurt. Garnish with extra raspberries, if you like. Serve immediately.

Per serving: 90 calories, 4 g protein, 18 g carbohydrates, 1 g fat, 1 g saturated fat, 5 mg cholesterol, 2 g fiber, 75 mg sodium

FRESH IDEAS

For extra kick, add some fresh herbs to your favorite smoothie—chopped parsley, crushed mint, or some feathery branches of dill or fennel, for example.

Carrot-Orange Juice

Wake up to this immune-boosting antioxidant cocktail that supplies all your vitamin A for the day and more than half your requirement for vitamin C.

2 SERVINGS

Prep 5 min

- 1½ cups fresh or bottled carrot juice, chilled
- ⅔ cup fresh-squeezed orange juice (3 oranges)
- ½ -inch-thick slice peeled fresh ginger

In bowl, mix carrot juice and orange juice. Crush ginger in garlic press to fill ½ teaspoon. Stir crushed ginger into juice mixture and serve. (If making ahead, stir before serving.)

Per serving: 75 calories, 2 g protein, 17 g carbohydrates, 0 g fat, 0 g saturated fat, 0 mg cholesterol, 0 g fiber, 93 mg sodium

Tomato Smoothie

This "savory smoothie" is a surefire bone-builder, thanks to calcium from the yogurt and vitamin C from fresh tomatoes.

2 SERVINGS

Prep 5 min

- 1 cup plain low-fat yogurt
- 2 large ripe plum tomatoes, peeled, seeded, and chopped
- ½ teaspoon dried basil, crumbled
- ¼ teaspoon salt

In blender, whirl yogurt, tomatoes, basil, and salt until very smooth, 2 minutes. Serve over ice, if desired.

Per serving: 91 calories, 7 g protein, 12 g carbohydrates, 2 g fat, 1 g saturated fat, 7mg cholesterol, 1 g fiber, 382 mg sodium

HINT **helpful HINT** HINT HINT HINT HINT HINT HINT

If you don't have a blender or food processor, you can still whip up smoothies with a wire whisk in a deep bowl.

FRESH IDEAS

For a summer starter, serve either of these drinks in a bowl as a cold soup.
Without being served on ice, the Spicy Vegetable Cocktail is very like a gazpacho
and the Orange-Tomato Blush, with a little plain low-fat yogurt whisked into it,
is like a Scandinavian fruit soup.

Spicy Vegetable Cocktail

The cancer-fighting phytochemical lycopene is highly concentrated in commercial tomato products like tomato juice.

4 SERVINGS

Prep 8 min

> **3** cups tomato juice
> **¼** cup coarsely chopped, seeded green bell pepper
> **1** scallion, trimmed to 5 inches, thinly sliced
> **1** tablespoon coarsely chopped parsley
> **1** tablespoon horseradish
> **1** teaspoon Worcestershire sauce
> **½** teaspoon sugar
> **½** teaspoon hot red pepper sauce, or to taste
> Celery stalks and lemon slices, for garnish
> *(optional)*

1 In blender, whirl tomato juice, green pepper, scallion, parsley, horseradish, Worcestershire, sugar, and hot pepper sauce until smooth, 2 to 3 minutes.

2 Serve over ice. Garnish with celery and lemon, if desired.

Per serving: 46 calories, 2 g protein, 9 g carbohydrates, 0 g fat, 0 g saturated fat, 0 mg cholesterol, 1 g fiber, 687 mg sodium

DID YOU KNOW ● ● ●

. . . that you need a special appliance to make your own vegetable juices? Blenders and food processors can puree vegetables to a consistency suitable for soups, but to separate out a vegetable's liquid, you need a juice extractor. Some extractors will also press juice out of oranges and other citrus fruits, but that is a separate process.

Orange-Tomato Blush

This wonderfully tangy drink, packed with energy-yielding carbohydrates, is refreshing for breakfast or brunch or as a pick-me-up at any time of day. It also makes an excellent alcohol-free alternative to a cocktail before lunch or dinner.

4 SERVINGS

Prep 25 min

> **1** ripe mango, peeled and coarsely chopped
> **1** pound tomatoes, skinned, halved and seeded
> **1½** pound watermelon, peeled, seeded and cut into chunks
> Grated zest and juice of 1 orange
> Grated zest and juice of 1 lime
> Ice
> **Orange and lime slices** *(optional)*

1 In a food processor or blender, puree mango, tomatoes, watermelon, orange and lime zest and juice until smooth. (You may have to do this in 2 batches.)

2 Half fill 4 large glasses with ice. Fill with orange-tomato blush. Garnish with orange and lime slices, if you like. Serve immediately.

Per serving: 130 calories, 4 g protein, 29 g carbohydrates, 1 g fat, 0 g saturated fat, 0 mg cholesterol, 3 g fiber, 90 mg sodium

VEGETABLES FOR VITALITY

FRESH IDEAS

Mix up the vegetables you put on your hors d'oeuvres tray. Try fennel sticks, jicama slices, endive leaves, kohlrabi juliennes, tiny purple carrots, and bok choy ribs with any of your favorite dips.

Steamed Vegetable Platter with Peanut Dip

This high-fiber party platter is super high in flavor.

8 SERVINGS

Prep 20 min ◆ **Cook** 20 min

- ⅔ **cup water**
- ⅓ **cup creamy peanut butter**
- 1 **clove garlic, minced**
- 2 **teaspoons grated fresh ginger**
- 2 **medium scallions, chopped**
- 2 **tablespoons packed brown sugar**
- 2 **tablespoons soy sauce**
- ⅛ **teaspoon chili powder**
- 1 **tablespoon fresh-squeezed lemon juice**
- 6 **large carrots, peeled, halved lengthwise, cut in 3 x ¼-inch sticks or 16 baby carrots with stems, scraped**
- 2 **large red or yellow bell peppers, halved, seeded, sliced ¼-inch thick**
- ½ **pound snow peas, trimmed or ½ pound green beans, trimmed**
- 8 **radishes, sliced thin**

1 For peanut dip: In small saucepan, bring water to boil. Stir in peanut butter, garlic, ginger, scallions, sugar, soy sauce, and chili powder. Simmer 2 minutes. Remove from heat. Stir in lemon juice. Set aside to cool slightly or refrigerate until ready to serve.

2 In a large saucepan with a steaming basket, bring water to a boil. Fill a sink with ice water. Steam carrots for 3 minutes, lift out and plunge into ice water to cool. Steam bell peppers for 1 minute, lift out, and plunge into ice water to cool. Steam snow peas or beans for 2 minutes, lift out, and plunge into ice water to cool. Drain vegetables and dry with paper towels.

3 On serving platter, arrange carrots, bell peppers, and snow peas or green beans with peanut dip in small bowl in center. Add radishes for garnish and contrast.

Per serving: 136 calories, 5 g protein, 19 g carbohydrates, 6 g fat, 1 g saturated fat, 0 mg cholesterol, 5 g fiber, 305 mg sodium

Creamy Spinach Dip

Leafy green vegetables like spinach are rich in folate, which helps protect against heart disease and birth defects.

6 SERVINGS

Prep 10 min

- 1 **box (10 ounces) frozen chopped spinach, thawed and squeezed dry**
- 1 **cup plain low-fat yogurt**
- ½ **cup reduced-fat mayonnaise**
- 2 **teaspoons dried dill**
- ½ **teaspoon celery seed**
- ⅛ **teaspoon salt**
- 1 **clove garlic, crushed**

In food processor, whirl spinach, yogurt, mayonnaise, dill, celery seed, salt, and garlic until smooth and creamy. Refrigerate for an hour before serving.

Per serving: 106 calories, 4 g protein, 7 g carbohydrates, 8 g fat, 2 g saturated fat, 9 mg cholesterol, 2 g fiber, 273 mg sodium

HINT **helpful HINT** HINT HINT HINT HINT HINT HINT HINT

Always make dips well ahead of time. Sitting in the refrigerator an hour or more not only allows a dip to chill properly, but it also allows the flavors to develop more fully and better complement each other.

VEGETABLES FOR VITALITY

Chiles con Queso with Vegetable Dippers

Antioxidant-rich fresh vegetables replace the usual chip dippers in this crowd-pleasing starter.

8 SERVINGS

Prep 20 min ◆ **Cook** 12 min

  2 **teaspoons olive oil**
  1 **green bell pepper, seeded and chopped**
  1 **medium onion, chopped**
  1 **can (4½ ounces) chopped green chiles**
  1 **cup chopped tomato**
1½ **teaspoons ground cumin**
  ½ **teaspoon salt**
  8 **ounces cream cheese**
  3 **tablespoons chopped cilantro**
  2 **teaspoons hot red pepper sauce**
  1 **red bell pepper, seeded and sliced**
  2 **small carrots, peeled and cut in sticks**
    Stalk celery, cut into sticks

1 In large nonstick skillet over medium heat, heat oil. Add green pepper and onion. Sauté until softened, 5 minutes. Add chiles, tomato, cumin, and salt. Cook 3 minutes.

2 Add cheese, cilantro, and hot sauce. Reduce heat to low. Cook, stirring, until cheese melts and mixture is creamy, 2 to 3 minutes. Serve warm with raw red pepper, carrots, and celery.

Per serving: 147 calories, 4 g protein, 9 g carbohydrates, 11 g fat, 6 g saturated fat, 31 mg cholesterol, 3 g fiber, 339 mg sodium

Grilled Tomato & Bell Pepper Salsa

Red and yellow peppers top the list of great sources of vitamin C.

6 SERVINGS

Prep 20 min ◆ **Cook** 12 min

  2 **firm-ripe tomatoes**
  1 **small onion, cut into ¾-inch-thick slices**
  2 **teaspoons olive oil**
  1 **ear corn, inner layer of husk intact**
  1 **small red bell pepper, seeded and finely chopped**
  1 **small yellow bell pepper, seeded and finely chopped**
  2 **cloves garlic, finely chopped**
  ½ **teaspoon ground cumin**
  ½ **teaspoon dried oregano, crumbled**
  ½ **teaspoon salt**
  ¼ **teaspoon chili powder**
  2 **tablespoons chopped cilantro**

1 Heat grill to medium hot or preheat broiler. Brush tomatoes and onion with oil. Place tomatoes, onion, and corn on grill or broiler pan.

2 Grill or broil 4 inches from heat, turning frequently, until lightly browned, 10 to 12 minutes.

3 When cool enough to handle, finely chop tomatoes and onion. Remove husk from corn and cut kernels from cob.

4 In serving bowl, combine tomatoes, onion, corn, red pepper, yellow pepper, garlic, cumin, oregano, salt, chili powder, and cilantro. Refrigerate until ready to serve.

Per serving: 48 calories, 1 g protein, 8 g carbohydrates, 2 g fat, 0 g saturated fat, 0 mg cholesterol, 2 g fiber, 202 mg sodium

DID YOU KNOW ● ● ●

. . .that not everybody likes cilantro? No herb with such a signature taste can please every palate. If you or your family are not cilantro fans, try substituting flat Italian parsley, chervil, or dill in your next batch of salsa, tablespoon for tablespoon.

DID YOU KNOW ● ● ●

. . . that mushrooms contain compounds called triterpenoids, which seem to fight cancer by inhibiting certain steps in the formation of tumors? Cooking mushrooms breaks down their fibrous cell walls, making some of their nutrients more available to the body.

Crostini with Artichokes & Tomato

A fast and flavorful way to boost your vitamin C intake.

4 SERVINGS (2 CROSTINI PER SERVING)

Prep 10 min ◆ **Cook** 2 min

- 1 jar (6 ounces) marinated artichokes, well drained and coarsely chopped
- 1 large tomato, seeded and coarsely chopped
- ¼ cup pitted black olives, coarsely chopped
- 2 tablespoons chopped parsley
- 1 tablespoon olive oil
- 1 small clove garlic, passed through a garlic press
- ¼ teaspoon salt
- ⅛ teaspoon black pepper
- 8 thin slices Italian bread, lightly toasted

1 In medium bowl, combine artichokes, tomato, olives, parsley, oil, garlic, salt, and pepper.

2 Just before serving, divide artichoke mixture equally among toast slices.

Per serving: 197 calories, 5 g protein, 27 g carbohydrates, 9 g fat, 1 g saturated fat, 0 mg cholesterol, 3 g fiber, 591 mg sodium

HINT **helpful HINT** HINT HINT HINT HINT HINT HINT

Crostini, like bruschetta, are cut from good French or Italian breads. Crostini are usually smaller—¹/₂-inch thick and no more than 2 inches in diameter, an easy hors d'oeuvre bite. Bruschetta are ³/₄-inch thick and the overall diameter is larger. Both can be topped and served as an hors d'oeuvre with drinks. Bruschetta are a more generous first course.

Vegetable-Stuffed Mushrooms

Start any meal with this fiber-packed first course.

4 SERVINGS

Prep 20 min ◆ **Cook** 20 min

- 24 large or 12 extra-large mushrooms, stems removed
- 2 teaspoons vegetable oil
- 1 onion, finely chopped
- 3 cloves garlic, minced
- 1 carrot, finely chopped
- 1 red bell pepper, finely chopped
- ½ cup chicken broth
- ½ teaspoon dried oregano
- 3 tablespoons grated Parmesan cheese
- 2 tablespoons chopped parsley

1 Preheat oven to 400°F. In a medium pot of boiling water, cook the mushroom caps for 2 minutes to blanch. Drain on paper towels.

2 In large skillet over moderate heat, heat oil. Add onion and garlic, and sauté for 5 minutes. Add carrot and pepper, and cook for 4 minutes. Add broth and oregano, and cook for 4 minutes or until the vegetables are very soft. Remove from heat; stir in Parmesan and parsley.

3 Spoon mixture into the mushroom caps and place on baking sheet

4 Bake 10 minutes or until piping hot.

Per serving: 90 calories, 6 g protein, 9 g carbohydrates, 5 g fat, 1 g saturated fat, 5 mg cholesterol, 2 g fiber, 120 mg sodium

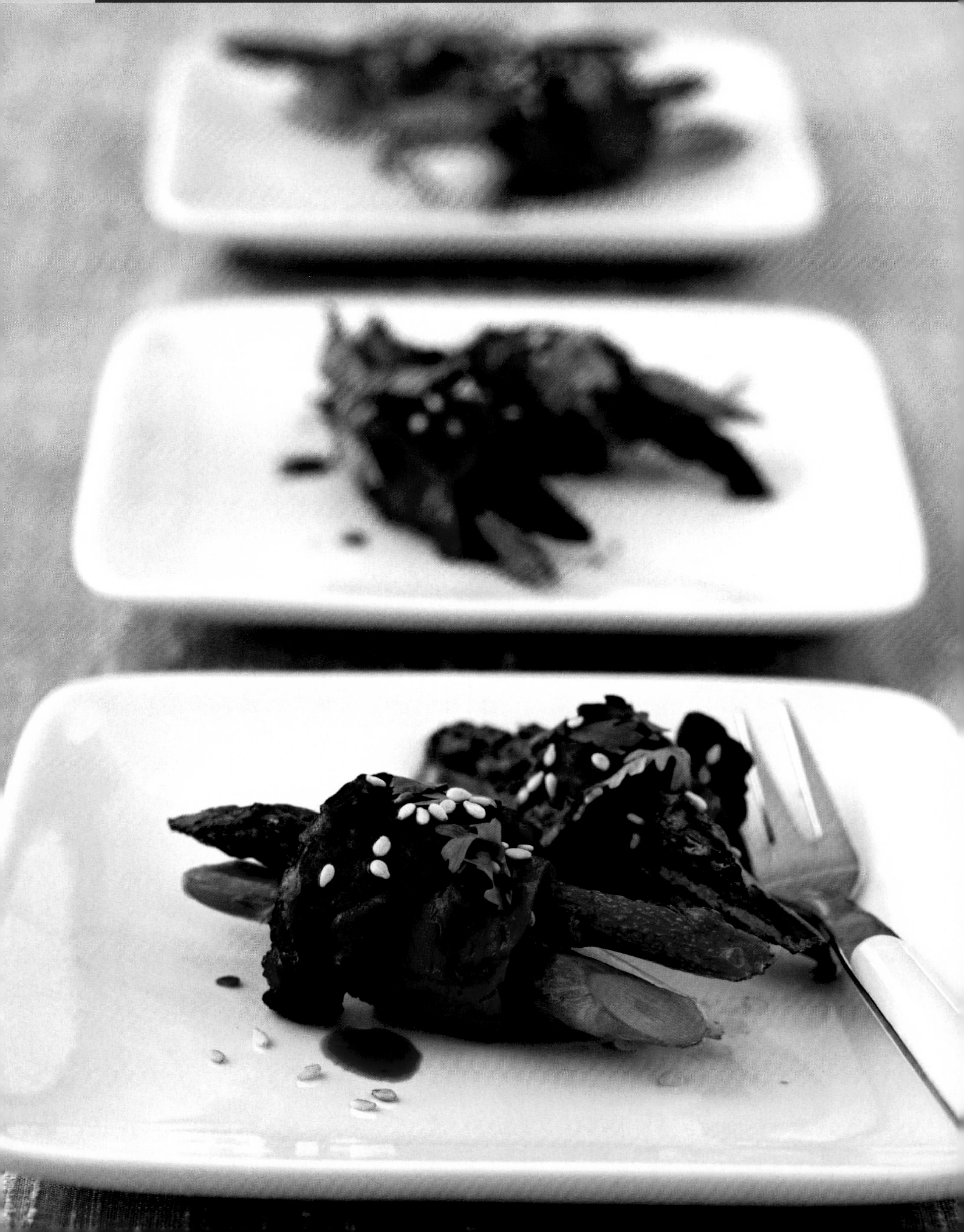

Beef, Scallion & Asparagus Roll-Ups

The green tops of scallions are a good source of vitamin C and beta-carotene, antioxidants that protect against all types of chronic disease.

4 SERVINGS (2 ROLL-UPS PER SERVING)

Prep 15 min ◆ **Cook** 6 min

- **8 asparagus stalks, trimmed to 6-inch lengths**
- **8 thin slices sirloin steak (¼ pound total)**
- **4 scallions, trimmed to 6-inch lengths**
- **2 teaspoons vegetable oil**
- **3 tablespoons bottled teriyaki sauce**
- **1 tablespoon sesame seeds, toasted**
- **1 tablespoon chopped cilantro**

1 Heat saucepan of water to a boil. Cut each asparagus stalk in half. Blanch in boiling water 1 minute, and then drain. Meanwhile, pound sirloin slices to ⅛-inch thickness. Cut each scallion into two 3-inch pieces.

2 Place 2 pieces of asparagus and 1 piece scallion near one end of each beef strip. Roll beef around middle of vegetables to form 8 bundles.

3 In large nonstick skillet over medium-high heat, heat oil. Add rolls. Brown 2 minutes, turning rolls frequently. Add teriyaki sauce, lower heat to medium, and boil 3 minutes.

4 Transfer rolls to serving platter. Sprinkle with sesame seeds and cilantro.

Per serving: 91 calories, 7 g protein, 4 g carbohydrates, 5 g fat, 1 g saturated fat, 16 mg cholesterol, 1 g fiber, 533 mg sodium

DID YOU KNOW ● ● ●

. . . that when you see the word "negamaki" on a Japanese restaurant menu, it refers to beef roll-ups, such as the Beef, Scallion & Asparagus Roll-Ups in the recipe above?

Pita Pizzas

Eating sweet peppers can help reduce your risk of stroke because they're rich in vitamin C.

4 SERVINGS

Prep 10 min ◆ **Cook** 3 min

- **½ cup thinly sliced roasted red bell peppers**
  (see page 295)
- **¼ teaspoon crushed fennel seeds or dried oregano, crumbled**
- **¼ teaspoon salt**
- **⅛ teaspoon black pepper**
- **1 ounce reduced-fat mozzarella cheese, shredded (about ¼ cup)**
- **½ ounce Gruyère or Jarlsberg cheese, shredded (about 2 tablespoons)**
- **2 whole-wheat pita breads (4 inches)**
- **8 teaspoons bottled tomato sauce or pizza sauce**
- **½ small red onion, thinly sliced**

1 Preheat broiler.

2 In small bowl, combine red peppers, fennel or oregano, salt, and pepper. In second bowl, combine mozzarella and Gruyère.

3 Separate each pita bread into 2 flat rounds. Place rounds, rough side up, on baking sheet. Broil 4 inches from heat until golden brown around edges, about 1 minute. Remove from broiler.

4 Spread 2 teaspoons sauce over each pita, covering edges. Spoon 2 tablespoons red pepper mixture over each pita. Sprinkle with cheese, dividing equally, then add onion in rings.

5 Broil until cheese is melted and pizzas are hot, about 2 minutes.

Per serving: 137 calories, 7 g protein, 23 g carbohydrates, 3 g fat, 2 g saturated fat, 7 mg cholesterol, 3 g fiber, 475 mg sodium

VEGETABLES FOR VITALITY

Baked Spinach-Stuffed Clams

Clams are packed with iron for healthy blood and zinc for a strong immune system.

4 SERVINGS

Prep 15 min ◆ **Cook** 25 min

- 12 **cherrystone or other hardshell clams**
- 3 **teaspoons olive oil**
- ¼ **cup finely chopped onion**
- 2 **cloves garlic, minced**
- 4 **teaspoons flour**
- ⅔ **cup fat-free half & half**
- ⅛ **teaspoon cayenne pepper**
- ⅓ **cup frozen chopped spinach, well drained**
- ⅓ **cup fresh bread crumbs**
- 4 **teaspoons grated Parmesan cheese**

1 In large skillet with ½ inch of water, place clams. Bring to a boil, cover, and cook 4 minutes or until clams open. (Start checking after 2 minutes and remove clams as they open; discard any that do not.) Transfer clams to bowl; when cool enough to handle, remove top shell halves and discard. Place shell halves with clams attached on baking sheet.

2 Preheat oven to 450°F. In small saucepan, heat 2 teaspoons oil over low heat. Add onion and garlic, and sauté for 5 minutes or until soft. Whisk in flour and cook for 1 minute. Whisk in half & half, salt, and cayenne, and cook for 3 minutes or until lightly thickened. Stir in spinach. Spoon spinach mixture over clams.

3 In small bowl, toss together bread crumbs and cheese. Top clams with bread-crumb mixture and drizzle with remaining teaspoon oil. Bake just until clams are bubbly and hot, about 5 minutes.

Per serving: 150 calories, 9 g protein, 16 g carbohydrates, 5 g fat, 1g saturated fat, 16 mg cholesterol, 1 g fiber, 330 mg sodium

Grilled Eggplant & Tomato Sandwiches

You'll get heart-protective nutrients in every bite.

6 SERVINGS

Prep 15 min ◆ **Cook** 12 min

- 2 **ounces goat cheese, crumbled**
- 1 **tablespoon snipped fresh chives or finely chopped green scallion tops**
- ¼ **cup dry bread crumbs**
- 2 **tablespoons grated Parmesan cheese**
- ½ **teaspoon dried basil, crumbled**
- 1 **large egg**
- 1 **large egg white**
- ¼ **teaspoon salt**
- 12 **slices ¼-inch-thick peeled eggplant**
- 6 **thin slices tomato, blotted dry**
- 2 **tablespoons olive oil**

1 In small bowl, mix goat cheese and chives. In pie plate, combine crumbs, cheese, and basil. In second pie plate, beat egg, egg white, and salt.

2 Spread about 2 teaspoons goat cheese mixture on eggplant slice. Top with tomato slice and another eggplant slice. Repeat to make 5 more sandwiches.

3 Dip each sandwich in egg, then crumb mixture to coat both sides. Place on wax paper.

4 In large nonstick skillet over medium-low heat, heat about 1½ tablespoons oil. Add sandwiches in single layer, working in batches if necessary. Cook until fork-tender and golden brown, 10 to 12 minutes, turning over halfway through cooking. Add more oil as needed if skillet gets dry. Serve warm.

Per serving: 133 calories, 6 g protein, 6 g carbohydrates, 10 g fat, 4 g saturated fat, 47 mg cholesterol, 1 g fiber, 213 mg sodium

FRESH IDEAS

For a sharper taste, substitute feta cheese or a more aged goat's milk or sheep's milk cheese for mild goat cheese in recipes. Goat's milk and sheep's milk are higher in fat than whole cow's milk, but lower in cholesterol. The longer these cheeses are aged, the tarter they become. Feta, made from either sheep's or goat's milk, is brined and needs to be rinsed in fresh cold water to cut down the salt.

on the menu

These Tex-Mex snacks are delicious eaten plain, but to make them more
festive, top with a spoonful of salsa, a dollop of yogurt or sour cream, and
a sprig of cilantro. To fill out a lunch, add a green salad and a dish of fruit
sherbet for dessert.

Chile-Cheese Quesadillas with Tomatoes

Chiles contain phytonutrients that protect against cancer and other chronic diseases.

4 SERVINGS (3 WEDGES PER SERVING)

Prep 15 min ◆ **Cook** 12 min

- **6 flour tortillas (8 inches)**
- **1 large tomato, seeded and finely chopped**
- **1 cup shredded Monterey Jack or cheddar cheese**
- **1 can (4.5 ounces) chopped mild chiles**
- **1 tablespoon chopped cilantro**
- **¼ teaspoon salt**
- **⅛ teaspoon black pepper**

1 Preheat oven to 200°F.

2 Place 3 tortillas on work surface. Sprinkle equally with tomato, cheese, chiles, cilantro, salt, and pepper. Place remaining tortillas on top. Gently press quesadillas to flatten.

3 Coat large nonstick skillet with nonstick cooking spray. Heat over medium-high heat. Place one quesadilla at a time in skillet. Cook until lightly browned on both sides and cheese is melted, about 2 minutes per side. Transfer to baking sheet; place in oven to keep warm. Repeat with the remaining quesadillas. To serve, cut each quesadilla into 4 wedges.

Per serving: 359 calories, 14 g protein, 44 g carbohydrates, 14 g fat, 7 g saturated fat, 25 mg cholesterol, 4 g fiber, 769 mg sodium

DID YOU KNOW ● ● ●

. . . that pan-grilled sandwiches in Italy are called panini? Very much like our classic grilled cheese sandwiches, they contain a different cheese—mozzarella instead of cheddar—and a different fat—olive oil instead of butter. The Italian sandwich can be varied with herbs and other ingredients, such as mushrooms or olives.

Pan-Grilled Tomato, Mozzarella & Basil Sandwich

Fresh green herbs like basil contain small amounts of protective antioxidant nutrients such as vitamin C and beta-carotene.

4 SANDWICHES

Prep 10 min ◆ **Cook** 4 min

- **4 thin slices mozzarella cheese (4 ounces total)**
- **8 thin slices tomato, seeded**
- **8 thin slices red onion**
- **8 basil leaves, shredded**
- **8 small slices Italian sandwich bread**
- **¼ teaspoon salt**
- **⅛ teaspoon black pepper**
- **4 teaspoons olive oil**

1 Blot mozzarella and tomato with paper towels.

2 Place 1 mozzarella slice, 2 tomato slices, 2 onion slices, and 2 shredded basil leaves on each of 4 slices of bread. Sprinkle with salt and pepper. Top with remaining bread.

3 In large nonstick skillet over medium heat, heat oil. Add sandwiches to skillet. Cook, firmly pressing down with spatula, until lightly browned, about 2 minutes. Turn sandwiches over. Cook, pressing down, until sandwich is browned and cheese is melted, about 2 minutes.

Per sandwich: 206 calories, 8 g protein, 17 g carbohydrates, 12 g fat, 5 g saturated fat, 23 mg cholesterol, 1 g fiber, 343 mg sodium

VEGETABLES FOR VITALITY

Bean & Vegetable Tostadas

Fiber from beans and vegetables keeps your digestive system healthy and can help lower your cholesterol.

6 TOSTADAS

Prep 15 min ◆ **Cook** 10 min

- 6 **corn tortillas (6 inches)**
- **Nonstick cooking spray**
- 1 **can (15 ounces) black beans, drained and rinsed**
- 1 **can (11 ounces) canned corn kernels, drained and rinsed**
- 1 **small tomato, cored and chopped (about ½ cup)**
- 2 **tablespoons finely chopped red onion**
- 1 **small jalapeño pepper, seeded and finely chopped**
- 2 **tablespoons chopped cilantro**
- 1 **tablespoon fresh-squeezed lime juice**
- ½ **teaspoon salt**
- ⅛ to ¼ **teaspoon hot red pepper sauce**
- 1 **small ripe avocado, pitted, peeled, and chopped**

1 Preheat oven 450°F. Place tortillas in single layer on baking sheets. Coat both sides of tortillas with cooking spray. Bake until lightly browned and crisp, about 10 minutes, flipping tortillas over halfway through. Transfer to wire racks and let cool.

2 In large bowl, stir together beans, corn, tomato, onion, jalapeño, cilantro, lime juice, salt, and hot sauce. Gently fold in avocado. Spoon ½ cup onto each tortilla.

Per tostada: 130 calories, 5 g protein, 26 g carbohydrates, 1 g fat, 0 g saturated fat, 0 mg cholesterol, 5 g fiber, 390 mg sodium

Corned Beef & Cabbage Calzones

Cabbage and other members of the cruciferous vegetable family help protect against cancers of the breast and prostate.

12 CALZONES

Prep 20 min ◆ **Cook** 35 min

- 2 **teaspoons vegetable oil**
- 1 **large onion, finely chopped**
- 3 **cups shredded green cabbage (½ of small head)**
- 1 **carrot, peeled and chopped**
- 2 **teaspoons Dijon mustard**
- ¼ **teaspoon salt**
- ⅛ **teaspoon black pepper**
- 1 **cup shredded part-skim Jarlsberg cheese (4 ounces)**
- ¼ **cup chopped deli corned beef (about 2 ounces)**
- **Half of 32-ounce package frozen pizza dough, thawed**

1 Preheat oven to 400°F.

2 In large nonstick skillet over medium heat, heat vegetable oil. Add onion. Sauté until slightly softened, about 3 minutes. Stir in cabbage, carrot, mustard, salt, and pepper. Cover and reduce heat to low. Cook until cabbage is wilted, 10 to 15 minutes, adding water if necessary to prevent sticking. Uncover and cook 1 minute, stirring. Let cool slightly. Stir in cheese and corned beef.

3 Shape dough into 12-inch-long log on lightly floured board, adding flour as needed to prevent sticking. Divide into 12 equal pieces. Roll or pat out 1 piece of dough into 6-inch circle. Spoon ¼ cup filling over lower half of round. Fold dough over to enclose filling. Press edges firmly to seal. Crimp edges with fork. Transfer to ungreased baking sheet. Repeat with remaining filling and dough.

4 Bake until heated through and golden brown, about 20 minutes. Cool on wire rack 15 minutes. (If you want to make calzones ahead, wrap the unbaked pies in plastic and keep in the refrigerator for up to 3 days before baking.)

Per calzone: 166 calories, 8 g protein, 23 g carbohydrates, 5 g fat, 2 g saturated fat, 9 mg cholesterol, 2 g fiber, 373 mg sodium

on the menu

*For a hearty lunch serve two Corned Beef & Cabbage Calzones per person
with a crisp green salad on the side and Pumpkin Spice Ice Cream (page 284)
for dessert.*

VEGETABLES FOR VITALITY

on the menu

To make four servings for lunch, cut each wrap in half. To serve as finger food at a party or for a snack, cut each wrap into 6 equal-sized pieces.

Avocado-Turkey Wraps

Avocado is rich in heart-protective monounsaturated fats and vitamin E.

12 MINI-WRAPS

Prep 10 min

- 3 tablespoons reduced-fat mayonnaise
- 1 tablespoon coarse-grain Dijon mustard
- 2 flour tortillas (10 inches)
- 1 ripe avocado, pitted, peeled, and cut lengthwise into thin slices
- 8 ounces thinly sliced cooked turkey breast
- 1 jar (12 ounces) roasted red peppers, drained and cut into strips

1 In small bowl, combine mayonnaise and mustard. Lay tortillas on work surface. Spread mayonnaise mixture evenly over surface of tortillas, dividing equally.

2 Place avocado slices on top, leaving ½-inch border around edge. Top with turkey and pepper strips.

3 Roll up each tortilla tightly and place, seam side down, on cutting board. Trim ends of wraps evenly with serrated knife. Cut each wrap into 6 equal pieces. Place, cut side down, on serving platter.

Per mini-wrap: 99 calories, 7 g protein, 9 g carbohydrates, 4 g fat, 1 g saturated fat, 17 mg cholesterol, 2 g fiber, 126 mg sodium

helpful HINT

Large pita rounds, lavosh, and other thin, flat breads can also be used to make sandwich wraps. Although it may look better to layer the ingredients separately in a wrap, it is often more practical to mix some of them together so the filling stays intact and the wrap is easier to eat. For instance, instead of slicing the avocado for these Avocado-Turkey Wraps, mash it with the mayonnaise and mustard to make a thick spread that will help keep the other ingredients in place. If necessary, hold a wrap together with a toothpick.

Herbed Cheese Bagels

A little parsley adds a hint of freshness and color to dishes. When used in quantity, its unique flavor can really be appreciated. It also makes a healthy contribution of vitamin C.

4 SERVINGS

Prep 10 min

- 3½ ounces reduced-fat cream cheese
- 2 scallions, thinly sliced
- ½ cup parsley, finely chopped
- 2 tablespoons chopped fresh dill
- 1 tablespoon chopped fresh tarragon
- Salt and pepper to taste
- 4 bagels
- ½ cucumber, thinly sliced
- 3 tomatoes, thinly sliced
- 1 red onion, thinly sliced

1 In a bowl, combine cream cheese, scallions, parsley, dill, and tarragon. Add salt and pepper to taste and mix until well blended.

2 Slice bagels in half horizontally. Spread cheese mixture on bagel bases. Layer cucumber, tomato, and onion slices on the cheese and cover with tops of bagels. Serve immediately.

Per bagel: 280 calories, 11g protein, 50g carbohydrates, 7 g fat, 3 g saturated fat, 15 mg cholesterol, 9 g fiber, 290 mg sodium

FRESH IDEAS

For a mild herb flavor, reduce the quantity of parsley to 2 tablespoons. Alternatively, for a peppery flavor, finely chop 1 bunch watercress, tough stalks discarded, and use instead of parsley.

VEGETABLES FOR VITALITY

Roasted Vegetable Baguettes with Feta Cheese

Feta cheese can be high in fat and salt, but because it has such a strong flavor, a little goes a long way. The peppers, onion, and zucchini will keep your vitamin C count high to fight cholesterol and prevent clogged arteries.

4 SERVINGS

Prep 45 min

> 2 **red bell peppers, roasted, seeded, and peeled** *(see page 295)***, and quartered lengthwise**
> 4 **short French baguettes or rolls, about (4½ ounces) each, halved horizontally**
> 1 **red onion, cut into small wedges**
> 2 **large zucchini, thickly sliced diagonally**
> 2 to 3 **garlic cloves, chopped** *(optional)*
> 3 **sprigs fresh rosemary**
> 1 **tablespoon extra-virgin olive oil**
>   **Salt and pepper**
> 6 **ounces feta cheese**

1 Preheat broiler.

2 Lightly toast the cut sides of French bread under broiler. Remove the bread and set aside on a board.

3 Remove the broiler rack and discard any crumbs from the bottom of the broiler pan. Put onion, zucchini, and garlic, if using, in the pan. Sprinkle with leaves from the rosemary sprigs and drizzle with the oil. Add salt and pepper to taste, and cook for 8 to 10 minutes, turning vegetables once, or until browned on both sides.

4 Using a small, sharp knife, cut pepper into thick slices. Arrange pepper and zucchini mixture over bottom halves of toasted bread, spooning all the pan juices from the zucchini over. Arrange, side by side, in broiler pan.

5 Crumble feta cheese over vegetables and broil for 3 to 4 minutes or until cheese is slightly browned. Top with the remaining bread halves. Cut in half at an angle and serve immediately.

Per serving: 260 calories, 13 g protein, 29 g carbohydrates, 12 g fat, 5 g saturated fat, 15 mg cholesterol, 5 g fiber, 730 mg sodium

HINT **helpful HINT** HINT HINT HINT HINT HINT HINT HINT

Baguettes, loved for their wonderful crusts and chewy texture, do not keep well because they are made without fat. Buy them fresh—on the way home for dinner—and use them right away. If that isn't possible, freeze fresh baguettes for later use.

FRESH IDEAS

Drizzle a little balsamic vinegar over the grilled vegetable mixture before adding the feta. Fresh thyme can be used instead of rosemary. Use pita breads or thickly sliced rye bread instead of baguettes.

Taco with Homemade Salsa & Guacamole

Quick and easy to make, this filling and colorful main course is low in saturated fat but high in flavor. It is a great recipe to tempt even the most ardent of meat-eaters into enjoying a vegetable-based meal.

4 SERVINGS

Prep 10 min ◆ Cook 20 min

- 2 tablespoons extra-virgin olive oil
- 1 onion, finely chopped
- 1 eggplant (10 ounces), cubed
- 1 butternut squash (1½ pounds), halved, seeded, peeled and cubed
- 1 large zucchini (6 ounces), cubed
- ¼ teaspoon chili powder
- ½ teaspoon ground cumin
- 1 garlic clove, crushed
- 1 can (14½ ounces), tomatoes
- 1 large ripe avocado
  Juice of ½ lime
- 3 ripe tomatoes, diced
- ½ red onion, finely chopped
- ¼ cup chopped cilantro
- 8 taco shells
- 8 ounces plain low-fat yogurt
  Lime wedges and fresh cilantro for garnish

1 In large saucepan over medium-high heat, heat oil. Add white onion and eggplant, and sauté, stirring frequently, until vegetables are lightly browned.

2 Add squash and zucchini. Stir in chile powder, cumin, and garlic. Pour in canned tomatoes with their juice. Add salt and pepper to taste. Heat to boiling, breaking up tomatoes with wooden spoon. Cover and simmer 15 minutes, stirring occasionally, until squash is just tender. Check during cooking and add water, if needed, to prevent vegetables from sticking.

3 Meanwhile, preheat oven to 350°F. To make guacamole, halve and pit avocado, scoop out flesh into a bowl and mash with lime juice. To make salsa, in a separate bowl, mix together fresh tomatoes, red onion, and cilantro. Set guacamole and salsa aside.

4 Put taco shells on baking sheet and warm in oven for 3 to 4 minutes. Transfer shells to serving plates. Fill with eggplant mixture. Top with guacamole, yogurt, and salsa. Garnish with lime wedges and cilantro, and serve.

Per serving: 420 calories, 8 g protein, 56 g carbohydrates, 21 g fat, 3 g saturated fat, 0 mg cholesterol, 15 g fiber, 150 mg sodium

DID YOU KNOW ● ● ●

. . .that when tomatoes were first introduced to Europeans, they were eyed suspiciously and suspected of having aphrodisiac properties? Nutritionists now know that these "love apples," as they were called, do have benefits for the heart, but not in the romantic sense.

Roasted Vegetable Tart

Every slice is rich in fiber and vital nutrients such as vitamin C and beta-carotene.

6 SERVINGS

Prep 25 min ◆ **Cook** 50 min

- 1 unbaked prepared pie crust (9 inches)
- 1 small (12 ounces) butternut squash, peeled
- 1 large zucchini, cut into ¼-inch-thick slices
- 1 medium red onion, cut into ¼-inch-thick slices
- 1 tablespoon plus 1 teaspoon olive oil
- ½ teaspoon salt
- ¼ cup grated Parmesan cheese
- 3 tablespoons chopped basil
- 1 jar (6 ounces) roasted red peppers, drained and cut into strips

1 Heat oven to 400°F. With a rolling pin, reshape round crust into a square and place it in an 8-inch baking pan. Fold over edges and crimp to make a decorative edge. Prick bottom with fork. Line pie crust with foil and fill with pie weights or dried beans. Bake 15 minutes. Remove foil and weights. Bake until golden, 5 to 10 minutes. Leave oven on.

2 Meanwhile, slice long neck of squash crosswise into ¼-inch-thick rounds until reaching seeded end. Scoop out seeds from rest of squash. Slice squash into rings. In large bowl, combine squash, zucchini, onion, 1 tablespoon oil, and salt .

3 Arrange squash and half the onion in single layer on baking sheet. Arrange zucchini and remaining onion in single layer on second baking sheet. Roast until zucchini is tender, 10 to 12 minutes. Remove zucchini from baking sheet. Continue roasting squash and onion just until tender, 5 minutes longer. Reduce oven temperature to 250°F.

4 Just before serving, assemble tart. Sprinkle bottom of pie shell with 1 tablespoon cheese. Top with even layer of zucchini, half the onion, 1 tablespoon cheese, and 1 tablespoon basil. Next layer squash, remaining onion, 1 tablespoon cheese, and 1 tablespoon basil. Arrange roasted pepper on top. Brush with remaining teaspoon oil. Sprinkle with remaining tablespoon cheese. Heat tart in oven 10 minutes. Sprinkle with remaining tablespoon basil and serve.

Per serving: 189 calories, 4 g protein, 19 g carbohydrates, 11 g fat, 3 g saturated fat, 3 mg cholesterol, 3 g fiber, 561 mg sodium

Tuna-Olive Polenta Pie

Tomatoes and bell peppers add vitamins C, E and B$_6$, as well as folate to this cornmeal-based pizza.

4 SERVINGS

Prep 30 min ◆ **Cook** 10–12 min

- 12 ounces instant polenta
- 1 tablespoon chopped fresh thyme
- 3 tablespoons chopped parsley
- 1 tablespoon extra-virgin olive oil
- 1 can (14½ ounces) tomatoes, chopped
- 1 roasted yellow bell pepper (see page 295), **halved, seeded, and sliced**
- 1 can (6½ ounces) tuna in spring water, drained and flaked
- 1 container (8 ounces) ricotta cheese
- 12 black olives, pitted and halved
- 1 to 2 teaspoons fresh thyme leaves, for garnish

1 Preheat broiler. Coat 12-inch pizza pan with nonstick cooking spray. Cook polenta according to package directions. Remove from heat and stir in thyme, parsley, and salt and pepper to taste. Spoon polenta onto pizza pan, making a smooth round with raised edges. Brush edges with olive oil. Set aside.

2 Put tomatoes in a saucepan with their juice and bring to a boil. Simmer over moderate heat for 6–8 minutes, stirring occasionally, until most of liquid has evaporated, leaving a fairly thick sauce.

3 Spread tomato sauce over polenta base and top with the pepper strips, tuna, ricotta, and olives. Broil pie six inches form heat for 10 minutes or until bubbling and golden brown. Garnish with thyme leaves and serve.

Per serving: 440 calories, 25 g protein, 61 g carbohydrates, 9 g fat, 4 g saturated fat, 35 mg cholesterol, 7 g fiber, 360 mg sodium

VEGETABLES FOR VITALITY

Italian Spinach Pie

Eat plenty of spinach to help keep your heart in tip-top shape with vitamins A and C and folate.

6 SERVINGS

Prep 10 min ◆ **Cook** 38 min

- 1 tablespoon olive oil
- 2 medium leeks, white part only, halved lengthwise, thinly sliced, and rinsed
- 1 box (10 ounces) chopped spinach, thawed and squeezed dry
- 1 cup cooked long-grain white rice
- 3 large eggs
- 1 cup grated Parmesan cheese
- ½ teaspoon dried marjoram, crumbled
- ½ teaspoon salt
- ¼ teaspoon black pepper

1 In medium nonstick skillet over medium heat, heat oil. Add leeks. Sauté until softened, about 8 minutes. Set aside.

2 Preheat oven to 375°F. Lightly coat 9-inch glass pie plate with nonstick cooking spray.

3 In medium bowl, combine leeks, spinach, rice, eggs, ¾ cup Parmesan, marjoram, salt, and pepper. Spoon into prepared plate and smooth top. Sprinkle with remaining ¼ cup Parmesan.

4 Bake until firm and browned, about 30 minutes. Serve warm or at room temperature, cut into wedges.

Per serving: 174 calories, 11 g protein, 13 g carbohydrates, 9 g fat, 4 g saturated fat, 117 mg cholesterol, 2 g fiber, 524 mg sodium

Zucchini-Carrot Crustless Quiche Squares

Carrots are super-rich in the disease-fighting antioxidant beta-carotene, which your body uses to make vitamin A.

16 SMALL SQUARES

Prep 15 min ◆ **Cook** 1 hr

- 1 teaspoon olive oil
- 1 large onion, finely chopped
- 1 large zucchini, cut into ½-inch cubes
- ½ teaspoon salt
- 2 large eggs
- ¼ cup milk
- 3 medium carrots, peeled, grated, and blotted dry
- 1 cup shredded cheddar cheese
- 1 tablespoon chopped dill

1 Heat oven to 375°F. Lightly coat 8-inch square or round baking pan with nonstick cooking spray. In large nonstick skillet over medium heat, heat oil. Add onion. Sauté until slightly softened, 3 minutes. Add zucchini. Increase heat to medium-high and sauté until zucchini is soft and all liquid has evaporated, 7 to 10 minutes. Stir in ¼ teaspoon of the salt. Remove from heat.

2 In large bowl, beat eggs, milk, and remaining ¼ teaspoon salt. Add carrots, zucchini, cheese, and dill. Spread in prepared pan.

3 Bake until quiche is just set in center, 45 minutes. Transfer to wire rack. Let cool at least 10 minutes before cutting. Serve warm or at room temperature.

Per square: 54 calories, 3 g protein, 3 g carbohydrates, 3 g fat, 2 g saturated fat, 35 mg cholesterol, 1 g fiber, 128 mg sodium

FRESH IDEAS

You can make a healthy, low-fat vegetable crust for a quiche using russet potatoes. First grate enough potato to make 2 cups after you have squeezed out the liquid. In a medium bowl, mix the grated potato with some diced onion, ¼ cup flour, a beaten egg, and salt and pepper. Spread this mixture into a greased pie pan and bake in a 375°F oven for 10 minutes. Fill with the quiche filling and return to oven for 45 minutes or until it is set.

on the menu

By cutting the Zucchini-Carrot Crustless Quiche Squares into just four portions instead of 16, you have a tasty main course for lunch, both nutritious and low-calorie. Finish off the meal with a crisp baguette, a salad, and a healthy dessert, such as Sweet & Spicy Carrot Pie with Nut Crust (page 277).

VEGETABLES FOR VITALITY

Cheese-Filled Spinach Terrine with Red Bell Peppers & Leeks

Vitamin C from the red peppers in this vegetable appetizer helps your body absorb more iron from the spinach. Folate from the peppers and leeks helps renew red blood cells.

12 SERVINGS

Prep 30 min ◆ **Cook** 1 hr 10 min

- 1 tablespoon olive oil
- 2 leeks, cut in ½-inch pieces and rinsed
- 2 cloves garlic, minced
- 1¼ pounds spinach, stems removed
- 1 cup whole milk
- 2 medium red bell peppers, seeded and cut in ¼-inch pieces
- 1½ teaspoons salt
- 1 teaspoon curry powder
- ¾ teaspoon black pepper
- 1 cup shredded part-skim mozzarella cheese
- 5 large eggs

1 Preheat oven to 350°F. Lightly coat 9 x 5-inch loaf pan with nonstick cooking spray. Line bottom of pan with wax paper. Coat paper with cooking spray.

2 In large nonstick skillet over medium heat, heat oil. Add leeks and garlic. Sauté until softened, 7 minutes. Remove to large bowl.

3 Wash spinach, leaving some water clinging to leaves. Place in same skillet over medium-low heat. Cover. Cook until spinach wilts, 2 minutes. Add to bowl with leeks.

4 Place leek-spinach mixture in food processor with ¼ cup milk. Whirl until smooth. Return mixture to bowl. Add bell peppers, salt, curry powder, black pepper, and cheese.

5 In small bowl, beat eggs lightly with remaining ¾ cup milk. Stir into spinach mixture. Pour into prepared loaf pan. Place loaf pan in larger baking dish. Fill larger dish halfway with hot water.

6 Bake 1 hour. Remove loaf pan from water bath. Let cool completely. Refrigerate until ready to serve.

7 To serve, unmold loaf onto platter and remove wax paper.

Per serving: 102 calories, 7 g protein, 7 g carbohydrate, 6 g fat, 2 g saturated fat, 97 mg cholesterol, 2 g fiber, 361 mg sodium

on the menu

Spinach terrine can be served as an elegant first course or as part of a cocktail party buffet, where it can be offered with crackers or French bread rounds.

GREAT SAVORY
soups

VEGETABLES FOR VITALITY

Gazpacho

This slightly spicy summer refresher is loaded with lycopene, a cancer-fighting phytochemical found in tomatoes and tomato products.

4 SERVINGS

Prep 25 min ◆ **Refrigerate** 1 hr

- 4 cups tomato juice
- 4 plum tomatoes, seeded and coarsely chopped
- 1 cucumber, peeled, seeded, and coarsely chopped
- 1 small yellow bell pepper, seeded and coarsely chopped
- 3 scallions, finely chopped
- ¼ cup fresh-squeezed lemon juice
- ¼ cup coarsely chopped fresh basil
- 1 clove garlic, minced
- ¼ teaspoon salt
- ¼ teaspoon black pepper
- ¼ teaspoon hot red pepper sauce

In large bowl or pitcher, combine tomato juice, tomatoes, cucumber, bell pepper, scallions, lemon juice, basil, garlic, salt, pepper, and pepper sauce. Refrigerate for at least 1 hour before serving cold.

Per serving: 76 calories, 3 g protein, 15 g carbohydrates, 0 g fat, 0 g saturated fat, 0 mg cholesterol, 2 g fiber, 1,020 mg sodium

DID YOU KNOW ● ● ●

. . .that cold soups taste better if you remove them from the refrigerator about 15 minutes before you serve them? Extreme cold dulls flavor and that short amount of time takes the icy edge off.

Summer Borscht

Beets provide the B vitamin folate, while cabbage and onions boost the vitamin C content of this cool classic.

6 SERVINGS

Prep 25 min ◆ **Cook** 50 min

- 8 cups water
- 2 celery stalks, chopped
- 1 carrot, peeled and chopped
- 1 onion, quartered
- 3 cloves garlic, minced
- 4 sprigs parsley
- 2 bay leaves
- ½ teaspoon salt
- 4 medium beets
- 1 small turnip
- 2 teaspoons olive oil
- 1 medium onion, minced
- 2 cups thinly sliced green cabbage
- 2 tablespoons finely chopped dill
- 1½ tablespoons fresh-squeezed lemon juice
- ¼ cup reduced-fat sour cream

1 In a large pot, combine water, celery, carrot, quartered onion, garlic, parsley, bay leaves, and salt. Bring to a boil. Reduce heat. Simmer, covered, 25 minutes. While broth is simmering, peel beets and turnip, adding peels to pot of broth. Cut beets and turnip into small pieces.

2 In large pot over medium heat, heat oil. Add minced onion. Sauté until softened, 5 minutes. Stir in beets, turnip, and cabbage. Strain broth and add. Simmer, uncovered, until beets are just tender, 20 minutes.

3 Remove from heat. Stir in dill and lemon juice. Let cool to room temperature. Cover and refrigerate until cold. Just before serving, whisk in sour cream.

Per serving: 71 calories, 2 g protein, 11 g carbohydrates, 3 g fat, 1 g saturated fat, 4 mg cholesterol, 3 g fiber, 223 mg sodium

HINT **helpful HINT** HINT HINT HINT HINT HINT HINT

For a quicker version of this cold beet soup, substitute two quarts of store-bought vegetable broth for the homemade broth used in this recipe. You can also use packaged, pre-shredded cabbage and canned beets.

on the menu

Some old-world cooks like the combination of cold borscht with warm boiled potatoes, seasoned with fresh chopped chives and served on a separate plate. Instead of mixing the sour cream into the soup, these cooks pass it for use with the potatoes too. With a slice of Pumpkin Maple Cheesecake (page 274) for dessert, the cold borscht and warm potatoes would make a lovely summer lunch.

DID YOU KNOW ● ● ●

. . .that next to beets, carrots are the sweetest vegetable?
That may be why so many children who don't like other vegetables
like them. And people who are counting carbohydrates should enjoy
carrots in moderation.

Carrot Soup with Dill

You get four times your daily requirement for vitamin A in just one bowl of this smooth, savory soup, plus vitamin C, potassium, and fiber.

4 SERVINGS

Prep 10 min ◆ **Cook** 45 min

- 1 tablespoon vegetable oil
- 1 onion, coarsely chopped
- 1 clove garlic, minced
- 2 cans (14½ ounces each) reduced-sodium, fat-free chicken broth
- 1¼ pound carrots peeled and coarsely chopped (4 cups)
- ½ teaspoon dried thyme, crumbled
- ¼ teaspoon salt
- ¼ teaspoon white pepper
- ¼ cup plain low-fat yogurt
- 1 tablespoon finely chopped dill

1 In medium saucepan over medium heat, heat oil. Add onion and garlic. Sauté until softened, 5 minutes. Add broth, carrots, and thyme. Simmer, uncovered, until vegetables are very tender, about 40 minutes.

2 In batches, puree soup in blender. Add salt and pepper. To serve hot, ladle into bowls and garnish each bowl with yogurt and dill. To serve cold, remove from heat and let cool to room temperature. Cover and refrigerate until cold. Garnish just before serving.

Per serving: 135 calories, 6 g protein, 20 g carbohydrates, 4 g fat, 0 g saturated fat, 1 mg cholesterol, 5 g fiber, 773 mg sodium

HINT **helpful HINT** HINT HINT HINT HINT HINT HINT

An equal amount of any type of pureed winter squash, such as turban, butternut, or acorn, or pureed fresh pumpkin can be used in place of canned pumpkin in just about any recipe. All of these orange-fleshed vegetables, although their flavors are distinct, are deliciously complemented by the same seasonings—herbs, spices, citrus juices, and zest.

Pumpkin Bisque

Pumpkin is a rich source of fiber and vitamins A and C.

4 SERVINGS

Prep 10 min ◆ **Cook** 45 min

- 1 tablespoon vegetable oil
- 1 small onion, finely chopped
- 2 carrots, peeled and finely chopped
- 2 celery stalks, finely chopped
- ¼ cup tomato paste
- 2 cans (14½ ounces each) reduced-sodium, fat-free chicken broth
- 1 bay leaf
- ½ teaspoon dried thyme, crumbled
- 1 can (15 ounces) solid-pack pumpkin puree
- ¼ cup half-and-half
- ¼ teaspoon salt
- ¼ teaspoon white pepper
  Sliced lime and chopped coriander, for garnish *(optional)*

1 In large saucepan over medium heat, heat oil. Add onion, carrot, and celery. Sauté until softened, 5 minutes. Stir in tomato paste. Cook 1 minute. Add broth, bay leaf, and thyme. Simmer, uncovered, until vegetables are very tender, about 30 minutes.

2 Stir in pumpkin. Cook 5 minutes longer. Remove bay leaf.

3 In blender or food processor, puree soup in batches. Pour soup back into saucepan. Add half-and-half. Bring to a simmer. Add salt and pepper. If too thick, add a little water. Garnish with lime and coriander before serving.

Per serving: 131 calories, 6 g protein, 16 g carbohydrates, 6 g fat, 1 g saturated fat, 6 mg cholesterol, 6 g fiber, 725 mg sodium

Asparagus Soup

Asparagus is a top source of folate, a B vitamin best known for helping to prevent heart disease and birth defects.

6 SERVINGS

Prep 20 min ◆ **Cook** 50 min

- 2 **pounds asparagus, trimmed**
- 1 **tablespoon vegetable oil**
- 1 **teaspoon butter**
- 2 **leeks, pale green and white parts only, rinsed and finely chopped**
- ½ **onion, finely chopped**
- 2 **cloves garlic, minced**
- 3 **tablespoons uncooked long-grain white rice**
  Grated zest from 1 lemon
- 3 **cans (14½ ounces each) reduced-sodium, fat-free chicken broth**
- ½ **teaspoon salt**
- ¼ **teaspoon black pepper**
- ½ **teaspoon dried tarragon, crumbled**
- 3 **tablespoons plain yogurt**

1 Slice tips from asparagus. In medium saucepan blanch tips in boiling water 1 minute. Drain. Coarsely chop remaining asparagus.

2 In large saucepan over medium heat, heat oil and butter. Add leeks, onion, and garlic. Sauté until softened, 5 minutes. Add chopped asparagus. Cook, covered, 10 minutes.

3 Add rice, lemon zest, broth, salt, and pepper. Simmer, partially covered, 30 minutes.

4 In food processor or blender, puree soup in batches. Return to saucepan. Stir in tarragon and reserved asparagus tips. Simmer 3 minutes. Remove from heat. Stir in yogurt and serve.

Per serving: 111 calories, 6 g protein, 15 g carbohydrates, 4 g fat, 1 g saturated fat, 2 mg cholesterol, 2 g fiber, 757 mg sodium

on the menu

Both asparagus and cauliflower go well with the flavor of mustard, so if you want to serve either of these soups as part of a classic soup-and-sandwich combo, ham on rye with a dab of Dijon would make a perfect pairing.

Cauliflower Soup with Gruyère

Satisfy your daily requirement for vitamin C with a single serving.

4 SERVINGS

Prep 15 min ◆ **Cook** 35 min

- 1 **tablespoon vegetable oil**
- 1 **small leek, white part only, rinsed and coarsely chopped**
- 1 **medium onion, finely chopped**
- 2 **cans (14½ ounces) reduced-sodium, fat-free chicken broth**
- ½ **head cauliflower, coarsely chopped (about 4 cups)**
- ½ **teaspoon dried thyme, crumbled**
- ½ **teaspoon ground cumin**
- ¼ **teaspoon white pepper**
- ⅔ **cup shredded Gruyère cheese**

1 In large saucepan over medium-high heat, heat oil. Add leek and onion. Sauté until softened, 5 minutes. Add broth, cauliflower, thyme, and cumin. Simmer, uncovered, until cauliflower is tender, about 30 minutes.

2 Add pepper to soup. Ladle soup into individual bowls and sprinkle cheese over each serving.

Per serving: 162 calories, 11 g protein, 10 g carbohydrates, 10 g fat, 4 g saturated fat, 20 mg cholesterol, 4 g fiber, 700 mg sodium.

Creamy Greens Soup

Mild-flavored collard greens and Swiss chard add a powerful blast of beta-carotene to every sip of this smooth, creamy soup. Leafy green vegetables are also high in vitamin K, which helps prevent excessive bleeding.

8 SERVINGS

Prep 25 min ◆ **Cook** 1 hr

- 2 teaspoons olive oil
- 2 leeks, pale green and white parts only, rinsed and coarsely chopped
- 1 medium onion, coarsely chopped
- 2 cloves garlic, minced
- 1 small bunch collard greens, stemmed and coarsely chopped
- 1 small bunch Swiss chard, stemmed and coarsely chopped
- 2 medium Yukon Gold or all-purpose potatoes, unpeeled and coarsely chopped
- 1 carrot, peeled and coarsely chopped
- 2 cans (14½ ounces each) reduced-sodium, fat-free chicken broth
- 1 teaspoon salt
- ½ cup half-and-half

1 In large pot over medium heat, heat oil. Add leeks and onion. Sauté until softened, about 5 minutes. Add garlic; sauté 2 minutes. Add collard greens, Swiss chard, potatoes, and carrot. Stir in broth, 4 cups water, and salt. Simmer, partially covered, 50 minutes.

2 In blender or food processor, puree soup in small batches. Return to pot. Stir in half-and-half. Heat just until warmed through.

Per serving: 124 calories, 5 g protein, 20 g carbohydrates, 4 g fat, 2 g saturated fat, 7 mg cholesterol, 5 g fiber, 459 mg sodium

Classic Corn Chowder with Two Kinds of Peppers

Sweet bell peppers and mild chiles pump up the flavor—and the vitamin C content—of this hearty favorite.

6 SERVINGS

Prep 15 min ◆ **Cook** 50 min

- 3 slices turkey bacon
- 1 tablespoon olive oil
- 1 large onion, finely chopped
- ½ pound all-purpose potatoes, unpeeled and cut into ½-inch cubes
- 2 cans (14½ ounces each) reduced-sodium, fat-free chicken broth
- 1 can (15¼ ounces) corn kernels, drained
- 1 red bell pepper, seeded and finely chopped
- 2 cups low-fat (2%) milk
- ½ teaspoon salt
- 1 tablespoon canned chopped mild green chiles

1 In large saucepan cook bacon until crisp, about 6 minutes. Transfer to paper towel to drain.

2 Heat oil in same pan over medium heat. Add onion. Sauté until softened, 5 minutes. Add potatoes and broth. Simmer, partially covered, until potatoes are tender, about 20 minutes. Stir in corn. Simmer 5 minutes.

3 Transfer half of potatoes and corn with a little liquid to food processor. Puree. Return to saucepan. Add red pepper, milk, and salt. Cover and simmer 10 minutes.

4 Finely chop bacon. Stir into chowder with chiles. Heat through and serve.

Per serving: 166 calories, 8 g protein, 22 g carbohydrates, 6 g fat, 2 g saturated fat, 13 mg cholesterol, 3 g fiber, 849 mg sodium

FRESH IDEAS

Other mild-tasting greens such as spinach, beet tops, or kale can be substituted for the Swiss chard and collard greens in the Creamy Greens Soup. For a vegetarian soup, you can substitute a vegetable stock or bouillon for the chicken broth.

on the menu

Kick-start a barbecue or Tex-Mex-style meal with a cup of this old-fashioned corn chowder. For added flourish and flavor, top the soup with fresh sprigs of cilantro.

Summer Garden Soup

A mélange of vegetables ensures you're getting a variety of vitamins and minerals in every spoonful.

6 SERVINGS

Prep 25 min ◆ **Cook** 45 min

- **2 teaspoons olive oil**
- **1 medium onion, finely chopped**
- **1 large stalk celery, finely chopped**
- **2 teaspoons finely chopped, peeled fresh ginger**
- **¼ pound green beans, cut into ½-inch pieces**
- **2 medium potatoes, unpeeled and cut into ½-inch cubes**
- **1 large carrot, peeled and cut into ½-inch cubes**
- **1 medium yellow summer squash, quartered lengthwise, seeded, and cut into ½-inch cubes**
- **1 bay leaf**
- **¾ teaspoon salt**
- **¾ cup fresh or frozen green peas**
- **2 plum tomatoes, seeded and coarsely chopped**
- **2 tablespoons finely chopped fresh basil leaves**
- **1½ teaspoons finely chopped fresh thyme leaves**

1 In large pot over medium heat, heat oil. Add onion, celery, and ginger. Sauté until very tender, 10 minutes. Add green beans, potatoes, carrot, squash, 8 cups water, bay leaf, and salt. Simmer, covered, 20 minutes.

2 Uncover soup. Simmer 15 minutes. For last 5 minutes, add peas, tomatoes, basil, and thyme. Remove bay leaf before serving.

Per serving: 88 calories, 3 g protein, 17 g carbohydrates, 2 g fat, 0 g saturated fat, 0 mg cholesterol, 4 g fiber, 307 mg sodium

FRESH 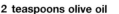 IDEAS

To turn Summer Garden Soup into a main dish for lunch or a light supper, stir small pieces of cooked chicken or ham into the pot just before serving.

HINT **helpful HINT** HINT HINT HINT HINT HINT HINT

You can cook the vegetables for Roasted Vegetable Soup right alongside a meat entrée. Since meats require longer oven time, you won't have to rush to put the soup together while the meat finishes. It can rest on top of the oven while you serve the soup.

Roasted Vegetable Soup

Carrot juice in place of broth sweetens the pot and boosts the beta-carotene content of this hearty soup.

4 SERVINGS

Prep 10 min ◆ **Cook** 40 min

- **1 tablespoon olive oil**
- **5 cloves garlic, peeled**
- **¾ pound all-purpose potatoes, unpeeled and cut into ½-inch cubes**
- **2 green bell peppers, seeded and cut into ½-inch squares**
- **½ teaspoon dried rosemary, crumbled**
- **1 yellow summer squash, halved lengthwise and cut into ½-inch cubes**
- **1 large red onion, cut into ½-inch cubes**
- **1½ cups vegetable broth or carrot juice**
- **¾ pound tomatoes, diced**
- **1 teaspoon dried tarragon, crumbled**
- **¾ teaspoon salt**

1 Preheat oven to 450°F. In large roasting pan, combine oil and garlic. Roast 5 minutes. Add potatoes, peppers, and rosemary. Toss to coat. Roast until potatoes begin to soften, 15 minutes.

2 Stir in squash and onion. Roast 15 minutes longer.

3 In large saucepan, combine broth, tomatoes, tarragon, and salt. Heat to a boil over medium heat. Add roasted vegetables.

4 Pour 1 cup water into roasting pan, scraping up any browned bits from bottom of pan. Pour pan juices into saucepan. Simmer 2 minutes and serve.

Per serving: 229 calories, 7 g protein, 45 g carbohydrates, 5 g fat, 1 g saturated fat, 0 mg cholesterol, 7 g fiber, 833 mg sodium

Greek Spinach, Egg & Lemon Soup

A traditional Greek combination is made healthier with fewer egg yolks, reduced-fat broth, and brown rice without compromising the rich flavor and velvety texture.

4 SERVINGS

Prep 5 min ◆ **Cook** 10 min

- 3 cups reduced-sodium, fat-free chicken broth
- 3 scallions, thinly sliced
- 3 cloves garlic, minced
- 1 package (10 ounces) frozen chopped spinach
- ½ teaspoon oregano
- 1 cup cooked brown rice
- 1 teaspoon grated lemon zest
- 3 tablespoons fresh lemon juice
- ½ teaspoon salt
- 1 large egg plus 2 egg whites

1 In medium saucepan, combine ¼ cup broth, scallions, and garlic. Cook over medium heat until scallions are tender, about 2 minutes.

2 Add remaining 2¾ cups broth, spinach, and oregano, and bring to a boil. Reduce to a simmer, cover, and cook until spinach is tender, about 5 minutes.

3 Stir in rice, lemon zest, lemon juice, and salt, and return to a simmer. Remove ½ cup hot liquid and whisk into whole egg and egg whites in medium bowl. Whisking constantly, pour warmed egg mixture into simmering soup.

Per serving: 114 calories, 8 g protein, 17 g carbohydrates, 2 g fat, 1 g saturated fat, 53 mg cholesterol, 3 g fiber, 728 mg sodium

Tomato Egg Drop Soup

An infusion of garlic adds rich flavor and cancer-fighting power to this Cuban-style broth.

6 SERVINGS

Prep 10 min ◆ **Cook** 16 min

- 1 tablespoon olive oil
- 1 small onion, finely chopped
- 6 cloves garlic, minced
- 4 ripe tomatoes, seeded and finely chopped
- 2 cans (14½ ounces each) reduced-sodium, fat-free chicken broth
- 1 bay leaf
- 1 teaspoon salt
- 2 large eggs, lightly beaten
- 6 slices (1 inch thick) Italian semolina bread, toasted
- 3 tablespoons coarsely chopped parsley

1 In large saucepan over medium heat, heat oil. Add onion. Sauté until softened, 5 minutes. Add garlic. Sauté 30 seconds. Stir in tomatoes. Sauté 1 minute.

2 Add broth, bay leaf, and salt. Reduce heat to low. Simmer, uncovered, 10 minutes. Remove from heat. Remove bay leaf. Stir in eggs. Place one slice of bread in each serving bowl. Ladle in hot soup. Sprinkle with parsley.

Per serving: 135 calories, 7 g protein, 17 g carbohydrates, 5 g fat, 1 g saturated fat, 71 mg cholesterol, 2 g fiber, 897 mg sodium

helpful HINT

Egg yolks enrich and thicken soups, but they also add fat and cholesterol. If this is a concern, substitute 2 egg whites for every whole egg called for in a soup recipe or use 1 whole egg and substitute the egg whites for a second or third egg.

on the menu

A light first course like Tomato Egg Drop Soup is the perfect start to any meal featuring roast meat as the main dish and a starchy side dish like potatoes. Finish with a fruit sorbet or pineapple wedges for dessert.

on the menu

This soup serves six as a first course or four as a light main dish. If you serve it as an entrée, round out the meal with a crisp romaine lettuce salad topped with an herb-flavored vinaigrette, and a bowl of fresh strawberries and pineapple chunks for dessert.

Chicken-Tomato Soup with Tortillas

Scallions, tomatoes, chiles, and fresh lime juice team up to make this zesty soup a good source of vitamin C.

6 SERVINGS

Prep 20 min ◆ **Cook** 50 min

- 1 **whole bone-in chicken breast, skin removed**
- 8 **cups reduced-sodium, fat-free chicken broth**
- 3 **cloves garlic**
- 1 **teaspoon salt**
- 1 **teaspoon black pepper**
- 1 **teaspoon dried oregano, crumbled**
- 1 **tablespoon olive oil**
- 5 **scallions, coarsely chopped**
- 1 **can (4½ ounces) green chiles, drained**
- 4 **medium tomatoes, coarsely chopped**
- ½ **cup fresh-squeezed lime juice**
- 4 **corn tortillas (6 inches),
  sliced into 3 x ¼-inch strips, toasted**
- 3 **tablespoons chopped cilantro**

1 Place chicken, broth, 2 cloves garlic, salt, pepper, and oregano in medium saucepan. Simmer, uncovered, 25 minutes.

2 Remove chicken from pot. Remove and discard bones. Cut chicken into large chunks. Strain and reserve broth.

3 In large saucepan over medium heat, heat oil. Mince remaining garlic. Add to saucepan along with scallions. Sauté until softened, 5 minutes. Add chiles, tomatoes, and strained broth. Simmer, partially covered, 15 minutes. (Recipe can be made ahead up to this point.)

4 Add chicken chunks, lime juice, and toasted tortilla strips. Simmer 5 minutes. Garnish with cilantro.

Per serving: 200 calories, 25 g protein, 11 g carbohydrates, 5 g fat, 1 g saturated fat, 60 mg cholesterol, 2 g fiber, 550 mg sodium.

DID YOU KNOW ● ● ●

...that chicken soup really does help fight colds? Laboratory studies show that it slows the migration of neutrophils, which cause inflammation at the infection site, giving relief to sore throats and runny noses.

Country-Style Chicken Vegetable Soup with Noodles

Root vegetables add earthy flavor and a mix of antioxidant nutrients to help protect against chronic disease.

4 SERVINGS

Prep 15 min ◆ **Cook** 45 min

- 1 **tablespoon vegetable oil**
- 1 **medium onion, coarsely chopped**
- 3 **carrots, peeled and diced**
- 1 **medium celery stalk, diced**
- 2 **cans (14½ ounces each) reduced-sodium,
  fat-free chicken broth**
- 1 **can (14½ ounces) diced tomatoes**
- ½ **pound bone-in chicken breast, skin removed**
- 1 **small turnip, peeled and diced**
- 1 **teaspoon dried basil, crumbled**
- 1½ **cups thin noodles**
- ¼ **teaspoon black pepper**

1 In large saucepan over medium heat, heat oil. Add onion, carrots, and celery. Sauté until softened, 5 minutes. Add broth, tomatoes, chicken breast, turnip, and basil. Simmer, uncovered, until chicken is cooked through, 30 minutes.

2 Remove chicken from saucepan. Remove and discard bones. Coarsely chop chicken. Return to soup. Add noodles. Cook until noodles are tender, 4 minutes. Add pepper.

Per serving: 283 calories, 19 g protein, 41 g carbohydrates, 5 g fat, 1 g saturated fat, 25 mg cholesterol, 5 g fiber, 828 mg sodium.

Turkey, Spinach & Rice in Roasted Garlic Broth

A combination of enriched rice, fresh spinach, and lean turkey makes this a particularly healthful source of the B vitamins your body needs to produce energy.

4 SERVINGS

Prep 15 min ◆ **Cook** 1 hr

- 2 medium whole heads garlic, unpeeled
- 2 tablespoons tomato paste
- 2 cans (14½ ounces each) reduced-sodium, fat-free chicken or turkey broth
- 1 cup cooked turkey cubes
- 1 cup cooked long-grain white rice
- ¾ pound spinach, stemmed and coarsely chopped
- ¼ teaspoon black pepper
- ¼ teaspoon hot pepper flakes, or to taste
- 1 tablespoon fresh-squeezed lemon juice

1 Preheat oven to 400°F.

2 Cut top third off garlic heads. Wrap each head in foil. Bake until very soft, about 50 minutes. Let cool. Remove foil. Squeeze out pulp into small bowl.

3 In large saucepan, stir together garlic pulp and tomato paste. Stir in broth. Bring to a boil. Add turkey, rice, spinach, pepper, and pepper flakes. Simmer, uncovered, 8 minutes. Just before serving, stir in lemon juice.

Per serving: 197 calories, 19 g protein, 24 g carbohydrates, 4 g fat, 1 g saturated fat, 30 mg cholesterol, 3 g fiber, 208 mg sodium

White Bean Soup with Spinach, Parsley, Sage & Parmesan

Spinach and beans provide folate for fighting heart disease and preventing birth defects in the early weeks of pregnancy.

4 SERVINGS

Prep 5 min ◆ **Cook** 25 min

- 1 tablespoon vegetable oil
- 4 ounces mild or hot Italian-style turkey sausage, casings removed
- 2 cloves garlic, minced
- 1 teaspoon dried sage, crumbled
- 1 can (19 ounces) cannellini beans, drained and rinsed
- 1 can (14½ ounces) reduced-sodium, fat-free chicken broth
- 4 cups torn spinach leaves or ½ of 10-ounce box chopped frozen spinach
- ¼ teaspoon salt
- ⅛ teaspoon black pepper
- 2 tablespoons finely chopped parsley
- 1 tablespoon fresh-squeezed lemon juice
- ¼ cup grated Parmesan cheese

1 In large nonstick saucepan over medium heat, heat oil. Add sausage. Cook, stirring to break up clumps, until browned, 3 minutes. Remove meat to paper towel.

2 In same pan, cook garlic and sage 30 seconds. Add beans, broth, and 1½ cups water. Simmer, uncovered, 10 minutes.

3 In food processor, puree half the beans with a few spoonfuls of broth. Return bean mixture to pan. Add sausage, spinach, salt, and pepper. Simmer, uncovered, 10 minutes. Stir in parsley and lemon juice. Sprinkle with cheese before serving.

Per serving: 173 calories, 12 g protein, 15 g carbohydrates, 7 g fat, 1 g saturated fat, 21 mg cholesterol, 4 g fiber, 890 mg sodium

HINT **helpful HINT** HINT HINT HINT HINT HINT HINT

Most soups will thicken if they are made ahead, refrigerated, and reheated before serving. If a soup gets too thick, simply stir in enough extra broth or water to get the desired consistency.

VEGETABLES FOR VITALITY

FRESH IDEAS

Other sausages can be used in place of the hot Italian-style turkey sausage in this recipe. Other greens, such as kale or collards, can also be used in place of the spinach. To speed up preparation, use frozen chopped versions of longer-cooking greens instead of fresh.

Portuguese Kale Soup with Sausage

The combination of fresh kale, carrots, and red bell pepper in this soup guarantees a rich variety of important vitamins and minerals.

8 SERVINGS

Prep 15 min ◆ **Cook** 55 min

- ½ **pound hot Italian-style turkey sausages**
- 1 **tablespoon vegetable oil**
- 1 **small onion, coarsely chopped**
- 2 **cloves garlic, minced**
- 1 **teaspoon cinnamon**
- ½ **teaspoon ground allspice**
- 1¼ **teaspoon salt**
- ¼ **pound fresh kale, stemmed and torn into small pieces**
- 2 **carrots, peeled, halved lengthwise, and thinly sliced crosswise**
- 1 **small red bell pepper, seeded and diced**
- 2 **cans (14½ ounces each) reduced-sodium, fat-free chicken broth**
- 1 **can (19 ounces) chickpeas, drained and rinsed**
- ¼ **cup grated Parmesan cheese**

1 Place sausages in small skillet with ¼ inch of water. Prick sausages with knife point. Gently boil, turning sausages occasionally, until water evaporates, about 8 minutes. Sauté until browned, about 5 minutes. Remove from skillet and let stand 5 minutes. Trim off any loose casing. Cut into ½-inch-thick slices.

2 In large saucepan over medium heat, heat oil. Add onion. Sauté until softened and lightly golden, 7 minutes. Stir in garlic, cinnamon, allspice, and salt. Sauté 1 minute.

3 Stir in kale, carrots, bell pepper, and broth. Add sausage slices. Simmer, partially covered, until vegetables are tender, 30 minutes.

4 Stir in chickpeas. Heat through. Garnish each serving with cheese.

Per serving: 128 calories, 10 g protein, 12 g carbohydrates, 5 g fat, 1 g saturated fat, 19 mg cholesterol, 3 g fiber, 660 mg sodium

Quick Fish Chowder with Tomato & Fennel

Tomato products, such as the canned stewed tomatoes used in this soup, are concentrated sources of lycopene, a phytochemical that helps fight prostate cancer.

4 SERVINGS

Prep 8 minutes ◆ **Cook** 25 min

- 1 **tablespoon olive oil**
- 1 **medium onion, coarsely chopped**
- 2 **cloves garlic, minced**
- 1 **teaspoon fennel seeds**
- 2 **cups bottled clam juice**
- 1 **can (14½ ounces) stewed tomatoes**
- ½ **cup dry white wine**
- ½ **pound red potatoes, unpeeled, cut into small dice**
- 1 **pound firm fish fillets, such as cod or scrod, cut into 8 pieces**
- ¼ **cup coarsely chopped parsley**

1 In large saucepan over medium-high heat, heat oil. Add onion and garlic. Sauté until softened, 5 minutes. Add fennel seeds. Sauté 30 seconds. Add clam juice, tomatoes, wine, and potatoes. Simmer, uncovered, until potatoes are tender, 15 minutes.

2 Add fish and parsley. Bring to a gentle boil. Remove from heat and serve immediately.

Per serving: 215 calories, 26 g protein, 16 g carbohydrates, 4 g fat, 1 g saturated fat, 50 mg cholesterol, 4 g fiber, 569 mg sodium

FRESH IDEAS

For a seafood chowder flavor, you can substitute two 8-ounce bottles of clam juice for the chicken broth in this *Root Vegetable Chowder* recipe.

Root Vegetable Chowder with Bacon Bits

How many helpful vitamins and minerals can you squeeze into one serving of soup? Plenty, when the soup is this nutritious blend of sweet potatoes, carrots, onions, potatoes, and other powerful vegetables.

4 SERVINGS

Prep 25 min ◆ **Cook** 45 min

- 2 teaspoons olive oil
- 1 large onion, finely chopped
- 2 stalks celery, coarsely chopped
- 1¼ teaspoons dried thyme, crumbled
- 2 medium carrots, peeled and coarsely chopped
- 1 large yam or sweet potato, peeled and coarsely chopped
- 1 medium parsnip, peeled and coarsely chopped
- 1 large red potato, peeled and coarsely chopped
- ½ green bell pepper, seeded and coarsely chopped
- 1 can (14½ ounces) reduced-sodium, low-fat chicken broth or vegetable broth
- ½ teaspoon salt
- 1⅔ cups reduced-fat (2%) milk
- 1 tablespoon balsamic vinegar
- 3 strips turkey bacon, cooked and coarsely chopped

1 In large saucepan over medium heat, heat oil. Add onion, celery, and thyme. Sauté until softened, 5 minutes. Add carrots, yam, parsnip, potato, green pepper, chicken broth, and salt. Add just enough water to cover ingredients. Simmer, covered, until vegetables are tender, about 30 minutes.

2 In blender, puree half the soup until smooth. Return puree to saucepan. Stir in milk. Gently heat. Add vinegar. Sprinkle with bacon before serving.

Per serving: 269 calories, 9 g protein, 45 g carbohydrates, 7 g fat, 2 g saturated fat, 21 mg cholesterol, 7 g fiber, 774 mg sodium

Cabbage & Kielbasa Soup

The cancer-fighting potential of cruciferous vegetables such as cabbage elevates the status of this once-humble soup to the level of nutritional superstar.

6 SERVINGS

Prep 15 min ◆ **Cook** 55 min

- 1 tablespoon vegetable oil
- ½ pound reduced-fat kielbasa sausage, diced
- 1 medium onion, coarsely chopped
- 4 cloves garlic, minced
- 2 cans (14½ ounces each) reduced-sodium, fat-free beef broth
- 1¼ cups water
- ½ medium head Savoy cabbage, coarsely chopped (about 4½ cups)
- 2 medium red potatoes, unpeeled, diced
- 2 medium carrots, peeled and diced
- 1 medium beet, peeled and diced
- 3 tablespoons finely chopped dill
- 1 bay leaf
- 1 tablespoon red-wine vinegar

1 In large saucepan over medium-high heat, heat oil. Add kielbasa. Sauté until browned, about 5 minutes. Add onion and garlic. Sauté until tender, 5 minutes.

2 Add broth, water, cabbage, potatoes, carrots, beet, dill, and bay leaf. Simmer, covered, until vegetables are very tender, 45 minutes. Stir in vinegar. Remove bay leaf and serve.

Per serving: 140 calories, 10 g protein, 17 g carbohydrates, 3 g fat, 0 g saturated fat, 10 mg cholesterol, 3 g fiber, 404 mg sodium

Chinese Beef Soup
with Barley & Spinach

Ordinary herbs and spices used in cooking often make their own contribution to good health.
Both the ginger and fennel seeds in this meaty soup, for example, help soothe the digestive tract.

6 SERVINGS

Prep 10 min ◆ **Cook** 1 hr 45 min

- 1½ **pounds beef stew meat,**
  trimmed and cut into 1-inch cubes
- 1 **onion, finely chopped**
- 4 **cloves garlic, minced**
- 1 **can (14½ ounces) reduced-sodium,**
  fat-free beef broth
- ¼ **cup soy sauce**
- 1 **piece ginger (2 inches),**
  peeled and cut into 4 pieces
- 1 **teaspoon fennel seeds**
- ½ **teaspoon salt**
- 1 **cup uncooked barley**
- 12 **cups stemmed spinach leaves**
- 2 **scallions, thinly sliced** (optional)

1 In large saucepan, combine beef, onion, garlic, 6 cups water, broth, soy sauce, ginger, fennel seeds, and salt. Bring to a boil over medium heat.

2 Stir in barley. Lower heat and simmer, covered, until beef is very tender, 1½ hours.

3 Stir in spinach. Simmer 2 minutes. Remove ginger pieces. Garnish with scallion, if desired.

Per serving: 314 calories, 30 g protein, 28 g carbohydrates, 9 g fat, 3 g saturated fat, 71 mg cholesterol, 8 g fiber, 952 mg sodium

HINT **helpful HINT** HINT HINT HINT HINT HINT HINT

To peel fresh ginger, first cut off any knobs or bumps. Using a small, sharp knife or vegetable peeler, pare the skin from the root along the section that you need. Then slice or dice the ginger as the recipe requires. Wrap and store any remaining ginger in the freezer.

MAIN COURSE poultry DISHES

Millennium Chef's Salad

A nutritional makeover updates this classic main dish salad to include dark leafy greens, colorful roasted peppers, lean, fresh chicken breast, and creamy, natural goat cheese.

6 SERVINGS

Prep 15 min ◆ **Cook** 15 min

- 6 **chicken tenderloins or 2 boneless, skinless chicken breasts**
- 3 **cups romaine or other dark green lettuce**
- 3 **cups baby spinach leaves**
- 6 **ounces thinly sliced smoked lean ham, cut into strips**
- 1 **roasted yellow bell pepper** (see page 295)**, seeded and cut lengthwise into thin strips**
- 1 **roasted orange bell pepper** (see page 295)**, seeded and cut lengthwise into thin strips**
- 18 **grape or cherry tomatoes, halved**
- 3 **ounces goat cheese, crumbled**
- ½ **cup extra-virgin olive oil**
- ¼ **cup balsamic vinegar**
- 1 **teaspoon Dijon mustard**
- 1 **clove garlic, minced**
- ¾ **teaspoon dried tarragon, crumbled**
- ¼ **teaspoon salt**

1 In medium saucepan, in lightly salted water, gently simmer chicken, uncovered, until cooked through, 10 minutes. Drain well.

2 To serve, divide lettuce leaves evenly among serving plates. Top each with ½ cup spinach, mounded in center. Cut chicken lengthwise into thin strips. Arrange chicken, ham, bell peppers, tomatoes, and cheese on each salad.

3 In small bowl, whisk together oil, vinegar, mustard, garlic, tarragon, and salt to make dressing. Serve with salad.

Per serving: 331 calories, 18 g protein, 12 g carbohydrates, 25 g fat, 7 g saturated fat, 45 mg cholesterol, 2 g fiber, 587 mg sodium

FRESH IDEAS

Chef's salads can include any combination of meats, vegetables, and cheese. You can substitute lean roast beef or turkey for some or all of the chicken and ham and add more salad vegetables, such as sliced cucumber and radishes, to the mix. In place of goat cheese, try crumbled feta or cubes of Swiss or Havarti cheese.

Grilled Chicken Salad

Treat your taste buds to this tangy mix of antioxidant-rich fresh fruit, salad veggies, and lean chicken breast.

4 SERVINGS

Prep 15 min ◆ **Refrigerate** 30 min ◆ **Cook** 6 min

- ¼ **cup orange juice**
- 3 **tablespoons fresh-squeezed lime juice**
- 2 **tablespoons olive oil**
- 1 **tablespoon white-wine vinegar**
- ½ **teaspoon Dijon mustard**
- ¾ **teaspoon salt**
- ⅛ **teaspoon black pepper**
- ¾ **pound boneless, skinless chicken breasts**
- 1 **mango, peeled, pitted, and cut into thin wedges**
- 1 **tomato, cored and cut into thin wedges**
- ½ **cucumber, seeded and thinly sliced**
- ½ **cup thinly sliced red onion**
- 4 **cups mixed salad greens**

1 In small bowl, whisk together orange juice, lime juice, oil, vinegar, mustard, salt and pepper. Transfer ¼ cup of dressing to another small bowl. Add chicken breasts and turn to coat. Refrigerate, covered, 30 minutes to 1 hour. Reserve remaining dressing.

2 Preheat grill to medium-hot or preheat broiler. Grill or broil chicken until browned on one side, 3 minutes. Baste with marinade from bowl that held chicken. Turn over and grill until cooked through, 3 minutes. Transfer to cutting board. Let stand 5 minutes. Cut into thick slices.

3 Meanwhile, in large bowl, combine remaining dressing, mango, tomato, cucumber, and onion. Add grilled chicken. Serve over greens.

Per serving: 220 calories, 19 g protein, 17 g carbohydrates, 9 g fat, 2 g saturated fat, 47 mg cholesterol, 3 g fiber, 512 mg sodium

VEGETABLES FOR VITALITY

Skewered Teriyaki Chicken & Vegetables

Kebabs are a fun and easy way to feature a variety of healthy vegetables in one meal.

4 SERVINGS

Prep 20 min ◆ **Refrigerate** 30 min ◆ **Cook** 14 min

- 1 **pound boneless, skinless chicken thighs, cut into 1-inch chunks**
- ½ **cup bottled teriyaki baste and glaze**
- 1 **medium zucchini, quartered lengthwise and cut crosswise into ¼-inch-thick pieces**
- 1 **large red bell pepper, cut into 1-inch squares**
- 4 **scallions, trimmed and cut crosswise in half**
- 8 **canned whole water chestnuts, drained and rinsed**

1 In small bowl, combine chicken and ¼ cup of the teriyaki baste. Refrigerate, covered, 30 minutes.

2 Preheat grill to medium-hot or preheat broiler. Alternately thread chicken, zucchini, red pepper, scallions, and water chestnuts on eight 12-inch metal skewers. Thread a water chestnut on the end of each skewer. Brush with some of remaining teriyaki baste.

3 Grill or broil skewers 4 inches from heat, turning often and brushing with baste, until vegetables are crisp-tender and chicken is cooked through, 12 to 14 minutes.

Per serving: 212 calories, 23 g protein, 10 g carbohydrates, 9 g fat, 2 g saturated fat, 74 mg cholesterol, 1 g fiber, 1,452 mg sodium

Grilled Chicken Breast with Corn & Pepper Relish

Black beans add heart-healthy soluble fiber and rich, satisfying flavor to the Mexican-style relish mix.

4 SERVINGS

Prep 20 min ◆ **Cook** 8 min

- 2 **cloves garlic, minced**
- 2 **teaspoons chili powder**
- ¼ **teaspoon salt**
- 3 **tablespoons fresh-squeezed lime juice**
- 2 **tablespoons vegetable oil**
- 1½ **pounds boneless, skinless chicken breasts, pounded ⅜ inch thick**
- ¾ **cup reduced-sodium, fat-free chicken broth**
- 1⅓ **cups fresh, drained canned, or thawed frozen corn kernels**
- 1 **cup diced, seeded, roasted red bell pepper** (see page 295)
- ⅔ **cup canned black beans, drained and rinsed**
- 2 **tablespoons coarsely chopped red onion**
- 1 **jalapeño chile, seeded and finely chopped**
- ¼ **teaspoon salt**
- 3 **tablespoons chopped cilantro**

1 In medium bowl, stir together garlic, chili powder, salt, 2 tablespoons lime juice, and oil. Add chicken and rub with marinade. Let stand at room temperature no more than 15 minutes.

2 Preheat grill to medium-hot or preheat broiler.

3 Grill or broil chicken 3 inches from heat just until cooked through, 3 to 4 minutes per side.

4 To make relish: In large skillet, heat broth. Add corn kernels, bell pepper, black beans, onion, chile, and salt. Heat through. Just before serving, stir in cilantro and remaining lime juice. Serve chicken topped with relish.

Per serving: 375 calories, 40 g protein, 29 g carbohydrates, 12 g fat, 2 g saturated fat, 95 mg cholesterol, 5 g fiber, 521 mg sodium

FRESH IDEAS

This chicken breast with corn and pepper relish can be just as delicious served cold on a hot summer night.

on the menu

Finish up with fresh sliced strawberries topped with frozen raspberries pureed in a blender or food processor.

Skillet Chicken with Carrots in Orange Sauce

Each serving satisfies a day's requirement for vitamin A, in the form of disease-fighting beta-carotene.

4 SERVINGS

Prep 10 min ◆ **Cook** 28 min

- 1 cup orange juice
- 3 tablespoons balsamic vinegar or red-wine vinegar
- 4 boneless, skinless chicken breast halves (about 1 pound)
- ¼ teaspoon salt
- ⅛ teaspoon black pepper
- ¼ cup all-purpose flour
- 2 tablespoons vegetable oil
- 4 scallions, thinly sliced
- ½ teaspoon ground coriander
- 4 medium carrots, peeled and cut into ¼-inch-thick slices
- 2 tablespoons chopped parsley

1 In small bowl, combine orange juice and vinegar.

2 Season chicken with salt and pepper. Coat with flour, heat oil in large nonstick skillet over medium heat. Add chicken. Cook until browned, about 3 minutes per side. Transfer to plate.

3 Add scallions, coriander, and ¼ cup of juice mixture to skillet, scraping up any browned bits from bottom of skillet. Cook 30 seconds. Add remaining juice mixture, carrots, and chicken. Bring to a boil. Cover skillet tightly, lower heat, and simmer until chicken is cooked through and carrots are tender, about 20 minutes.

4 Place a chicken breast on each of 4 plates. Spoon carrots and sauce over top. Garnish with parsley.

Per serving: 447 calories, 55 g protein, 23 g carbohydrates, 13 g fat, 2 g saturated fat, 145 mg cholesterol, 3 g fiber, 318 mg sodium

FRESH IDEAS

Just about any fresh vegetable can be used to make this Italian-style stir-fry, so feel free to substitute equal amounts of broccoli, green beans, or whatever else looks good on the salad bar.

Salad-Bar Italian Chicken Stir-Fry

A world of good nutrition awaits you at the supermarket salad bar, where you can pick up just the right amounts of pre-sliced veggies to make this dish.

4 SERVINGS

Prep 5 min ◆ **Cook** 12 min

- 2 tablespoons olive oil
- 1 pound boneless, skinless chicken breasts, cut in ½-inch-wide strips
- ½ teaspoon salt
- ¼ teaspoon black pepper
- 1½ cups sliced, seeded red, green, or yellow bell peppers
- 1½ cups sliced zucchini
- 2 cloves garlic, minced
- 1 cup cherry tomatoes, each halved
- ½ teaspoon dried oregano, crumbled
- 2 teaspoons balsamic vinegar

1 In large nonstick skillet over medium-high heat, heat oil. Add chicken. Sauté just until barely cooked through, 4 minutes. Sprinkle with ¼ teaspoon of the salt and pepper. Remove chicken from skillet.

2 In same skillet, sauté bell peppers and zucchini just until tender, 4 minutes. Sprinkle with remaining ¼ teaspoon salt. Add garlic. Sauté 30 seconds. Add tomatoes and oregano. Cook 1 minute. Return chicken pieces to skillet. Sprinkle with vinegar. Heat through.

Per serving: 209 calories, 24 g protein, 6 g carbohydrates, 10 g fat, 2 g saturated fat, 63 mg cholesterol, 2 g fiber, 352 mg sodium

VEGETABLES FOR VITALITY

Orange-Flavored Chicken with Sweet Pepper & Asparagus

There are plenty of B vitamins in every bite, to help your body use protein, carbohydrates, and fats, and to ensure maximum energy production, and vitamin C to control blood cholesterol.

4 SERVINGS

DID YOU KNOW ● ● ●

...that black walnuts are native to North America and require being run over with a car (or an equivalent pressure) to crack their hard outer hull? Much more common—and easier to shell—are English or Persian walnuts, now grown in California.

Prep 15 min ◆ **Cook** 10 min

- 1 orange
- 2 tablespoons rice wine or dry sherry
- 1 tablespoon soy sauce
- 1 teaspoon sugar
- 1¼ teaspoons cornstarch
- ¼ teaspoon red pepper flakes
- ½ pound asparagus, trimmed and cut into 2-inch pieces
- 1 tablespoon vegetable oil
- 1 pound boneless, skinless chicken breasts, cut into ½-inch-wide strips
- 1 tablespoon finely chopped, peeled fresh ginger
- 1 clove garlic, minced
- 1 red bell pepper, seeded and cut into strips
- 4 scallions, cut into 2-inch pieces
- ⅓ cup walnuts, chopped

1 Using vegetable peeler, peel four 3-inch-wide strips of zest from orange. Cut zest into thin strips. Squeeze juice from orange to make ¼ cup. In small bowl, stir together orange juice, wine, soy sauce, sugar, cornstarch, and pepper flakes.

2 In medium saucepan, steam asparagus just until tender, about 3 minutes.

3 In large nonstick skillet or wok over medium-high heat, heat oil. Add chicken. Stir-fry until no longer pink, about 4 minutes. Remove chicken to plate.

4 Add orange zest, ginger, and garlic to skillet. Stir-fry 30 seconds. Add bell pepper, scallions, and asparagus. Stir-fry 1 minute. Add juice mixture. Bring to a boil. Return chicken to pan. Stir-fry until heated through. Sprinkle with walnuts and serve at once.

Per serving: 268 calories, 26 g protein, 10 g carbohydrates, 12 g fat, 2 g saturated fat, 63 mg cholesterol, 2 g fiber, 291 mg sodium

Stir-Fried Chicken & Broccoli with Coconut Milk

This sweet and spicy Thai-style dish supplies a day's worth of vitamin C to protect you from infection, strengthen your blood vessels, and help your body to absorb iron.

4 SERVINGS

Prep 25 min ◆ **Cook** 8 min

- ½ cup reduced-fat coconut milk
  Grated zest of 1 lime
- 1 tablespoon fresh-squeezed lime juice
- 1 tablespoon soy sauce
- 1½ teaspoons grated, peeled fresh ginger
- 1 tablespoon light-brown sugar
- 1 teaspoon cornstarch
- ½ teaspoon Thai-style green curry paste
  (optional)
- 2½ tablespoons vegetable oil
- 1 onion, halved and cut crosswise into ½-inch-thick slices
- 6 cloves garlic, minced
- ¾ pound broccoli, cut into small florets and stems thinly sliced
- ½ pound mushrooms, each halved
- ¾ pound boneless, skinless chicken breasts, cut in 1½-inch-long strips
- ¼ cup chopped basil leaves

1 In small bowl, combine coconut milk, lime zest, lime juice, soy sauce, ginger, brown sugar, cornstarch, and curry paste, if using.

2 In large skillet or wok over high heat, heat 1½ tablespoons of the oil. Add onion and garlic. Stir-fry until slightly softened, 2 minutes. Add broccoli and mushrooms. Stir-fry 2 minutes. Transfer to bowl.

3 Add remaining 1 tablespoon oil to skillet. Add chicken. Stir-fry until lightly golden, 2 minutes. Add coconut milk and broccoli mixture. Cover and simmer until chicken is cooked through and vegetables are crisp-tender, about 2 minutes.

4 Add basil. Serve at once.

Per serving: 272 calories, 25 g protein, 16 g carbohydrates, 13 g fat, 4 g saturated fat, 49 mg cholesterol, 4 g fiber, 343 mg sodium

HINT **helpful HINT** HINT HINT HINT HINT HINT HINT

Thai curry paste is spicy-hot, so use it sparingly if you're not used to it. You can also add a little zing to this dish by adding ¼ teaspoon crushed red pepper flakes instead of the curry paste.

Mediterranean Chicken

Fennel, green beans, and white kidney beans add folate, calcium, and fiber to an earthy chicken dish.

4 SERVINGS

Prep 20 min ◆ **Cook** 1 hour

- 2 **tablespoons olive oil**
- 1 **whole chicken (about 3½ pounds), cut into 8 serving pieces, skin removed**
- ¼ **cup flour**
  Bulb fennel (1½ pounds), trimmed and sliced
- 4 **cloves garlic, slivered**
- 1 **cup chicken broth**
- 2 **tablespoons fresh lemon juice**
- ½ **teaspoon salt**
- ¼ **teaspoon each rosemary, thyme, and pepper**
- 1 **can (19 ounces) white kidney beans (cannellini), rinsed and drained**
- ½ **pound green beans, cut into 2-inch lengths**

1 Preheat oven to 350°F.

2 In Dutch oven, heat oil over medium-high heat. Dredge chicken in flour. Sauté until golden, 4 minutes per side. Transfer to plate.

3 Add fennel to pan, reduce heat to medium, and cook, stirring often, until fennel is golden, 7 minutes. Add garlic; cook 1 minute. Add broth, lemon juice, salt, rosemary, thyme, and pepper. Bring to a boil. Add chicken, cover, and place in oven.

4 Bake until chicken is done, about 35 minutes. Stir in kidney beans and green beans. Bake 5 more minutes.

Per serving: 780 Calories, 95 g protein, 42 g carbohydrates, 24 g fat, 5 g saturated fat, 280 mg cholesterol, 13 g fiber, 1090 mg sodium

Chicken Baked with 40 Cloves of Garlic

If garlic has all the cancer-, cholesterol-, and bacteria-fighting properties that its proponents claim, this is just about the healthiest dish you can eat.

8 SERVINGS

Prep 25 min ◆ **Cook** 1 hour 15 min

- 6 **tablespoons olive oil**
- 2 **whole chickens (about 3½ pounds each), each cut into 8 serving pieces, skin removed**
- ⅓ **cup flour**
- 40 **cloves garlic, unpeeled**
- 3 **stalks celery, halved lengthwise and cut crosswise into 1-inch lengths**
- 4 **sprigs fresh rosemary or 1 teaspoon dried**
- 3 **sprigs fresh thyme or ½ teaspoon dried**
- 1 **cup dry vermouth or white wine**
- 1 **cup chicken broth**
- 1½ **teaspoons salt**

1 Preheat oven to 350°F. In large skillet, over medium heat, heat 2 tablespoons of oil. Dredge chicken in flour, shaking off excess. Add one-third of chicken to pan and sauté 4 minutes per side or until golden brown. Transfer to 10 x 14-inch roasting pan. Repeat sautéing in two more batches, using 2 tablespoons of oil per batch, cooking until golden brown and transferring to roasting pan.

2 Add garlic, celery, rosemary, and thyme to skillet, and cook 1 minute. Add vermouth. Increase heat to high, bring to a boil, and cook 2 minutes to evaporate alcohol. Add broth and salt to skillet, and bring to a boil. Remove from heat. Pour vegetables and cooking liquid over chicken in roasting pan. Cover pan with foil.

3 Bake until chicken is cooked through and garlic is meltingly tender, 45 minutes.

4 Spoon chicken and garlic onto dinner plates.

Per serving: 660 Calories, 87 g protein, 13 g carbohydrates, 23 g fat, 5 g saturated fat, 280 mg cholesterol, 1 g fiber, 700mg sodium

DID YOU KNOW ● ● ●

. . . that when garlic enjoys long, slow cooking—45 minutes or more in the oven—it loses its characteristic bite and offensive odor and gives quite a different flavor to whatever it has been cooked with?

Chicken Stew with Winter Squash & White Beans

This hearty, satisfying cold-weather comforter is rich in folate, fiber, and flavor.

6 SERVINGS

Prep 15 min ◆ **Cook** 1 hr

- 1 tablespoon olive oil
- 3 pounds chicken parts
- ½ teaspoon salt
- ¼ teaspoon black pepper
- 1 medium onion, coarsely chopped
- 4 cloves garlic, peeled and each halved
- 1 cup white wine
- 2 tablespoons tomato paste
- 2 bay leaves
- ½ teaspoon dried thyme, crumbled
- 1 can (15½ ounces) cannellini beans, drained and rinsed
- 1½ pounds butternut squash, seeded, peeled, and cut into 1½-inch pieces

1 Preheat oven to 350°F.

2 In large flameproof casserole over medium-high heat, heat oil. Season chicken with ¼ teaspoon of the salt and pepper. In batches if necessary, brown chicken in casserole, about 6 minutes. Transfer to plate.

3 Lower heat to medium. Add onion and garlic. Sauté until slightly softened, about 3 minutes. Add wine. Scrape up any browned bits from bottom. Stir in tomato paste, bay leaves, thyme, and remaining ¼ teaspoon salt. Add chicken. Bring to a boil. Cover.

4 Move casserole to oven and bake 20 minutes.

5 Stir in beans and squash. Cover. Bake until chicken and squash are tender, 20 to 30 minutes. Discard bay leaves.

Per serving: 381 calories, 29 g protein, 19 g carbohydrates, 21 g fat, 5 g saturated fat, 75 mg cholesterol, 5 g fiber, 330 mg sodium

HINT **helpful HINT** HINT HINT HINT HINT HINT HINT

To cut the saturated fat in these dishes in half, remove the skin from the chicken pieces and hens and discard before eating. You can discard even more fat in the stew by refrigerating it overnight and lifting off the congealed fat the next day before reheating and serving it.

Cornish Hens with Honey-Glazed Root Vegetables

This fiber-rich combination of sweet potatoes, parsnips, and celery root protects your digestive tract.

4 SERVINGS

Prep 15 min ◆ **Cook** 1 hr

- 2 large sweet potatoes, peeled and cut into 1-inch chunks
- 2 large parsnips, peeled and cut into 1-inch chunks
- 1 large celery root, peeled and cut into 1-inch chunks
- 1 medium red onion, quartered
- 2 teaspoons fresh thyme or 1 teaspoon dried thyme, crumbled
- ½ teaspoon salt
- ½ teaspoon black pepper
- 2 tablespoons olive oil
- 2 Cornish hens (about 1¼ pounds each)
- ½ teaspoon paprika
- 2 tablespoons honey

1 Preheat oven to 350°F. Place oven rack in lowest position.

2 In large roasting pan or 2 smaller pans, combine potatoes, parsnips, celery root, onion, thyme, salt, pepper, and oil. Nestle hens, breast side up, in among vegetables. Sprinkle hens with paprika.

3 Bake 50 minutes, stirring vegetables occasionally. Stir honey into vegetables. Bake until hens are cooked through and vegetables are fork-tender, 10 to 15 minutes. Cut each hen in half to serve.

Per serving: 630 calories, 45 g protein, 50 g carbohydrates, 28 g fat, 7 g saturated fat, 134 mg cholesterol, 8 g fiber, 715 mg sodium

VEGETABLES FOR VITALITY

Poached Chicken with Seasonal Vegetables

Use any combination of healthful veggies in this simple all-in-one supper dish.

4 SERVINGS

Prep 10 min ◆ **Cook** 25 min

- **4 boneless, skinless chicken breasts (1¼ pounds)**
- **3 cups chicken broth**
- **3 tablespoons dry sherry, or dry white wine**
- **1 bouquet garni (parsley, thyme, and bay leaf)**
- **1½ pounds mixed vegetables, such as asparagus, corn on the cob, broccoli, carrots, cauliflower, leeks, and savoy cabbage**
- **Chopped fresh parsley to garnish**

1 In large flameproof casserole or a deep frying pan, combine chicken breasts, broth, sherry or wine, and bouquet garni. Bring to a boil. Lower heat, cover, and poach chicken for 20 minutes, skimming off foam as necessary.

2 Meanwhile, cut all vegetables into bite-size pieces.

3 After chicken has been poaching 20 minutes, add vegetables to pan. Cover and continue cooking until the vegetables are tender and chicken juices run clear when breasts are pierced, about 5 minutes. Remove bouquet garni.

4 Spoon broth and vegetables into large, shallow serving bowls and top with chicken, whole or sliced as you prefer. Sprinkle with parsley and serve.

Per serving: 340 calories, 32 g protein, 14 g carbohydrates, 17 g fat, 6 g saturated fat, 90 g cholesterol, 3 g fiber, 180 g sodium

Turkey Cutlets with Green Beans & Sweet Onion Sauce

A delicious way to boost your veggie count: sautéed turkey on a bed of green beans with onions on top.

4 SERVINGS

Prep 15 min ◆ **Cook** 13 min

- **2 tablespoons grated orange zest**
- **½ cup fresh orange juice**
- **2 teaspoons grated lemon zest**
- **¼ cup fresh lemon juice**
- **3 tablespoons golden honey**
- **½ teaspoon freshly ground black pepper**
- **4 small boneless skinless turkey breast cutlets (4 ounces each)**
- **1 pound green beans or French haricots verts**
- **2 tablespoons unsalted butter**
- **1 extra-large yellow onion, slivered (1½ cups)**
- **2 large shallots, sliced**
- **2 large garlic cloves, minced**

1 In small bowl, whisk orange zest and juice, lemon zest and juice, honey, and pepper. Set aside.

2 Place cutlets, 1 at a time, between 2 sheets of plastic wrap. Pound until ½-inch thick. Sprinkle both sides with ¼ teaspoon salt.

3 Half-fill medium-size saucepan with water. Add remaining salt and bring to a boil over medium-high heat. Add green beans and cook just until beans turn bright green, 3 minutes. Drain, transfer to a platter, and keep warm.

4 Meanwhile, in large nonstick skillet over medium-high heat, melt butter. Add onion, shallots, and garlic; sauté for 2 minutes or just until the onion is transparent, but not brown. Using a slotted spoon, transfer to a plate.

5 Sauté turkey in same skillet for 3 minutes on each side. Arrange on top of the beans on the platter and keep hot. Pour juice and zest mixture into skillet, add onion mixture, and boil 2 minutes. Spoon over turkey and serve.

Per serving: 315 calories, 29 g protein, 37 g carbohydrates, 7 g fat, 4 g saturated fat, 86 mg cholesterol, 4 g fiber, 587 mg sodium

Chicken Breasts Stuffed with Spinach & Cheese

The phytochemical-rich filling fights chronic disease and helps protect your eyesight.

6 SERVINGS

Prep 20 min ◆ **Cook** 35 min

- 6 boneless, skinless chicken breast halves (about 1½ pounds)
- ¾ teaspoon salt
- ¼ teaspoon black pepper
- ½ teaspoon dried basil, crumbled
- 1 box (10 ounces) frozen leaf spinach, thawed and squeezed dry
- 6 roasted red bell pepper halves *(recipe page 295)*
- 6 thin slices reduced-fat Jarlsberg or Swiss cheese (4 ounces)
- ½ cup low-fat buttermilk
- 2 cups fresh whole-wheat bread crumbs

1 Preheat oven to 425°F. Coat rimmed baking sheet with nonstick cooking spray.

2 Flatten each chicken breast between plastic wrap to ⅛-inch thickness. Season one side with salt, pepper, and basil. Top each with spinach, red pepper, and cheese, dividing equally, and leaving ¼-inch border around edge. Roll up breasts around filling and secure with toothpick.

3 Dip each breast in buttermilk, then coat evenly with crumbs. Place, seam side down, on baking sheet.

4 Bake until chicken is cooked through and crumb coating is browned, about 35 minutes. Remove toothpicks, and serve.

Per serving: 236 calories, 31 g protein, 10 g carbohydrates, 8 g fat, 4 g saturated fat, 76 mg cholesterol, 2 g fiber, 518 mg sodium

Chicken Pot Pie with Chunky Vegetables

This classic comfort food has a healthful, new-age twist: a higher ratio of vegetables to meat.

6 SERVINGS

Prep 25 min ◆ **Cook** 45 min

- 2 tablespoons olive oil
- 3 leeks, rinsed, white and pale green parts coarsely chopped
- 2 celery stalks, coarsely chopped
- 2 large carrots, peeled and thickly sliced
- 1 large red potato, unpeeled and cut into bite-size chunks
- 1 cup thickly sliced mushrooms
- 3 tablespoons all-purpose flour
- ½ teaspoon dried thyme, crumbled
- ¼ teaspoon salt
- 1 can (14½ ounces) reduced-sodium, fat-free chicken broth
- 2 cups bite-size pieces cooked chicken
- 1 cup fresh or frozen green peas
  Prepackaged pastry for single-crust 9-inch pie
- 1 large egg whisked with 1 tablespoon milk for glaze

1 In large saucepan over medium heat, heat oil. Add leeks, celery, carrots, and potato. Cook, stirring occasionally, 5 minutes. Add mushrooms. Cook, stirring occasionally, 5 minutes. Stir in flour, thyme, and salt until blended. Stir in broth. Increase heat to medium-high. Cook, stirring, until thickened, about 2 minutes. Stir in chicken and peas. Transfer to 9- or 10-inch deep-dish pie plate. Let cool to room temperature.

2 Preheat oven to 400°F.

3 Unfold pastry, checking its fit on top of pie plate. Brush underside of pastry with glaze and place over filling. Trim edge and flute pastry, if desired. Brush top of pastry with glaze. Cut four 1-inch slits in center of pastry to vent steam.

4 Bake until filling is bubbly and pastry is golden brown, 25 to 30 minutes. Let stand at least 10 minutes before serving.

Per serving: 393 calories, 22 g protein, 39 g carbohydrates, 16 g fat, 5 g saturated fat, 82 mg cholesterol, 4 g fiber, 500 mg sodium

on the menu

Start a fall dinner with a creamy tomato bisque, follow with this hearty pot pie and a simple green salad, and end the meal with a light lemon mousse.

Turkey Drumsticks with Lentils, Carrots & Tomatoes

Lentils, like all legumes, are rich in soluble fiber, making this low-fat meal even healthier for your heart.

4 SERVINGS

Prep 10 min ◆ **Cook** 1½

- 1 tablespoon olive oil
- 4 turkey drumsticks (3 pounds), skin removed
- 1 teaspoon salt
- ¼ teaspoon black pepper
- 1 large onion, finely chopped
- 2 carrots, peeled and finely chopped
- 2 cloves garlic, minced
- ¾ cup dried lentils
- 1 can (14½ ounces) reduced-sodium, fat-free chicken broth
- 1 can (14½ ounces) diced tomatoes in juice
- 1 teaspoon dried rosemary, crumbled
- 1 tablespoon fresh-squeezed lemon juice

1 In nonstick Dutch oven or very large, deep skillet over medium-high heat, heat oil. Add drumsticks. Season with ½ teaspoon of the salt and ⅛ teaspoon of the pepper. Cook until browned all over, 10 to 15 minutes. Transfer drumsticks to plate. Cover with foil.

2 Add onion to skillet. Sauté until slightly softened, 3 minutes. Add carrots. Sauté 3 minutes. Add garlic. Sauté 30 seconds. Stir in lentils, broth, remaining ½ teaspoon salt, and remaining ⅛ teaspoon pepper. Bring to a boil, then lower heat and simmer, covered, 20 minutes.

3 Stir in tomatoes with their juice and rosemary. Top with drumsticks. Cover tightly. Continue to simmer until lentils are tender and drumsticks are cooked through, 30 to 45 minutes. Add a little water if mixture becomes too dry. Transfer drumsticks to serving plates. Stir lemon juice into lentil mixture. Simmer, uncovered, 3 minutes. Serve with turkey.

Per serving: 483 calories, 62 g protein, 35 g carbohydrates, 10 g fat, 3 g saturated fat, 201 mg cholesterol, 12 g fiber, 1,144 mg sodium

Tex-Mex Turkey Casserole

Vitamins C, B₆, E, and folate fill this hearty dish.

6 SERVINGS

Prep 15 min ◆ **Cook** 55 min

- 1 tablespoon vegetable oil
- 1 onion, coarsely chopped
- 1 tablespoon chili powder
- ½ teaspoon cinnamon
- ¼ teaspoon salt
- 3 tablespoons all-purpose flour
- 1 can (14½ ounces) diced tomatoes with mild green chiles
- 1 can (14½ ounces) reduced-sodium, fat-free chicken broth
- ½ pound piece of deli oven-roasted turkey, sliced ½ inch thick and cut into ½-inch-thick cubes
- 2 zucchini, cut into ½-inch cubes
- 1 cup frozen corn kernels
- 1½ cups cooked long-grain white rice
- 4 ounces reduced-fat Monterey Jack cheese, shredded

1 Preheat oven to 350°F. In large saucepan over medium heat, heat oil. Add onion. Sauté until softened, 5 minutes. Stir in chili powder, cinnamon, salt, and flour. Cook, stirring, 2 minutes. Stir in tomatoes and broth. Cook, stirring, until slightly thickened, about 2 minutes. Off heat, stir in turkey, zucchini, corn, and rice. Pour into ungreased 9 x 9 x 2-inch-square baking dish. (Recipe can be prepared ahead to this point.)

2 Bake until bubbly, about 40 minutes. Sprinkle with cheese. Bake until cheese is melted, 5 minutes. Let stand 5 minutes before serving.

Per serving: 264 calories, 20 g protein, 29 g carbohydrates, 8 g fat, 3 g saturated fat, 47 mg cholesterol, 3 g fiber, 831 mg sodium

Asian Vegetable-Packed Turkey Burgers

Grated carrot is the secret ingredient that boosts both the flavor and the antioxidant power of these low-fat, low-calorie poultry patties.

6 BURGERS

Prep 10 min ◆ **Cook** 10 min

1½ **pounds lean ground turkey (7% fat)**
  2 **carrots, peeled and finely shredded**
  3 **scallions, finely chopped**
  2 **tablespoons soy sauce**
  2 **teaspoons finely chopped, peeled fresh ginger**
  ¼ **teaspoon salt**
  ¼ **teaspoon black pepper**

  1 Preheat broiler.

  2 In medium bowl, combine turkey, carrots, scallions, soy sauce, ginger, salt, and pepper. Shape into 6 equal patties.

  3 Broil burgers 4 inches from heat for 5 minutes. Turn over and broil just until no longer pink in center, 4 to 5 minutes.

Per burger: 135 calories, 16 g protein, 3 g carbohydrates, 6 g fat, 2 g saturated fat, 67 mg cholesterol, 1 g fiber, 498 mg sodium

on the menu

Serve on a roll with lettuce and tomato, just like any burger, or serve on a bed of thin noodles with shreds of scallion and red pepper, tossed with a few drops of dark sesame oil. Cucumbers sprinkled with rice vinegar make a refreshing side dish.

MAIN COURSE meat DISHES

Beefy Green Salad

When it comes to salad greens, the more deeply colored they are, the more vitamins and minerals they contain.

4 SERVINGS

Prep 20 min ◆ **Cook** 2 min

- 1 cup parsley leaves
- 1 tablespoon capers, drained
- 1 tablespoon prepared mustard
- 1 tablespoon white wine vinegar
- 1 clove garlic, peeled
- 3 tablespoons olive oil
- 2 tablespoons reduced-sodium, fat-free chicken broth
- 1 tablespoon vegetable oil
- 1 pound beef top round steak, cut into 3 x ¼-inch strips
- 1 head romaine lettuce or spinach leaves, torn into bite-size pieces
- 1 large red bell pepper, seeded and cut into strips
- ½ medium red onion, thinly sliced

1 In food processor or blender, combine parsley leaves, capers, prepared mustard, vinegar, garlic, olive oil, and broth. Whirl until smooth to make dressing

2 In medium nonstick skillet over high heat, heat oil. Add beef. Sauté just until pink, about 2 minutes. Transfer to plate. Let cool.

3 In serving bowl or platter, combine romaine, bell pepper, and onion. Top with beef strips. Serve with dressing.

Per serving: 339 calories, 27 g protein, 8 g carbohydrates, 23 g fat, 5 g saturated fat, 65 mg cholesterol, 4 g fiber, 187 mg sodium

Beef Salad Niçoise

In this hearty French-style salad, slices of iron-rich rump steak top a mixture of colorful, vitamin-packed vegetables in a tangy Dijon mustard dressing.

4 SERVINGS

Prep 15 min ◆ **Cook** 30 min

- 1 thick-cut lean rump steak (12 ounces), trimmed
  Salt and pepper
- ¼ teaspoon dried herbes de Provence, or to taste
- 1 pound small new potatoes, scrubbed
- ½ pound green beans, trimmed
- ½ pound frozen lima beans, thawed
- ½ pint cherry tomatoes, halved
- ½ cup mixed pitted black and green olives
- 2 tablespoons snipped chives
- 3 tablespoons chopped parsley
- 2 tablespoons extra-virgin olive oil
- 1 tablespoon red wine vinegar
- 2 teaspoons Dijon mustard
- 4 cups baby spinach leaves
- 4 cups torn lettuce leaves

1 Pat steak dry with paper towel. Season on both sides with salt, pepper, and herbes de Provence. Set aside.

2 In large saucepan of boiling water, cook potatoes 10 minutes. Add green and lima beans. Cook for 5 minutes or until all vegetables are just tender. Drain and rinse with cold water to cool slightly.

3 In large bowl, combine potatoes, beans, tomatoes, olives, chives, and parsley. Set aside.

4 Heat ridged cast-iron grill pan or nonstick frying pan over medium-high heat until hot. Grill steak 3 minutes on each side or until cooked to desired doneness. Remove to plate and let stand 5 minutes.

5 Meanwhile, combine oil, vinegar, and mustard in screw-top jar with 2 tablespoons water. Season with salt and pepper. Shake dressing to mix well.

6 Cut steak into ¼-inch-thick slices. Add to vegetables. Pour any juices that have collected on the plate into the dressing. Pour dressing over meat and vegetables and toss well. In large salad bowl, combine spinach and lettuce leaves. Spoon steak salad over greens and serve immediately.

Per serving: 500 calories, 35 g protein, 51 g carbohydrates, 19 g fat, 3 g saturated fat, 50 g cholesterol, 17 g fiber, 890 g sodium

on the menu

A full Niçoise salad has all the elements you need for a delicious, healthy dinner.
For contrast, you might want to start with a hot consommé, and for dessert, try
some Camembert cheese with a baguette and fresh pears.

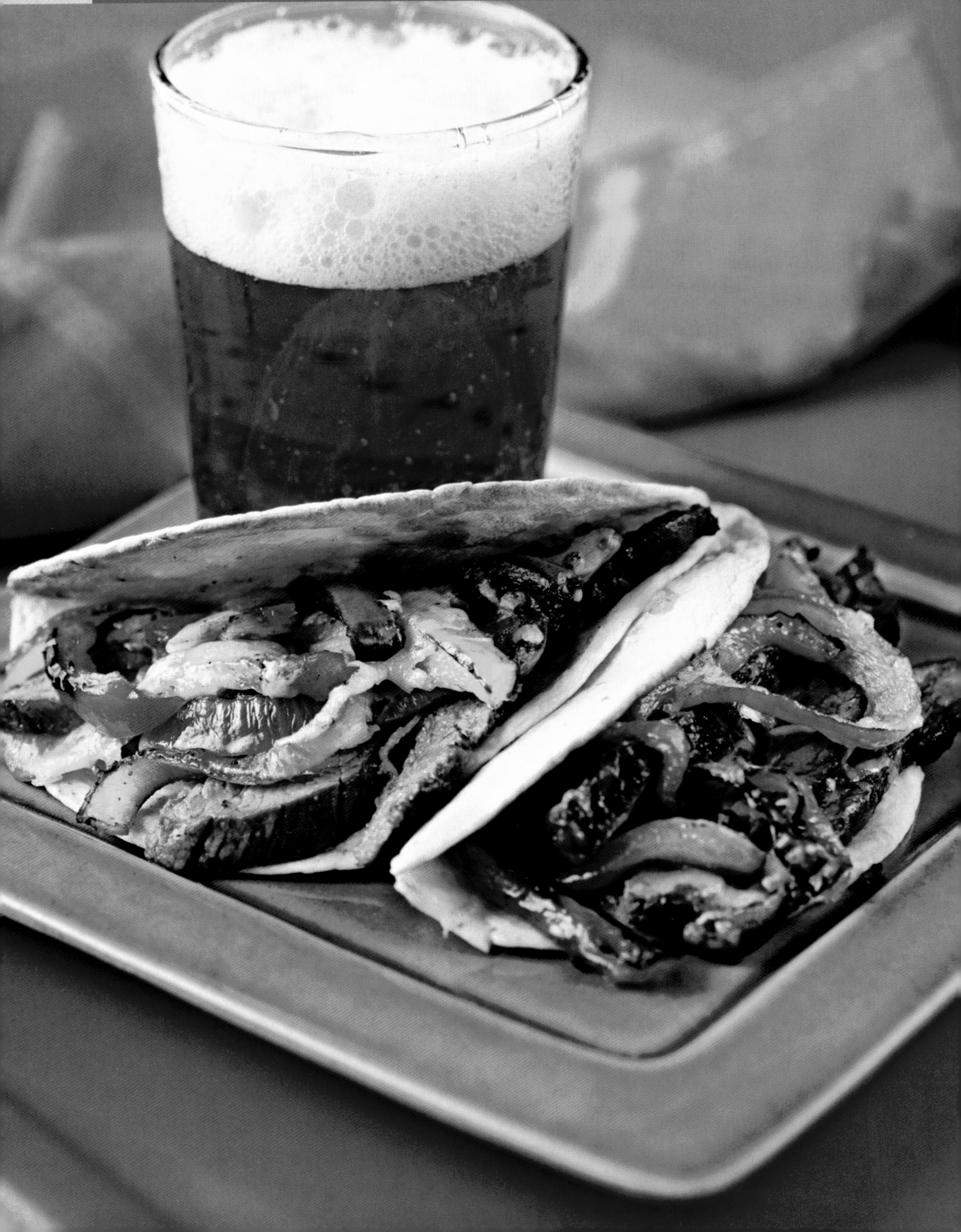

Beef, Onion & Pepper Fajitas

A fajita is a tortilla wrapped around meat and an assortment of vegetables, which means it's naturally loaded with vitamins, minerals, and phytochemicals.

8 FAJITAS

Prep 15 min ◆ **Marinate** 1 to 2 hr ◆ **Cook** 12 min

- 1 flank steak (about 1 pound)
- 1 red onion, sliced
- 1 small red bell pepper, seeded and cut into thin strips
- 1 small green bell pepper, seeded and cut into thin strips
- 1 small yellow bell pepper, seeded and cut into thin strips
- 4 cloves garlic, minced
- ½ cup fresh lime juice
- 2 tablespoons olive oil
- 2 tablespoons balsamic vinegar
- 1 teaspoon ground cumin
- ½ teaspoon salt
- ¼ teaspoon black pepper
- 1 serrano or jalapeño chile pepper, seeded and finely chopped
- 8 flour tortillas (6 inches), warmed following package directions
- ¼ pound Monterey Jack cheese, shredded

1 In shallow baking dish, combine steak, onion, and bell peppers. In small bowl, whisk together garlic, lime juice, oil, vinegar, cumin, salt, pepper, and chile. Pour over steak mixture. Toss to coat. Refrigerate, covered, 1 to 2 hours.

2 Preheat broiler.

3 Broil steak on broiler-pan rack 4 inches from heat 2 minutes each side. Add onion and bell peppers to rack. Spoon remaining marinade over steak and vegetables. Broil, turning meat and vegetables over occasionally, until meat is cooked to desired doneness and vegetables are crisp-tender, 6 to 8 minutes longer. Let meat stand 5 minutes.

4 Cut meat diagonally across grain into thin slices. Place on warmed tortillas, dividing equally, with onion and peppers. Top with cheese. Place under broiler just until cheese melts, about 30 seconds. Fold tortillas over filling and serve.

Per fajita: 293 calories, 18 g protein, 24 g carbohydrates, 14 g fat, 6 g saturated fat, 40 mg cholesterol, 2 g fiber, 411 mg sodium

Thai-Style Beef Sandwich

Vitamin-packed coleslaw enriches this beef sandwich.

4 SERVINGS

Prep 10 min ◆ **Marinate** 30 min ◆ **Cook** 10 min

- 2 tablespoons tomato paste
- ½ cup fresh lime juice (about 3 limes)
- 1½ teaspoons ground coriander
- 1 pound well-trimmed flank steak
- 1 teaspoon sugar
- I teaspoon salt
- I teaspoon red pepper flakes
- 3 cups shredded green cabbage (12 ounces)
- 2 carrots, shredded
- 1 large red bell pepper, cut into matchsticks
- ½ cup chopped cilantro
- ⅓ cup chopped fresh mint
- 4 hard rolls, halved crosswise

1 In shallow glass dish, stir together tomato paste, half the lime juice, and coriander. Add flank steak, turning to coat. Refrigerate for 30 minutes.

2 In large bowl, whisk together remaining ¼ cup lime juice, sugar, salt, and pepper flakes. Add cabbage, carrots, bell pepper, cilantro, and mint; toss well to combine. Refrigerate coleslaw until serving time.

3 Preheat broiler. Remove steak from marinade. Broil 6 inches from heat for 4 minutes per side for medium-rare, brushing any remaining marinade over steak halfway through cooking time. Let stand for 10 minutes. Cut thin, diagonal slices across the grain.

4 To serve, spoon coleslaw on bottom half of each roll. Cover with steak and top halves of rolls.

Per serving: 420 calories, 32 g protein, 47 g carbohydrates, 13 g fat, 5 g saturated fat, 55 mg cholesterol, 7 g fiber, 890 mg sodium

Stir-Fried Beef with Broccoli, Snow Peas, Peppers & Shiitake Mushrooms

Mushrooms supply selenium and potassium, essential minerals that help reduce your risk of stroke. Broccoli, snow peas, and peppers give you megadoses of vitamin C and phytochemicals to fight cancer.

4 SERVINGS

Prep 20 min ◆ **Marinate** 20 min ◆ **Cook** 13 min

- **3 tablespoons soy sauce**
- **2 teaspoons packed dark-brown sugar**
- **1 pound beef round steak, cut across grain into ⅛-inch-thick strips**
- **1 small head broccoli, cut into 4-inch long florets (about 2 firmly packed cups)**
- **2 tablespoons vegetable oil**
- **2 cups sliced shiitake mushroom caps**
- **1 red bell pepper, seeded and thinly sliced**
- **1 cup snow peas, stems and strings removed**
- **4 scallions, cut diagonally into ¼-inch pieces**
- **1 tablespoon minced garlic**
- **1 tablespoon finely chopped, peeled fresh ginger**
  Pinch red pepper flakes
- **⅓ cup reduced-sodium, fat-free chicken broth**
- **1 tablespoon balsamic vinegar**
- **2 teaspoons cornstarch**

1 In medium bowl, stir together 1 tablespoon of the soy sauce and brown sugar. Add beef. Toss to coat. Marinate at room temperature 20 minutes.

2 Steam broccoli until crisp-tender, 3 to 4 minutes. Cool under cold running water. Drain.

3 In large nonstick skillet or wok over high heat, heat oil. Add meat. Stir-fry just until pink, about 2 minutes. Transfer from skillet with slotted spoon.

4 Add mushrooms, bell pepper, snow peas, scallions, garlic, ginger, and pepper flakes to skillet. Stir-fry until snow peas are crisp-tender, 3 to 4 minutes.

5 Stir together broth, remaining 2 tablespoons soy sauce, vinegar, and cornstarch in small bowl until smooth. Add to skillet. Bring to a boil (mixture will be very thick). Add broccoli. Cook just until heated through, about 2 minutes.

6 Drain beef. Add to skillet. Heat through, about 30 seconds. Serve immediately.

Per serving: 301 calories, 30 g protein, 21 g carbohydrates, 12 g fat, 2 g saturated fat, 66 mg cholesterol, 4 g fiber, 838 mg sodium

FRESH IDEAS

A beef stir-fry can accommodate many different vegetables and seasonings. Here are a few to try:
- *Asparagus, sugar snaps, and radishes with scallions and lemon zest*
- *Multi-pepper—red, yellow, green—with basil and garlic*
- *Green beans, baby corn, and zucchini with shallots, tarragon, and dill*

Grilled Steak with Tomatoes, Onions & Portobello Mushrooms

Round out the nutritional profile of a juicy, iron-rich steak by topping it with a classic combination of vitamin- and phytochemical-rich vegetables. The results are delectable!

4 SERVINGS

Prep 15 min ◆ **Cook** 15 min

- 2 teaspoons olive oil
- 2 cloves garlic, minced
- 4 slices (½ inch thick) red onion
- 4 large portobello mushrooms, stems removed
  Nonstick olive-oil cooking spray
- 2 boneless rib-eye steaks (12 ounces each)
- ½ teaspoon salt
- ¼ teaspoon black pepper
- 3 ripe tomatoes
  Fresh chives or parsley, finely chopped
  (optional)

1 Heat grill to high. Meanwhile, in small skillet over medium heat, heat oil. Add garlic. Sauté 2 minutes. Transfer oil and garlic to large bowl.

2 Coat onion slices and mushroom caps on both sides with cooking spray.

3 Grill onion and mushrooms just until browned, about 2 minutes each side. Cut mushrooms into thick slices. Add mushrooms and onion to garlic oil. Toss to coat.

4 Cut steaks crosswise into two equal-size pieces. Pat dry. Season with salt and pepper. Coat lightly with cooking spray.

5 Grill steaks until seared and browned grill marks appear, 3 to 4 minutes. Turn steaks over. Grill 2 to 3 minutes for medium-rare, or until desired doneness.

6 To serve, cut each tomato into 6 slices. Arrange 3 slices on top of each cooked steak. Top with mushroom-onion mixture. Sprinkle with chives, if desired.

Per serving: 305 calories, 23 g protein, 8 g carbohydrates, 20 g fat, 7 g saturated fat, 67 mg cholesterol, 2 g fiber, 159 mg sodium

helpful HINT

Any dish that can be grilled can also be broiled. Preheat the broiler and adjust the rack and broiler pan so the food will be 3 to 4 inches from the heat source. Follow the same directions and times as for grilling.

DID YOU KNOW ● ● ●

. . . that cooked fresh mushrooms have almost three times the niacin and potassium, twice the iron, and 15 times the riboflavin of a comparable amount of canned mushrooms?

on the menu

This flank steak roll is equally delicious served as the centerpiece of a sit-down hot meal or as one of several tempting dishes on a cold buffet. For the hot meal, serve the beef roll with mashed sweet potatoes and a grapefruit and greens salad in a citrus vinaigrette. For a cold dinner, add crusty hot bread and a mixed green salad.

Flank Steak Roll with Spinach, Carrots & Red Pepper

Each slice of this easily prepared entrée is a mosaic of color, flavor, and powerful nutrients that will protect your health.

6 SERVINGS

Prep 15 min ◆ **Marinate** 2 to 4 hr ◆ **Cook** 40 min

- ½ cup red wine
- ⅓ cup reduced-sodium soy sauce
- 2 tablespoons sugar
- 1 teaspoon garlic powder
- 1½ pounds flank steak, butterflied
- 6 ounces fresh baby spinach leaves
- 4 scallions, coarsely chopped
- ⅛ teaspoon salt
- 2½ cups grated peeled carrots (about 1 pound carrots)
- 1 jar (12 ounces) roasted red peppers, drained

1 In large resealable plastic bag or container, combine red wine, soy sauce, sugar, and garlic powder. Add steak. Turn to coat. Refrigerate at least 2 hours or up to 4 hours.

2 Meanwhile, rinse spinach and leave some water clinging to leaves. Place in large pot over medium heat. Cook, stirring often, just until wilted, about 1 minute. Transfer to plate. Let cool.

3 Preheat oven to 375°F.

4 Remove meat from marinade. Pat dry. Set marinade aside. Spread spinach in even layer over steak. Top with scallions. Sprinkle with salt. Layer carrots on top, then roasted peppers. Starting at one long side of steak, roll up meat tightly to enclose filling. Secure seam in several spots with toothpicks. Place roll, seam side down, in shallow baking pan. Brush top with marinade.

5 Roast 15 minutes. Spoon any juices in pan over top of meat. Roast 20 minutes longer for medium-rare or until desired doneness. Let meat stand 10 minutes.

6 Meanwhile, in small saucepan, boil remaining marinade just until it's thick enough to coat a spoon. Strain and set aside.

7 Cut meat diagonally into ¼-inch-thick slices. Drizzle a little marinade on each plate. Top with steak slices.

Per serving: 229 calories, 21 g protein, 15 g carbohydrates, 9 g fat, 4 g saturated fat, 48 mg cholesterol, 2 g fiber, 738 mg sodium

Orange Beef with Broccoli

Broccoli and bell pepper serve up vitamin C in this dish.

4 SERVINGS

Prep 20 min ◆ **Marinate** 30 min ◆ **Cook** 15 min

- 2 teaspoons cornstarch
- ¼ cup dry sherry
- 2 tablespoons reduced-sodium soy sauce
- ¼ teaspoon baking soda
- 12 ounces flank steak, cut into thin strips
- 4 teaspoons olive oil
- 4 tablespoons finely slivered orange zest
- ¼ teaspoon crushed red pepper flakes
- 5 cups broccoli florets and stems
- 1 red bell pepper, cut into matchsticks
- 4 scallions, thinly sliced
- 3 cloves garlic, minced
- 1 cup jicama matchsticks

1 In medium bowl, whisk together cornstarch, sherry, soy sauce, and baking soda. Add steak, tossing to coat. Refrigerate 30 minutes.

2 In large nonstick skillet over medium heat, heat 3 teaspoons oil. Reserving marinade, add beef, half of orange zest, and pepper flakes to skillet. Stir-fry until beef is just cooked, 3 minutes. Transfer to plate.

3 Add remaining oil, broccoli, bell pepper, scallions, and garlic to skillet. Cook 3 minutes. Add ½ cup water. Cook until broccoli is crisp-tender, 2 minutes.

4 Stir ⅓ cup water and reserved marinade into skillet. Bring to boil. Cook, stirring, 1 minute. Return beef to skillet. Add jicama. Cook until beef is heated through, 1 minute. Garnish with remaining orange zest.

Per serving: 284 calories, 21 g protein, 16 g carbohydrates, 14 g fat, 4.4 g saturated fat, 16 mg cholesterol, 5.3 g fiber, 473 mg sodium

VEGETABLES FOR VITALITY

Moroccan Beef Stew with Sweet Potatoes, Chickpeas & Dried Fruit

Chickpeas add low-fat protein to this North African beef hotpot. Sweet potatoes add vitamin C, beta-carotene, and plenty of fiber. The dried apricots and raisins offer a sweet taste note, made more provocative by a mix of Middle Eastern spices.

6 SERVINGS

Prep 15 min ◆ **Cook** 1 hr 50 min

- 1 tablespoon vegetable oil
- 1 pound beef bottom round steak, cut into 1-inch cubes
- 1 onion, finely chopped
- 4 cloves garlic, minced
- ½ teaspoon ground ginger
- ½ teaspoon cinnamon
- ½ teaspoon ground nutmeg
- ½ teaspoon ground turmeric
- ½ teaspoon salt
- ¼ teaspoon black pepper
- ½ cup chopped dried apricots
- ¼ cup golden or dark seedless raisins
- 2 sweet potatoes, peeled and cut into ¾-inch chunks
- 3 cups reduced-sodium, fat-free chicken broth
- 1 can (15 ounces) chickpeas, drained and rinsed
  Thinly sliced strips scallion greens
  Thin strips orange zest

1 In large nonstick saucepan or pot over medium-high heat, heat oil. Working in batches, add beef and brown on all sides, 3 to 4 minutes per batch. Transfer meat to plate as it browns. Add onion to saucepan. Cook until softened, 5 minutes, adding a spoonful of water, if needed, to prevent sticking.

2 Add garlic, ginger, cinnamon, nutmeg, turmeric, salt, and pepper. Cook 1 minute. Add apricots, raisins, potatoes, reserved beef, and broth. Cover and simmer until meat is very tender, 1½ hours.

3 Stir in chickpeas. Heat through. Garnish with scallion and orange zest.

Per serving: 330 calories, 18 g protein, 37 g carbohydrates, 12 g fat, 4 g saturated fat, 48 mg cholesterol, 5 g fiber, 812 mg sodium

FRESH IDEAS

You can substitute chunks of winter squash or baby carrots for the sweet potatoes in this stew without significantly changing the flavor or nutritional value.

Classic Veal Stew with Mushrooms, Carrots, Shallots & Beer

This heart-healthy main dish is high in vitamins, minerals, and fiber, and low in saturated fat. It is also, despite its heart-healthy virtues, a mouthwatering take on the traditional beef carbonara, so popular in Belgium.

4 SERVINGS

Prep 15 min ◆ **Cook** 1½ hr

- **1 pound stewing veal, cut into 1-inch pieces**
- **¾ teaspoon salt**
- **¼ teaspoon black pepper**
- **2 tablespoons vegetable oil**
- **2 portobello mushrooms, stems removed and caps cut into 1-inch dice**
- **8 large shallots (or 1 onion), finely chopped**
- **2 tablespoons all-purpose flour**
- **1 bottle dark beer**
- **1 tablespoon white wine vinegar**
- **½ teaspoon dried thyme, crumbled**
- **1 pound large carrots, peeled and cut into 2-inch lengths**

1 Pat veal dry. Season with ¼ teaspoon of the salt and pepper.

2 In large flameproof casserole over high heat, heat oil. Working in batches, add veal and brown on all sides, 3 to 4 minutes per batch. Transfer veal to plate.

3 Lower heat to medium. Add mushrooms and shallots to casserole. Sauté until shallots are just golden, about 5 minutes. Stir in flour. Add veal, beer, vinegar, thyme, and remaining ½ teaspoon salt. Bring to a boil. Add carrots. Cover. Lower heat. Simmer until veal is tender, about 1¼ hours.

4 Transfer veal, carrots, and mushrooms to serving dish. Boil sauce to reduce to about 1¼ cups. Pour over veal.

Per serving: 310 calories, 26 g protein, 21 g carbohydrates, 11 g fat, 2 g saturated fat, 95 mg cholesterol, 3 g fiber, 490 mg sodium

DID YOU KNOW ● ● ●

. . .that shallots are a member of the onion family with a complex flavor all their own? It can be described as being delicate and savory, milder than garlic, but sweeter than onions.

Cider-Braised Ham with Yams & Apple

High-fiber yams and modern lean pork are combined in a tasty low-fat, low-calorie dish.

4 SERVINGS

Prep 15 min ◆ **Cook** 30 min

- **1 cup plus 1 tablespoon apple cider**
- **1 tablespoon Dijon mustard**
- **1 tablespoon finely chopped, peeled fresh ginger**
- **½ teaspoon ground cloves**
- **1 yam or sweet potato, peeled and cut into ⅛-inch-thick slices**
- **1 pound lean ham steak**
- **1 Granny Smith apple, peeled, cored, and cut into 12 wedges**
- **1 tablespoon cornstarch**
- **½ cup diagonally sliced green part of scallions**

1 In large skillet, stir together 1 cup of the cider, mustard, ginger, and cloves. Bring to a simmer. Add yam slices. Cover tightly and simmer until partially tender, 15 minutes.

2 Add ham steak, covering with yam slices. Arrange apple wedges over top. Cover and simmer until apples and yam are tender and ham is heated through, 10 to 15 minutes.

3 Meanwhile, in small bowl, stir together cornstarch and the 1 tablespoon of cider until well blended.

4 With slotted spoon, remove ham, yams, and apple to platter. Cover with foil to keep warm.

5 Stir a little of hot pan liquid into cornstarch mixture until smooth. Stir cornstarch mixture into skillet. Cook over medium heat, stirring, until slightly thickened, about 1 minute.

6 Divide ham, yams, and apples among 4 plates. Spoon skillet sauce over. Garnish with scallions.

Per serving: 211 calories, 18 g protein, 25 g carbohydrates, 4 g fat, 1 g saturated fat, 38 mg cholesterol, 2 g fiber, 1,188 mg sodium

FRESH IDEAS

Adding fresh fruit to a meat dish is a great way to include more vitamins and fiber in a meal. Sliced pears, halved kumquats, orange sections, or pineapple chunks could be used in this recipe in place of the apple.

Sausage & Rice-Stuffed Bell Peppers

Sweet peppers are chock-full of vitamin C and other nutrients that boost your immune system and fight chronic disease.

4 SERVINGS

Prep 15 min ◆ **Cook** 45 min

- **4 large bell peppers, any colors**
- **10 ounces sweet Italian sausages**
- **1 teaspoon dried oregano, crumbled**
- **1½ cups cooked white rice**
- **1 carrot, peeled and grated**
- **½ cup shredded mild cheddar cheese**
- **1½ cups prepared tomato sauce, warmed** *(optional)*

1 Cut peppers in half through stem end. Scrape out membranes and seeds. Steam peppers 5 minutes to soften slightly. Finely chop usable part of pepper tops.

2 Heat large nonstick skillet over medium heat. Remove sausage from casings and crumble into skillet. Add chopped pepper and oregano. Cook until sausage is browned and cooked through, breaking up with wooden spoon, about 3 minutes. Remove skillet from heat. Stir in rice, carrot, and cheese.

3 Preheat oven to 375°F.

4 Place peppers in 9-inch-square baking dish. Fill each pepper with rice mixture, packing in mixture with small spoon. Cover with foil.

5 Bake until peppers are tender, 25 to 30 minutes. Serve with tomato sauce, if desired.

Per serving: 306 calories, 14 g protein, 31 g carbohydrates, 15 g fat, 6 g saturated fat, 43 mg cholesterol, 4 g fiber, 435 mg sodium

Pork & Pinto Bean Chili

Typical Southwestern ingredients—tomatoes, peppers, and garlic—flavor this high-fiber phytochemical-rich stew.

6 SERVINGS

Prep 20 min ◆ **Cook** 2 hr

- 1½ **pounds pork stew meat, such as shoulder, cut into ½-inch cubes**
- ½ **cup all-purpose flour**
- 2 **tablespoons vegetable oil**
- 1 **large onion, finely chopped**
- 1 **green bell pepper, seeded and coarsely chopped**
- 1 **jalapeño chile, seeded and finely chopped**
- 3 **cloves garlic, minced**
- 1 **can (28 ounces) plum tomatoes with juice, coarsely chopped**
- 1 **cup reduced-sodium, fat-free chicken broth**
- 3 **tablespoons chili powder**
- ¼ **teaspoon salt**
- 2 **cans (15 ounces each) pinto beans, drained and rinsed**

1 Coat pork with flour. Shake off excess flour.

2 In large nonstick saucepan over medium-high heat, heat oil. Working in batches, add pork and brown on all sides, about 5 minutes per batch. Transfer pork to plate as it browns.

3 Lower heat to medium. Add onion, bell pepper, jalapeño, and garlic. Cook until onion is softened, about 5 minutes. Return pork to pan. Add tomatoes, broth, chili powder, and salt. Simmer 1 hour, stirring occasionally. Stir in beans. Simmer until meat is tender and sauce is thickened, about 40 minutes. If sauce becomes too thick, thin with a little water.

Per serving: 298 calories, 25 g protein, 24 g carbohydrates, 11 g fat, 3 g saturated fat, 56 mg cholesterol, 7 g fiber, 583 mg sodium

Pork Chops with Fresh Sauerkraut

When you make sauerkraut yourself, cabbage retains its fresh flavor, and much more of its nutritional power.

4 SERVINGS

Prep 15 min ◆ **Cook** 55 min

- 1 **tablespoon vegetable oil**
- 4 **pork chops (about 6 ounces each)**
- ¾ **teaspoon salt**
- ¼ **teaspoon black pepper**
- 1 **medium onion, thinly sliced**
- 1 **cup coarsely chopped, peeled carrot**
- 2 **cloves garlic, sliced**
- 1 **cup white wine**
- 6 **cups shredded Savoy cabbage (1 small head)**
- 1 **bay leaf**
- 3 **whole cloves**
- 2 **tablespoon white wine vinegar**
- 1 **teaspoon sugar**

1 In large nonstick skillet over medium-high heat, heat oil. Season chops with ¼ teaspoon of the salt and pepper. Add chops to skillet. Sauté until well browned on both sides, about 3 minutes per side. Transfer chops to plate.

2 Lower heat to medium. Add onion, carrot, and garlic to skillet. Sauté until onion is softened, about 5 minutes. Add wine. Bring to a boil. Stir in cabbage, bay leaf, and cloves. Cover. Simmer over medium-low heat until cabbage is tender, 20 to 30 minutes.

3 Stir vinegar, sugar, and remaining ½ teaspoon salt into cabbage mixture. Add pork chops. Cover. Continue simmering until pork is just cooked through, about 10 minutes. Serve with boiled potatoes, if desired.

Per serving: 275 calories, 29 g protein, 13 g carbohydrates, 12 g fat, 3 g saturated fat, 73 mg cholesterol, 5 g fiber, 524 mg sodium

helpful HINT

Store-bought chili powder is a blend of ground, dried chile peppers, oregano, and cumin. You can make your own by trying different dried chiles. In a heavy skillet over medium heat, toast the chiles for 2 minutes, shaking the pan often. Let cool, then remove seeds, stems, and inner veins. In a blender, grind the chiles to a fine powder. Store in an airtight container.

DID YOU KNOW ● ● ●

   ...that cabbage is one of the oldest cultivated vegetables and
the grandfather of all the brassicas, such as broccoli, Brussels
sprouts, cauliflower, and kale? It is thought to have originated
along the coasts of temperate northern Europe and moved across
continents from there.

Stir-Fried Ginger Pork with Bok Choy & Garlic

Bok choy supplies the same vitamins and disease-fighting antioxidants as other cabbages, the same potassium and fiber, and much, much higher amounts of calcium and beta-carotene.

4 SERVINGS

Prep 15 min ◆ **Marinate** 15 min ◆ **Cook** 10 min

- **3 tablespoons dry sherry or rice wine**
- **2 tablespoons soy sauce**
- **1 tablespoon cornstarch**
- **1 teaspoon dark sesame oil**
- **1 teaspoon light-brown sugar**
- **¼ teaspoon black pepper**
- **1 boneless pork tenderloin (about 1 pound), cut into ⅛-inch-thick slices**
- **2 tablespoons vegetable oil**
- **5 cups coarsely chopped bok choy**
- **2 cloves garlic, minced**

1 In medium bowl, stir together 1½ tablespoons of the sherry, soy sauce, cornstarch, sesame oil, sugar, and pepper. Add pork. Toss to coat. Marinate at room temperature for 15 minutes.

2 In large nonstick skillet or wok over high heat, heat 1 tablespoon of the oil. Add bok choy. Stir-fry 2 minutes. Cover. Cook until wilted, about 2 minutes. Transfer bok choy to plate. Pour out liquid left in skillet.

3 Add remaining 1 tablespoon oil to skillet. Add garlic. Sauté 15 seconds. Add pork mixture. Stir-fry until just cooked through, 3 to 4 minutes. Add bok choy and remaining sherry. Cook until heated through. Serve immediately.

Per serving: *267 calories, 25 g protein, 5 g carbohydrates, 16 g fat, 4 g saturated fat, 64 mg cholesterol, 2 g fiber, 536 mg sodium*

DID YOU KNOW ● ● ●

. . .that bok choy leaves can be braised like any other greens and bok choy stems can be cut up and used for seasoning in soups and stews just like celery stalks?

FRESH IDEAS

You can make a mouthwatering ginger pork stir-fry with other vegetables than bok choy. Try substituting broccoli spears, snow peas, green beans, or sliced turnips for a nice change.

Orange-Glazed Roast Pork Tenderloin with Sweet Potatoes, Onions, Carrots & Apples

Lean pork tenderloin pairs well with sweet vegetables such as carrots and sweet potatoes, heart savers that are high in fiber and beta-carotene. Onions and apples add vitamin C and folate to the nutritional mix.

4 SERVINGS

Prep 20 min ◆ Marinate 2 hr ◆ **Cook** 55 min

- ½ cup orange juice concentrate
- 1 teaspoon honey
- ½ teaspoon ground cumin
- ¼ teaspoon cinnamon
- ¼ teaspoon chili powder
- 1 pork tenderloin (1¼ pounds)
- 1 tablespoon vegetable oil
- 2 medium sweet potatoes, peeled and cut in ½-inch pieces
- 1 medium onion, cut into ½-inch pieces
- 2 medium carrots, peeled and cut in ½-inch pieces
- 2 medium apples, cored, peeled, and cut into 1-inch pieces
- ½ teaspoon salt
- ½ cup dry white wine
- 1 tablespoon butter

1 In large bowl, combine orange juice concentrate, honey, cumin, cinnamon, and chili powder. Add pork. Turn to coat. Cover and refrigerate for at least 2 hours or up to 24 hours, turning pork occasionally.

2 Preheat oven to 350°F.

3 In very large ovenproof skillet over medium-high heat, heat oil. Transfer pork from marinade to skillet. Brown on all sides, about 5 minutes. Transfer to plate. Clean skillet.

4 Add sweet potatoes, onion, carrots, apples, salt, and white wine to skillet. Place pork on top of vegetables. Brush with marinade. Cover with foil.

5 Roast pork until instant-read meat thermometer inserted in center registers 155°F, about 40 minutes.

6 Transfer pork to cutting board. Let stand 5 minutes. Stir butter into vegetables in skillet. Slice pork and serve with vegetables.

Per serving: 397 calories, 33 g protein, 36 g carbohydrates, 14 g fat, 5 g saturated fat, 103 mg cholesterol, 4 g fiber, 354 mg sodium

on the menu

Calcium-rich mustard greens would be a good foil for the sweet-flavored vegetables and fruits that are cooked around the pork roast. For dessert, a slice of watermelon would be refreshing.

VEGETABLES FOR VITALITY

Skillet Okra with Ground Lamb & Tomato

Okra helps fight heart disease because it contains pectin and other soluble fibers that lower cholesterol.

4 SERVINGS

Prep 10 min ◆ **Cook** 35 min

- 1 tablespoon olive oil
- 2 onions, finely chopped
- 2 cloves garlic, minced
- ½ pound ground lamb
- 1 tomato, seeded and finely chopped
- ¼ cup tomato paste
- ¾ teaspoon salt
- ⅛ teaspoon black pepper
- 1 pound okra, trimmed
- 2 tablespoons fresh-squeezed lemon juice
- 1 tablespoon finely chopped cilantro *(optional)*

1 In large nonstick skillet over medium heat, heat oil. Add onions. Sauté until softened, about 5 minutes. Add garlic. Sauté 1 minute. Add lamb. Cook, breaking up meat with wooden spoon, until browned, about 5 minutes. Drain off any fat.

2 Stir in tomato, 1 cup water, tomato paste, salt, and pepper. Top with okra. Sprinkle with lemon juice. Cover. Cook until okra is tender, 15 minutes. Uncover. Simmer 5 minutes to reduce liquid. Sprinkle with cilantro before serving, if desired.

Per serving: 245 calories, 15 g protein, 21 g carbohydrates, 12 g fat, 4 g saturated fat, 41 mg cholesterol, 6 g fiber, 492 mg sodium

Country Lamb & Vegetable Cobbler

If you enjoy hearty stews topped with dumplings or crumbly pastry, you'll love this low-fat version with many more vegetables than cubes of meat.

4 SERVINGS

Prep 20 min ◆ **Cook** 1 hour

- 1 pound lean lamb steak, trimmed and cut into 1-inch cubes
- 1 pound carrots, thickly sliced
- 4 large stalks celery, thickly sliced
- 1 pound leeks, thickly sliced
- 12 ounces strong dry cider
- 1 can (14½ ounces) reduced-sodium, fat-free chicken broth
- Salt and pepper
- 1 box (10 ounces) frozen peas, thawed
- Several sprigs fresh rosemary, sage and thyme, tied together to make a bouquet garni

FOR THE TOPPING
- 1 cup sifted self-rising white flour
- ¼ cup chopped fresh parsley and sage combined
- ½ teaspoon salt
- ⅛ teaspoon pepper
- ½ cup reduced-fat sour cream
- 1 to 2 teaspoons low-fat milk *(optional)*

1 In large flameproof casserole, dry-fry lamb over medium-high heat until lightly browned, 6 to 8 minutes, stirring frequently. Add carrots, celery, and leeks. Cook 4 minutes, stirring occasionally.

2 Add cider, broth, and salt and pepper to taste. Bring to a boil. Reduce heat to low, cover and simmer until vegetables are tender, 20 to 25 minutes.

3 Meanwhile, heat oven to 400°F. Prepare pastry topping: In medium bowl, stir together flour, parsley, sage, salt, and pepper. Stir in sour cream and mix until firm dough forms. If dough is too dry, add 1 or 2 teaspoons milk. Roll out dough to ½-inch thickness. Cut into 16 triangles.

4 Add peas and bouquet garni to casserole. Arrange triangles on top, covering surface.

5 Bake until topping is well risen and golden brown, 25 to 30 minutes.

Per serving: 530 calories, 35 g protein, 73 g carbohydrates, 12 g fat, 5g saturated fat, 90 g cholesterol, 9 g fiber, 750 g sodium

on the menu

With all the vegetables, meat, and pastry in the lamb cobbler, you need add very little extra to make a meal. For company, you might start with a cream of pumpkin soup and finish with fresh fruit and a selection of your favorite cheeses.

New Irish Stew with Carrots, Potatoes, Onions, Leeks, Turnips & Peas

This classic celebratory dish gets a nutrition update—the proportion of vegetables to meat has been raised considerably and the mixture of simmering flavors is a melody of good tastes and smells, as well as vitamins and antioxidants.

6 SERVINGS

Prep 20 min ◆ **Cook** 1½ hr

- **2 teaspoons vegetable oil**
- **1 pound boneless lamb shoulder, cut into 1-inch chunks**
- **4 red or Yukon Gold potatoes, unpeeled and coarsely chopped**
- **3 carrots, peeled and cut into bite-size chunks**
- **2 onions, coarsely chopped**
- **2 leeks, rinsed and white and pale green parts coarsely chopped**
- **1 large turnip, peeled and coarsely chopped**
- **2 tablespoons all-purpose flour**
- **1 bay leaf**
- **½ teaspoon dried rosemary**
- **1 teaspoon salt**
- **¼ teaspoon black pepper**
- **1 cup green peas, fresh or frozen**

1 In large nonstick pot or deep skillet over medium-high heat, heat oil. Working in batches, add meat and brown on all sides, about 5 minutes per batch. Transfer meat to medium bowl as it browns.

2 Add potatoes, carrots, onions, leeks, and turnip to pot. Cook 10 minutes, stirring occasionally. Stir in flour until blended. Add 3 cups water, bay leaf, rosemary, salt, and pepper. Bring to a boil. Reduce heat. Add meat. Simmer, uncovered, stirring occasionally, until meat is tender, 50 to 60 minutes. Add peas. Simmer 5 minutes, and serve.

Per serving: 270 calories, 18 g protein, 30 g carbohydrates, 9 g fat, 3 g saturated fat, 45 mg cholesterol, 6 g fiber, 510 mg sodium

on the menu

Serve this stew with a good loaf of Irish soda bread to sop up the good-to-the-last-drop juices. Finish the meal with No-Bake Pumpkin Pie with Gingersnap Crust (page 274) and a round of Irish coffee.

MAIN COURSE seafood DISHES

Stir-Fried Shrimp & Snow Peas

The vitamin E in shrimp and vitamin C in snow peas make an award-winning combination for boosting immunity.

4 SERVINGS

Prep 10 min   **Cook** 8 min

- 1 tablespoon plus 2 teaspoons vegetable oil
- ¼ pound snow peas
- 1 small red bell pepper, seeded and julienned
- ¼ teaspoon salt
- 1 pound medium shrimp, shelled and deveined
- 3 scallions, finely chopped
- ½ teaspoon red pepper flakes
- 2 cloves garlic, minced
- 1 tablespoon finely chopped, peeled fresh ginger
- 3 tablespoons reduced-sodium soy sauce
- 1 tablespoon fresh-squeezed lemon juice
- 1 tablespoon grated lemon zest

1 In large nonstick skillet or wok over medium heat, heat the 2 teaspoons of oil. Add snow peas, bell pepper, and salt. Stir-fry until crisp-tender, 3 minutes. Transfer to plate.

2 In same skillet, heat remaining tablespoon of oil. Add shrimp, scallions, and pepper flakes. Stir-fry 1½ minutes. Add garlic and ginger. Stir-fry 1 minute. Add soy sauce and lemon juice. Stir-fry until shrimp are curled and cooked through, about 1 minute.

3 Add snow peas and bell pepper to skillet. Stir-fry just long enough to heat through, about 30 seconds. Stir in lemon zest and serve.

Per serving: 169 calories, 20 g protein, 6 g carbohydrates, 7 g fat, 1 g saturated fat, 168 mg cholesterol, 2 g fiber, 795 mg sodium

Tex-Mex Grilled Shrimp Salad

Avocado, shrimp, and olive oil are all rich in vitamin E, which protects your heart and helps improve immunity.

4 SERVINGS

Prep 15 min   **Cook** 6 min

- 12 medium shrimp (about ¾ pound), peeled and deveined
- ¼ teaspoon salt
- ¼ teaspoon black pepper
  Nonstick olive-oil cooking spray
- ⅔ cup cooked corn kernels, fresh, drained canned, or thawed frozen
- 1 avocado, peeled, pitted, and sliced
- 12 grape tomatoes, each halved
- ¼ cup finely chopped red onion
- 2 tablespoons coarsely chopped, bottled pickled jalapeño chiles
- 2 tablespoons pickled jalapeño liquid
- ¾ teaspoon ground cumin
- 1 tablespoon olive oil
- 16 bite-size tortilla chips
- 2 tablespoons chopped cilantro
- ¼ cup reduced-fat sour cream

1 Preheat grill to hot or preheat broiler. Season shrimp with salt and pepper. Coat with cooking spray.

2 Grill or broil shrimp 4 inches from heat until curled and bright pink, 2 to 3 minutes each side. Let cool slightly.

3 Meanwhile, in large bowl, combine corn, avocado, tomatoes, onion, pickled jalapeños and liquid, cumin, and oil. Let stand 5 minutes. Fold in shrimp, tortilla chips, and cilantro.

4 Divide salad among 4 serving plates. Top each with sour cream. Serve at once.

Per serving: 238 calories, 17 g protein, 17 g carbohydrates, 13 g fat, 3 g saturated fat, 130 mg cholesterol, 6 g fiber, 437 mg sodium

FRESH IDEAS

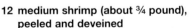

Pickled jalapeños give this salad its punch. They are packed in a liquid that you can use to spice up homemade salsas, salad dressings, soups, and stews.

Scallops Florentine

The word "Florentine" in its title means a recipe is made with spinach, and that means the dish is rich in all the vitamins, minerals, and phytochemicals that make leafy green vegetables so good for you.

4 SERVINGS

Prep 10 min   **Cook** 12 min

- ¾ **pound fresh spinach**
- 2 **tablespoons olive oil**
- 1½ **pounds sea scallops**
- 2 **cloves garlic, minced**
- 1 **teaspoon grated lemon zest**
- 1 **cup reduced-sodium, fat-free chicken broth**
- 1 **cup frozen peas, thawed**
- 1 **tablespoon fresh-squeezed lemon juice**
- ¼ **teaspoon salt**
- ¼ **teaspoon black pepper**

1 Steam spinach just until wilted, 3 minutes. Cool under cold running water. Squeeze dry.

2 In large nonstick skillet over high heat, heat oil. Add scallops. Sauté until still slightly uncooked in center, 2 minutes per side. Transfer to plate.

3 Lower heat to medium. Add garlic and lemon zest to skillet. Cook 30 seconds. Add chicken broth and peas. Simmer 3 minutes. Add spinach, scallops, lemon juice, salt, and pepper. Cook just until heated though. Serve in shallow bowls.

Per serving: 286 calories, 31 g protein, 13 g carbohydrates, 13 g fat, 2 g saturated fat, 52 mg cholesterol, 4 g fiber, 550 mg sodium

DID YOU KNOW ● ● ●

. . . that scallops contain about twice as much omega-3 fatty acids as water-packed light tuna? Omega-3 fatty acids help suppress inflammatory compounds in the body and improve cardiovascular health.

on the menu

Serve over—or with—steaming hot rice that's been cooked in chicken broth. Sliced ripe tomatoes make a perfect side dish. Offer sliced fresh fruit for dessert.

Shrimp with Fennel

Shrimp's vitamin B$_{12}$ is matched by the vitamin C in the fennel, tomatoes, and onion.

4 SERVINGS

Prep 15 min   **Cook** 30 min

- 1 **tablespoon extra-virgin olive oil**
- 1 **large onion, chopped**
- 1 **bulb fennel, chopped**
- 1 **large garlic clove, crushed**
- 1 **can (14½ ounces) tomatoes in juice, chopped**
- ½ **cup fish stock**
- ½ **tablespoon fennel seeds**
  Finely grated zest and juice of ½ orange
- 1 **cup long-grain rice**
  Pinch of saffron threads
- 1 **pound peeled jumbo shrimp**
  Fresh basil leaves to garnish

1 In large nonstick frying pan, heat oil over medium heat. Add onion, fennel, and garlic. Cook, stirring occasionally, until vegetables are soft, 5 minutes. Add tomatoes with their juice, fish stock, fennel seeds, and orange zest and juice. Season with salt and pepper. Bring to a boil, stirring. Reduce heat to low and partially cover pan. Simmer 12 minutes.

2 Meanwhile, cook rice according to package directions, adding crushed saffron to boiling water.

3 Bring tomato sauce back to a boil. Place shrimp on top of sauce, cover pan tightly, and cook over low heat until shrimp are done, 3 to 4 minutes.

4 Divide rice among serving bowls. Top with shrimp and tomato sauce. Sprinkle with basil.

Per serving: 380 calories, 30 g protein, 49 g carbohydrates, 7 g fat, 1 g saturated fat, 175 g cholesterol, 5 g fiber, 400 g sodium

VEGETABLES FOR VITALITY

Sea Scallop & Cherry Tomato Sauté

Sizzling, protein-rich scallops and tiny tomatoes, packed with vitamin C, go from skillet to table in minutes.

4 SERVINGS

Prep 5 min   **Cook** 10 min

  1 pound sea scallops
  4 teaspoons cornstarch
  2 teaspoons olive oil
  3 cloves garlic, minced
  1 pint cherry tomatoes
  ⅔ cup dry vermouth, white wine, or chicken broth
  ½ teaspoon salt
  ⅓ cup chopped fresh basil
  1 tablespoon cold water

1 Dredge scallops in 3 teaspoons of the cornstarch, shaking off excess. In large nonstick skillet over medium heat, heat oil. Add scallops and sauté until golden brown and cooked through, about 3 minutes. With slotted spoon, transfer scallops to bowl.

2 Add garlic to pan and cook 1 minute. Add tomatoes and cook until they begin to collapse, about 4 minutes. Add vermouth, salt, and basil to pan. Bring to a boil and cook for 1 minute.

3 Meanwhile, stir together remaining 1 teaspoon cornstarch and cold water in small bowl. Add cornstarch mixture to pan and cook, stirring, until sauce is slightly thickened, about 1 minute.

4 Return scallops to pan, reduce to a simmer, and cook just until heated through, about 1 minute.

Per serving: 176 calories, 20 g protein, 10 g carbohydrate, 4 g fat, 1 g saturated fat, 37 mg cholesterol, 1 g fiber, 483 mg sodium

Crab Gumbo

The fibrous gums and pectins found in okra help lower cholesterol and provide protection against stomach ulcers.

4 SERVINGS

Prep 10 min   **Cook** 35 min

  2 tablespoons vegetable oil
  ½ pound okra, cut into ½-inch-thick slices
  1 medium onion, coarsely chopped
  1 red bell pepper, seeded and diced
  1 green bell pepper, seeded and diced
  ½ cup diced baked ham (about 3 ounces)
  2 cloves garlic, minced
  1 can (14½ ounces) stewed tomatoes
  1 can (14½ ounces) reduced-sodium, fat-free chicken broth plus enough water to equal 2 cups
  1 pound cooked lump crabmeat
  ¼ teaspoon hot red-pepper sauce
  ¼ teaspoon salt
  ¼ teaspoon black pepper

1 In large saucepan over medium-high heat, heat oil. Add okra, onion, red and green bell peppers, and ham. Sauté until okra is tender and no longer sticky, about 10 minutes.

2 Add garlic. Sauté 1 minute. Add tomatoes and chicken broth mixture. Simmer, uncovered, 20 minutes.

3 Stir in crabmeat, pepper sauce, salt, and pepper. Gently heat through and serve.

Per serving: 293 calories, 31 g protein, 18 g carbohydrates, 11 g fat, 1 g saturated fat, 126 mg cholesterol, 5 g fiber, 1,006 mg sodium

DID YOU KNOW ● ● ●

. . . that gumbo got its name from the African word "quinbombo," which means okra to anyone who lives in the Congo? What goes into a gumbo is pretty much up to the individual cook; okra, however, is usually an ingredient in this hearty and spicy stew that is now considered a classic in the American South.

on the menu

This delectable summer salad is a treat that requires little embellishment. You might want to start with a small bowl of cold potato soup and finish with a dish of lime sherbet and some lace cookies.

Cool Seafood Salad with Pineapple & Pepper

This light, fresh, summery dish simply screams good health—even the dressing is packed with cancer-fighting phytochemicals.

4 SERVINGS

Prep 20 min ◇ **Refrigerate** 15 min ◇ **Cook** 7 min

- 2 tablespoons orange juice
- 1 tablespoon fresh-squeezed lime juice
- 1 teaspoon grated peeled fresh ginger
- ¼ teaspoon chili powder
- ¼ teaspoon salt
- 3 tablespoons vegetable oil
- 1 tablespoon olive oil
- 2 tablespoons chopped fresh basil
- ½ pound large shrimp, peeled and deveined
- ½ pound scallops
- ½ pound cooked lump crabmeat
- ½ large pineapple, peeled, cored, and cut into 1-inch pieces
- 1 large red bell pepper, seeded and cut into ½-inch squares
- ½ head romaine lettuce, separated into leaves

1 In large bowl, stir together orange juice, lime juice, ginger, chili powder, and salt. Whisk in vegetable oil and olive oil. Stir in basil.

2 Steam shrimp until curled and bright pink, 3 to 4 minutes. Drain. Add to dressing bowl. Toss to combine.

3 Steam scallops until opaque, about 3 minutes. Drain. Add to shrimp. Refrigerate at least 15 minutes.

4 Add crabmeat to shrimp mixture. Gently stir in pineapple and bell pepper. Serve on romaine leaves.

Per serving: 326 calories, 30 g protein, 14 g carbohydrates, 17 g fat, 2 g saturated fat, 154 mg cholesterol, 3 g fiber, 488 mg sodium

HINT helpful HINT HINT HINT HINT HINT HINT HINT HINT

> *Almost any dish made with shellfish can also be made with a firm-fleshed fish. Fillet of monkfish, cut into bite-size chunks, is a great substitute for shrimp, scallops, lobster, and/or crabmeat because it has a taste reminiscent of shellfish. Halibut, mahi-mahi, salmon, shark, swordfish, and tuna can all be used as substitutes in recipes calling for shellfish.*

Asian Steamed Fish Fillets with Vegetable Sticks

A combination of some of the most healthful of all foods— low-fat fish and vitamin-packed vegetables—is cooked by one of the most healthful of all cooking techniques— steaming—to make a dynamite meal.

4 SERVINGS

Prep 15 min ◇ **Cook** 12 min

- 1½ pounds halibut or other firm-fleshed white fish fillets, in 4 pieces
- 2 tablespoons soy sauce
- 2 tablespoons white wine or sake
- 1 thin slice fresh ginger, peeled and cut in thin sticks
- 2 medium carrots, peeled and cut into 3 x ¼-inch sticks
- 2 ounces snow peas, cut in half lengthwise
- ½ yellow bell pepper, seeded and cut into thin sticks

1 Place fillets in baking dish that will fit inside large steamer basket or on rack that will fit into large skillet. In small cup, stir together soy sauce and white wine. Pour over fish. Top with ginger and carrots.

2 Fill skillet with 1 inch of water. Bring to a simmer. Place steamer basket or wire rack in skillet. Place baking dish containing fish in basket or on rack. Cover skillet or basket. Steam 5 to 6 minutes. Add snow peas and yellow pepper to baking dish. Cover. Steam until fish flakes when touched with fork and vegetables are crisp-tender, about 5 minutes. Serve at once.

Per serving: 175 calories, 32 g protein, 7 g carbohydrates, 3 g fat, 0 g saturated fat, 45 mg cholesterol, 2 g fiber, 558 mg sodium

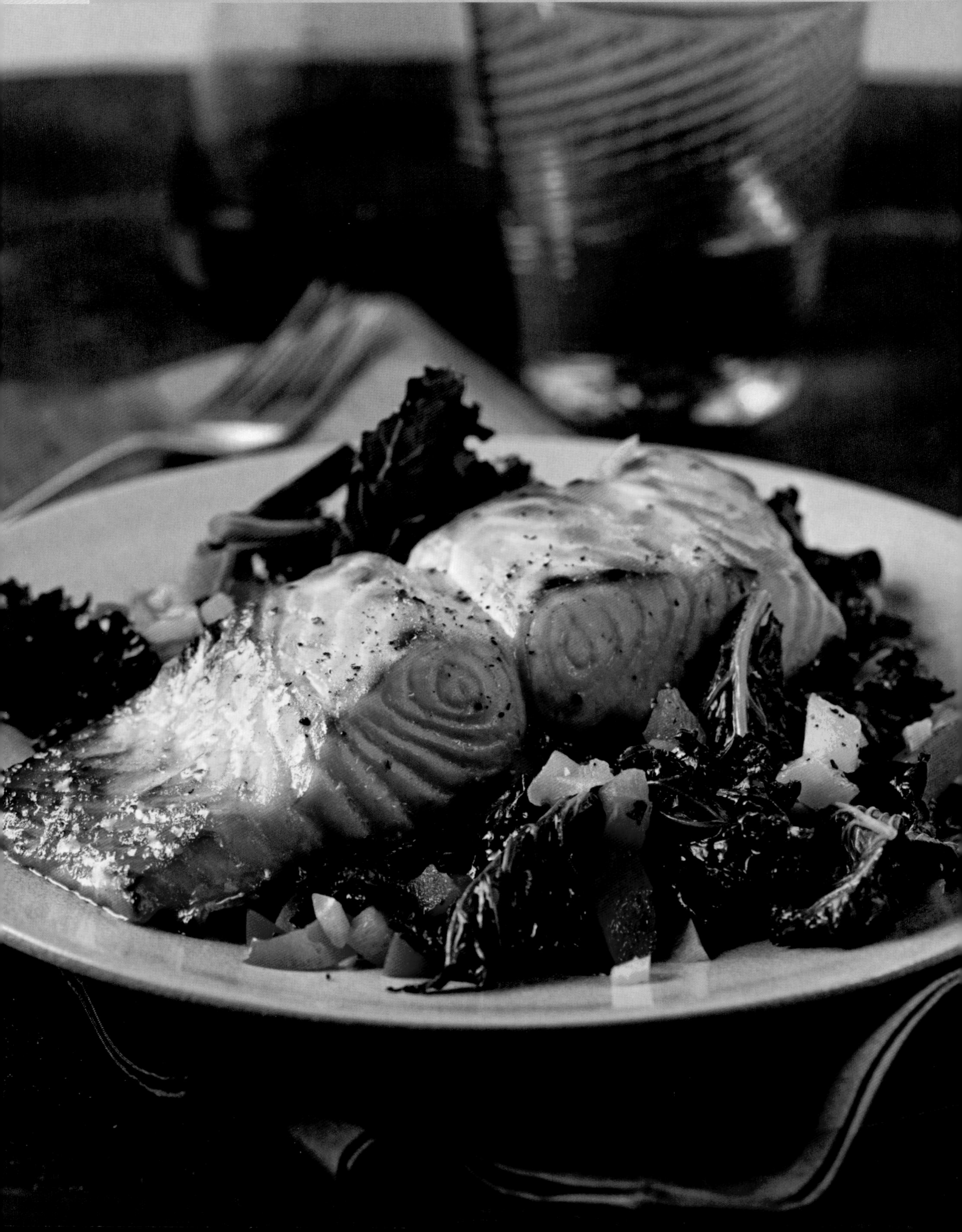

Salmon on a Bed of Greens

*Calcium-rich kale provides a bone-building—and delicious—
base for a fish fillet.*

4 SERVINGS

Prep 15 min ◆ **Refrigerate** 30 min ◆ **Cook** 16 min

¼ **cup grapefruit juice**

1½ **tablespoons mustard**

1½ **tablespoons honey**

¼ **teaspoon red pepper flakes**

4 **salmon fillets (6 ounces each)**

1½ **pounds kale, large stems removed
   and leaves chopped**

3 **tablespoons olive oil**

½ **red bell pepper, seeded and finely chopped**

½ **yellow pepper, seeded and finely chopped**

1 In baking dish large enough to hold fish fillets
in single layer, combine grapefruit juice, mustard,
honey, and pepper flakes. Add salmon to dish,
turning to coat both sides with marinade. Refrigerate,
covered, 30 minutes.

2 Preheat broiler.

3 In large pot, bring 2 quarts of water to a boil.
Add kale. Return water to boil and cook 5 minutes.
Drain well. Squeeze out excess water.

4 Heat olive oil in large skillet over medium heat.
Add red and yellow bell peppers. Sauté 1 minute. Add
kale. Sauté until peppers and kale are tender, about
3 minutes. Remove skillet from heat and keep warm.

5 Remove salmon from marinade. Place, skin
side down, on rack in foil-lined broiler pan. Reserve
marinade.

6 Broil salmon 4 inches from heat for 3 minutes.
Brush on remaining marinade. Broil until fish is opaque
and flakes when touched with knife, 3 to 4 minutes.
(If fish begins to brown too much, drop to lower rack
in broiler.) Serve salmon on bed of kale and peppers.

*Per serving: 402 calories, 41 g protein, 21 g carbohydrates, 18 g fat,
3 g saturated fat, 97 mg cholesterol, 3 g fiber, 233 mg sodium*

HINT helpful HINT HINT HINT HINT HINT HINT HINT

*Almost any baked fish will release liquids, so
don't be surprised to find a puddle at the bottom
of your casserole dish. Simply spoon these pan
juices over the fish to add back flavor and
moisture.*

Baked Cod Casserole with Potatoes, Tomatoes & Arugula

*A one-dish meal, tailor-made for the health of your heart.
with lean fish and lots of vitamin-rich vegetables.*

4 SERVINGS

Prep 20 min ◆ **Cook** 38 min

1 **pound red potatoes,
   unpeeled and cut in ½-inch-thick slices**

1 **onion, thinly sliced**

1 **tablespoon olive oil**

½ **teaspoon salt**

4 **plum tomatoes, seeded and coarsely chopped**

3 **cloves garlic, minced**

½ **teaspoon dried oregano, crumbled**

1½ **cups arugula leaves**

1 **pound cod, scrod, halibut, or other thick,
   firm-fleshed white fish steaks, cut into
   2-inch chunks**

1 Preheat oven to 350°F. In 13 x 9 x 2-inch baking
dish, combine potatoes, onion, oil, and ¼ teaspoon salt.

2 Bake 20 minutes, stirring mixture once.

3 Stir tomatoes, garlic, and oregano into potato
mixture. Spread arugula on top in even layer. Top with
cod. Sprinkle with remaining ¼ teaspoon salt.

4 Bake, covered with aluminum foil, just until fish
is cooked through, 15 to 18 minutes. Transfer fish and
vegetable mixture to serving plates. Spoon pan juices
over each serving.

*Per serving: 213 calories, 22 g protein, 21 g carbohydrates, 5 g fat,
1 g saturated fat, 43 mg cholesterol, 4 g fiber, 363 mg sodium*

VEGETABLES FOR VITALITY

Grilled Tuna Steak with Corn, Tomato & Zucchini

Together, the tuna and vegetables in this dish provide a complete collection of antioxidant vitamins A, C, and E. Tuna and other fatty fish are high in omega-3 fatty acids, which are thought to protect against heart disease.

4 SERVINGS

Prep 20 min   **Cook** 10 min

- 1¼ **pounds tuna steaks (1 inch thick)**
- ½ **teaspoon salt**
- ¼ **teaspoon black pepper**
- ¼ **cup apricot jam**
- 1 **tablespoon Dijon mustard**
- 1 **ear of corn, husked and cut into 8 equal pieces**
- 2 **tomatoes, cored and each cut into 8 equal wedges**
- 2 **medium zucchini, each quartered lengthwise and cut crosswise into ¼-inch-thick slices**
- 2 **cloves garlic, minced**
- 2 **serrano chiles, seeded and finely chopped**
- 4 **teaspoons olive oil**

1 Preheat grill to medium-hot or preheat broiler.

2 Season tuna steaks with ¼ teaspoon of the salt and ⅛ teaspoon of the pepper. In small cup, stir together jam and mustard. Spread one side of tuna steaks with half the jam mixture.

3 In center of each of four 12-inch squares of foil, place corn, tomato, and zucchini, dividing equally. Sprinkle evenly with garlic, remaining ¼ teaspoon salt and ⅛ teaspoon pepper, chiles, and oil. Fold edges of foil over to form tightly sealed packets.

4 Grill or broil tuna and foil packets 4 inches from heat for 4 minutes. Turn tuna over. Spread with remaining jam mixture. Cook until tuna is opaque in center and begins to flake when touched with fork, 4 to 6 minutes. Carefully open vegetable packets and serve with tuna.

Per serving: 302 calories, 35 g protein, 27 g carbohydrates, 7 g fat, 1 g saturated fat, 62 mg cholesterol, 3 g fiber, 458 mg sodium

HINT **helpful HINT** HINT HINT HINT HINT HINT HINT HINT

Bluefish, mackerel, salmon, swordfish, or mako shark can be substituted in just about any recipe that calls for fresh tuna, but you may have to adjust the cooking time.

Roast Trout & Potatoes

A bed of watercress adds vitamins and fresh flavor.

4 SERVINGS

Prep 20 min   **Cook** 40 minutes

- 1½ **pounds potatoes, quartered**
- 1 **tablespoon olive oil**
- 4 **small trout (10 ounces each), cleaned Sprigs fresh tarragon**
- 1 **orange, cut into 16 half slices**
- 1 **lemon, cut into 16 half slices**
- ¼ **cup orange juice**
- 1 **cucumber, peeled**
- 6 **ounces plain low-fat yogurt**
- 2 **tablespoons chopped fresh mint**
- ¼ **pound watercress, washed and trimmed**

1 Preheat oven to 400°F. In large saucepan, combine potatoes and enough water to cover. Bring to a boil. Reduce heat and simmer 5 minutes. Drain and return potatoes to pan. Drizzle oil over potatoes and toss to coat. Lay potatoes out on a baking sheet. Roast, turning several times, until tender, about 25 minutes.

2 Season inside of trout with tarragon, salt, and pepper. Cut four 12-inch squares of foil. Divide half the fruit slices among foil squares, lay fish on top, and cover with remaining slices. Sprinkle orange juice over.

3 Wrap fish in foil and seal packets. Lay packets on second baking sheet. Bake 20 minutes. Meanwhile, grate cucumber into sieve and press out excess water. In small bowl, mix cucumber, yogurt, and mint.

4 Arrange fish and potatoes on plates. Garnish with watercress, fruit slices, and cucumber sauce.

Per serving: 430 calories, 40 g protein, 43 g carbohydrates, 12 g fat, 3 g saturated fat, 165 g cholesterol, 6 g fiber, 160 g sodium

VEGETABLES FOR VITALITY

Caribbean Seafood Curry Stew with Bell Peppers, Ginger & Scallions

Ginger, curry powder, hot pepper flakes, and ground allspice contribute a unique blend of health-protective phytochemicals that are just as powerful as those found in any fruit or vegetable. But this stew also has bell peppers and scallions to add vitamins C, B$_6$, and folate to the mix.

4 SERVINGS

Prep 30 min • **Cook** 30 min

- 2 teaspoons olive oil
- 6 thin scallions, finely chopped
- 1 yellow bell pepper, seeded and coarsely chopped
- 1 tablespoon finely chopped, peeled fresh ginger
- 1½ teaspoons curry powder
- ¼ to ½ teaspoon hot red pepper flakes
- ¼ teaspoon ground allspice
- 2 tablespoons reduced-sodium soy sauce
- 1½ tablespoons brown sugar
- ¼ teaspoon salt
- 1 can (14 ounces) reduced-fat coconut milk
- 3 plum tomatoes, quartered lengthwise and seeded
- ½ pound halibut steaks, skin removed and steaks cut into 2-inch chunks
- ½ pound medium shrimp, peeled and deveined
- 2 tablespoons chopped cilantro
- 1 tablespoon fresh-squeezed lime juice

1 In large saucepot over medium heat, heat oil. Add scallions, bell pepper, and ginger. Sauté until softened, 5 minutes. Add curry powder, pepper flakes to taste, and allspice. Sauté 2 minutes. Stir in soy sauce, brown sugar, and salt. Stir in coconut milk and tomatoes. Gently simmer, uncovered, 15 minutes.

2 Add halibut and shrimp to stew mixture. Gently simmer, uncovered, just until fish is cooked through, 5 to 8 minutes. Stir in cilantro and lime juice and serve.

Per serving: 223 calories, 22 g protein, 17 g carbohydrates, 9 g fat, 4 g saturated fat, 99 mg cholesterol, 2 g fiber, 605 mg sodium

DID YOU KNOW ● ● ●

. . .that shellfish may have received a bad rap about cholesterol? Mussels are the lowest and scallops are next, both having lower cholesterol than a lean turkey breast. Of the shellfish, shrimp are highest in cholesterol but they are still a low-fat source of protein.

HINT **helpful HINT** HINT HINT HINT HINT HINT HINT

To make Caribbean Seafood Curry Stew ahead of time, follow the directions through cooking the seafood in step 2. Allow stew to cool to room temperature, then refrigerate for up to one day. Reheat, then stir in cilantro and lime juice.

MAIN COURSE pasta DISHES

Pasta with No-Cook Vegetable Sauce

When the sauce is made from finely chopped raw vegetables, the dish retains the vitamin C and B that can be lost in long cooking.

4 SERVINGS

Prep 15 min ◆ **Cook** 12 min

- 8 ounces rotelle pasta
- 1 medium zucchini, cut into ¼-inch dice
- 1 medium yellow bell pepper, seeded and cut into ¼-inch dice
- 2 large tomatoes, cut into ¼-inch dice
- 2 tablespoons olive oil
- ¼ cup chopped fresh basil
- ¾ teaspoon salt
- ½ teaspoon black pepper
- 2 tablespoons grated Parmesan cheese

1 In large pot of lightly salted boiling water, cook rotelle until tender, following package directions.

2 Meanwhile, combine zucchini, yellow pepper, tomatoes, oil, basil, salt, pepper, and cheese in large serving bowl.

3 Drain rotelle. Add to vegetables in serving bowl. Gently toss, and serve.

Per serving: 303 calories, 10 g protein, 47 g carbohydrates, 9 g fat, 2 g saturated fat, 2 mg cholesterol, 5 g fiber, 772 mg sodium

DID YOU KNOW ● ● ●

...that almost any dish made with fresh vegetables can be called primavera? The word means springtime in Italian.

Pasta Primavera

Get seven vegetables in one dish! You're bound to get a bounty of vitamins and minerals.

4 SERVINGS

Prep 15 min ◆ **Cook** 25 min

- 2 tablespoons olive oil
- 4 plum tomatoes, coarsely chopped
- 1 medium carrot, peeled and cut into ¼-inch-thick slices
- 2 cloves garlic, sliced
- 1 cup sliced mushrooms
- ¾ cup reduced-sodium, fat-free chicken broth or vegetable broth
- 1 pound asparagus, trimmed, cut into ½-inch pieces, and blanched
- 1 cup frozen peas, thawed
- 1 medium yellow summer squash, cut into ¼-inch-thick slices
- ¼ cup minced fresh basil
- ¼ cup grated Parmesan cheese
- 8 ounces fettuccine pasta

1 In medium nonstick saucepan, heat oil over medium heat. Add tomatoes, carrot, and garlic. Cook 10 minutes. Add mushrooms and broth. Cook 10 minutes. Add asparagus, peas, and squash. Cook until all the vegetables are tender, about 2 minutes. Add basil and cheese. Cover and set aside to keep warm.

2 Meanwhile, in large pot of lightly salted boiling water, cook fettuccine until tender, following package directions. Drain. Place in serving bowl. Add vegetable sauce. Toss to mix. Serve at once.

Per serving: 386 calories, 16 g protein, 60 g carbohydrates, 11 g fat, 3 g saturated fat, 5 mg cholesterol, 8 g fiber, 542 mg sodium

FRESH IDEAS

You can try any combination of vegetables and herbs that you want for a pasta sauce. Sauté them in a little olive oil, add broth for liquid, and sprinkle with Parmesan. Some ideas:

- *Arugula, broccoli, leeks, and tarragon*
- *Eggplant, broccoli rabe, garlic, and oregano*
- *Green beans, sugar snaps, fennel, and parsley*

Fusilli with Pan-Roasted Vegetables

Just one serving of this richly flavored pasta supplies more than one-third of the daily recommendation for fiber.

4 SERVINGS

Prep 20 min ◆ **Cook** 25 min

- 2 tablespoons olive oil
- 1 large sweet onion, cut into thin wedges
- 1 yellow bell pepper, seeded and chopped
- 1 small butternut squash (1¼ pounds), peeled, seeded, and cut into 1-inch chunks
- ½ teaspoon salt
- ¼ cup minced fresh basil
- 5 cloves garlic, minced
- 1 cup grape or cherry tomatoes, each cut in half
- 4 cups fresh baby spinach, tough stems removed
- 4 cups reduced-sodium, fat-free chicken broth
- 8 ounces fusilli pasta

1 In large nonstick skillet over medium heat, heat 1 tablespoon of the oil. Add onion and bell pepper. Sauté until softened, about 5 minutes. Add squash, ¼ teaspoon of the salt, the basil, and half the garlic. Cover and cook, stirring occasionally, 8 minutes. Increase heat to high. Cook, uncovered, stirring occasionally, until vegetables brown slightly and squash is just tender, 5 to 7 minutes. Transfer squash mixture to large bowl. Add tomatoes to bowl.

2 In same skillet, heat remaining tablespoon oil over medium heat. Add remaining garlic, ¼ teaspoon salt, and the spinach. Cook, stirring occasionally, until spinach wilts, about 2 minutes. Add spinach to squash mixture.

3 Meanwhile, in large pot, bring broth and 2 cups water to a boil. Add fusilli. Cook until tender, following package directions. Reserve ½ cup cooking liquid. Drain fusilli. Combine fusilli, squash mixture, and reserved cooking liquid, and serve.

Per serving: 372 calories, 12 g protein, 66 g carbohydrates, 9 g fat, 1 g saturated fat, 1 mg cholesterol, 9 g fiber, 485 mg sodium

Sausage & Pepper Pasta

Sweet peppers contain phytochemicals that protect against heart disease, stroke, and cancer and also boost immunity.

4 SERVINGS

Prep 10 min ◆ **Cook** 15 min

- 2 tablespoons olive oil
- ½ pound chicken sausages, sliced
- 2 medium onions, thinly sliced
- 2 large red or orange bell peppers, seeded and thinly sliced
- 1 large green bell pepper, seeded and thinly sliced
- 2 cloves garlic, minced
- 1 teaspoon dried basil, crumbled
- ½ cup pitted black olives
- 1 tablespoon balsamic vinegar
- ¼ teaspoon salt
- ¼ teaspoon black pepper
- 8 ounces rotelle or farfalle pasta
  Grated Parmesan cheese

1 In large nonstick skillet, heat oil over medium-high heat. Add sausages and onions. Sauté until onion is softened and lightly golden, about 5 minutes. Add bell peppers, garlic, and basil. Sauté until peppers are very tender, about 10 minutes. Remove from heat. Stir in olives, vinegar, salt, and pepper.

2 Meanwhile, in large pot of lightly salted boiling water, cook rotelle until tender, following package directions. Drain, reserving ¼ cup of the cooking water. Toss rotelle with sausage mixture and reserved cooking water. Serve with grated Parmesan cheese on the side.

Per serving: 443 calories, 19 g protein, 57 g carbohydrates, 16 g fat, 3 g saturated fat, 35 mg cholesterol, 3 g fiber, 933 mg sodium

VEGETABLES FOR VITALITY

Creamy Bow Ties with Green Peas & Sun-Dried Tomatoes

Peas add muscle-building protein to this dish, along with B vitamins for energy production.

4 SERVINGS

Prep 10 min ◆ **Cook** 15 min

- 8 ounces farfalle pasta
- 1 tablespoon olive oil
- 1 tablespoon butter or margarine
- 1 cup finely chopped onion
- 3 cloves garlic, minced
- ½ teaspoon dried oregano, crumbled
- ¼ teaspoon dried marjoram, crumbled
- 1½ tablespoons all-purpose flour
- 1 cup reduced-sodium, fat-free chicken broth or vegetable broth
- 1 cup fresh or frozen petite green peas
- ⅔ cup sun-dried tomato halves, thinly sliced
- ⅓ cup grated Parmesan cheese

1 In large pot of lightly salted boiling water, cook farfalle until tender, following package directions.

2 Meanwhile, in large nonstick skillet over medium heat, heat oil and butter. Add onion, garlic, oregano, and marjoram. Sauté until onion is softened, about 5 minutes. Stir in flour until blended. Whisk in broth. Heat, stirring, until thickened, 2 to 3 minutes. Stir in peas and tomatoes. Cook just until peas are tender, about 5 minutes. Remove from heat. Stir in 3 tablespoons of the Parmesan.

3 Drain farfalle, reserving ½ cup of the cooking water. Toss farfalle with vegetable mixture and reserved cooking water. Sprinkle with remaining Parmesan, and serve.

Per serving: 380 calories, 16 g protein, 60 g carbohydrates, 10 g fat, 4 g saturated fat, 13 mg cholesterol, 6 g fiber, 647 mg sodium

HINT   helpful HINT   HINT HINT HINT HINT HINT HINT

Most pasta recipes are finished off with a fresh grating of Parmesan cheese. Food experts agree that Parmigiano-Reggiano is the best of the best. You can buy a wedge of this hard Italian cheese at a specialty food store and grate it yourself as needed.

Linguine with Spinach Pesto

A sauce made with spinach contains phytochemicals that add extra protection against age-related blindness.

8 SERVINGS

Prep 15 min ◆ **Cook** 12 min

- 1 pound linguine pasta
- 3 cups fresh baby spinach, tough stems removed
- ½ cup fresh basil leaves
- 3 cloves garlic
- 3 tablespoons walnuts
- 3 tablespoons olive oil
- ⅓ cup fresh-squeezed lemon juice
- ¾ teaspoon salt
- ½ teaspoon black pepper
- 2 medium red bell peppers, seeded and cut into ¼-inch dice
- 4 plum tomatoes, cut into ¼-inch dice
- ¼ cup grated Parmesan cheese

1 In large pot of lightly salted boiling water, cook linguine until tender, following package directions.

2 Meanwhile, to make pesto, combine spinach, basil, garlic, and walnuts in food processor. Process until finely chopped. With machine running, add olive oil, lemon juice, salt, and pepper. Process until smooth.

3 Drain linguine. Transfer to large serving bowl. Add spinach pesto, red bell peppers, and tomatoes. Toss to mix. Sprinkle with Parmesan cheese.

Per serving: 300 calories, 10 g protein, 48 g carbohydrates, 8 g fat, 2 g saturated fat, 2 mg cholesterol, 3 g fiber, 420 mg sodium

on the menu

This refreshing pasta dish doesn't require much more than a simple salad of mixed greens in a vinaigrette and a light fruit compote for dessert to make a satisfying—and healthful—meal.

VEGETABLES FOR VITALITY

Penne with Fresh Tomato Sauce & Grilled Eggplant

Cooking tomatoes in olive oil helps release the cancer-fighting phytochemical lycopene. First salting it, and then grilling instead of frying it keeps eggplant from absorbing more oil than it should and reduces the total fat in this recipe.

4 SERVINGS

on the menu

Serve with slices of smoked mozzarella cheese and toasted Italian bread topped with roasted garlic (page 313).

Prep 15 min ◆ **Stand** 30 min ◆ **Cook** 35 min

- **1 pound eggplant, cut lengthwise into ¾-inch-thick slices**
- **½ teaspoon salt**
- **2 tablespoons olive oil**
- **4 cloves garlic, thinly sliced**
- **1½ pounds ripe plum tomatoes, halved, seeded, and coarsely chopped**
- **1 teaspoon chopped fresh oregano or ½ teaspoon dried, crumbled**
- **2 teaspoons balsamic vinegar**
- **½ teaspoon sugar**
- **Nonstick olive-oil cooking spray**
- **8 ounces penne pasta**
- **¼ cup shaved or shredded Parmesan cheese**

1 Sprinkle eggplant slices with ¼ teaspoon salt. Let stand a least 30 minutes to draw out liquid.

2 Meanwhile, in large nonstick skillet, heat oil over medium-low heat. Add garlic. Cook, stirring, 1 minute.

3 Add tomatoes, oregano, and remaining ¼ teaspoon salt to oil in skillet. Increase heat to medium. Cook just until tomatoes are softened, about 6 minutes. Stir in vinegar and sugar. Cook 30 seconds longer.

4 Preheat grill or broiler. Rinse eggplant slices; pat dry. Lightly coat both sides of eggplant with cooking spray.

5 Grill or broil eggplant 4 inches from heat until softened and, if grilling, dark grill marks appear, about 5 minutes each side. Set aside to cool slightly.

6 Meanwhile, in large pot of lightly salted boiling water, cook penne until tender, following package directions. Drain. Toss with tomato mixture. Coarsely chop eggplant. Add to pasta mixture. Stir in Parmesan. Serve hot or at room temperature.

Per serving: 362 calories, 13 g protein, 59 g carbohydrates, 10 g fat, 2 g saturated fat, 4 mg cholesterol, 7 g fiber, 406 mg sodium

Rigatoni with Broccoli Rabe, Cherry Tomatoes & Roasted Garlic

The terrific amount of vitamin C in this combination of broccoli rabe, yellow bell pepper, onion, and tomatoes boosts your immune system to help your body fight infection. Broccoli rabe also has cancer-fighting phytochemicals.

4 SERVINGS

Prep 10 min ◆ **Cook** 12 min

- 12 **ounces rigatoni pasta**
- 2 **small bunches broccoli rabe, tough stems removed and leaves cut crosswise into 1-inch-wide pieces**
- 1 **tablespoon olive oil**
- 1 **red onion, halved and thinly sliced crosswise**
- 1 **yellow bell pepper, seeded and cut lengthwise into thin strips**
- 2 **scallions, thinly sliced on diagonal**
- ½ **cup golden raisins**
- ¼ **teaspoon red pepper flakes**
- ¼ **teaspoon salt**
- 8 **cloves roasted garlic** *(see page 313)*
- 12 **cherry tomatoes, each halved**
-    **Pinch ground nutmeg**
- ¼ **teaspoon black pepper**
- ¼ **cup grated Parmesan cheese**

1 In large pot of lightly salted boiling water, cook rigatoni until tender, following package directions. Add broccoli rabe to pasta pot for last 5 minutes of cooking time. Drain pasta and broccoli rabe.

2 Meanwhile, in large nonstick skillet, heat oil over medium-high heat. Add red onion, bell pepper, scallions, raisins, pepper flakes, and salt. Sauté until vegetables are crisp-tender, about 4 minutes. Add roasted garlic. Sauté 1 minute. Remove from heat.

3 Return pasta and broccoli rabe to pot. Add bell pepper mixture, tomatoes, and nutmeg. Sprinkle with black pepper and cheese, and serve.

Per serving: 514 calories, 21 g protein, 98 g carbohydrates, 7 g fat, 2 g saturated fat, 4 mg cholesterol, 6 g fiber, 506 mg sodium

DID YOU KNOW ● ● ●

. . .that golden and brown raisins are made from the same Thompson seedless grapes? Golden raisins are oven-dried and treated with sulfur dioxide to keep them from darkening. Brown raisins are sun-dried.

Pasta with Shrimp & Cherry Tomatoes

In colder months, when good fresh vegetables are harder to find, cherry tomatoes fill the gap. In addition to great flavor, they provide plenty of vitamin C plus vitamin A in the form of beta-carotene.

4 SERVINGS

Prep 10 min ◆ **Cook** 12 min

- 8 ounces orecchiette or medium pasta shells
- 2 tablespoons olive oil
- 1 pound medium shrimp, cleaned
- 3 cloves garlic, minced
- 4 flat canned anchovy fillets
- ½ teaspoon red pepper flakes, or to taste
- 4 cups red cherry or grape tomatoes, each cut in half
- 3 tablespoons fresh oregano leaves or 1 teaspoon dried, crumbled
- ½ cup pitted green olives
- 2 tablespoons drained capers
- ¼ teaspoon black pepper

1 In large pot of lightly salted boiling water, cook pasta shells until tender, following package directions.

2 Meanwhile, in large nonstick skillet, heat 1 tablespoon of the oil over medium-high heat. Add shrimp and one third of the garlic. Sauté until shrimp just turn pink and curl, 2 to 3 minutes. Transfer from skillet to plate.

3 In same skillet, heat remaining 1 tablespoon oil. Add remaining garlic, anchovies, and pepper flakes. Sauté until garlic is softened, about 30 seconds. Do not let it brown. Add tomatoes and oregano. Sauté until tomatoes are softened, 3 to 4 minutes. Add cooked shrimp, olives, and capers.

4 Drain pasta well. Toss with shrimp and tomato mixture. Sprinkle with black pepper.

Per serving: 419 calories, 21 g protein, 53 g carbohydrates, 14 g fat, 2 g saturated fat, 129 mg cholesterol, 3 g fiber, 1,141 mg sodium

on the menu

To round out the meal, serve a romaine lettuce salad with a Caesar dressing, a whole-wheat baguette, and a platter of fresh apples and favorite cheeses for dessert.

Pasta Salad with Arugula, Tomatoes & Smoked Cheese

Like all dark green, leafy vegetables, arugula can help lower your risk of having a stroke.

4 SERVINGS

Prep 15 min ◆ **Cook** 10 min

- 8 ounces penne or rotelle pasta
- 12 ounces cherry tomatoes, each halved
- ½ small red onion, thinly sliced
- 4 ounces arugula, chopped
- 3 ounces smoked mozzarella cheese, cut into ½-inch cubes
- 2 tablespoon sun-dried tomatoes, finely chopped and soaked in boiling water 10 minutes
- 2 tablespoons chopped pitted black olives
- 1 tablespoon olive oil
- 1 tablespoon balsamic vinegar
- ½ teaspoon salt
- ¼ teaspoon black pepper

1 In large saucepan of lightly salted water, boil pasta until tender, following package directions. Drain and rinse under cold running water.

2 In large bowl, combine tomatoes, onion, arugula, cheese, sun-dried tomatoes, olives, and cold pasta.

3 In small bowl, whisk together olive oil, balsamic vinegar, salt, and pepper. Add to pasta mixture. Toss well. Serve immediately.

Per serving: 368 calories, 15 g protein, 50 g carbohydrates, 13 g fat, 5 g saturated fat, 23 mg cholesterol, 4 g fiber, 573 mg sodium

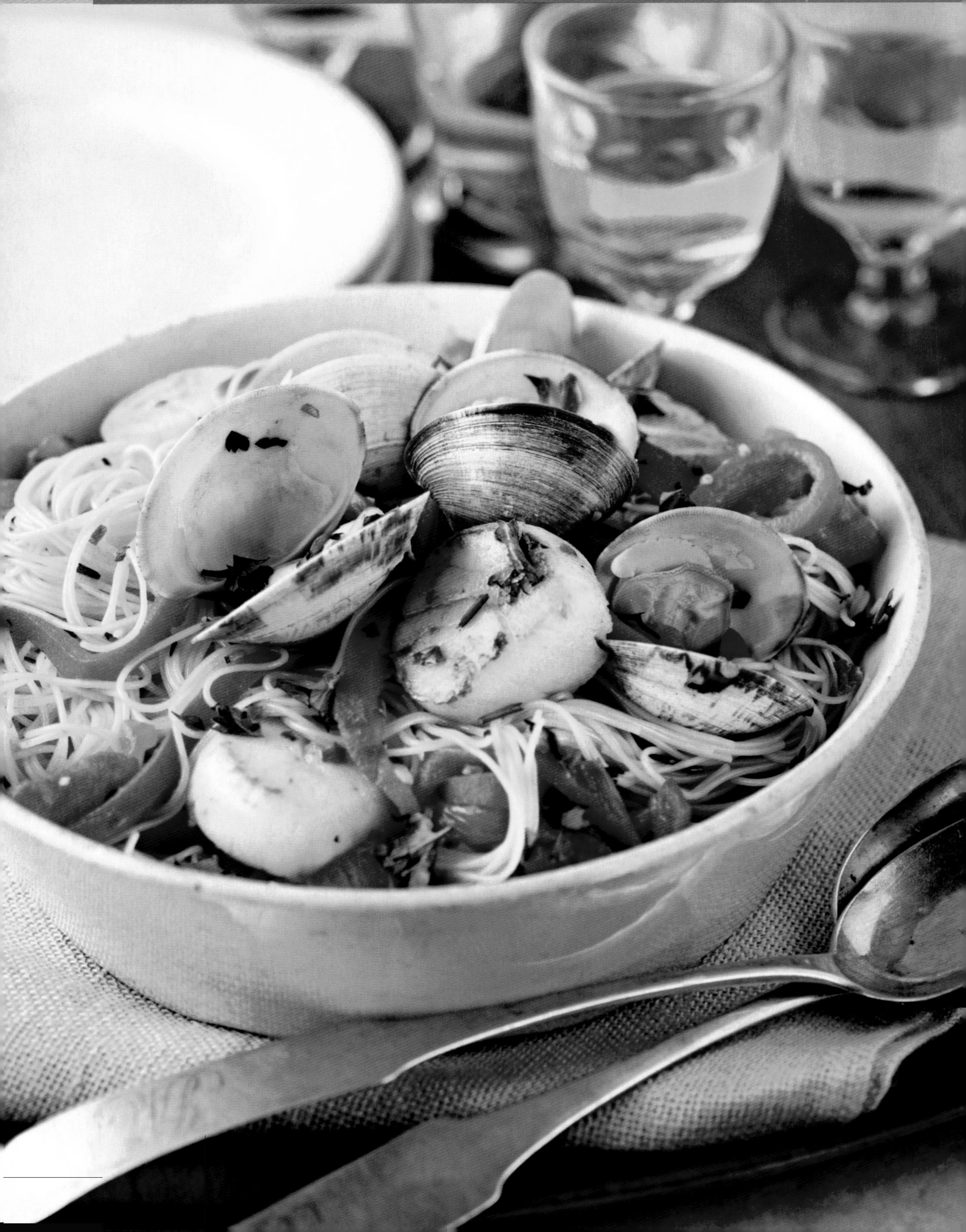

Angel Hair with Clams & Roasted Pepper

Any dish made with peppers is rich in cancer-fighting antioxidants; a good amount of parsley adds more beta carotene and vitamin C to the mix.

4 SERVINGS

Prep 10 min ◆ **Cook** 25 min

- 2 tablespoons olive oil
- ½ pound scallops
- 2 cloves garlic
- ½ cup dry white wine
- Pinch red pepper flakes
- 2 dozen littleneck clams, scrubbed
- 1 can (14½ ounces) diced tomatoes
- 1 teaspoon salt
- 1 cup thinly sliced roasted red bell pepper (see page 295)
- ⅓ cup coarsely chopped flat-leaf parsley
- 12 ounces angel-hair pasta

1 In large nonstick saucepan over medium-high heat, heat oil. Add scallops. Cook until almost cooked through, about 4 minutes. Transfer scallops to plate.

2 Add garlic to pan. Cook 15 seconds. Add wine, pepper flakes, and clams. Cover. Reduce heat to medium. Cook until clams have all opened, about 8 minutes. Transfer clams with slotted spoon to bowl. Discard any unopened clams.

3 Add tomatoes with can liquid to pan. Boil until reduced to 1½ cups, about 10 minutes. Stir in roasted pepper, clams, scallops, and parsley.

4 Meanwhile, in large pot of lightly salted boiling water, cook angel hair until tender, following package directions. Drain well. Add to sauce in pan. Serve at once.

Per serving: 526 calories, 35 g protein, 76 g carbohydrates, 9 g fat, 1 g saturated fat, 55 mg cholesterol, 5 g fiber, 638 mg sodium

FRESH IDEAS

The tomatoes, pepper, and white wine in Angel Hair with Clams & Roasted Pepper are classic foils for many kinds of seafood. You can substitute ½ pound of any firm-fleshed white fish, such as cod or haddock, for the scallops or try ½ pound shellfish, such as shrimp or crab, instead of the clams in this recipe.

Linguine with Shiitake Mushrooms, Sweet Pepper & Ham

Mushrooms help keep your blood pressure on an even keel.

6 SERVINGS

Prep 10 min ◆ **Cook** 18 min

- 2 tablespoons olive oil
- 1 yellow bell pepper, trimmed, seeded and cut into ¼-inch dice
- ½ pound shiitake mushroom caps, cut into ¼-inch-thick strips
- 4 ounces lean ham, finely chopped
- 2 cloves garlic, minced
- 1 can (28 ounces) whole tomatoes, drained and chopped
- ½ teaspoon dried basil, crumbled
- ¼ teaspoon salt
- ¼ teaspoon black pepper
- 12 ounces linguine pasta
- Grated Parmesan cheese *(optional)*

1 In large nonstick saucepan over medium high-heat, heat oil. Add bell pepper, mushrooms, ham, and garlic. Sauté until mushrooms are tender, 6 to 8 minutes. Add tomatoes and basil. Cook until thickened, about 10 minutes. Stir in salt and pepper.

2 Meanwhile, in large pot of lightly salted boiling water, cook linguine until tender, following package directions. Drain. Add to sauce in saucepan. Serve with Parmesan on the side, if you like.

Per serving: 309 calories, 13 g protein, 49 g carbohydrates, 6 g fat, 1 g saturated fat, 9 mg cholesterol, 3 g fiber, 638 mg sodium

Asian Noodle Salad

A Thai-style seasoning combination of basil, mint, and cilantro leaves adds vitamin C and carotenoids to a dish that's already packed with vitamins, minerals, fiber, and protective phytochemicals.

6 SERVINGS

Prep 15 min ◆ **Cook** 10 min

- 12 ounces whole-wheat linguine
- ½ pound snow peas, halved lengthwise
- 3 medium carrots, peeled, cut into 2-inch lengths, and cut lengthwise into thin slices
- 2 cups packed fresh basil leaves
- ½ cup packed fresh mint leaves
- ¼ cup packed fresh cilantro leaves
- 2 cloves garlic
- 2 tablespoons dark sesame oil
- 1 tablespoon vegetable oil
- ¼ teaspoon red pepper flakes
- ½ teaspoon salt
- 1 red bell pepper, seeded and cut into slivers
- 3 scallions, finely chopped
- 2 tablespoons chopped unsalted dry-roasted peanuts

1 Cook linguine in large pot of lightly salted boiling water until tender, following package directions. For last 2 minutes of cooking, add snow peas and carrots. Drain in colander. Rinse under cold running water. Drain well.

2 Meanwhile, in small food processor, pulse together basil, mint, cilantro, garlic, sesame oil, vegetable oil, pepper flakes, and ¼ teaspoon of the salt until a paste forms.

3 In large bowl, combine linguine, snow peas, carrots, bell pepper, scallions, basil mixture, and remaining salt. Serve at room temperature or chilled. Garnish with peanuts.

Per serving: 321 calories, 12 g protein, 52 g carbohydrates, 10 g fat, 1 g saturated fat, 0 mg cholesterol, 11 g fiber, 355 mg sodium

on the menu

This salad stands alone as a lunch dish or even a light supper dish. For a more substantial salad, add shredded cooked chicken, pork, or beef. This salad is also an excellent side dish to roasted or grilled meat or poultry.

Tagliatelle with Veggies & Blue Cheese

Broccoli and cauliflower add flavor, texture, and—most important—nutrients galore to this quick dish.

4 SERVINGS

Prep 10 min ◆ **Cook** 15 min

- 8 ounces spinach tagliatelle
- 8 ounces broccoli florets, cut up
- 8 ounces cauliflower florets, cut up
- 6 ounces blue cheese, rind removed, diced
  Freshly grated nutmeg
  Salt and black pepper

1 In large pot of lightly salted boiling water, cook pasta until al dente, following package directions. Add broccoli and cauliflower for last 3 minutes of cooking time. In large colander, drain pasta and vegetables .

2 Rinse out pot and return to burner over low heat. Add cheese. Cook, stirring often, until cheese melts into smooth sauce.

3 Add pasta and vegetables and stir gently to coat well and heat through. Season to taste with nutmeg, salt, and black pepper. Serve immediately.

Per serving: 490 calories, 26 g protein, 58 g carbohydrates, 18 g fat, 10g saturated fat, 110 g cholesterol, 7 g fiber, 850 g sodium

Buckwheat Noodles with Tofu & Green Vegetables

Tofu adds blood-building iron and bone-strengthening calcium to this Asian-style entrée. Watercress supplies beta-carotene and vitamin C, two important antioxidants for fighting disease. Zucchini and scallions offer more vitamin C and folate for proper tissue growth.

4 SERVINGS

Prep 15 min ◆ **Cook** 15 min

- 1 tablespoon vegetable oil
- 4 scallions, chopped
- 4 cloves garlic, minced
- 1 medium zucchini, halved lengthwise and cut crosswise into ¼-inch-thick slices
- ½ cup vegetable broth or reduced-sodium, fat-free chicken broth
- 2 tablespoons reduced-sodium soy sauce
- 2 teaspoons cornstarch
- 1 teaspoon dark sesame oil
- 6 ounces extra-firm tofu, cut in cubes
- 6 ounces buckwheat (soba) noodles
- 1 cup packed watercress, tough stems removed
- 2 tablespoons chopped cilantro

1 In large nonstick skillet over medium-high heat, heat oil. Reserve some of dark green parts of scallions for garnish. Add remaining scallions, garlic, and zucchini to skillet. Sauté until softened, about 5 minutes.

2 Meanwhile, in small bowl, whisk together broth, soy sauce, cornstarch, and sesame oil until smooth.

3 Add tofu and broth mixture to skillet. Heat to a boil, stirring constantly, until sauce thickens, 1 to 2 minutes. Remove from heat.

4 In large pot of lightly salted boiling water, cook noodles until tender, following package directions. Reserve ¼ cup cooking liquid. Drain noodles. Rinse noodles under cold running water.

5 Combine noodles, zucchini-tofu mixture, reserved cooking liquid, watercress, and cilantro in large bowl. Toss gently. Garnish with reserved scallions.

Per serving: 262 calories, 14 g protein, 40 g carbohydrates, 7 g fat 1 g saturated fat, 0 mg cholesterol, 7 g fiber, 642 mg sodium

FRESH IDEAS

If you're in a specialty foods store or well-stocked supermarket that carries flavored tofu, look for Thai-style or five-spice tofu to use in Asian recipes. The flavored tofu adds depth to the taste of the finished dish.

Shanghai Noodles
with Cabbage, Pork & Peas

Cabbage contains phytochemicals that fight breast and other hormone-related cancers and, along with peas, scallions, and sprouts, supplies plenty of vitamin C, a prime antioxidant for fighting free radicals and repairing molecular damage in the body.

6 SERVINGS

Prep 20 min ◆ **Marinate** 15 min ◆ **Cook** 12 min

- 12 ounces linguine pasta
- 12 ounces boneless pork loin
- 1 tablespoon dry sherry or rice wine
- 1 tablespoon soy sauce
- 2 teaspoons sugar
- 1 tablespoon vegetable oil
- 2 cloves garlic, minced
- 2 teaspoons finely chopped, peeled fresh ginger
- 3 cups coarsely shredded napa (Chinese) cabbage
- 1 cup frozen peas, thawed
- 6 scallions, cut into 2-inch lengths and thinly sliced lengthwise
- ¾ cup reduced-sodium, fat-free chicken broth
- 2 tablespoons bottled oyster sauce
- 1½ teaspoons cornstarch mixed with 2 teaspoons water
- ½ cup fresh bean sprouts
- 1 teaspoon dark sesame oil

1 In large pot of lightly salted boiling water, cook linguine until tender, following package directions. Drain and cool under cold running water. Reserve.

2 Meanwhile, cut pork into ⅛-inch-thick slices across grain. Cut slices into bite-size pieces.

3 In medium bowl, stir together sherry, soy sauce, and sugar. Add pork and toss to coat. Marinate at room temperature 15 minutes.

4 In large nonstick skillet over medium-high heat, heat 2 teaspoons of the oil. Add garlic and ginger. Stir-fry 15 seconds. Add pork mixture. Stir-fry just until cooked through, 3 to 4 minutes. Transfer pork to a plate.

5 Add remaining 1 teaspoon oil to skillet. Add cabbage. Stir-fry over medium-high heat, 2 minutes. Add peas and scallions. Stir-fry 1 minute. Add broth and oyster sauce. Bring to a boil. Stir in cornstarch mixture. Lower heat. Simmer until sauce is thickened, about 30 seconds. Add pork and linguine. Cook just until heated through, 1 to 2 minutes. Stir in bean sprouts and sesame oil. Serve at once.

Per serving: 358 calories, 22 g protein, 52 g carbohydrates, 7 g fat, 2 g saturated fat, 33 mg cholesterol, 4 g fiber, 403 mg sodium

DID YOU KNOW ● ● ●

. . .that cornstarch has twice the thickening power of wheat flour? Nor does it need fat to make a smooth paste before being mixed into a liquid—just a small amount of cold water. This can cut calories —and lumps—from sauces and gravies.

Cheese Tortellini with Pumpkin & Ricotta

A warm and hearty dish to serve in cold-weather months, when pumpkins and winter squashes are among the most powerfully nutritious vegetables on the market.

4 SERVINGS

Prep 15 min ◆ **Cook** 30 min

- 1 **tablespoon olive oil**
- 1 **medium onion, finely chopped**
- 1½ **pounds sugar pumpkin or butternut squash, seeded, peeled, and cut into ¾-inch cubes (about 4 cups)**
- ½ **cup reduced-sodium, fat-free chicken broth or vegetable broth**
- 1 **teaspoon leaf sage, crumbled**
- ½ **teaspoon salt**
- ⅛ **teaspoon black pepper**
- 12 **ounces cheese tortellini**
- ½ **cup part-skim ricotta cheese**
- ⅓ **cup grated Romano cheese**
- 1 **tablespoon finely chopped flat-leaf parsley**

1 In large nonstick saucepan over medium heat, heat oil. Add onion. Cook until golden, about 10 minutes. Add pumpkin, broth, sage, salt, and pepper. Cover. Cook just until pumpkin is tender, about 20 minutes.

2 Meanwhile, in large pot of lightly salted water, cook tortellini until tender, following package directions. Drain. Toss with ricotta in large bowl.

3 Add pumpkin, Romano cheese, and parsley to tortellini mixture. Gently toss to combine. Serve at once.

Per serving: 305 calories, 15 g protein, 36 g carbohydrates, 12 g fat, 3 g saturated fat, 27 mg cholesterol, 5 g fiber, 945 mg sodium

Meat Tortellini with Roasted Red Bell Pepper Sauce

Roasted peppers from a jar provide a significant amount of beta-carotene and vitamin C, proving that convenience food can indeed be healthful when you make smart choices.

4 SERVINGS

Prep 5 min ◆ **Cook** 10 min

- 12 **ounces meat-filled tortellini**
- 1 **jar (12 ounces) roasted red bell peppers**
- 2 **cloves garlic**
- 2 **tablespoons olive oil**
- 1 **tablespoon reduced-sodium soy sauce**
- 1 **tablespoon cold butter, cut into small pieces**
- 3 **tablespoons shredded fresh basil leaves**

1 In large pot of lightly salted boiling water, cook tortellini until tender, following package directions.

2 Meanwhile, in food processor, combine red peppers and their liquid, garlic, oil, and soy sauce. Process until pureed. Transfer to medium saucepan. Simmer over low heat 10 minutes.

3 Drain tortellini. Just before serving, whisk cold butter into red pepper puree. Stir in basil. Add tortellini to red pepper sauce. Toss to combine, and serve.

Per serving: 285 calories, 12 g protein, 21 g carbohydrates, 17 g fat, 6 g saturated fat, 116 mg cholesterol, 1 g fiber, 657 mg sodium

HINT **helpful HINT** HINT HINT HINT HINT HINT HINT HINT

Romano is a hard Italian grating cheese made from sheep's milk. It has a sharper flavor than Parmesan, a hard grating cheese made from cow's milk. You can substitute Parmesan in any recipe that calls for Romano. Or you can mix the two. A third Italian hard grating cheese, Asiago, is made from cow's milk and has a flavor that falls somewhere between Parmesan and Romano. All three have their adherents. Experiment to find what you like best.

on the menu

Serve Meat Tortellini with Roasted Bell Pepper Sauce with a crisp green salad
and a side dish of sautéed broccoli rabe. End the meal with chocolate sorbet.

Stuffed Giant Pasta Shells

A creamy classic packed with vitamins and minerals.

4 SERVINGS

Prep 45 min   ◆   **Cook** 30 min

- **1 pound spinach, trimmed and rinsed**
- **3 zucchini, thinly sliced**
- **4 cloves garlic, finely chopped**
- **1 can (14½ ounces) vegetable broth**
- **8 ounces ricotta cheese**
- **3 ounces coarsely chopped walnuts**
- **1/4 cup grated Parmesan cheese**
- **3 tablespoons each chopped fresh marjoram, chives, and basil**
- **1 egg, lightly beaten**
- **12 giant pasta shells, cooked al dente**
- **2 ounces Edam cheese, grated**

1 In large saucepan, place spinach with rinse water clinging to leaves. Cover, cook over high heat, shaking pan often, 3 minutes. Drain, cool, and set aside.

2 In same saucepan, combine zucchini, half the garlic, and broth. Bring to a boil; boil until just tender, 3 minutes. Place zucchini, broth, half the ricotta, walnuts, 2 tablespoons Parmesan cheese, and salt and pepper to taste in food processor. Puree until smooth.

3 Squeeze spinach dry and coarsely chop. In medium bowl, mix spinach with marjoram, chives, basil, remaining garlic and ricotta cheese, and egg.

4 Preheat oven to 375°F. Stuff pasta with spinach mixture. Arrange in baking dish. Pour zucchini sauce over shells. Sprinkle with remaining Parmesan. Cover dish. Bake 30 minutes. Sprinkle Edam cheese over. Let stand 5 minutes before serving.

Per serving: 750 calories, 43 g protein, 83 g carbohydrates, 30 g fat, 11 g saturated fat, 95 g cholesterol, 8.5 g fiber, 450 g sodium

Spinach-Stuffed Manicotti with Mushrooms

Here's a tasty, one-dish meal that scores high in good nutrition and high in good flavor.

4 SERVINGS

Prep 25 min   ◆   **Cook** 40 min

- **8 manicotti or cannelloni shells**
- **2 teaspoons olive oil**
- **1 small onion, finely chopped**
- **1 package (10 ounces) frozen chopped spinach, thawed**
- **1 cup part-skim ricotta cheese**
- **4 ounces part-skim mozzarella cheese, shredded**
- **¼ cup grated Parmesan cheese**
- **1 teaspoon dried basil, crumbled**
- **¼ teaspoon garlic powder**
- **¼ teaspoon salt**
- **1¼ cups prepared tomato sauce**
- **10 ounces mushrooms, sliced**

1 In large pot of lightly salted boiling water, cook manicotti 8 minutes. Drain. Let cool slightly.

2 Meanwhile, in medium nonstick skillet over medium heat, heat 1 teaspoon of the oil. Add onion. Sauté until softened, 5 minutes.

3 In colander, briefly drain spinach, letting it retain some liquid. In large bowl stir together spinach, ricotta, mozzarella, Parmesan, basil, garlic powder, and salt.

4 Preheat oven to 350°F.

5 Spread ¼ cup tomato sauce over bottom of 13 x 9 x 2-inch baking dish. Stuff each manicotti shell at both ends with spinach mixture to fill completely. Arrange manicotti in single layer in baking dish. Top with remaining tomato sauce. Cover with foil.

6 Bake until heated through, about 30 minutes.

7 About 5 minutes before end of baking time, in skillet over medium heat, heat remaining teaspoon oil. Add mushrooms. Sauté just until slightly softened, about 2 minutes. Serve manicotti topped with mushrooms.

Per serving: 382 calories, 26 g protein, 40 g carbohydrates, 14 g fat, 7 g saturated fat, 37 mg cholesterol, 5 g fiber, 1,111 mg sodium

Baked Pasta with Garlic & Greens

Here's an easy and delicious way to get more garlic into your diet and give your immune system a helping hand.

8 SERVINGS

Prep 15 min ◆ **Cook** 50 min

- **1 pound penne or rigatoni pasta**
- **1 tablespoon olive oil**
- **6 cloves garlic, thinly sliced**
- **1 package (10 ounces) frozen kale or collard greens, thawed and well drained**
- **3 cups prepared tomato sauce**
- **1 cup part-skim ricotta cheese**
- **1 cup shredded part-skim mozzarella cheese**
  Kalamata olives for garnish

1 Preheat oven to 350°. Lightly coat 2-quart baking dish with nonstick cooking spray.

2 In large pot of lightly salted boiling water, cook penne until tender, following package directions.

3 Meanwhile, in medium nonstick skillet over medium-low heat, heat oil. Add garlic. Sauté until golden, about 5 minutes. Add kale. Heat through, about 5 minutes. Transfer to large bowl. Stir in tomato sauce and ricotta cheese.

4 Drain penne. Add to bowl. Mix well. Scrape into baking dish. Top with mozzarella cheese. Cover with foil.

5 Bake 25 minutes. Remove foil. Bake until lightly golden, about 10 minutes. Garnish with olives.

Per serving: 341 calories, 17 g protein, 53 g carbohydrates, 8 g fat, 4 g saturated fat, 18 mg cholesterol, 4 g fiber, 810 mg sodium

Creamy Mac 'n' Cheese with Tomatoes

An old-fashioned comfort food gets a flavor enhancement and vitamin boost from grated carrots and sliced tomatoes.

8 SERVINGS

Prep 15 min ◆ **Cook** 30 min

- **1 pound elbow macaroni**
- **3 tablespoons vegetable oil**
- **4 scallions, coarsely chopped**
- **¼ teaspoon salt**
- **¼ cup all-purpose flour**
- **4 cups low-fat (1%) milk, warmed**
- **2 tablespoons Dijon mustard**
- **2 cups shredded reduced-fat sharp cheddar cheese**
- **1 cup shredded reduced-fat Monterey Jack cheese**
- **½ cup grated Parmesan cheese**
- **1 medium carrot, peeled and coarsely grated**
- **2 tomatoes, cored and sliced**
- **1 cup fresh whole-wheat bread crumbs**

1 In large pot of lightly salted boiling water, cook macaroni until tender, following package directions. Drain well. Return to pot.

2 Meanwhile, in large nonstick saucepan over medium heat, heat oil. Add scallions and salt. Cook, stirring, occasionally, 3 minutes. Gradually stir in flour. Cook 1 minute. Gradually stir in 1 cup of the milk until well blended, with no lumps. Gradually stir in remaining milk. Bring to a boil. Lower heat. Simmer, stirring, until lightly thickened, 2 to 3 minutes. Remove from heat. Stir in mustard. Stir in cheddar, Monterey Jack, and ¼ cup of the Parmesan.

3 Preheat oven to 375°F. Lightly coat 13 x 9 x 2-inch baking dish with nonstick cooking spray.

4 Fold carrot and cheese sauce into macaroni. Scrape into prepared baking dish. Arrange tomatoes in single layer over top. Combine remaining ¼ cup Parmesan and crumbs in small bowl. Sprinkle over tomatoes.

5 Bake until filling is bubbly and topping is lightly browned, about 20 minutes. Let stand 10 minutes before serving.

Per serving: 502 calories, 26 g protein, 60 g carbohydrates, 19 g fat, 9 g saturated fat, 39 mg cholesterol, 3 g fiber, 862 mg sodium

FRESH IDEAS

You can use any short to medium-size stubby pasta shape in this Mac 'n' Cheese dish, including radiatore, rotelle, short fusilli, wagon wheels, ziti, penne, or farfalle (butterfly shape). For children, there are racket shapes and cartoon characters and, around holidays, turkeys, Pilgrims, stars, Christmas trees, angels, and musical notes.

Quick & Easy One-Step Spinach Lasagna

Save time with no-boil lasagna noodles, bottled tomato sauce, and frozen spinach—
all processed "fast" foods that are good for you because they still supply plenty of essential
vitamins and cancer-defeating phytochemicals.

8 SERVINGS

Prep 20 min ◆ **Cook** 45 min

- 3 **cups part-skim ricotta cheese**
- 1 **cup grated Parmesan cheese**
- 1 **large egg**
- 4 **cups bottled chunky tomato pasta sauce**
- 12 **oven-ready, no-boil lasagna noodles (from 8-ounce package)**
- 2 **boxes (10 ounces each) frozen chopped spinach, thawed and squeezed dry**
- 1 **cup shredded part-skim mozzarella cheese**

1 Preheat oven to 350°F. Coat 13 x 9 x 2-inch baking dish with nonstick cooking spray.

2 In medium bowl, stir together ricotta, Parmesan, and egg.

3 Spread 1 cup pasta sauce over bottom of baking dish. Arrange 3 lasagna noodles side by side in dish. Spread 1¼ cups ricotta mixture over top of noodles. Top with a third of the spinach. Repeat layering two more times with sauce, noodles, ricotta mixture, and spinach. Top with remaining 3 noodles. Spread remaining 1 cup sauce over top. Gently press lasagna noodles down into dish, so sauce comes up around sides. Cover dish with foil.

4 Bake 35 minutes. Uncover. Sprinkle with mozzarella. Bake until cheese is melted and filling is bubbly, about 10 minutes. Let stand 10 minutes before cutting into rectangles.

Per serving: 456 calories, 26 g protein, 50 g carbohydrates, 17 g fat, 9 g saturated fat, 72 mg cholesterol, 6 g fiber, 1,009 mg sodium

FRESH ❧ IDEAS

You can make one-step lasagna with other favorite ingredients too. Just follow the recipe above with a few changes:
- *Use ¹/₂ pound sliced pepperoni sausage and ¹/₂ pound sliced mushrooms for the spinach layers*
- *Use frozen chopped broccoli and some diced ham for the spinach layer and substitute shredded Jarlsberg for the mozzarella*

HINT **helpful HINT** HINT HINT HINT HINT HINT HINT

For convenience, Quick & Easy One-Step Spinach Lasagna uses no-boil lasagna noodles that are precooked and then dehydrated at the pasta factory. Recipes that call for precooked noodles are specially developed to include enough liquid to surround and rehydrate the noodles, either by calling for more tomato sauce or for water in addition to the sauce.

The convenience of no-boil lasagna noodles is twofold: You get to skip the separate step of cooking pasta, and the rigidity of the noodles makes it easier to assemble the layers. Also, there are no "puddles" at the bottom of the lasagna dish when you use precooked noodles, because the noodles soak up the added liquid.

DID YOU KNOW ● ● ●

...that the Arabs introduced dried pasta into Europe via Sicily, an early Arab colony? A Sicilian word "maccaruni," which translates as "made into a dough by force," is the origin of our word macaroni. Kneading durum wheat into pasta does, indeed, take force (men in Sicily used to do it with their feet) and some Sicilian lasagnas still include raisins and spices more Arab than Italian.

VEGETABLES FOR VITALITY

Quick Baked Ziti with Ground Turkey, Onions, Tomatoes, Green Beans & Broccoli

Canned tomatoes are a rich source of the phytochemical lycopene, which can help battle prostate cancer and other chronic diseases. Broccoli adds beta-carotene, sulforaphane, and indoles to the anti-disease mix as well as vitamin C. Green beans offer vitamin C, folate, iron, and more beta-carotene.

6 SERVINGS

Prep 10 min ◆ **Cook** 40 min

- 8 **ounces ziti pasta**
- 2 **teaspoons olive oil**
- 1 **large onion, chopped**
- 2 **cans (14½ ounces each) diced tomatoes with basil, garlic, oregano**
- ¾ **pound ground turkey**
- ½ **teaspoon salt**
- ½ **teaspoon dried thyme, crumbled**
- 1 **box (10 ounces) frozen French-cut green beans, thawed**
- 1 **box (10 ounces) frozen broccoli spears, thawed and chopped**
- ½ **cup reduced-fat sour cream**
- ½ **cup shredded Parmesan cheese**

1 In large pot of lightly salted water, cook ziti until tender, following package directions. Drain. Transfer to large bowl.

2 Meanwhile, in large nonstick skillet over medium-high heat, heat 1 teaspoon of the oil. Add onion. Sauté until softened, 5 minutes. Add tomatoes. Cook until liquid is reduced by half, 3 to 5 minutes. Stir tomato mixture into pasta.

3 Return skillet to medium-high heat. Add remaining teaspoon oil. Coarsely crumble ground turkey into skillet. Sprinkle with salt and thyme. Cook turkey, stirring, until lightly browned and just cooked through, about 4 minutes.

4 Stir turkey, green beans, broccoli, and sour cream into ziti mixture. Spread in 13 x 9 x 2-inch baking pan. Sprinkle with Parmesan.

5 Bake until edges of pasta are golden and cheese melts, 20 to 25 minutes.

Per serving: 396 calories, 24 g protein, 49 g carbohydrates, 12 g fat, 5 g saturated fat, 54 mg cholesterol, 5 g fiber, 1,182 mg sodium

DID YOU KNOW ● ● ●

...that the per capita consumption of pasta in the United States is 30 pounds a year? Although the U.S. still imports some pasta from Italy, it is manufacturing almost all of what is consumed domestically and even exporting some pasta to Asia.

MAIN COURSE
vegetarian
DISHES

VEGETABLES FOR VITALITY

Stuffed Zucchini Gratin

These zucchini "boats," filled with ricotta and Gruyère cheese, are a good source of bone-saving calcium.

4 SERVINGS

Prep 15 min ◆ **Cook** 23 min

- **4 medium zucchini**
- **1 cup part-skim ricotta cheese**
- **1 large egg, lightly beaten**
- **¼ cup shredded Gruyère cheese**
- **1 teaspoon all-purpose flour**
- **½ teaspoon dried thyme, crumbled**
- **¼ teaspoon salt**
- **¼ teaspoon black pepper**
- **1 can (15 ounces) corn kernels, drained and rinsed**
- **2 teaspoons vegetable oil**
- **4 scallions, thinly sliced**
- **1 plum tomato, seeded and coarsely chopped**

1 Preheat broiler. Cover baking sheet with aluminum foil.

2 In large pot of lightly salted boiling water, cook zucchini until softened, about 5 minutes. Drain. Rinse under cold running water.

3 Halve zucchini lengthwise. Scoop out centers, leaving about ⅓-inch-thick shell. Coarsely chop flesh. Place zucchini shells on baking sheet.

4 In medium bowl, stir together ricotta, egg, cheese, flour, thyme, salt, pepper, and corn.

5 In medium nonstick skillet over medium-high heat, heat oil. Add chopped zucchini, scallions, and tomato. Sauté until light golden and mixture is dry, about 8 minutes. Let cool slightly. Stir into ricotta mixture. Spoon into zucchini halves.

6 Broil 6 inches from heat until heated through and filling is lightly browned, about 10 minutes. Let stand 10 minutes before serving.

Per serving: 329 calories, 15 g protein, 49 g carbohydrates, 10 g fat, 6 g saturated fat, 23 mg cholesterol, 10 g fiber, 743 mg sodium

on the menu

These high-protein zucchini "boats" can center a lunch or a dinner with the addition of seven-grain rolls, a tomato salad, and Pumpkin Maple Cheesecake (page 274) for dessert.

Couscous-Stuffed Peppers

Chickpeas and couscous combine to give this low-calorie dish a high protein score.

6 SERVINGS

Prep 20 min ◆ **Cook** 30 min

- **6 large bell peppers (red, yellow, orange, or green)**
- **1 tablespoon vegetable oil**
- **1 small zucchini, finely chopped**
- **2 cloves garlic, minced**
- **1 tablespoon fresh-squeezed lemon juice**
- **2 cups cooked couscous**
- **1 can (15 ounces) chickpeas, drained and rinsed**
- **1 ripe tomato, seeded and finely chopped**
- **1 teaspoon dried oregano, crumbled**
- **½ teaspoon salt**
- **¼ teaspoon black pepper**
- **½ cup crumbled feta cheese**

1 Slice tops off peppers to make lids. Scoop out membranes and seeds and discard. In large saucepan of lightly salted boiling water, simmer peppers and lids covered, 5 minutes. Drain.

2 Preheat oven to 350°F.

3 Heat oil in medium saucepan over medium heat. Add zucchini and garlic. Sauté 2 minutes. Stir in lemon juice. Cook 1 minute and remove from heat. Stir in couscous, chickpeas, tomato, oregano, salt, and pepper. Stir in cheese. Fill each pepper with couscous mixture. Place upright in shallow baking dish. Cover with pepper tops.

4 Bake just until filling is heated through, about 20 minutes.

Per serving: 207 calories, 8 g protein, 36 g carbohydrates, 4 g fat, 1 g saturated fat, 3 mg cholesterol, 7 g fiber, 307 mg sodium

Barley Risotto with Asparagus & Mushrooms

To reduce saturated fat, olive oil replaces the butter traditionally used in this Italian-style rice dish.

4 SERVINGS

Prep 15 min ◆ **Cook** 40 min

- 2 cans (14½ ounces each) reduced-sodium, fat-free chicken broth
- 2 tablespoons olive oil
- 1 onion, finely chopped
- 8 ounces mushrooms, preferably mixture of wild varieties, coarsely chopped
- 2 cloves garlic, minced
- 1 cup pearl barley
- 8 ounces asparagus, trimmed, and cut into bite-size pieces, leaving tips whole
- ½ cup grated Parmesan cheese

1 In medium saucepan, heat broth and 2 cups water to just below a simmer. Cover; keep at a simmer.

2 In large deep nonstick skillet over medium heat, heat oil. Sauté onion until slightly softened, 3 minutes. Add mushrooms and garlic. Sauté until mushrooms are softened, 5 minutes. Stir in barley. Stir in 2 cups hot broth mixture. Simmer, covered, 15 minutes.

3 Meanwhile, blanch asparagus tips in the pot of hot broth for 2 minutes. Transfer with slotted spoon to plate.

4 Add more hot broth to barley mixture, ½ cup at a time, stirring frequently. Let each batch of liquid be absorbed before adding more. When adding the last batch of liquid, stir in asparagus stem pieces. Stir in Parmesan. Serve risotto topped with asparagus tips.

Per serving: 329 calories, 15 g protein, 49 g carbohydrates, 10 g fat, 2 g saturated fat, 23 mg cholesterol, 10 g fiber, 743 mg sodium

Vegetable Pot Pie

You won't miss the meat when you bite into this flavorful, vitamin-packed pie enriched with bits of cheddar cheese.

6 SERVINGS

Prep 20 min ◆ **Cook** 55 min

- 2 tablespoons butter
- 2 celery stalks, coarsely chopped
- 1 yellow onion, coarsely chopped
- 1 large carrot, peeled and cut into small chunks
- 1 small red bell pepper, seeded and coarsely chopped
- ¾ teaspoon dried thyme, crumbled
- 3 tablespoons all-purpose flour
- 1 cup vegetable broth or bouillon
- 1 cup broccoli florets
- 1 cup cauliflower florets
- 1 cup frozen pearl onions
- 2 ounces cheddar cheese, cut into small cubes
  Lattice pastry top or plain pastry circle for one-crust 9-inch pie

1 In large nonstick saucepan over medium heat, melt butter. Add celery, onion, carrot, pepper, and thyme. Sauté until vegetables are tender, 10 minutes.

2 Stir in flour until well blended. Stir in broth. Increase heat to medium-high. Add broccoli, cauliflower, and pearl onions. Bring to boil, then lower heat and simmer, uncovered, 15 minutes. Remove saucepan from heat. (If making filling ahead, let cool to room temperature. Cover and refrigerate.)

3 Preheat oven to 400°F.

4 Spread vegetable mixture in 9-inch glass or ceramic pie plate. Top with cheese. Cover filling with pastry. Trim edges. (If crust is not lattice, cut 6 long slits in it to vent steam.) Place dish on baking sheet.

5 Bake until pastry is golden and filling is bubbly, 25 to 30 minutes. Let stand 10 minutes before serving.

Per serving: 296 calories, 7 g protein, 32 g carbohydrates, 17 g fat, 8 g saturated fat, 27 mg cholesterol, 4 g fiber, 408 mg sodium

helpful HINT

To make a lattice pie crust, roll out a piece of dough 5 or 6 inches wide and longer than the pie plate by 2 inches. Cut into ½-inch strips(10 or 12 are plenty). Start at a side to weave strips over the pie, bending back strips made in one direction to allow you to lay strips in the other direction. When weaving is finished, trim the ends.

Carrot-Zucchini Soufflé

What an elegant way to get your antioxidants!

8 SERVINGS

Prep 15 min ◆ **Cook** 1hr 5 min

- 1 **pound carrots, peeled and cut into ½-inch-thick slices**
- 2 **tablespoons vegetable oil**
- ¼ **cup coarsely chopped onion**
- 2 **tablespoons all-purpose flour**
- ½ **cup reduced-fat (1%) milk**
- 4 **large eggs, separated**
- 1 **medium zucchini, grated**
- ½ **teaspoon salt**
- ¼ **teaspoon black pepper**
- ¼ **teaspoon ground nutmeg**

1 In medium saucepan, steam carrots until tender, about 20 minutes. Puree in food processor.

2 Preheat oven to 400°F. Coat 8-cup soufflé dish with nonstick cooking spray.

3 Heat oil in small saucepan over medium heat. Add onion. Sauté until softened, about 5 minutes. Stir in flour. Cook, stirring occasionally, 1 minute. Stir in milk. Bring to a boil, stirring constantly. Transfer to large bowl. Stir in carrots and egg yolks. Fold in zucchini. Stir in salt, pepper, and nutmeg.

4 In medium bowl beat egg whites until soft peaks form. Fold whites, a third at a time, into vegetable mixture. Spoon into prepared dish.

5 Bake until puffed and golden, 30 to 40 minutes. Serve at once.

Per serving: 116 calories, 5 g protein, 10 g carbohydrates, 6 g fat, 2 g saturated fat, 109 mg cholesterol, 2 g fiber, 215 mg sodium

DID YOU KNOW ● ● ●

. . .that the slightest amount of fat from butter, oil, or egg yolk will keep egg whites from whipping up into soft peaks? Make sure the bowl is clean and egg whites are completely separated from yolks.

Broccoli & Corn Pudding

Sure proof that creamy comfort food can be good for you!

6 SERVINGS

Prep 15 min ◆ **Cook** 1¼ hr

- 3 **cups broccoli florets**
- 2 **teaspoons vegetable oil**
- 1 **small onion, finely chopped**
- 2 **tablespoons all-purpose flour**
- 1 **cup evaporated nonfat milk**
- 1 **cup low-fat milk (1%)**
- 3 **large eggs, lightly beaten**
- ½ **cup shredded reduced-fat cheddar cheese**
- 1 **can (15½ ounces) corn kernels, drained**
- ¾ **teaspoon salt**
- ⅛ **teaspoon black pepper**
- ⅛ **teaspoon ground allspice**

1 Preheat oven to 350°. Lightly coat 2-quart baking dish or casserole with nonstick cooking spray.

2 Place broccoli and ¼ cup water in microwavable bowl. Cover loosely with wax paper. Microwave 4 minutes. Let cool. Drain. Coarsely chop.

3 Heat oil in medium nonstick saucepan over medium-low heat. Add onion. Cook, covered, until softened, about 6 minutes. Stir in flour until well blended. Stir in evaporated milk and low-fat milk until blended. Continue stirring until mixture thickens slightly, 3 to 4 minutes. Remove from heat. Whisk in eggs and cheese. Stir in broccoli, corn, salt, pepper, and allspice. Pour into prepared dish. Place dish into larger baking pan. Pour boiling water into large pan to come halfway up side of dish.

4 Bake until knife inserted into center comes out clean, 55 to 60 minutes.

Per serving: 192 calories, 13 g protein, 21 g carbohydrates, 7 g fat, 3 g saturated fat, 116 mg cholesterol, 2 g fiber, 583 mg sodium

Thai-Style Stir-Fry

A seasoning combination of ginger, chiles, garlic, and scallions provides powerful flavor and powerful antioxidant protection against chronic disease.

4 SERVINGS

Prep 15 min ◆ **Cook** 6 min

- ½ cup vegetable broth
- ¼ cup fresh-squeezed lime juice
- 2 tablespoons reduced-sodium soy sauce
- 2 teaspoons sugar
- 2 teaspoons cornstarch
- 2 tablespoons vegetable oil
- 4 cloves garlic, minced
- 1 tablespoon finely chopped, peeled fresh ginger
- 2 serrano or jalapeño chiles, seeded and finely chopped
- 1 red bell pepper, seeded and cut into ½-inch squares
- 4 scallions, thinly sliced
- 1 medium zucchini, diced
- 12 bottled baby corn, rinsed
- ¼ pound Chinese or napa cabbage, shredded
- 1 pound firm tofu, cut into ½-inch cubes

1 In small bowl, whisk together broth, lime juice, soy sauce, sugar, and cornstarch until smooth.

2 In large nonstick skillet or wok over medium-high heat, heat 2 teaspoons of the oil. Add garlic, ginger, and chiles. Stir-fry 30 seconds. Add to broth mixture.

3 In skillet heat remaining oil. Add bell pepper, scallions, and zucchini. Stir-fry until crisp-tender, 2 to 3 minutes. Add corn and cabbage. Stir-fry 1 minute. Add tofu and broth mixture. Cover and simmer 2 minutes. Serve at once.

Per serving: 196 calories, 11 g protein, 16 g carbohydrates, 10 g fat, 1 g saturated fat, 0 mg cholesterol, 2.4 g fiber, 502 mg sodium

Fried Rice with Tofu & Vegetables

One of the tastiest ways to incorporate high-quality vegetable protein from tofu into your diet.

SERVES 4

Prep 20 min ◆ **Marinate** 1 hr ◆ **Cook** 20 min

- 1 cup dry white wine or chicken broth
- ¼ cup light soy sauce
- 2 tablespoons honey
- 1 tablespoon grated peeled fresh ginger
- 12 ounces extra-firm tofu, cut into 1-inch cubes
- 1 cup long-grain white rice
- 2 garlic cloves, minced
- 1 package (16 ounces) frozen mixed Chinese vegetables, slightly thawed
- 5 scallions, cut into 2-inch pieces
- ¼ teaspoon pepper
- 1 large egg, lightly beaten

1 In large, zip-close plastic bag, combine wine, 1 tablespoon of the soy sauce, honey, and 1 teaspoon ginger. Add tofu, press out excess air, close bag, and shake gently to coat. Marinate in refrigerator 1 hour, turning occasionally.

2 Cook rice according to package directions; keep warm. Meanwhile, lightly coat wok or large deep skillet with nonstick cooking spray and set over high heat until hot but not smoking.

3 Stir-fry garlic and remaining ginger until fragrant, about 1 minute. Add mixed vegetables, half of scallions, rice, remaining soy sauce, and pepper. Stir-fry until mixed vegetables are heated through, about 4 minutes. Push ingredients to one side of wok, and then pour in beaten egg. Cook egg until almost set, cutting egg into strips with heatproof spatula.

4 Pour marinade into small saucepan. Boil over high heat 2 minutes. Add tofu and marinade to wok. Stir-fry until tofu is heated through, about 4 minutes. Sprinkle with remaining scallions.

Per serving: 442 calories, 21 g protein, 61 g carbohydrates, 9 g fat, 2 g saturated fat, 53 mg cholesterol, 3 g fiber, 668 mg sodium

DID YOU KNOW ● ● ●

. . .that tofu is sometimes called the "cheese of Asia"? It is
made by coagulating the protein of soybeans into curds and has a
high calcium, high protein, and high fat content. It even looks like
farmer's cheese. But, unlike cheese, it is bland and adds no flavor
of its own to recipes.

Chili with White Beans, Tomatoes & Corn

Clear your arteries, boost your immunity, and lower your risk of developing cancer. That's what the fiber in beans, the vitamins C and E in tomatoes, the vitamin C in carrots, and the vitamins C, B_6, and folate in peppers can do. Who would have thought such a fun food could provide so many health benefits?

6 SERVINGS

Prep 15 min ◆ **Cook** 50 min

- 2 tablespoons vegetable oil
- 1 large onion, finely chopped
- 1 red bell pepper, seeded and coarsely chopped
- 1 small carrot, peeled and diced
- 1 small celery stalk, diced
- 4 cloves garlic, minced
- 3 tablespoons chili powder
- 2 tablespoons sweet paprika
- 2 teaspoons dried oregano, crumbled
- 1 teaspoon ground cumin
- 1 can (28 ounces) whole tomatoes with their liquid, chopped
- 2 cans (19 ounces each) cannellini beans, drained and rinsed
- 1 can (15 ounces) black beans, drained and rinsed
- 1 cup water
- ¼ cup reduced-sodium soy sauce
- 1 box (10 ounces) corn kernels

1 In large nonstick saucepan over medium-high heat, heat oil. Add onion, bell pepper, carrot, celery, and garlic. Cook until vegetables are softened, about 5 minutes. Stir in chili powder, paprika, oregano, and cumin. Cook 1 minute.

2 Add tomatoes, beans, water, and soy sauce to saucepan. Simmer, uncovered, 30 minutes, stirring occasionally. Stir in corn. Simmer 10 minutes more.

Per serving: 274 calories, 15 g protein, 48 g carbohydrates, 7 g fat, 1 g saturated fat, 0 mg cholesterol, 13 g fiber, 856 mg sodium

on the menu

This hefty vegetarian chili calls for some Carrot-Flecked Corn Bread (page 259), a big tossed green salad, and some Bourbon-Squash Cake (page 270) with coffee to make a meal.

FRESH IDEAS

Black beans, white beans, and yellow corn provide a hearty foundation for this protein-rich vegetarian chili. But any bean will do in this Tex-Mex stew, and you can also substitute an equal amount of canned (or cooked from dry) lentils for the beans used in this recipe. If you do use lentils, add them with the corn near the end of cooking, and simmer just for the final 10 minutes.

on the menu

This sophisticated sandwich mix of mushrooms, asparagus, and goat cheese calls for a baby spinach and watercress salad with an orange vinaigrette and a cappuccino for dessert.

VEGETABLES FOR VITALITY

Vegetable Tart Provençal

This charming tart, with thyme-flavored pastry, makes a very tasty carrier for a selection of nutrition-packed vegetables: onions with vitamin C and folate; zucchini with more vitamin C; tomatoes with vitamins C and E, as well as antioxidants beta-carotene and lycopene to fight off cancer and heart disease.

4 SERVINGS

Prep 20 min ◆ **Cook** 47 min

- **2 large sweet Vidalia onions, sliced**
- **1½ cups all-purpose flour**
- **1½ teaspoons chopped fresh thyme**
- **½ teaspoon salt**
- **⅓ cup ice water**
- **2 tablespoons olive oil**
- **2 medium zucchini (8 ounces each)**
- **4 medium tomatoes, cut into ¼-inch-thick slices**
- **2 tablespoons grated Parmesan cheese**

1 Coat large nonstick skillet with nonstick cooking spray and set over medium-high heat until hot. Reduce heat to medium-low, add onions, and sauté until very soft and golden, 20 minutes. Transfer to plate.

2 Preheat oven to 400°F. In large bowl, mix flour, thyme, and ¼ teaspoon of the salt. Stir in water and oil just until soft dough forms. Lightly sprinkle work surface with flour and pat out dough into 16 x 10-inch rectangle or 13-inch round. Fold in half and transfer to 12 x 6-inch tart pan or 9-inch round tart pan with removable bottom. Trim edges.

3 Cut zucchini diagonally into long, 1-inch-thick slices. Lightly coat skillet again with cooking spray and set over medium heat. Add zucchini and sauté until golden, 5 to 7 minutes.

4 Arrange zucchini, tomatoes, and onions in rows on pastry, standing them up and overlapping them slightly. Sprinkle with remaining salt and Parmesan. Bake until crust is golden, about 20 minutes. Serve hot, warm, or at room temperature.

Per serving: 305 calories, 9 g protein, 49 g carbohydrates, 9 g fat, 2 g saturated fat, 2 mg cholesterol, 5 g fiber, 354 mg sodium

DID YOU KNOW ● ● ●

...that the term "Provençal" refers to an area of southern France on the Mediterranean called Provence? There, olives, tomatoes, onions, garlic, and dozens of herbs like rosemary, thyme, and marjoram grow in profusion and form the basis of a robust cuisine loved all over the world.

vegetables
on the SIDE

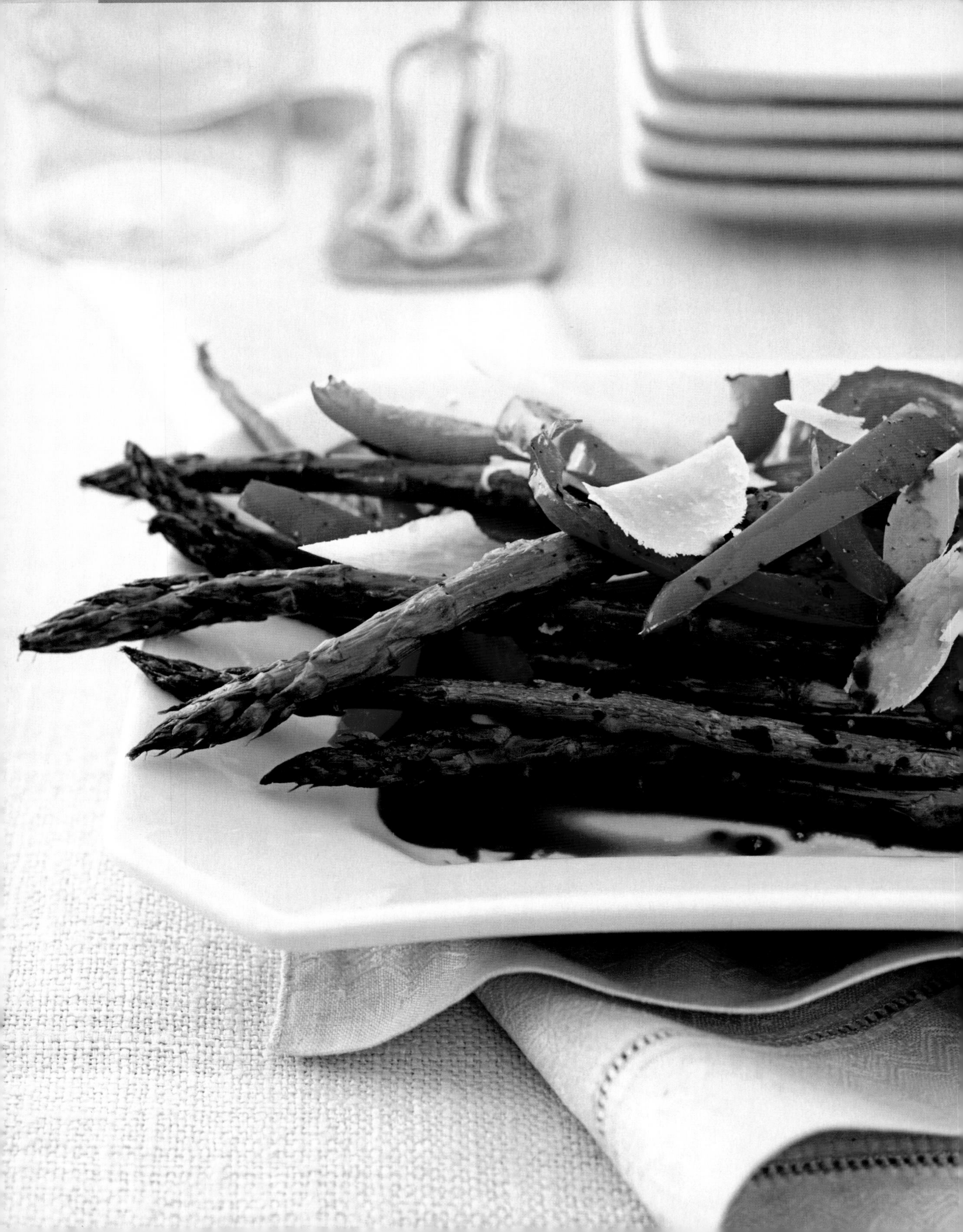

Roast Asparagus & Red Pepper with Parmesan

This fresh vegetable combo is packed with powerful antioxidants and protective vitamins that help fight chronic diseases such as cancer and heart disease.

4 SERVINGS

Prep 10 min ◆ **Cook** 12 min

- **1 pound asparagus, trimmed and bottom half of stalks thinly peeled**
- **1 red bell pepper, seeded and cut lengthwise into thin strips**
- **1 tablespoon olive oil**
- **1 tablespoon balsamic vinegar**
- **1 ounce Parmesan cheese, in one piece**
- **¼ teaspoon black pepper**

1 Preheat oven to 500°F.

2 Place asparagus and bell pepper strips in large shallow baking pan. Drizzle with oil. Toss to coat.

3 Roast until crisp-tender, 10 to 12 minutes, turning occasionally. Transfer to serving dish.

4 Sprinkle with vinegar. Toss to coat. Using a vegetable peeler, shave cheese into thin curls over vegetables. Season with pepper.

Per serving: 86 calories, 5 g protein, 5 g carbohydrates, 6 g fat, 2 g saturated fat, 6 mg cholesterol, 2 g fiber, 140 mg sodium

HINT **helpful HINT** HINT HINT HINT HINT HINT HINT

Roast vegetables are the perfect accompaniment for roast meat or poultry And they are easy to work into the cooking agenda. When the roast beef, for example, goes into the oven, prepare the vegetables and place in a roasting pan with oil and seasonings. When the beef comes out of the oven, turn up the heat and put in the vegetables. They will have plenty of time to cook while the meat rests before it is ready to carve. Just turn the vegetables once or twice to be sure they brown evenly.

Stir-Fried Asparagus & Snow Peas

You can't go wrong with a green vegetable mix like this one, loaded with nutrients that help fight birth defects and at the same time prevent age-related diseases.

6 SERVINGS

Prep 10 min ◆ **Cook** 4 min

- **1 tablespoon olive oil**
- **1 pound asparagus, trimmed, bottom half of stalks thinly peeled, stalks cut diagonally into 1-inch lengths, leaving tips about 2 inches long**
- **¼ pound snow peas**
- **4 scallions, thinly sliced**
- **¼ teaspoon salt**
- **⅛ teaspoon black pepper**
- **1 small clove garlic, minced**
- **1 teaspoon grated lemon zest**
- **2 tablespoons finely chopped parsley**

In large nonstick skillet or wok over medium-high heat, heat oil. Add asparagus, snow peas, scallions, salt, and pepper. Stir-fry until vegetables are almost crisp-tender, 2 to 3 minutes. Add garlic, zest, and parsley. Stir-fry 1 minute. Serve at once.

Per serving: 42 calories, 2 g protein, 4 g carbohydrates, 3 g fat, 0 g saturated fat, 0 mg cholesterol, 1 g fiber, 104 mg sodium

VEGETABLES FOR VITALITY

Balsamic Beets with Toasted Pecans

Beets boost energy like no other vegetable, because they are so high in natural sugars.

4 SERVINGS

Prep 5 min ◆ **Cook** 10 min

- 3 **tablespoons chopped pecans**
- 2 **tablespoons balsamic vinegar**
- 1 **teaspoon sugar**
- 2 **teaspoons butter or margarine**
- 3 **medium beets, steamed, peeled, and sliced or 1 jar (15 ounces) sliced beets, drained**

1 In medium nonstick skillet over medium heat, toast pecans, stirring often, until browned, about 4 minutes. Transfer to plate.

2 In same skillet over medium-low heat, cook vinegar, sugar, and butter. Add beets. Cook, stirring often, until beets are heated through and all liquid is absorbed, about 5 minutes. Top with pecans. Serve at once.

Per serving: 86 calories, 1 g protein, 8 g carbohydrates, 6 g fat, 2 g saturated fat, 5 mg cholesterol, 2 g fiber, 140 mg sodium

Broccoli & Cauliflower with Cream Sauce

Carrot juice is the antioxidant-rich "secret ingredient" that makes the sauce as healthful as the vegetables.

4 SERVINGS

Prep 10 min ◆ **Cook** 13 min

- ½ **cup carrot juice**
- 3 **tablespoons reduced-fat sour cream**
- 2 **cups broccoli florets**
- 2 **cups cauliflower florets**

1 In small saucepan over high heat, boil carrot juice until reduced to ¼ cup, about 8 minutes. Remove from heat. Whisk in sour cream.

2 Steam broccoli and cauliflower until crisp-tender, about 5 minutes. Transfer to serving dish. Serve with sour cream sauce.

Per serving: 44 calories, 3 g protein, 6 g carbohydrates, 2 g fat, 1 g saturated fat, 4 mg cholesterol, 2 g fiber, 45 mg sodium

HINT **helpful HINT** HINT HINT HINT HINT HINT HINT

Beets will keep their color better if you add lemon juice or vinegar to the cooking water. Beet stains are all but impossible to remove from cutting boards, so to save your surfaces, peel steamed beets by cutting off both ends over the sink and then holding them under cold running water while you remove the skins. Before slicing beets, coat the cutting board lightly with nonstick cooking spray. This may not prevent staining altogether, but it will help.

on the menu

You can drizzle the broccoli and cauliflower with creamy carrot sauce, or serve the sauce separately in a small bowl and let people use it as a dip.

VEGETABLES FOR VITALITY

Broccoli-Potato Puree

Mashed potatoes take a colorful and nutritious twist when mixed with phytochemical- and vitamin-rich broccoli, not to mention the extra vitamin C and folate from the scallions. This recipe keeps the fat down to two tablespoons for six people by using the vegetable cooking water to help puree the potatoes (and salvage some vitamins).

6 SERVINGS

Prep 15 min ◆ **Cook** 15 min

- 1 **pound broccoli, trimmed and coarsely chopped**
- ½ **pound russet potatoes, peeled and diced**
- 4 **scallions, thinly sliced**
- 1½ **quarts water**
- 1 **teaspoon salt**
- ¼ **teaspoon black pepper**
- 2 **tablespoons butter**
- ¼ **cup fresh-squeezed lemon juice**

1 In a large pot, cook broccoli, potatoes, and scallions in 1½ quarts of simmering water until vegetables are very tender, about 15 minutes. Drain, reserving ½ cup cooking liquid.

2 Combine vegetables with reserved cooking liquid in food processor. Pulse until mixture is almost smooth. Whirl in salt, pepper, butter, and lemon juice. Serve at once.

Per serving: 92 calories, 3 g protein, 13 g carbohydrates, 4 g fat, 2 g saturated fat, 10 mg cholesterol, 3 g fiber, 508 mg sodium

HINT **helpful HINT** HINT HINT HINT HINT HINT HINT

Even though russet, or Idaho, potatoes are used mostly for baking and frying, they also make excellent mashed potatoes. Because they are drier and higher in starch than other varieties of potato, they can be whipped in a food processor without turning gummy.

FRESH IDEAS

Substitute greens such as spinach or kale for the broccoli in this recipe.

Braised Broccoli Rabe with Garlic & Parmesan

Broccoli rabe provides the same powerful nutrients as regular broccoli. Here it is prepared in the way that is most traditional in the southern part of Italy where it is native.

4 SERVINGS

Prep 10 min ◆ **Cook** 25 min

- 1 tablespoon olive oil
- 4 cloves garlic, thinly sliced
- 2 pounds broccoli rabe, tough stems removed
- 1 teaspoon salt
- ¼ teaspoon crushed red pepper flakes
- 2 cups water
- 3 tablespoons grated Parmesan cheese

1 In large nonstick skillet over medium-low heat, heat oil. Add garlic. Cook, stirring often, until softened, about 5 minutes. Do not let burn.

2 Add broccoli rabe, salt, pepper flakes, and water. Simmer, covered, 8 minutes. Uncover. Cook until tender, about 7 minutes. Drain off excess liquid, if necessary.

3 Sprinkle with Parmesan. Serve at once.

Per serving: 84 calories, 6 g protein, 8 g carbohydrates, 5 g fat, 1 g saturated fat, 3 mg cholesterol, 0 g fiber, 684 mg sodium

DID YOU KNOW ● ● ●

...that extra-virgin olive oil comes from the first cold pressing of the olives and has the least acid? It also has the best flavor, but virgin and pure olive oils, which are milder in taste and less expensive to buy, are acceptable in most recipes. Avoid olive oil labeled "pomace"; it is chemically extracted in the third pressing of the olives and doesn't have good flavor. For the same price, you are better off with a neutral oil like canola that has no taste of its own.

on the menu

Serve broccoli rabe with sweet Italian sausage, browned in a skillet with seedless grapes. Add crisp bread to soak up juices and top off the meal with a cup of lemon sorbet.

VEGETABLES FOR VITALITY

Stir-Fried Bok Choy with Sugar Snap Peas

Bok choy has more of the disease-fighting antioxidant beta-carotene than other types of cabbage. This flavorful vegetable is also low in calories, has no fat, and is a rich source of fiber and vitamin C.

4 SERVINGS

Prep 10 min ◆ **Cook** 10 min

- 2 teaspoons olive oil
- 1 carrot, cut into matchsticks
- 2 tablespoons slivered fresh ginger
- 1 pound bok choy, cut into ½-inch-wide slices
- 8 ounces sugar snap peas, trimmed
- 3 tablespoons orange juice concentrate
- 1 tablespoon light-brown sugar
- 1 tablespoon reduced-sodium soy sauce
- ½ teaspoon salt
- 1 teaspoon cornstarch blended with 1 tablespoon water

1 In large nonstick skillet over medium heat, heat ¼ cup water and oil. Add carrot and ginger, and cook, stirring frequently, until carrot is crisp-tender, about 3 minutes.

2 Add bok choy, sugar snap peas, orange juice concentrate, brown sugar, soy sauce, and salt. Cover and cook 3 minutes, or until bok choy begins to wilt.

3 Uncover and cook, stirring frequently, until bok choy is crisp-tender, about 2 minutes. Stir in cornstarch mixture and cook, stirring constantly, until vegetables are evenly coated, about 1 minute.

Per serving: 109 calories, 4 g protein, 19 g carbohydrates, 2.5 g fat, 0.5 g saturated fat, 0 mg cholesterol, 3 g fiber, 630 mg sodium

Mustard-Glazed Brussels Sprouts & New Potatoes

Cancer-fighting phytochemicals abound in this dish, even in the dressing's shallots!

4 SERVINGS

Prep 10 min ◆ **Cook** 15 min

- 10 ounces Brussels sprouts, halved if large
- 12 ounces red or white new potatoes, unpeeled and halved if large
- 1 tablespoon olive oil
- 1 tablespoon finely chopped shallots or onion
- 2 ounces lean ham or prosciutto, trimmed and diced
- 2 teaspoons Dijon mustard
- ¼ teaspoon salt
- ⅛ teaspoon black pepper

1 Steam Brussels sprouts and new potatoes until tender, 8 to 10 minutes. Drain.

2 Heat oil in large nonstick skillet over medium-high heat. Add shallots. Sauté until softened, 2 to 3 minutes. Stir in ham and mustard. Add Brussels sprouts, potatoes, salt, and pepper. Heat through, about 2 minutes. Serve at once.

Per serving: 133 calories, 7 g protein, 18 g carbohydrates, 5 g fat, 1 g saturated fat, 7 mg cholesterol, 4 g fiber, 413 mg sodium

FRESH IDEAS

When you're cooking a member of the cabbage family—and that includes Brussels sprouts, broccoli, bok choy, and cauliflower—you can always use the seasoning from one dish to flavor another. For instance, any of these vegetables can be steamed and served with the simple mustard sauce prepared for this Brussels sprouts and potato mixture.

on the menu

Mustard-Glazed Brussels Sprouts & New Potatoes is a hearty side dish for a roast turkey or duck. A mixed green salad would lighten the menu. Try fresh fruit—melon or grapes—for dessert.

on the menu

*Braised Cabbage with Apple & Caraway goes well with pork chops
or a loin roast, asparagus, mashed potatoes, and—for dessert—a lemon tart.*

Braised Cabbage with Apple & Caraway

The protective phytochemicals in cabbage are particularly effective against hormone-related diseases such as breast cancer.

6 SERVINGS

Prep 15 min ◆ **Cook** 15 min

- 2 **teaspoons vegetable oil**
- 1 **small onion, finely chopped**
- ¾ **teaspoon caraway seeds**
- 1 **pound green cabbage, cored and thinly sliced (6½ cups)**
- 1 **tablespoon rice wine vinegar or cider vinegar**
- ½ **teaspoon salt**
- 2 **small crisp red apples such as Gala, Braeburn, or Empire, cored and cut into small cubes**
- 1 **teaspoon honey**
- 2 **tablespoons chopped walnuts, toasted**
  (optional)

1 Heat oil in large nonstick skillet over medium heat. Add onion and caraway seeds. Sauté until onion is softened, about 5 minutes.

2 Stir in cabbage, vinegar, and salt. Cover. Cook just until cabbage wilts, about 4 minutes. Uncover. Increase heat to high. Add apples and honey. Cook, stirring frequently, until apples are crisp-tender and most of liquid cooks off, 4 to 6 minutes. Transfer to serving plate. Top with walnuts, if desired, and serve.

Per serving: 67 calories, 2 g protein, 13 g carbohydrates, 2 g fat, 0 g saturated fat, 0 mg cholesterol, 4 g fiber, 212 mg sodium

HINT **helpful HINT** HINT HINT HINT HINT HINT HINT

Most apples are suitable for both cooking and eating, but some varieties work better in recipes than others. Cooking apples, such as Granny Smiths and Rome Beauties, are generally firmer and tarter than eating varieties. Cooking apples can withstand longer cooking times without disintegrating. This matters when you're baking apples or using them in a pie, but it's not so important when you're adding apples to a quick sauté.

Sweet & Sour Red Cabbage

Cooked cabbage has even more cancer-fighting power than raw cabbage, because its protective phytochemicals are made more available by heating.

6 SERVINGS

Prep 5 min ◆ **Cook** 30 min

- 1 **tablespoon vegetable oil**
- 1 **medium onion, thinly sliced**
- 1 **small head red cabbage, cored and coarsely shredded (about 6 cups)**
- ½ **cup red wine**
- 4 **whole allspice**
- 2 **tablespoons red wine vinegar**
- 1 **tablespoon light-brown sugar**
- ½ **teaspoon salt**

1 Heat oil in large nonstick saucepan over medium-high heat. Add onion. Sauté until softened, about 5 minutes. Add cabbage, red wine, and allspice. Cover. Cook over medium-low heat until tender, about 20 minutes. Add vinegar, brown sugar, and salt.

2 Bring to a boil. Cook, uncovered, stirring occasionally, until almost all liquid is evaporated, about 5 minutes.

Per serving: 52 calories, 1 g protein, 7 g carbohydrates, 3 g fat, 0 g saturated fat, 0 mg cholesterol, 2 g fiber, 208 mg sodium

VEGETABLES FOR VITALITY

Chinese Cabbage with Ginger

All members of the cabbage family contain phytochemicals that help fight cancer.

4 SERVINGS

Prep 10 min ◆ **Cook** 6 min

- 1 tablespoon vegetable oil
- 1 tablespoon finely chopped, peeled fresh ginger
- 6 cups coarsely chopped Chinese (napa) cabbage or bok choy
- ¼ teaspoon salt
- ¼ cup reduced-sodium, fat-free chicken broth or vegetable broth
- 1 tablespoon chopped roasted peanuts

1 Heat large nonstick skillet or wok over high heat. Add oil and ginger. Cook 30 seconds. Add cabbage. Stir-fry 2 minutes. Add salt and broth. Cover. Cook until almost wilted, about 2 minutes.

2 Remove skillet from heat. Let stand, covered, 1 minute. Sprinkle with peanuts and serve.

Per serving: 70 calories, 2 g protein, 4 g carbohydrates, 5 g fat, 1 g saturated fat, 0 mg cholesterol, 2 g fiber, 240 mg sodium

on the menu

Carrots Parmesan are good enough for company. Serve them with a baked ham, dilled new potatoes, and strawberries and fresh pineapple for dessert.

Carrots Parmesan

In every serving, there's plenty of vitamin A, in the health-protective form of beta-carotene.

6 SERVINGS

Prep 6 min ◆ **Cook** 30 min

- 2 tablespoons olive oil
- 1 pound carrots, peeled and cut diagonally into ¼-inch-thick slices
- ¼ teaspoon salt
- ¼ teaspoon black pepper
- 2 tablespoons grated Parmesan cheese

1 In medium nonstick saucepan over medium-low heat, heat oil. Add carrots. Cover. Cook just until carrots are tender, about 15 minutes.

2 Increase heat to medium. Cook, uncovered, until carrots are lightly browned, stirring occasionally, about 15 minutes. Season with salt and pepper. Sprinkle with Parmesan just before serving.

Per serving: 82 calories, 2 g protein, 10 g carbohydrates, 5 g fat, 0 g saturated fat, 1 mg cholesterol, 3 g fiber, 177 mg sodium

HINT helpful HINT HINT HINT HINT HINT HINT HINT

One secret to successful stir-frying is to get the wok hot before adding the oil. This helps prevent the food from sticking to the side of the wok. It's a trick that also works when cooking with a cast-iron or regular metal skillet. If you have more food to stir-fry than the wok can comfortably handle, it's better to cook in batches than to crowd the pot. If there are too many vegetables in the wok, they will start to steam and lose the tender-crisp texture you expect from a stir-fry.

Braised Carrot, Celery & Fennel

Celery and fennel add unbeatable flavor to this dish; carrots, however, add the unbeatable health benefits.

4 SERVINGS

Prep 10 min ◆ **Cook** 18 min

- 4 **carrots, peeled, halved lengthwise, and cut into 2½ x ¼-inch pieces**
- 3 **celery ribs, peeled and cut into 2½ x ¼-inch pieces**
- 1 **small red onion, thinly sliced**
- ½ **fennel bulb, cored and thinly sliced**
- 1 **can (14½ ounces) reduced-sodium, fat-free chicken broth**
  Salt and pepper
- 2 **teaspoons butter**

1. In large saucepan over medium-high heat, gently simmer carrots, celery, onion, and fennel in broth, covered, until vegetables are tender, about 15 minutes.

2. Uncover saucepan. Boil until liquid reduces slightly, 2 to 3 minutes. Season to taste with salt and pepper. Stir in butter, and serve.

Per serving: 77 calories, 3 g protein, 13 g carbohydrates, 2 g fat, 1 g saturated fat, 5 mg cholesterol, 4 g fiber, 616 mg sodium

helpful HINT

Combining vegetables can make a simple side dish into something much more exciting. Just be sure that you choose vegetables that will cook in the same amount of time. Some naturally do—parsnips and carrots, for example, or zucchini and tomatoes. Others can be matched if you parboil the one that needs more cooking, such as a potato, before you combine it with a faster-cooking leek. Or if you cut the longer-cooking vegetable, such as eggplant, into smaller pieces than a faster-cooking companion like green peppers. Use seasonings that suit both too.

Roasted Carrots with Rosemary

You can't beat the flavor or the health benefits of this earthy, yet sophisticated, quick and easy side dish.

6 SERVINGS

Prep 10 min ◆ **Cook** 20 min

- 1 **pound large carrots, peeled and cut into 2 x ¼-inch sticks**
- ¼ **teaspoon salt**
- 1½ **teaspoons olive oil**
- 1 **teaspoon minced fresh rosemary leaves or ½ teaspoon dried, crumbled**

1 Preheat oven to 400°F.

2 Mound carrot sticks on baking sheet. Sprinkle with salt and drizzle with oil. Gently toss. Spread out on sheet into single layer.

3 Roast 10 minutes. Stir in rosemary. Roast until crisp-tender and lightly browned in spots, 7 to 10 minutes.

Per serving: 44 calories, 1 g protein, 8 g carbohydrates, 1 g fat, 0 g saturated fat, 0 mg cholesterol, 2 g fiber, 136 mg sodium

on the menu

The wonderful intense flavor of rosemary roasted with carrots makes this a side dish that can stand up to a special feast—a standing rib roast of beef with Yorkshire pudding, for example, or a turkey stuffed with seasoned bread cubes, sausage, and chestnuts.

VEGETABLES FOR VITALITY

Braised Baby Vegetables

Slowly braising whole baby vegetables preserves their nutrients and enriches their flavors. Reducing the cooking juices in the final stages of braising creates a healthy sauce that also makes an attractive glaze.

4 SERVINGS

Prep 15 min ◆ **Cook** 25–30 min

- 2 tablespoons butter or olive oil
- 4 baby leeks (8 ounces), trimmed, halved lengthwise and well cleaned
- 8 ounces baby parsnips, trimmed and halved lengthwise
- 8 ounces baby carrots, trimmed
- 8 pickling-type onions or shallots, trimmed and peeled
- 4 ounces vegetable broth
- 1 teaspoon sugar
- 1 bay leaf
  Pepper

1 In a large saucepan or flameproof casserole over medium heat, melt butter. Add leeks, parsnips, carrots, and onions or shallots. Stir in broth, sugar, bay leaf and pepper to taste. Bring to a boil, cover, and reduce heat to low.

2 Cook for 10 minutes or until vegetables are barely tender. Remove lid and boil liquid for 2 to 3 minutes or until bubbling and reduced to a thick syrup-like glaze. Toss the vegetables in glaze, discard bay leaf, and serve immediately.

Per serving: 180 calories, 3 g protein, 128g carbohydrates, 7 g fat, 1g saturated fat, 0 mg cholesterol, 5g fiber, 42 mg sodium

Carrot & Parsnip Puree

Two vitamin-rich vegetables in one dish means that you get twice the health benefits.

4 SERVINGS

Prep 10 min ◆ **Cook** 20 min

- 3 large carrots, peeled and chopped
- 1 large parsnip, peeled and chopped
- ½ teaspoon salt
- 1 tablespoon butter or vegetable oil
- 1 teaspoon grated orange zest

1 In medium saucepan, combine carrots, parsnip, salt, and enough water to barely cover vegetables. Simmer, uncovered, until vegetables are very tender and most of liquid has evaporated, about 20 minutes.

2 Drain vegetables. Transfer to food processor or blender. Add butter and orange zest. Process until vegetables form a smooth puree.

Per serving: 82 calories, 1 g protein, 13 g carbohydrates, 3 g fat, 2 g saturated fat, 8 mg cholesterol, 3 g fiber, 408 mg sodium

FRESH IDEAS

When baby vegetables are not available, use ordinary vegetables and cut them into chunks or large pieces. For extra flavor, add grated zest and juice of 1 orange with the broth, or stir in snipped fresh chives or chopped parsley just before serving the vegetables.

DID YOU KNOW ● ● ●

. . .that baby vegetables can either be fully ripe miniature varieties of a vegetable or immature vegetables, picked before they are fully grown? All are nutritious, and most are tender, more delicate versions of their full-size relatives. About 45 types of baby vegetables are sold in North American markets. Baby avocados from California are about 3 inches long and have no seed. Baby artichokes, available in the spring, have no chokes. One baby cauliflower is 2 inches in diameter. And baby celery, available in fall and winter, is 7 inches long and packs a tastier wallop than mature celery.

on the menu

Serve Carrot & Parsnip Puree with roast beef or grilled fish and tender-crisp asparagus or sugar snap peas.

Whole Baked Cauliflower with Yogurt-Chive Sauce

Like broccoli, cabbage, and other cruciferous vegetables, cauliflower is a power vegetable, full of cancer-fighting phytochemicals as well as lots of vitamin C and folate and plenty of vitamin B_6 and potassium.

6 SERVINGS

Prep 10 min ◆ **Cook** 35 min

- ½ cup plain low-fat yogurt
- ¼ cup loosely packed minced fresh chives
- 1½ tablespoons Dijon mustard
- 1 head cauliflower
- 2 teaspoons olive oil
- 1 large shallot, minced
- ¼ teaspoon dried oregano, crumbled
- 1¼ cups fresh bread crumbs

1 In blender or food processor, puree yogurt, chives, and mustard to make sauce. If making sauce ahead, refrigerate.

2 Preheat oven to 350°F.

3 Trim leaves from base of cauliflower. Remove hard bottom stem, keeping remaining cauliflower whole. In large pot of lightly salted boiling water, cook cauliflower, fully submerged, until barely crisp-tender, about 6 minutes. Drain. Let cool slightly.

4 Heat oil in medium nonstick skillet over medium heat. Add shallot and oregano. Sauté 2 minutes. Stir in bread crumbs, mixing well to coat with oil and seasonings. Cook, stirring, until lightly browned, about 2 minutes.

5 If necessary, slightly level top of cauliflower so it can stand inverted in small baking dish. Place cauliflower, stem end up, in dish. Fill hollow of stem with crumb mixture.

6 Bake until bread crumbs are golden and cauliflower is fork-tender, 20 to 25 minutes. Serve with sauce.

Per serving: 83 calories, 4 g protein, 12 g carbohydrates, 3 g fat, 1 g saturated fat, 1 mg cholesterol, 3 g fiber, 289 mg sodium

on the menu

A whole head of cauliflower, smothered in fresh bread crumbs, makes an impressive display on a dinner table. Serve with grilled fish or a roast of lamb, tossed green salad, and pistachio ice cream for dessert.

Baked Collard Greens with Rice & Ham

This casserole contains a wide variety of vitamins, minerals, and phytochemicals that keep your heart healthy, your bones strong, and your immune system ready and able to fight cancer and other chronic diseases.

6 SERVINGS

Prep 10 min ◆ **Cook** 50 min

- 1 tablespoon vegetable oil
- 1 small onion, cut into ½-inch pieces
- 4 cloves garlic, coarsely chopped
- ¼ pound cooked ham, cut into ¼-inch pieces
- 4 cups chopped, steamed collard greens, drained
- 2 cups cooked white rice
- 1 can (15 ounces) chopped tomatoes, drained and liquid reserved
- 1 large egg, lightly beaten
- ¾ cup grated reduced-fat cheddar cheese
- 2 tablespoons hot red pepper sauce

1 Preheat oven to 350°F. Coat 2-quart covered casserole dish with nonstick cooking spray.

2 Heat oil in medium nonstick skillet over medium heat. Add onion and garlic. Sauté until softened, about 5 minutes. Add ham and collards. Sauté 2 minutes. Transfer to large bowl.

3 Add rice, tomatoes with ¾ cup reserved juice (or enough water to make ¾ cup liquid), egg, ½ cup of the cheddar cheese, and hot sauce to collard mixture. Stir to combine. Transfer to casserole dish, spreading evenly. Top with remaining ¼ cup cheese.

4 Bake, covered, 40 minutes. Let stand 5 minutes before serving.

Per serving: 198 calories, 13 g protein, 25 g carbohydrates, 6 g fat, 2 g saturated fat, 48 mg cholesterol, 4 g fiber, 576 mg sodium

HINT **helpful HINT** HINT HINT HINT HINT HINT HINT

Cook this casserole in the winter, when fresh collards are at their sweetest. Cut off and finely chop any collard stems that are thicker than a chopstick. Start cooking the chopped stems a few minutes before the leaves and thinner stems to be sure they are equally tender.

DID YOU KNOW ● ● ●

. . . that ham can be cured by both wet and dry methods? Most grocery store ham is wet-cured, soaked in or injected with brine. Specialty ham, such as country ham, Smithfield ham, or Parma ham (prosciutto), is dry-cured with a seasoned salt mixture that permeates the meat before it is washed, dried, smoked, and aged or just dried and aged.

VEGETABLES FOR VITALITY

Irish Mashed Potatoes with Cabbage & Leeks

Ordinary mashed potatoes are made super flavorful and super nutritious with the addition of cabbage and leeks and the health-defending phytochemicals they contain.

8 SERVINGS

Prep 15 min ◆ **Cook** 25 min

- 2 **pounds Yukon Gold potatoes, unpeeled and quartered**
- 2 **cans (14½ ounces each) reduced-sodium, fat-free chicken broth, plus cold water as needed**
- 1 **pound leeks, trimmed, thinly sliced, and rinsed**
- 1 **cup low fat (1%) milk**
- 3 **cloves garlic, crushed**
- 1 **bay leaf**
- 1 **pound green cabbage, cored and thinly sliced**
- ¼ **cup cold water**
- ¼ **teaspoon ground nutmeg**
- ¼ **teaspoon salt**
- ¼ **teaspoon white pepper**
- 2 **tablespoons unsalted butter**
- ¼ **cup minced chives**

1 In large saucepan, combine potatoes, broth, and water as needed to cover potatoes with liquid. Boil potatoes until tender, 20 to 25 minutes.

2 Meanwhile, in second large saucepan, combine leeks, milk, garlic, and bay leaf. Cover. Bring to boil and simmer until leeks are softened, 15 to 20 minutes. Drain, reserving leeks, milk, and garlic separately. Discard bay leaf.

3 In same saucepan, combine cabbage and ¼ cup water. Cover. Gently boil until tender, 10 to 15 minutes. Drain. Squeeze cabbage dry. Finely chop.

4 Drain potatoes and transfer to large bowl. Add milk and garlic to potatoes. Mash. Stir in leeks, cabbage, nutmeg, salt, pepper, and butter. Top with chives.

Per serving: 168 calories, 6 g protein, 29 g carbohydrates, 4 g fat, 2 g saturated fat, 9 mg cholesterol, 3 g fiber, 379 mg sodium

HINT **helpful HINT** HINT HINT HINT HINT HINT HINT

When a recipe calls for white pepper, it may be as much for appearance as for flavor. Chefs use white pepper on pale-colored foods. A white peppercorn is a ripened black peppercorn with milder flavor.

Potato & Pumpkin Gratin

This one-pot meal provides an excellent array of nutrients from many food groups. The vegetables supply plenty of fiber and a mixture of vitamins, including vitamin C from the potatoes, tomatoes, and onion and vitamin A from the pumpkin (as beta-carotene). The cheese is, of course, an excellent source of calcium as well as protein.

4 SERVINGS

Prep 45 min ◆ **Cook** 35–40 min

- 1 pound small all-purpose potatoes, halved
- 1½ pounds pumpkin
- ½ cup apple cider
- 10 ounces vegetable broth
- 1 small sprig of fresh rosemary
- 1 large red onion, halved and thinly sliced
- 3 beefsteak tomatoes, thickly sliced
- 2 sprigs fresh oregano, stalks discarded
- 12 cups grated Parmesan cheese
- 1 cup fresh white bread crumbs
- Salt and pepper

1 Preheat the oven to 350°F. In a medium saucepan, combine potatoes and water to cover. Bring to a boil. Cook for 15 to 20 minutes or until just tender. Drain.

2 In large saucepan, combine pumpkin, cider and broth. Add rosemary. Bring to a boil, partially cover pan, and simmer 15 minutes. Add onion and continue to cook for 10 minutes. Discard rosemary and add salt and pepper to taste.

3 Slice potatoes and arrange half of them over the bottom of a 2 quart ovenproof baking dish. Lay half the tomato slices on the potatoes and scatter half the oregano leaves over. Season to taste with salt and pepper, and sprinkle with half of the cheese.

4 Spoon cooked pumpkin on top, adding all the cooking liquid. Top with remaining potatoes, tomatoes and oregano. Mix remaining cheese with bread crumbs and sprinkle over top of vegetables.

5 Bake gratin for 35 to 40 minutes or until topping is crisp and golden brown. Serve hot.

Per serving: 480 calories, 30 g protein, 53 g carbohydrates, 18 g fat, 11 g saturated fat, 45 mg cholesterol, 6 g fiber, 370 mg sodium

FRESH IDEAS

Substitute 8 ounces mushrooms for the pumpkin, and omit the cider, broth, rosemary and onion. Halve or slice the mushrooms and mix them with 1 small bunch of scallions, chopped, then layer them in the gratin instead of the cooked pumpkin mixture. Increase baking time to 45–50 minutes. The mushrooms give up their liquid during baking to moisten the gratin slightly.

on the menu

Baked Sweet Potato "Fries" go especially well with veggie burgers or pork
entrées, including ham and sausages as well as chops and roasts.

Baked Sweet Potato "Fries"

Baked "fries" are the way to go when you're cutting back on fat. These baked sweet potato sticks are so flavorful, you'll never know the difference.

4 SERVINGS

Prep 7 min ◆ **Cook** 20 min

- 1 pound sweet potatoes, peeled and cut into ½-inch-thick "fries"
- 1 tablespoon vegetable oil
- ¼ teaspoon salt
- ¼ teaspoon black pepper

1 Preheat oven to 425°F. Lightly coat baking sheet with nonstick cooking spray.

2 In large bowl, combine sweet potatoes, oil, salt, and pepper. Toss to coat. Spread fries in single layer on baking sheet.

3 Bake 10 minutes. Turn fries over. Continue baking until tender and lightly browned, about 10 minutes longer.

Per serving: 102 calories, 1 g protein, 17 g carbohydrates, 4 g fat, 0 g saturated fat, 0 mg cholesterol, 2 g fiber, 152 mg sodium

---

HINT **helpful HINT** HINT HINT HINT HINT HINT HINT

Pure maple syrup has a smoother, more subtle flavor than imitation syrups, and is actually less sweet. You don't need the most expensive "fancy" or "light amber" grade of maple syrup, which is used in candy making. "Medium amber" is the best grade for table use. Cheap maple-flavored syrups are usually made from corn syrup, flavored with a little pure maple syrup; they are simply not as good as the real thing. If you heat maple syrup, it will go further. Keep open containers in the refrigerator.

Mashed Sweet Potatoes with Cinnamon & Maple Syrup

This subtly spiced side dish is a phenomenal source of beta-carotene, which helps lower the risk of heart disease, stroke, and cancer.

6 SERVINGS

Prep 10 min ◆ **Cook** 20 min

- 2 pounds sweet potatoes, peeled and chopped
- ½ teaspoon salt
- 1 cinnamon stick
- 2 tablespoons maple syrup
- 1½ tablespoons butter or vegetable oil

1 In medium saucepan, combine sweet potatoes, salt, cinnamon stick, and just enough water to cover potatoes. Boil, uncovered, stirring occasionally, until potatoes are tender, about 20 minutes. Drain. Discard cinnamon stick.

2 Transfer potatoes back to saucepan. Add 1½ tablespoons of the maple syrup and butter. Mash. Serve, drizzled with remaining maple syrup.

Per serving: 166 calories, 2 g protein, 33 g carbohydrates, 3 g fat, 2 g saturated fat, 8 mg cholesterol, 2 g fiber, 210 mg sodium

VEGETABLES FOR VITALITY

Ginger Candied Yams

There's twice the daily requirement for vitamin A in a single serving of this sweetly spiced dish.

4 SERVINGS

Prep 10 min ◆ **Cook** 25 min

- 2 tablespoons honey
- 1½ tablespoons vegetable oil
- 1 pound yams or sweet potatoes, peeled and cut into 1-inch pieces
- ½ teaspoon grated lemon zest
- ½ teaspoon grated, peeled fresh ginger
- ¼ teaspoon salt

1 In medium nonstick saucepan over medium heat, heat honey and oil until bubbling, about 1 minute. Add sweet potatoes. Cover. Cook over low heat until sweet potatoes begin to give off liquid, about 5 minutes. Add zest and ginger. Cook, covered, just until potatoes are tender, 10 to 15 minutes longer. Do not overcook.

2 Uncover saucepan. Add salt. Boil over medium-high heat until thickly glazed, about 5 minutes.

Per serving: 172 calories, 2 g protein, 30 g carbohydrates, 6 g fat, 0 g saturated fat, 0 mg cholesterol, 2 g fiber, 157 mg sodium

Twice-Baked Stuffed Sweet Potatoes

Use a half-and-half combination of butter and oil to maintain rich flavor while cutting back on the saturated fat that could hurt your heart.

4 SERVINGS

Prep 10 min ◆ **Cook** 1hr 10 min

- 2 large sweet potatoes (1½ pounds total)
- 1 can (8 ounces) crushed pineapple, drained
- 1 tablespoon vegetable oil
- 1 tablespoon butter
- 1 tablespoon light- or dark-brown sugar
- 1 teaspoon grated orange zest
- ½ teaspoon salt
- 2 tablespoons chopped pecans

1 Preheat oven to 350°F. Pierce each sweet potato twice with tip of knife.

2 Bake until soft, about 50 minutes. Set aside until cool enough to handle but still very warm. Reduce oven heat to 325°F.

3 Cut potatoes in half lengthwise. Scoop out flesh and place in medium bowl, being careful not to tear skin. Reserve skins. Add pineapple, oil, butter, sugar, zest, and salt to potato flesh. Whip with electric mixer or whisk until slightly fluffy.

4 Place skin shells on baking sheet. Fill with potato mixture, mounding each. Bake 15 minutes. Sprinkle with pecans. Bake 5 minutes longer.

Per serving: 236 calories, 2 g protein, 38 g carbohydrates, 9 g fat, 2 g saturated fat, 8 mg cholesterol, 4 g fiber, 303 mg sodium

HINT **helpful HINT** HINT HINT HINT HINT HINT HINT

Twice-Baked Stuffed Sweet Potatoes can be made up to a day ahead of time. Bake and stuff the potatoes as directed in the recipe through step 3. Place in a shallow dish, cover loosely and refrigerate. Remove from refrigerator 30 minutes before baking as directed in the recipe.

on the menu

*Spinach has a natural affinity for the flavor of sesame. This simple side dish
gets a double dose of sesame from lightly toasted seeds and intensely
flavored oil.*

Steamed Sesame Spinach

This simple side dish contains powerful phytochemicals that help keep your eyes healthy.

4 SERVINGS

Prep 10 min ◆ **Cook** 5 min

1 **pound spinach, stems removed**
⅛ **teaspoon red pepper flakes**
½ **teaspoon dark sesame oil**
1 **teaspoon salt**
1 **teaspoon fresh-squeezed lemon juice**
1 **tablespoon sesame seeds, toasted**

1 In medium saucepan, steam spinach with pepper flakes until tender, 3 to 5 minutes. Transfer to serving bowl.

2 Add sesame oil, salt, and lemon juice to spinach. Toss to mix. Sprinkle with sesame seeds. Serve at once.

Per serving: 38 calories, 3 g protein, 4 g carbohydrates, 2 g fat, 0 g saturated fat, 0 mg cholesterol, 3 g fiber, 643 mg sodium

HINT **helpful HINT** HINT HINT HINT HINT HINT HINT

When you're planning vegetable side dishes for a meal, consider both the style and flavor of the main dish, and the nutritional balance of the meal as a whole. Stick to a single type of cuisine, such as Mediterranean or Asian, unless you're familiar with the flavors of all the recipes you're using. Choose side dishes that are varied in color and texture. If one side dish features a green vegetable, complement it with other dishes that include orange, red, yellow or white vegetables. If one dish is soft and smooth, pick another that is crisp or crunchy. A little forethought helps to ensure a pleasant, satisfying, and well-rounded meal.

Roasted Tomatoes with Garlic & Herbs

Even in winter, when plum tomatoes are not at their best, these taste like a burst of summer. Slow-roasting fresh tomatoes in olive oil concentrates the cancer-fighting phytochemical lycopene and makes it more available to the body.

4 SERVINGS

Prep 10 min ◆ **Cook** 3 hrs

3 **pounds plum tomatoes, halved lengthwise**
2 **tablespoons olive oil**
5 **cloves garlic, finely chopped**
½ **cup finely chopped fresh basil**
2 **tablespoons minced fresh rosemary**
1 **teaspoon sugar**
l **teaspoon salt**

1 Preheat the oven to 250°F. Line a jelly-roll pan with foil.

2 In a large bowl, toss tomatoes with oil, garlic, basil, rosemary, sugar, and salt. Place tomatoes, cut side up, in prepared pan. Bake 3 hours, or until the tomatoes have collapsed and their skins have wrinkled.

3 Serve at room temperature or refrigerate and serve chilled.

Per serving: 148 calories, 4 g protein, 19 g carbohydrates, 8 g fat, 13 g saturated fat, 0 mg cholesterol, 5.4 g fiber, 468 mg sodium

HINT **helpful HINT** HINT HINT HINT HINT HINT HINT

Once baked, roasted tomatoes will keep for several days in the refrigerator. Eat them as is or use them in pasta sauces and salads.

Zucchini with Parsley, Garlic & Lemon

You'll get a hefty helping of vitamin C in every serving of this simple, tasty side dish.

4 SERVINGS

Prep 5 min ◆ **Cook** 8 min

2 teaspoons olive oil
1¼ pounds zucchini, halved lengthwise and cut crosswise into ½-inch-thick half-moons
1 tablespoon minced garlic
¼ teaspoon salt
2 tablespoons chopped parsley
2 teaspoons fresh-squeezed lemon juice

1 In large nonstick skillet over medium-high heat, heat oil. Add zucchini. Sauté 3 minutes. Add garlic. Sauté until zucchini is crisp-tender, 3 to 5 minutes.

2 Remove skillet from heat. Stir in salt, parsley, and lemon juice. Serve warm or at room temperature.

Per serving: 44 calories, 2 g protein, 5 g carbohydrates, 3 g fat, 0 g saturated fat, 0 mg cholesterol, 2 g fiber, 151 mg sodium

Grilled Zucchini, Peppers, Mushrooms & Onions with Balsamic Glaze

Boost your supply of vitamin C and B with this Mediterranean-style combination of veggies.

4 SERVINGS

Prep 10 min ◆ **Cook** 14 min

1 large red bell pepper, seeded and cut in 1-inch-wide strips
1 medium zucchini, cut into ½-inch-thick slices
1 medium red onion, cut into ½-inch-thick slices
2 medium portobello mushrooms, stems removed and caps cut into ¾-inch-wide strips
2 tablespoons extra-virgin olive oil
1 teaspoon dried oregano, crumbled
1 tablespoon balsamic vinegar
¼ teaspoon salt
¼ teaspoon black pepper

1 Preheat grill or broiler. Lightly coat grill or broiler-pan rack with nonstick cooking spray.

2 In large bowl combine bell pepper, zucchini, onion, and mushrooms. Sprinkle with oil and oregano. Toss to coat. Arrange vegetables in single layer on rack.

3 Grill or broil about 2 inches from heat until vegetables are just crisp-tender and lightly flecked with brown, 6 to 8 minutes. Turn over and cook on other side until done, about 4 to 6 minutes.

4 Arrange vegetables on platter. In small bowl, stir together balsamic vinegar, salt, and pepper. Brush over vegetables. Serve warm or at room temperature.

Per serving: 101 calories, 2 g protein, 8 g carbohydrates, 7 g fat, 1 g saturated fat, 0 mg cholesterol, 3 g fiber, 152 mg sodium

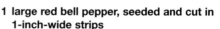

HINT **helpful HINT** HINT HINT HINT HINT HINT HINT HINT

Be sure to cut any vegetables you plan to grill into pieces that are consistent in size and no more than an inch thick, so they will all cook quickly and evenly. Soak the vegetable pieces in cold water for 15 to 30 minutes before brushing with oil and grilling to keep them from drying out.

on the menu

Grilled vegetables team up well with grilled bluefish, tuna, or sea bass. Grilling intensifies all the flavors. Finish the meal with country bread and a fresh-baked blueberry cobbler topped with vanilla ice cream.

Spring Vegetable Sauté with Tarragon

This dish features vitamin-rich asparagus, yellow squash, and snow peas, vegetables that are at their most flavorful and nutritious when they first arrive on the market in early spring. In fact, snow peas are so named because they are harvested in early spring, often while there is still some snow left on the ground.

4 SERVINGS

Prep 15 min ◆ **Cook** 4 min

- **1 tablespoon butter**
- **1 tablespoon vegetable oil**
- **1 bunch scallions, cut into 2-inch lengths**
- **1 medium yellow summer squash, unpeeled and cut into ¼-thick slices**
- **4 ounces snow peas, blanched**
- **1 small bunch asparagus, trimmed, cut into 4-inch pieces, and blanched**
- **½ teaspoon salt**
- **¼ teaspoon black pepper**
- **1 teaspoon chopped fresh tarragon or ½ teaspoon dried tarragon, crumbled**

1 In large nonstick skillet over medium-high heat, heat butter and oil. Add scallions and squash. Sauté 1 minute.

2 Add snow peas, asparagus, salt, and pepper. Cover. Cook until vegetables are heated through, about 2 minutes. Stir in tarragon. Serve at once.

Per serving: 96 calories, 3 g protein, 8 g carbohydrates, 7 g fat, 2 g saturated fat, 8 mg cholesterol, 3 g fiber, 310 mg sodium

FRESH IDEAS

This fresh vegetable mélange makes a great pasta topper. Double the amounts of oil and butter called for (so there's enough to coat pasta) and cut the vegetables in smaller pieces. Proceed as directed in the recipe, tossing vegetables with hot cooked spaghetti, thin linguine, or fusilli before serving.

on the menu

For a light and simple springtime meal, serve a spring vegetable sauté over rice seasoned with lemon zest, and warm slices of lean ham on the side.

Mixed Asian-Style Vegetables with Oyster Sauce, Garlic & Ginger

Side dishes that feature a wide variety of vegetables also feature a wide variety of essential nutrients and protective antioxidants. A seasoning mix of soy sauce, oyster sauce, lime juice, garlic, ginger, and fresh basil brings a taste of Thailand to this winning combination.

8 SERVINGS

Prep 20 min ◆ **Cook** 6 min

- 1 tablespoon reduced-sodium soy sauce
- 1 tablespoon oyster sauce
- 2 tablespoons fresh-squeezed lime juice
- 1 tablespoon sugar
- 2 tablespoons vegetable oil
- 4 cloves garlic, minced
- 2 serrano chiles or jalapeño chiles, seeded and thinly sliced diagonally
- 3 scallions, thinly sliced
- 1 red bell pepper, seeded and cut into ¼-inch pieces
- ¼ pound snow peas
- 1 Japanese eggplant, cut into ¼-inch cubes
- ¼ pound mushrooms, stems removed and caps cut into wedges
- 1 tablespoon finely chopped, peeled fresh ginger
- 3 small heads baby bok choy, cored and thinly sliced
- ½ cup loosely packed basil leaves, cut into thin shreds

1 In small bowl, stir together soy sauce, oyster sauce, lime juice, and sugar.

2 In large nonstick skillet or wok over medium-high heat, heat oil. Add garlic and chiles. Stir-fry 30 seconds. Add scallions, bell pepper, snow peas, eggplant, mushrooms, and ginger. Stir-fry 2 minutes. Add bok choy. Stir-fry until wilted, about 1 minute. Add soy sauce mixture. Stir-fry until all vegetables are crisp-tender, about 1 minute. Stir in basil and serve at once.

Per serving: 78 calories, 3 g protein, 9 g carbohydrates, 4 g fat, 0 g saturated fat, 0 mg cholesterol, 4 g fiber, 128 mg sodium

DID YOU KNOW ● ● ●

...that Asian oyster sauce, which is made from boiled oysters, doesn't have a fishy flavor? There are, however, many vegetarian brands on the market that are made from mushrooms and can be used with equal success.

Bulgur with Spring Vegetables

The nutlike taste of bulgur is a perfect foil for early-season vegetables. Bulgur provides a number of heart-nourishing compounds, including complex carbohydrates, protein, niacin, insoluble fiber, phytoestrogens, and vitamin E, all of which work to keep your cardiovascular system healthy.

6 SERVINGS

Prep 45 min ◆ **Cook** 10 min

- 1¼ **cups bulgur**
- 3½ **cups boiling water**
- 2 **tablespoons olive oil**
- 3 **tablespoons fresh lemon juice**
- I **teaspoon salt**
- ½ **teaspoon pepper**
- 2 **leeks, halved lengthwise, cut crosswise into 1-inch pieces, and well washed**
- 2 **cloves garlic, minced**
- 12 **asparagus spears, cut into 2-inch lengths**
- 1 **cup frozen peas**
- ¼ **cup chopped fresh mint**

1 In large heatproof bowl combine bulgur and boiling water. Let stand until bulgur is tender, about 30 minutes; stir after 15 minutes. Drain bulgur in large fine-meshed sieve to get rid of any remaining liquid.

2 In large bowl whisk together 1 tablespoon of oil, the lemon juice, salt, and pepper. Add drained bulgur and fluff with a fork.

3 In medium skillet over low heat, heat remaining 1 tablespoon oil. Add leeks and garlic to skillet and cook until leeks are tender, about 5 minutes. Transfer to bowl with bulgur.

4 In steamer set over a pan of boiling water, steam asparagus until tender, about 4 minutes. Add peas during final 30 seconds of steaming. Add vegetables to bowl of bulgur along with mint and toss to combine. Serve at room temperature or chilled.

Per serving: 188 calories, 6 g protein, 32 g carbohydrates, 5 g fat, 0.5 g saturated fat, 0 mg cholesterol, 8 g fiber, 330 mg sodium

on the menu

Serve this hearty side dish with lean sliced beef and roasted red peppers. Offer fresh figs for dessert.

Roasted Harvest Vegetables

This winter vegetable combination is rich in fiber, potassium, and beta-carotene.

4 SERVINGS

Prep 20 min ◆ **Cook** 45 min

- 3 **tablespoons olive oil**
- 6 **cloves garlic, thinly sliced**
- 3 **cups butternut squash chunks (1-inch)**
- 10 **ounces Brussels sprouts, trimmed and halved lengthwise**
- 8 **ounces fresh shiitake mushrooms, stems discarded and caps thickly sliced**
- 2 **large red apples, unpeeled, cut into 1-inch chunks**
- ¼ **cup oil-packed sun-dried tomatoes, drained and thinly sliced**
- 1 **teaspoon dried rosemary, minced**
- ½ **teaspoon salt**
- ¼ **cup grated Parmesan cheese**

1 Preheat oven to 400°F. In large roasting pan, combine olive oil and garlic. Heat 3 minutes in the oven. Add squash, Brussels sprouts, mushrooms, apples, sun-dried tomatoes, rosemary, and salt; toss to combine.

2 Roast 35 minutes, or until vegetables are tender, tossing vegetables every 10 minutes. Sprinkle Parmesan over vegetables, and roast 5 minutes longer.

Per serving: 292 calories, 8 g protein, 39 g carbohydrates, 14 g fat, 17 g saturated fat, 4 mg cholesterol, 9.3 g fiber, 464 mg sodium

VEGETABLES FOR VITALITY

Mediterranean Rice with Green Peas & Sun-Dried Tomatoes

Combining rice and peas helps boost the muscle-building protein in any meal.

6 SERVINGS

Prep 15 min ◆ **Cook** 20 min

- 1 can (14½ ounces) reduced-sodium, fat-free chicken broth
- 1½ cups fresh sweet peas or 1 package (10 ounces) frozen peas
- ½ cup sun-dried tomatoes, thinly sliced
- ¼ teaspoon salt
- 1 cup long-grain white rice

1 In medium saucepan over high heat, bring broth to a boil. Add peas, tomatoes, and salt. Bring back to a boil. Add rice and stir. Cover. Lower heat to bare simmer. Cook just until liquid is absorbed and rice is tender, about 15 minutes.

2 Remove saucepan from heat. Let stand 10 minutes. Uncover. Fluff with fork.

Per serving: 175 calories, 7 g protein, 36 g carbohydrates, 0 g fat, 0 g saturated fat, 0 mg cholesterol, 3 g fiber, 437 mg sodium

White Beans Stewed with Swiss Chard

Beans protect your heart with soluble fiber that helps lower cholesterol.

8 SERVINGS

Prep 10 min ◆ **Cook** 25 min

- 1 small bunch Swiss chard (about ½ pound)
- 2 tablespoons olive oil
- 1 small onion, finely chopped
- 1 carrot, peeled and finely chopped
- 1 teaspoon dried oregano, crumbled
- 1 bay leaf
- 2 cloves garlic, minced
- 1 cup reduced-sodium, fat-free chicken broth
- 2 cans (19½ ounces each) cannellini beans, drained and rinsed
- ½ teaspoon salt
- ⅛ teaspoon black pepper
- ½ cup grated Parmesan cheese

1 Remove tough stems from chard and finely chop. Coarsely chop leaves.

2 Heat oil in large nonstick skillet over medium heat. Add onion, carrot, oregano, and bay leaf. Sauté until onion and carrot are very soft, about 8 minutes. Add garlic. Sauté 30 seconds.

3 Add chard and broth to skillet. Cook, stirring occasionally, until chard just begins to wilt, about 2 minutes. Stir in beans. Simmer, covered, 10 minutes. Uncover and cook until chard is tender, 5 minutes. Season with salt and pepper. Remove bay leaf. Sprinkle with cheese and serve.

Per serving: 139 calories, 7 g protein, 16 g carbohydrates, 5 g fat, 1 g saturated fat, 4 mg cholesterol, 5 g fiber, 482 mg sodium

FRESH IDEAS

If you want to substitute another green for Swiss chard, try spinach or beet greens, which are both as mild as Swiss chard. Instead of cannellini beans, try chickpeas or pink beans. You can also experiment with the herbs you use—try thyme and parsley or chervil.

on the menu

This hearty side dish becomes a main dish when you add chopped cooked ham, chicken, turkey, pork, or scrambled egg to the mix.

Vegetable Fried Rice

Carrots, peppers, cabbage, and mushrooms join forces to help provide a balanced blend of vitamins and minerals that can only be found in a combination dish like this one, which features a variety of power vegetables.

6 SERVINGS

Prep 20 min ◆ **Cook** 20 min

- ¼ **cup reduced-sodium, fat-free chicken broth or vegetable broth**
- 2½ **tablespoons soy sauce**
- 1½ **teaspoons dark sesame oil**
- 1½ **tablespoons vegetable oil**
- 2 **carrots, peeled and cut into matchstick pieces**
- 1 **red bell pepper, seeded and coarsely chopped**
- 4 **scallions, thinly sliced (darker green tops reserved for garnish)**
- 2 **tablespoons finely chopped, peeled fresh ginger**
- 1 **cup quartered white, cremini, or shiitake mushrooms**
- 2 **cloves garlic, minced**
- 2 **cups sliced napa cabbage**
- ¼ **teaspoon salt**
- 3 **cups cooked long-grain white rice, chilled**

1 In small bowl, whisk together broth, soy sauce, and sesame oil.

2 In large, deep nonstick skillet or wok over medium-high heat, heat vegetable oil. Add carrots, bell pepper, white and pale green parts of scallions, and ginger. Cook until crisp-tender, stirring once, about 5 minutes.

3 Add mushrooms and garlic. Cook, stirring occasionally, 5 minutes. Add cabbage and salt. Cook, stirring, just until cabbage is slightly wilted, about 3 minutes. Stir in rice and soy sauce mixture. Cook, stirring occasionally, until rice is heated through, about 3 minutes. Slice darker green scallion tops. Sprinkle over rice before serving.

Per serving: 178 calories, 4 g protein, 29 g carbohydrates, 5 g fat, 1 g saturated fat, 0 mg cholesterol, 2 g fiber, 542 mg sodium

Basmati Rice with Kale & Butternut Squash

When it comes to vegetables that are high in fiber and antioxidant power, you just can't beat butternut squash.

6 SERVINGS

Prep 15 min ◆ **Cook** 16 min

- ½ **cup basmati rice**
- 1 **tablespoon curry powder**
- 1 **pound kale, tough stems removed and kale blanched**
- ½ **pound butternut squash, seeded, peeled, and cut in ¾-inch pieces**
- ¼ **cup raisins**
- 1 **cup reduced-fat coconut milk**
- ¾ **cup water**
- 1 **teaspoon salt**

1 Heat 12-inch nonstick skillet over medium-low heat. Add rice. Toast, stirring frequently, until lightly browned, about 3 minutes. Add curry powder. Cook, stirring, 1 minute.

2 Add kale, squash, raisins, coconut milk, water, and salt to skillet. Cover and simmer until liquid is absorbed and rice and squash are tender, about 12 minutes. Remove from heat. Let stand, covered, 5 minutes.

Per serving: 143 calories, 4 g protein, 29 g carbohydrates, 3 g fat, 1 g saturated fat, 0 mg cholesterol, 3 g fiber, 420 mg sodium

VEGETABLES FOR VITALITY

Tomato Chutney

Cooked tomatoes are one of the best sources of lycopene, a cancer-fighting phytochemical that is released when the food containing it is heated.

3 CUPS

Prep 20 min ◆ Cook 25 min

- 1¾ pounds plum tomatoes, seeded and coarsely chopped
- 2 celery stalks, coarsely chopped
- 1 red onion, coarsely chopped
- ½ cup golden raisins
- ⅓ cup packed light-brown sugar
- ⅓ cup cider vinegar
- 2 tablespoons finely chopped, peeled fresh ginger
- 2 tablespoons chopped, bottled pickled jalapeño chiles
- ¼ teaspoon ground allspice
- ¼ teaspoon salt
- 14 grape or small cherry tomatoes, each quartered

1 In large nonreactive saucepan, combine plum tomatoes, celery, onion, raisins, brown sugar, vinegar, ginger, chiles, allspice, and salt. Bring to a boil and then simmer, uncovered, stirring occasionally, until ingredients are tender and most of liquid has evaporated, 20 to 25 minutes.

2 Remove saucepan from heat. Stir in grape tomatoes. Let cool to room temperature. Place in storage dish, cover, and refrigerate at least 24 hours or up to one week.

Per 1/4 cup: 70 calories, 1 g protein, 17 g carbohydrates, 0 g fat, 0 g saturated fat, 0 mg cholesterol, 2 g fiber, 79 mg sodium

Pumpkin Pickles

Like sweet potatoes and most winter squash, pumpkin is loaded with beta-carotene, an antioxidant that protects against all types of chronic disease. Ginger, cinnamon, and peppercorns add sweet-and-spicy flavor and health protective phytochemicals of their own.

6 TO 8 HALF-PINTS

Prep 25 min ◆ Cook 20 min

- 1 lemon
- 5 cups sugar
- 3 cups cider vinegar
- ¼ cup finely chopped, peeled fresh ginger
- 2 cinnamon sticks
- 20 black peppercorns
- 1 tablespoon salt
- 1 sugar pumpkin (3 to 4 pounds), seeded, peeled, and cut into 1½ x ¾ x ¾-inch pieces

1 Using vegetable peeler, remove strips of zest from lemon. In large nonreactive saucepan, combine zest, sugar, vinegar, ginger, cinnamon, peppercorns, and salt. Simmer, stirring to dissolve sugar, 5 minutes. Add pumpkin. Simmer, stirring occasionally, until pumpkin is crisp-tender, about 15 minutes.

2 With slotted spoon, transfer pumpkin pickles to sterilized canning jars (you will need about 8 half-pint jars or 4 one-pint jars). Pour in cooking liquid to within ¼ inch of top of each jar. Seal. Refrigerate and use within one week, or sterilize jars following canning jar manufacturer's instructions for longer storage.

Per 1/2 cup: 30 calories, 1 g protein, 8 g carbohydrates, 0 g fat, 0 g saturated fat, 0 mg cholesterol, 1 g fiber, 208 mg sodium

FRESH IDEAS

There are many different types of chutney, but they all generally feature a single vegetable or fruit simmered in a spicy blend of seasonings. In this recipe, you could substitute two cups of cut-up unripe (hard) mango for the plum tomatoes. For mango chutney, omit the celery and grape tomatoes but otherwise follow the recipe as directed. Serve chutney with grilled meats, grains, rice, potatoes, and curry dishes. It is also a wonderful appetizer, served with cream cheese on crackers or wedges of toasted pita bread.

on the menu

This unusual condiment is a perfect side dish to serve at fall and winter dinners,
and it also makes an unusual and thoughtful hostess gift.

VEGETABLES FOR VITALITY

Sweet Corn & Bell Pepper Relish

Combine the convenience of canned corn and the fresh taste of sweet yellow and orange peppers for a fast-to-fix, flavorful side dish that's as nutritious as it is colorful. Canned corn contains ferulic acid, an antioxidant that destroys naturally occurring toxins in the body.

6 SERVINGS

Prep 10 min ◆ **Cook** 5 min

1½ **cup white vinegar**
¼ **cup sugar**
¾ **teaspoon dry mustard**
¼ **teaspoon salt**
2 **scallions, thinly sliced**
½ **small orange bell pepper, seeded and diced**
½ **small yellow bell pepper, seeded and diced**
1 **can (15 ounces) corn kernels, drained**

1 In small nonreactive saucepan, combine vinegar, sugar, dry mustard, and salt. Simmer 5 minutes. Remove from heat.

2 Stir in scallions, bell peppers and corn. Let cool. Refrigerate in covered container up to 1 week. Serve chilled or at room temperature.

Per Serving: 70 calories, 1 g protein, 16 g carbohydrates, 0 g fat, 0 g saturated fat, 0 mg cholesterol, 1 g fiber, 236 mg sodium

FRESH IDEAS

To spice up this relish, add a tablespoon or two of finely chopped jalapeño or other chile pepper.

on the menu

Since fresh corn is a summer vegetable, corn relishes are most often made for summer barbecues and picnics. But when you use canned or frozen corn kernels, the relish becomes a side dish you can serve year round with roasted meats, poultry and seafood.

SIDE-DISH
salads

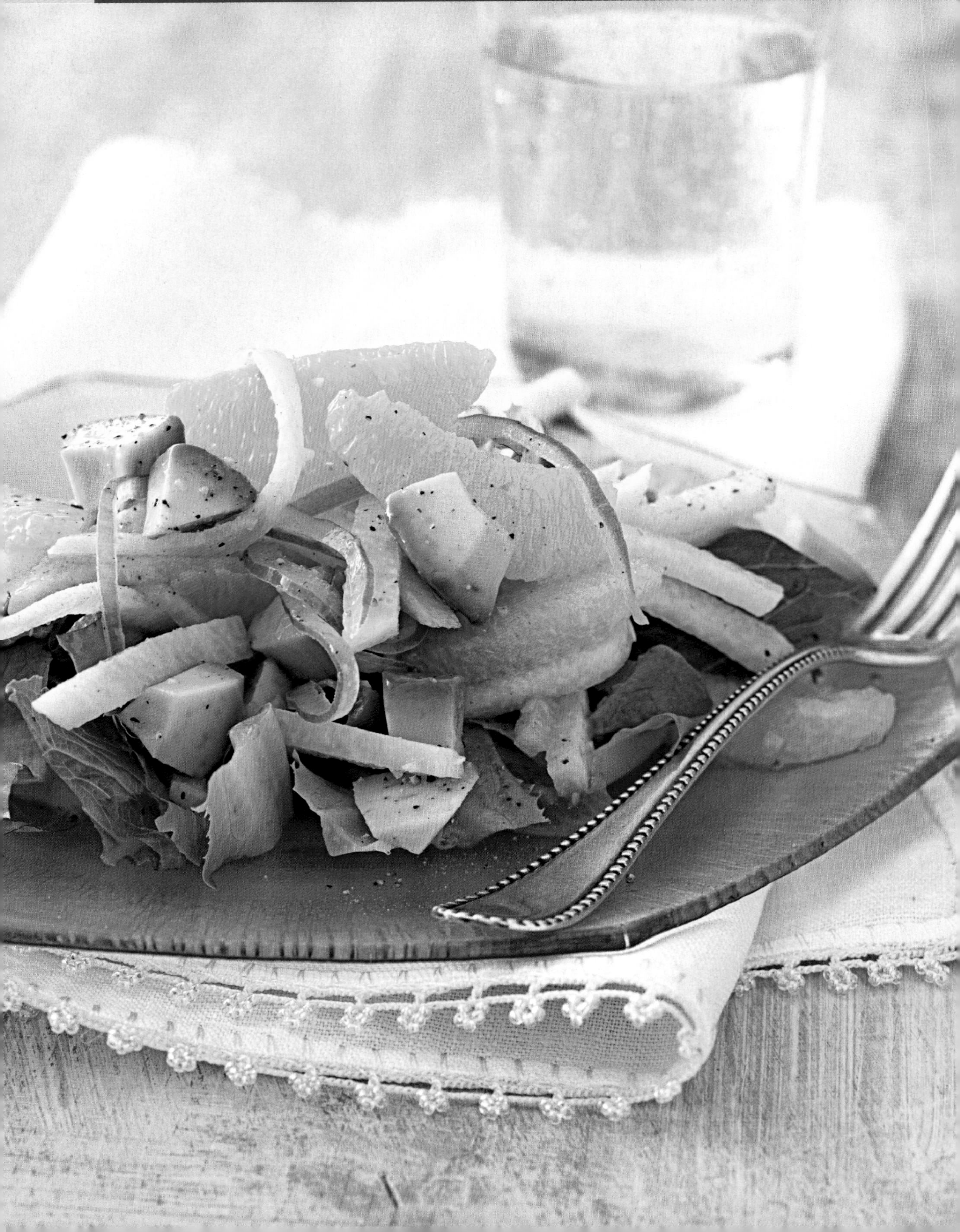

Avocado, Jicama & Orange Salad

A true health salad, this sweet and tangy Southwestern-style mix supplies all the antioxidant vitamins that protect your health, with a high dose of fiber for good measure.

6 SERVINGS

Prep 10 min ◆ **Refrigerate** 15 min

- 3 tablespoons olive oil
- 1 tablespoon fresh-squeezed lime juice
- 1 clove garlic, minced
- 1½ teaspoons white-wine vinegar
- ¼ teaspoon ground cumin
- ⅛ teaspoon salt
  - Pinch chili powder
- 8 ounces jicama, peeled and cut into 3 x ¼-inch strips
- 2 oranges, peeled and cut into sections
- 1 avocado, pitted, peeled, and cut into chunks
- ½ small red onion, thinly sliced crosswise
- 8 cups torn romaine lettuce

1 In small bowl, whisk together oil, lime juice, garlic, vinegar, cumin, salt and chili powder to make vinaigrette. In large bowl toss together jicama, oranges, avocado, onion, and vinaigrette. Refrigerate 15 minutes.

2 Serve salad on bed of romaine leaves.

Per serving: 156 calories, 3 g protein, 14 g carbohydrates, 12 g fat, 2 g saturated fat, 0 mg cholesterol, 7 g fiber, 57 mg sodium

helpful HINT

All the different ingredients for making Broccoli & Orange Salad, including the dressing, can be prepared several hours ahead and refrigerated separately. To serve, let come to room temperature, then assemble.

Broccoli & Orange Salad

Sulforaphane, the cancer-fighting substance that put broccoli on the phytochemical map, is most concentrated in the plant's florets.

4 SERVINGS

Prep 15 min ◆ **Cook** 3 min

- 1 small head broccoli, stalks removed for other use and head separated into small florets
- 2 tablespoons orange juice
- 2 teaspoons honey
- 2 teaspoons soy sauce
- 1 teaspoon cider vinegar
- 2 tablespoons vegetable oil
- 1 tablespoon chopped cilantro
- 1 orange, peeled, cut into ¼-inch-thick slices, slices halved and seeded
- ½ small red onion, cut crosswise into thin slices and separated
- 2 whole canned water chestnuts, thinly sliced
- ¼ teaspoon black pepper

1 In large pot of lightly salted water, cook broccoli florets until crisp-tender, 3 minutes. Drain in colander. Rinse under cold running water.

2 In small bowl, whisk together orange juice, honey, soy sauce, and vinegar. Whisk in oil. Stir in cilantro to complete vinaigrette.

3 In large bowl toss broccoli, orange, and vinaigrette. Arrange on plates. Top with onion and water chestnuts. Sprinkle with pepper.

Per serving: 119 calories, 3 g protein, 13 g carbohydrates, 7 g fat, 1 g saturated fat, 0 mg cholesterol, 3 g fiber, 174 mg sodium

VEGETABLES FOR VITALITY

Endive, Apple & Watercress Salad with Almonds

Watercress and endive are super sources of beta-carotene.

6 SERVINGS

Prep 10 min

- ⅓ cup plain low-fat yogurt
- 1 tablespoon reduced-fat mayonnaise
- 2 teaspoons honey
- 1 teaspoon Dijon mustard
- ¼ teaspoon curry powder
- ⅛ teaspoon ground ginger
- 1 bunch watercress, tough stems removed
- 1 large endive, halved lengthwise and cut crosswise into ½-inch-thick slices
- 1 McIntosh apple, halved, cored, and thinly sliced
- 2 tablespoons sliced or slivered almonds, toasted

In small bowl, whisk together yogurt, mayonnaise, honey, mustard, curry powder, and ginger to make dressing. In large bowl toss together watercress, endive, apple, and dressing. Top with almonds.

Per serving: 54 calories, 2 g protein, 8 g carbohydrates, 2 g fat, 0 g saturated fat, 2 mg cholesterol, 1 g fiber, 62 mg sodium

Cucumber, Radish & Snow Pea Salad

Snow peas and radishes are great sources of folate and vitamin C, nutrients that work together to protect the health of your heart.

4 SERVINGS

Prep 10 minutes

- 6 ounces snow peas, trimmed
- 1 tablespoon rice vinegar
- 2 teaspoons sugar
- 2 teaspoons soy sauce
- 1 teaspoon dark sesame oil
- ⅛ teaspoon salt
- 2 cucumbers, scored and thinly sliced
- 2 bunches radishes, thinly sliced
- 1 tablespoon sesame seeds, toasted *(optional)*

1 In saucepan of lightly salted boiling water, cook snow peas until crisp-tender, 2 to 3 minutes. Drain. Rinse under cold running water.

2 In small bowl, whisk together vinegar, sugar, soy sauce, sesame oil, and salt until sugar and salt are dissolved to make vinaigrette.

3 In large bowl, toss together snow peas, cucumbers, radishes, and vinaigrette. Sprinkle with sesame seeds, if using.

Per serving: 64 calories, 3 g protein, 10 g carbohydrates, 2 g fat, 0 g saturated fat, 0 mg cholesterol, 3 g fiber, 247 mg sodium

HINT **helpful HINT** HINT HINT HINT HINT HINT HINT HINT

To toast almonds, place the nuts in a small dry skillet. Cook over medium heat, shaking pan often, until almonds just begin to color. Remove from pan and cool before using.

DID YOU KNOW ● ● ●

. . .that radishes were first cultivated thousands of years ago in China? In ancient Greece they were so prized that gold replicas were made of them.

on the menu

This refreshing salad makes a cool first course before grilled chicken and corn on the cob. Finish off with wedges of cold watermelon.

Asparagus, Snow Pea & Tomato Salad with Ginger Dressing

This Asian-inspired vegetable mix is an excellent source of folate, beta-carotene, and vitamin C, three key nutrients for fighting cancer and heart disease.

6 SERVINGS

Prep 10 min ◆ **Cook** 7 min

- 1 tablespoon soy sauce
- 2 teaspoons rice vinegar
- 2 teaspoons fresh-squeezed lemon juice
- 1 teaspoon dark sesame oil
- 3 tablespoons vegetable oil
- 2 finely chopped scallions
- 1 tablespoon finely chopped, peeled fresh ginger
- ¼ pound snow peas
- 1 pound thin asparagus, trimmed
- 1 head romaine lettuce, cored and separated into leaves
- 4 plum tomatoes, cut into wedges
- ¼ cup walnuts, toasted and coarsely chopped

1 In a small bowl, whisk together soy sauce, rice vinegar, lemon juice, and sesame oil. Whisk in vegetable oil, then stir in scallions and ginger to complete dressing.

2 In large skillet of lightly salted boiling water, cook snow peas until crisp-tender, 2 to 3 minutes. Remove snow peas with slotted spoon to colander. Rinse under cold running water.

3 Add asparagus to boiling water in skillet. Cook until crisp-tender, 3 to 4 minutes. Drain in colander. Rinse under cold running water. In large bowls toss snow peas and asparagus separately with just enough dressing to lightly coat.

4 Arrange 3 or 4 romaine leaves on each serving plate. Top with snow peas, asparagus, and tomatoes. Garnish with walnuts. Pass remaining dressing.

Per serving: 146 calories, 5 g protein, 9 g carbohydrates, 12 g fat, 1 g saturated fat, 0 mg cholesterol, 4 g fiber, 200 mg sodium

Beefy Pasta Salad

A pretty and nutritious salad, bursting with flavor.

4 SERVINGS

Prep 25 min ◆ **Cook** 20 min

- 8 ounces rotelle or other small pasta shape
- 6 cups broccoli spears
- 10 ounces well-trimmed sirloin steak
- 1¼ cups plain fat-free yogurt
- 3 tablespoons light mayonnaise
- 1 tablespoon balsamic vinegar
- ¾ cup basil leaves
- 1 teaspoon salt
- 1 pound plum tomatoes, quartered
- 1 medium red onion, halved and thinly sliced

1 Cook pasta in large pot of boiling water according to package directions. Add broccoli spears during last 2 minutes of cooking; drain.

2 Meanwhile, preheat broiler. Broil steak 4 inches from heat for 4 minutes per side for medium, or until done to taste. Transfer steak to cutting board and thinly slice across the grain, on the diagonal.

3 Combine yogurt, mayonnaise, vinegar, basil, and salt in food processor and process until smooth. Transfer dressing to large serving bowl.

4 Add steak and any juices accumulated on cutting board and toss to coat. Add pasta, broccoli, tomatoes, and onion to bowl and toss again. (Recipe can be made ahead and refrigerated. Bring back to room temperature before serving.)

Per serving: 471 calories, 29g protein, 58 g carbohydrates, 15 g fat, 4.5 g saturated fat, 50 g cholesterol, 7 g fiber, 781 sodium

VEGETABLES FOR VITALITY

Green Vegetable Salad with Garlic & Ginger

Crisp, fat-free, and delicately flavored, these lightly steamed vegetables can be enjoyed hot or cold.

4 SERVINGS

Prep 20 min ◆ **Cook** 3-4 min

- ½ **pound broccoli**
- ½ **pound small bok choy, or other Chinese leaves**
- 4 **scallions**
- ¼ **pound sugar snaps, trimmed**
- 1 **small clove garlic, crushed**
- 1 **teaspoon finely grated ginger**
- 1 **teaspoon dark-brown sugar**
- 1 **tablespoon Thai fish sauce**

1 Fill steamer pot with water to just below basket. Bring water to a boil.

2 Cut broccoli into small florets, trimming stalks to about ½ inch. Peel remaining stalk and cut diagonally into ½-inch slices. Trim bok choy and slice stems. Trim scallions and cut diagonally into thin slices.

3 In large bowl, combine broccoli, bok choy, scallions, and sugar snaps. Add garlic and ginger and toss well. Transfer to steamer basket, cover and steam until vegetables are tender-crisp, 3 to 4 minutes.

4 In small cup, combine sugar and fish sauce, stirring until sugar dissolves. Arrange vegetables in serving dish and drizzle with this dressing. Serve hot, or let cool, then refrigerate until 10 minutes before serving.

Per serving: 50 calories, 4 g protein, 9 g carbohydrates, 0 g fat, 0 g saturated fat, 0 g cholesterol, 3 g fiber, 400 g sodium

Romaine Lettuce with Chunky Tomato Vinaigrette

Rarely will the dressing boost the vitamin content of a salad as much as this one made with chopped fresh tomatoes.

6 SERVINGS

Prep 12 min

- 2 **large ripe tomatoes, halved, seeded, and coarsely chopped**
- ⅓ **cup loosely packed fresh basil leaves**
- 2 **tablespoons ketchup**
- 2 **tablespoons olive oil**
- 1 **tablespoon balsamic vinegar**
- 1 **small clove garlic, minced**
- ½ **teaspoon salt**
- 1 **large head romaine lettuce, torn into bite-size pieces**
- ¼ **cup crumbled feta cheese**

In food processor, combine tomatoes, basil, ketchup, oil, vinegar, garlic and salt to make vinaigrette. Pulse with on/off motion until blended but still chunky. In large bowl, toss romaine with vinaigrette. Sprinkle with feta. Serve at once.

Per serving: 82 calories, 3 g protein, 5 g carbohydrates, 6 g fat, 2 g saturated fat, 6 mg cholesterol, 2 g fiber, 237 mg sodium

FRESH IDEAS

Chunky Tomato Vinaigrette also makes a quick and delicious topping for grilled meats and chicken, or any pasta. It can be made several hours ahead and kept refrigerated. You can embellish it on pasta with grated mozzarella, pitted black olives, or thin slices of a good hard salami.

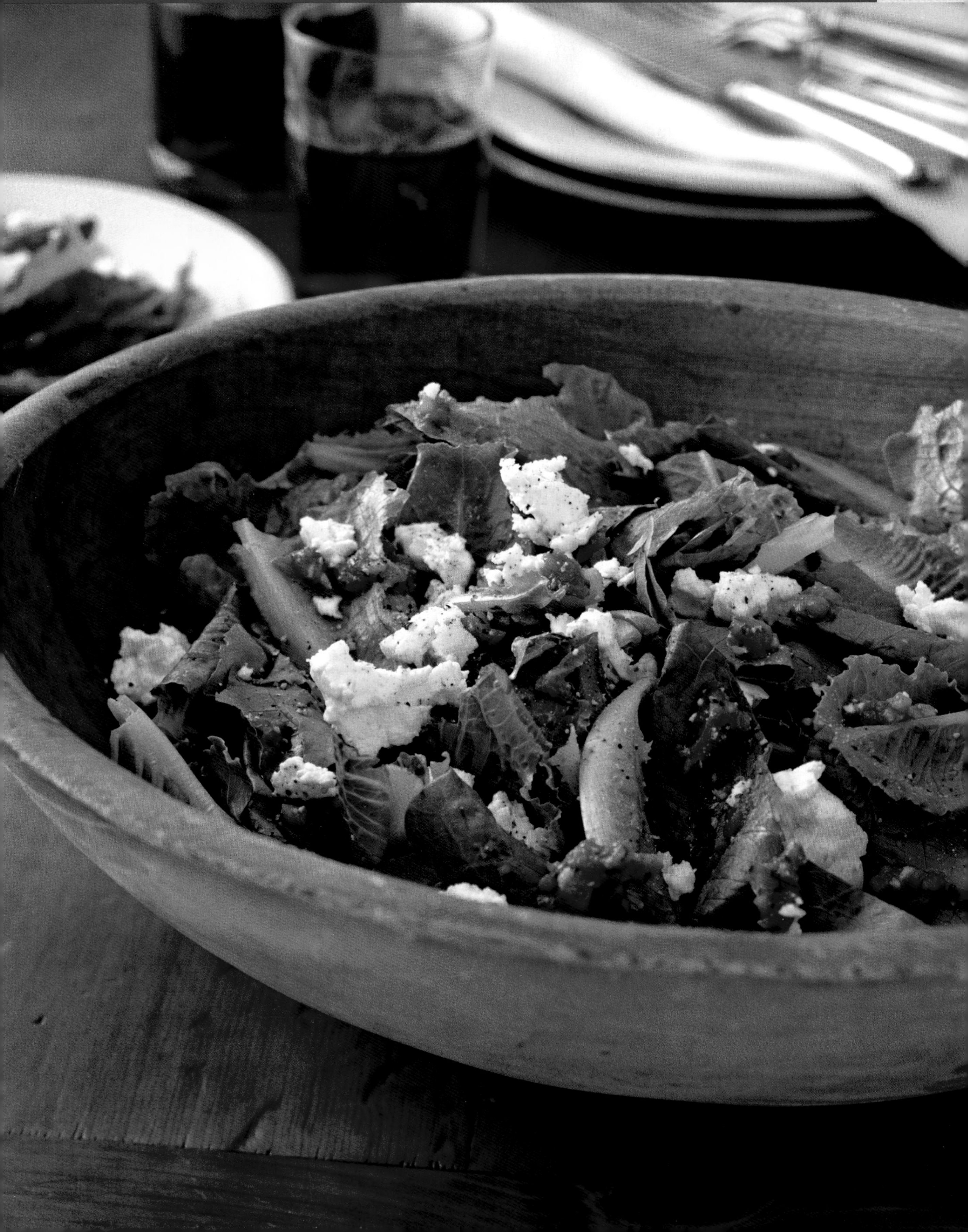

VEGETABLES FOR VITALITY

on the menu

Grilled chicken or fish goes well with this curry-flavored salad. Add some
Indian flat bread and finish off the meal with a cool fruit-flavored sorbet.

Three-Vegetable Salad with Curry Vinaigrette

Phytochemicals known as indoles, found in cauliflower and other cruciferous vegetables, may help protect against hormone-related cancers. Beans give you vitamin A for good vision, and both the beans and corn supply plenty of folate, important in the growth of new cells.

4 SERVINGS

Prep 10 min ◆ **Cook** 7 min

- 2 teaspoons curry powder
- ¼ cup fresh-squeezed lime juice
- ¼ teaspoon salt
- 3 tablespoons vegetable oil
- ½ pound green beans, trimmed and cut in half crosswise
- 1 small head cauliflower, stalks removed for other use and head separated into small florets
- 1 cup corn kernels, fresh or frozen, thawed

1 In small dry skillet, toast curry powder over medium-low heat, stirring frequently, until fragrant, about 1 minute. In small bowl whisk together lime juice, warm curry powder, and salt. Whisk in vegetable oil to finish vinaigrette.

2 In large saucepan of lightly salted boiling water, cook green beans until crisp-tender, about 3 minutes. Remove with slotted spoon to colander. Rinse under cold running water.

3 Add cauliflower florets to boiling water. Cook until crisp-tender, about 4 minutes. Drain in colander. Rinse under running cold water.

4 In large bowl, toss together green beans, cauliflower, corn, and vinaigrette. Serve chilled or at room temperature.

Per serving: 197 calories, 6 g protein, 22 g carbohydrates, 12 g fat, 1 g saturated fat, 0 mg cholesterol, 9 g fiber, 758 mg sodium

helpful HINT

Toasting curry powder in a dry skillet eliminates its rawness and enhances its flavor. Other spices, such as cumin and chili powder, also benefit from toasting, especially when added to foods that don't require further cooking.

Carrot-Almond Salad with Raspberry Vinaigrette

Beta-carotene, the phytochemical that gives carrots their deep orange color, helps boost your immune system.

4 SERVINGS

Prep 15 min ◆ **Cook** 8 min

- 2 tablespoons raspberry vinegar
- 1 tablespoon olive oil
- 1 tablespoon honey
- ¼ teaspoon salt
- ¼ teaspoon black pepper
- 1 pound carrots, peeled and diagonally cut into ¼-inch-thick ovals
- ¼ cup sliced almonds
- 1 scallion, trimmed to 6 inches, thinly sliced

1 In small bowl, whisk together vinegar, oil, honey, salt, and pepper for the vinaigrette. In medium pot, steam carrots just until tender, 6 to 8 minutes. Rinse under cold running water. Drain.

2 In medium bowl, toss together carrots, almonds, scallion, and vinaigrette.

Per serving: 134 calories, 3 g protein, 18 g carbohydrates, 6 g fat, 1 g saturated fat, 0 mg cholesterol, 4 g fiber, 204 mg sodium

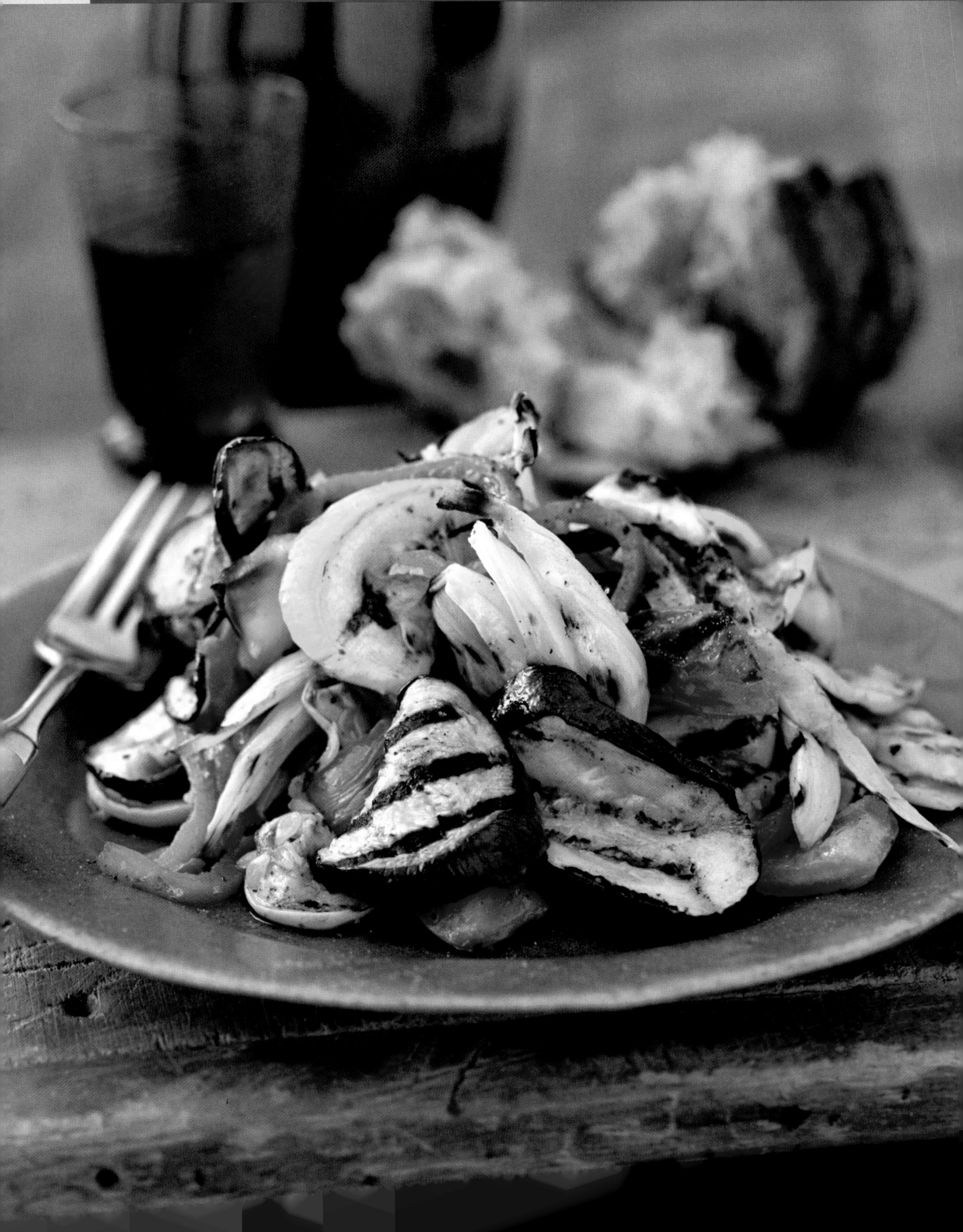

Grilled Vegetable Salad

Here's a Mediterranean mix that will keep your taste buds happy and your heart healthy at the same time.

6 SERVINGS

Prep 25 min ◆ **Cook** 15 min

- 1 small eggplant (¾ pound)
- 1 small bulb fennel (6 ounces), trimmed
- 1 medium yellow summer squash
- 1 medium zucchini
- ½ teaspoon salt
  Nonstick olive-oil cooking spray
- 1 small red bell pepper, halved through stem end and seeded
- 3 plum tomatoes, halved through stem end and seeded
- 2 tablespoons olive oil
- 2 cloves garlic, minced
- 1 teaspoon finely chopped fresh marjoram or ½ teaspoon dried marjoram, crumbled
- 1½ tablespoons balsamic vinegar

1 Preheat grill to medium-high heat. Slice eggplant, fennel, squash, and zucchini lengthwise into ½-inch-thick pieces. Sprinkle sliced vegetables with ¼ teaspoon of the salt. Coat all over with cooking spray.

2 Grill red pepper, skin side down, until blackened and blistered, 3 to 4 minutes.

3 Grill eggplant, fennel, squash, and zucchini on one side until grill marks are dark brown but vegetables are still very firm, about 4 minutes. Turn vegetables over. Grill until browned on other side and just tender, about 3 minutes for squash and zucchini, 5 to 6 minutes longer for eggplant and fennel.

4 Coat cut sides of tomatoes with cooking spray. Grill, cut sides down, just until light grill marks appear, about 3 minutes.

5 In small skillet over medium heat, heat oil. Add garlic, marjoram, and remaining ¼ teaspoon salt. Sauté 1 minute.

6 Peel grilled pepper. Cut in strips. Cut all remaining vegetables into bite-size chunks. Transfer to medium bowl. Add olive-oil mixture and vinegar. Toss to coat. Serve at room temperature.

Per serving: 85 calories, 2 g protein, 10 g carbohydrates, 5 g fat, 1 g saturated fat, 0 mg cholesterol, 4 g fiber, 211 mg sodium

Wilted Spinach Salad

An old favorite, updated. Lower-fat turkey bacon replaces regular bacon, whole-grain bread is used to make croutons, and phytochemical-rich tomato juice spikes the dressing.

4 SERVINGS

Prep 5 min ◆ **Cook** 5 min

- 8 cups fresh spinach leaves
- 2 tablespoons olive oil
- 1 red onion, thinly sliced
- ¼ cup tomato juice
- 1 tablespoon fresh-squeezed lemon juice
- 1 teaspoon Dijon mustard
- 1 small clove garlic, minced
- ¼ teaspoon salt
- ⅛ teaspoon black pepper.
- 2 slices turkey bacon, cooked and crumbled
- 2 slices multi-grain bread, trimmed, toasted, and cut into ½-inch cubes

1 Place spinach in large bowl. In large nonstick skillet over medium heat, heat olive oil. Add onion. Sauté 1 minute. Stir in tomato juice, lemon juice, mustard, garlic, salt, and pepper. Bring just to a boil, then remove from heat.

2 Pour hot dressing over spinach and toss to coat. Top with bacon and bread cubes. Serve warm.

Per serving: 140 calories, 5 g protein, 12 g carbohydrates, 9 g fat, 1 g saturated fat, 6 mg cholesterol, 3 g fiber, 435 mg sodium

Sweet Potato Salad with Raisins & Orange Dressing

A sweet and tangy mix of flavors, textures, and antioxidants that could help save your life.

4 SERVINGS

Prep 25 min ◆ **Cook** 20 min

> 1 pound sweet potatoes, peeled, quartered lengthwise, and cut crosswise into ½-inch-thick slices
> 3 tablespoons olive oil
> 1 tablespoon fresh-squeezed lemon juice
> 1 tablespoon orange juice
> 1 teaspoon honey
> ¼ teaspoon salt
> ¼ teaspoon black pepper
> 1 medium bunch arugula, torn into pieces
> 1 navel orange, peeled and cut into sections
> ½ small red onion, thinly sliced crosswise
> 3 tablespoons raisins

1 Preheat oven to 400°F. Line large baking pan with foil. Lightly coat with nonstick cooking spray. Toss sweet potatoes on pan with 1 tablespoon of oil. Spread in even layer. Roast potatoes until tender and lightly browned, about 20 minutes.

2 In small bowl, whisk together remaining 2 tablespoons olive oil, lemon juice, orange juice, honey, salt, and pepper. Taste dressing and add another 1 tablespoon lemon juice, if desired.

3 In large bowl, toss together warm potatoes and dressing. Add arugula, orange sections, onion, and raisins. Toss to mix.

Per serving: 219 calories, 3 g protein, 31 g carbohydrates, 11 g fat, 1 g saturated fat, 0 mg cholesterol, 4 g fiber, 163 mg sodium

FRESH IDEAS

> *To give the Roasted Eggplant & Tomato Salad some protein to make it into a main course lunch dish, add some sliced fresh mozzarella cheese before you drizzle on the dressing. Or serve it with slices of a good Italian salami on the side.*

Roasted Eggplant & Tomato Salad

Brushing vegetables with just a little oil and then roasting them is generally a healthier cooking technique than frying, particularly with a vegetable like eggplant, which soaks up oil like a sponge.

4 SERVINGS

Prep 15 min ◆ **Cook** 20 min

> 1 pound eggplant, cut crosswise into ½-inch-thick slices
> 1 pound plum tomatoes, cut into ½-inch-thick slices
> 2 tablespoons olive oil
> ¼ teaspoon salt
> ¼ teaspoon black pepper
> 1 small clove garlic
> 1 tablespoon red wine vinegar
> 15 small basil leaves

1 Preheat oven to 500°F. Line large baking pan with foil. Coat lightly with nonstick cooking spray. Arrange eggplant and tomato slices in one layer on foil. Brush with 1 tablespoon of the oil. Sprinkle with salt and pepper.

2 Roast until eggplant is softened and golden, 20 minutes. Let cool.

3 Put garlic through a press into a small bowl. Add remaining 1 tablespoon of olive oil and vinegar and whisk until blended to make dressing. To serve, overlap slices of tomato and eggplant with basil leaves. Brush with dressing.

Per serving: 115 calories, 2 g protein, 13 g carbohydrates, 7 g fat, 1 g saturated fat, 0 mg cholesterol, 4 g fiber, 160 mg sodium

Potato Salad with Sun-Dried Tomatoes, Scallions & Basil

Everyone's favorite outdoor party food is also an excellent source of vitamin C from all three vegetables.

6 SERVINGS

Prep 10 min ◆ **Cook** 15 min

- 1½ pounds small red potatoes, unpeeled and halved
- 2 tablespoons reduced-fat mayonnaise
- 2 teaspoons Dijon mustard
- ¼ cup low-fat buttermilk
- 2 scallions, thinly sliced
- ¼ cup chopped sun-dried tomatoes (not oil-packed)
- 8 basil leaves, shredded or finely chopped
- ½ teaspoon salt
- ¼ teaspoon black pepper

1 In large pot of lightly salted boiling water, cook potatoes until tender, 10 to 15 minutes. Drain well.

2 In small bowl, stir together mayonnaise and mustard. Stir in buttermilk to complete dressing.

3 In large bowl, combine potatoes, scallions, sun-dried tomatoes, basil, salt, and pepper. Add dressing. Toss to coat.

Per serving: 103 calories, 4 g protein, 17 g carbohydrates, 2 g fat, 0 g saturated fat, 2 mg cholesterol, 3 g fiber, 340 mg sodium

Carrot-Broccoli Slaw

Broccoli stalks are loaded with vitamin C for a healthy heart. The carrots give you beta-carotene for healthy skin and hair. The almonds provide thiamine for your metabolism. Here's a simple and delicious way to use them all.

6 SERVINGS

Prep 10 min

- ¼ cup reduced-fat mayonnaise
- 1 tablespoon white-wine vinegar
- 1 large bunch broccoli
- 3 medium carrots, peeled and grated
- ¼ cup sliced almonds, toasted
- 3 tablespoons chopped fresh parsley
- ⅛ teaspoon black pepper

1 In a small bowl, whisk together mayonnaise and vinegar to make dressing.

2 Cut off broccoli florets and reserve for another use. Peel stalks, then grate in food processor or by hand.

3 In large bowl, combine broccoli, carrots, and dressing. Stir in almonds, parsley, and pepper.

Per serving: 87 calories, 3 g protein, 8 g carbohydrates, 6 g fat, 1 g saturated fat, 3 mg cholesterol, 3 g fiber, 114 mg sodium

helpful HINT

Both the salads on this page would be great additions to a picnic. However, because they have mayonnaise in their dressings, they need to be kept chilled right up to the moment that they are served. Chill the salads thoroughly before you pack them. Put the chilled salad in a container with a close-fitting top and place in a well-insulated picnic bag big enough to hold ice or ice packs all around the container. Keep the picnic bag in the shade.

DID YOU KNOW ● ● ●

...that the name coleslaw comes from a Dutch word, "koolsla," which means cabbage salad? Recipes for this popular salad have always been open to improvisation from the basic cabbage (we now use carrots and broccoli, for example) to the dressing (mayonnaise to vinaigrette and many combinations in between).

Corn, Tomato & Basil Salad with Sweet Red Onion

A phytochemical in corn protects your eyes against age-related macular degeneration, which causes blindness. The tomatoes and onion provide cholesterol-fighting vitamin C.

6 SERVINGS

Prep 15 min

- 1 **tablespoon olive oil**
- 1 **teaspoon balsamic vinegar**
- ¼ **teaspoon salt**
- 2 **cups corn kernels, fresh or frozen, thawed**
- 2 **large ripe tomatoes, seeded and coarsely chopped**
- ½ **cup loosely packed fresh basil leaves, finely chopped**
- ¼ **cup minced red or sweet onion**

In large bowl whisk together oil, vinegar, and salt. If you're using fresh corn, blanch the kernels for 30 seconds in a large pot of boiling water before adding them to the salad. Stir in corn. Gently stir in tomatoes, basil, and onion. Serve at once.

Per serving: 77 calories, 2 g protein, 13 g carbohydrates, 3 g fat, 0 g saturated fat, 0 mg cholesterol, 2 g fiber, 102 mg sodium.

FRESH IDEAS

A fresh vegetable salad, almost like a salsa, can be made from any combination of vegetables, herbs, and vinaigrette. Pick from what looks tempting at the market and parboil vegetables that need it. Some combinations to try:
- *Carrots, celery, scallions, and dill*
- *Peas, turnips, bell peppers, and chives*
- *Potatoes, radishes, red onions, and parsley*

on the menu

Serve this simple, fresh salad with broiled fish or poultry and Baked Sweet Potato "Fries" (page 215). End the meal with a healthy slice of Carrot-Pineapple Cake (page 270), and an espresso coffee.

HEALTHY HOMEMADE
breads

Sweet Carrot-Raisin Muffins

Sunflower seeds add heart-protecting vitamin E.

12 MUFFINS

Prep 10 min ◆ **Cook** 15 min

- 1 cup all-purpose flour
- ½ cup whole-wheat flour
- ½ cup sugar
- 2 teaspoons baking powder
- ¼ teaspoon salt
- ½ teaspoon cinnamon
- ¼ teaspoon ground allspice
- ¼ teaspoon ground nutmeg
- ½ cup unsweetened applesauce
- ¼ cup vegetable oil
- 2 large eggs, lightly beaten
- 1 large carrot, peeled and finely shredded
- ½ cup raisins
- 2 tablespoons unsalted, shelled sunflower seeds

1 Preheat oven to 400°F. Coat 12 standard muffin-pan cups with nonstick cooking spray or line with paper liners.

2 In large bowl, combine all-purpose flour, whole-wheat flour, sugar, baking powder, salt, cinnamon, allspice, and nutmeg.

3 In medium bowl, combine applesauce, oil, and eggs. Fold in carrot and raisins. Stir in flour mixture until evenly moistened. Spoon into muffin cups, filling each two-thirds full. Sprinkle with sunflower seeds.

4 Bake until toothpick inserted in centers comes out clean, 15 minutes. Cool muffins in pan on wire rack. Turn out onto rack. Serve warm or at room temperature.

Per muffin: 177 calories, 3 g protein, 28 g carbohydrates, 6 g fat, 1 g saturated fat, 35 mg cholesterol, 2 g fiber, 126 mg sodium.

Orange-Yam Muffins with Pecan Streusel

You can use canned or fresh-cooked yams in this recipe for a megadose of beta-carotene.

12 MUFFINS

Prep 20 min ◆ **Cook** 22 min

FOR PECAN STREUSEL
- ¼ cup packed light brown sugar
- ¼ cup all-purpose flour
- ½ teaspoon cinnamon
- ⅛ teaspoon salt
- 2 tablespoons cut-up butter
- ⅓ cup chopped pecans

FOR MUFFINS
- 1¾ cups all-purpose flour
- 1 teaspoon baking powder
- 1 teaspoon baking soda
- 1 teaspoon cinnamon
- ¾ teaspoon ground ginger
- ½ teaspoon salt
- 1 cup mashed yam or sweet potato
- ⅓ cup packed light-brown sugar
- ¼ cup honey
- ¼ cup vegetable oil
- 1 tablespoon finely grated orange zest
- 2 large eggs, lightly beaten
- ½ cup low-fat buttermilk

1 Make Pecan Streusel: In medium bowl combine sugar, flour, cinnamon, and salt. Cut in butter with pastry blender until mixture is crumbly. Rub mixture briefly between fingertips to blend butter. Stir in pecans. Refrigerate while preparing muffins.

2 Preheat oven to 350°F. Coat 12 standard muffin-pan cups with nonstick cooking spray or line with paper liners. In small bowl, combine flour, baking powder, baking soda, cinnamon, ginger, and salt.

3 In medium bowl, stir together yam, sugar, honey, oil, and zest. Beat in eggs and buttermilk until well blended. Stir in flour mixture just until evenly moistened. Spoon into muffin cups, filling each two-thirds full. Sprinkle streusel over tops.

4 Bake until tops of muffins spring back when gently pressed, 20 to 22 minutes. Cool muffins in pan on wire rack. Turn out onto rack. Serve warm or at room temperature.

Per muffin: 253 calories, 4 g protein, 38 g carbohydrates, 10 g fat, 2 g saturated fat, 41 mg cholesterol, 2 g fiber, 286 mg sodium.

DID YOU KNOW ● ● ●

. . . that you can prepare muffin batter and spoon it into muffin cups the night before, then refrigerate the batter overnight and pop the pan into the oven to bake fresh muffins in the morning? It's a great way to make a busy morning's breakfast go smoothly.

Tomato Biscuits

Bits of fresh tomato add antioxidant power to these easy drop biscuits. Yogurt puts calcium in every bite.

12 BISCUITS

Prep 12 min ◆ **Cook** 12 min

- 1 medium tomato, seeded and finely chopped
- 2 cups all-purpose flour
- 1 tablespoon baking powder
- ½ teaspoon salt
- 1 cup low-fat plain yogurt
- ⅓ cup olive oil
- 2 tablespoons finely chopped scallion
- 1 tablespoon finely chopped sun-dried tomato

1 Preheat oven to 450°F. Lightly coat baking sheet with nonstick cooking spray. Drain chopped fresh tomato on paper towels.

2 In medium bowl, combine flour, baking powder, and salt. In small bowl combine yogurt and oil and stir into flour mixture until evenly moistened.

3 Stir fresh tomato, scallion, and sun-dried tomato into flour mixture. Drop dough, ¼ cup at a time, onto prepared baking sheet, for total of 12 biscuits.

4 Bake until tops are golden brown, about 12 minutes. Serve warm.

Per biscuit: 145 calories, 3 g protein, 18 g carbohydrates, 7 g fat, 1 g saturated fat, 1 mg cholesterol, 1 g fiber, 111 mg sodium.

FRESH ❧ IDEAS

Baking powder, vegetable oil, and yogurt are the ingredients that produce a tender, flaky biscuit. For browner tops, brush the biscuits with milk or oil before baking. For more flavor, add a couple of tablespoons of finely chopped ham, chives, or mild chile peppers to your biscuit batter.

HINT **helpful HINT** HINT HINT HINT HINT HINT HINT

To make Sweet Potato Biscuits even healthier for your heart, substitute 2 egg whites for the whole egg, and whole-wheat flour for some or all of the cup of white flour.

Sweet Potato Biscuits

These heart-helper biscuits are low in saturated fat because they're made with oil instead of butter.

12 BISCUITS

Prep 12 min ◆ **Cook** 15 min

- 1¾ cups all-purpose flour
- ¼ teaspoon salt
- 4 teaspoons ground baking powder
- Pinch nutmeg
- 1 cup mashed sweet potato or yam
- ¼ cup vegetable oil
- ¼ cup low-fat (1%) milk
- 1 large egg, lightly beaten
- 2 tablespoons light-brown sugar

1 Preheat oven to 425°F.

2 In small bowl, sift together flour, salt, baking powder, and nutmeg.

3 In medium bowl, stir together sweet potato, oil, milk, egg, and sugar. Stir in flour mixture just until evenly moistened.

4 Turn dough out onto well-floured surface. Pat dough out to ¾-inch-thick circle. Cut into rounds with 2½-inch biscuit cutter. Place rounds on baking sheet, about 1 inch apart. Gather up remaining dough, gently pat into a circle, and cut out remaining biscuits.

5 Bake until golden, 12 to 15 minutes. Serve warm.

Per biscuit: 143 calories, 3 g protein, 21 g carbohydrates, 6 g fat, 1 g saturated fat, 18 mg cholesterol, 1 g fiber, 186 mg sodium.

Carrot-Ginger Scones

This classic British-style biscuit gets a beta-carotene boost from grated carrot.

8 SCONES

Prep 15 min ◆ **Cook** 20 min

- 1½ cups all-purpose flour
- ¼ cup plus 2 teaspoons sugar
- 1½ teaspoons baking powder
- ½ teaspoon salt
- ¼ teaspoon baking soda
- 2 tablespoons crystallized ginger
- 6 tablespoons chilled butter, cut into small pieces
- 1 large carrot, peeled
- ½ cup low-fat buttermilk

1 Preheat oven to 400°F. Lightly coat baking sheet with nonstick cooking spray.

2 In food processor, combine flour, ¼ cup of the sugar, baking powder, salt, and baking soda. Pulse to mix. Add ginger. Pulse until ginger is finely ground. Add butter. Pulse until mixture resembles coarse cornmeal. Transfer to medium bowl.

3 Grate carrot in food processor. Add to flour mixture. Fold buttermilk into flour mixture just until evenly moistened.

4 Scrape soft dough onto well-floured surface. Knead briefly just until dough holds together. Pat out to 1-inch-thick round. Sprinkle top with remaining 2 teaspoons sugar.

5 Cut dough into 8 equal wedges. Arrange wedges, 1 inch apart, on prepared baking sheet.

6 Bake until golden, 18 to 20 minutes. Transfer to wire rack. Let cool.

Per scone: 203 calories, 3 g protein, 28 g carbohydrates, 9 g fat, 5 g saturated fat, 24 mg cholesterol, 1 g fiber, 278 mg sodium

Cranberry-Walnut Pumpkin Bread

Walnuts and walnut oil contain "good fats" that help keep your arteries clear and your heart healthy.

1 LOAF (ABOUT 16 SLICES)

Prep 15 min ◆ **Cook** 45 min

- 1¼ cups all-purpose flour
- 1 teaspoon ground ginger
- 1 teaspoon cinnamon
- ¾ teaspoon baking soda
- ¼ teaspoon salt
- 1 cup canned solid-pack unsweetened pumpkin
- ⅔ cup packed dark-brown sugar
- ¼ cup walnut oil or vegetable oil
- 2 large eggs, lightly beaten
- 1 teaspoon vanilla extract
- ½ cup walnuts, coarsely chopped
- ½ cup dried cranberries

1 Preheat oven to 350°F. Lightly coat 9 x 5-inch loaf pan with nonstick cooking spray.

2 In medium bowl, sift together flour, ginger, cinnamon, baking soda, and salt.

3 In another medium bowl, stir together pumpkin, sugar, oil, eggs, and vanilla until smooth. Stir in flour mixture just until evenly moistened. Stir in walnuts and cranberries. Spoon into prepared pan.

4 Bake until toothpick inserted in center comes out clean, about 45 minutes. Turn out onto wire rack. Let cool.

Per slice: 225 calories, 5 g protein, 34 g carbohydrates, 10 g fat, 0 g saturated fat, 40 mg cholesterol, 2 g fiber, 161 mg sodium

helpful HINT

Scones are sweet, rich, cakelike biscuits that are often served with afternoon tea. They are traditionally made with butter, sugar, eggs, and cream. In this recipe, the eggs are omitted, and buttermilk stands in for the cream to cut back a little on saturated fat without affecting the flavor.

FRESH IDEAS

Quick breads such as this Cranberry-Walnut Pumpkin Bread make great hostess gifts.
They are called quick breads because they have no yeast, so there's no rising time.
That means you can pop a loaf into the oven in minutes.

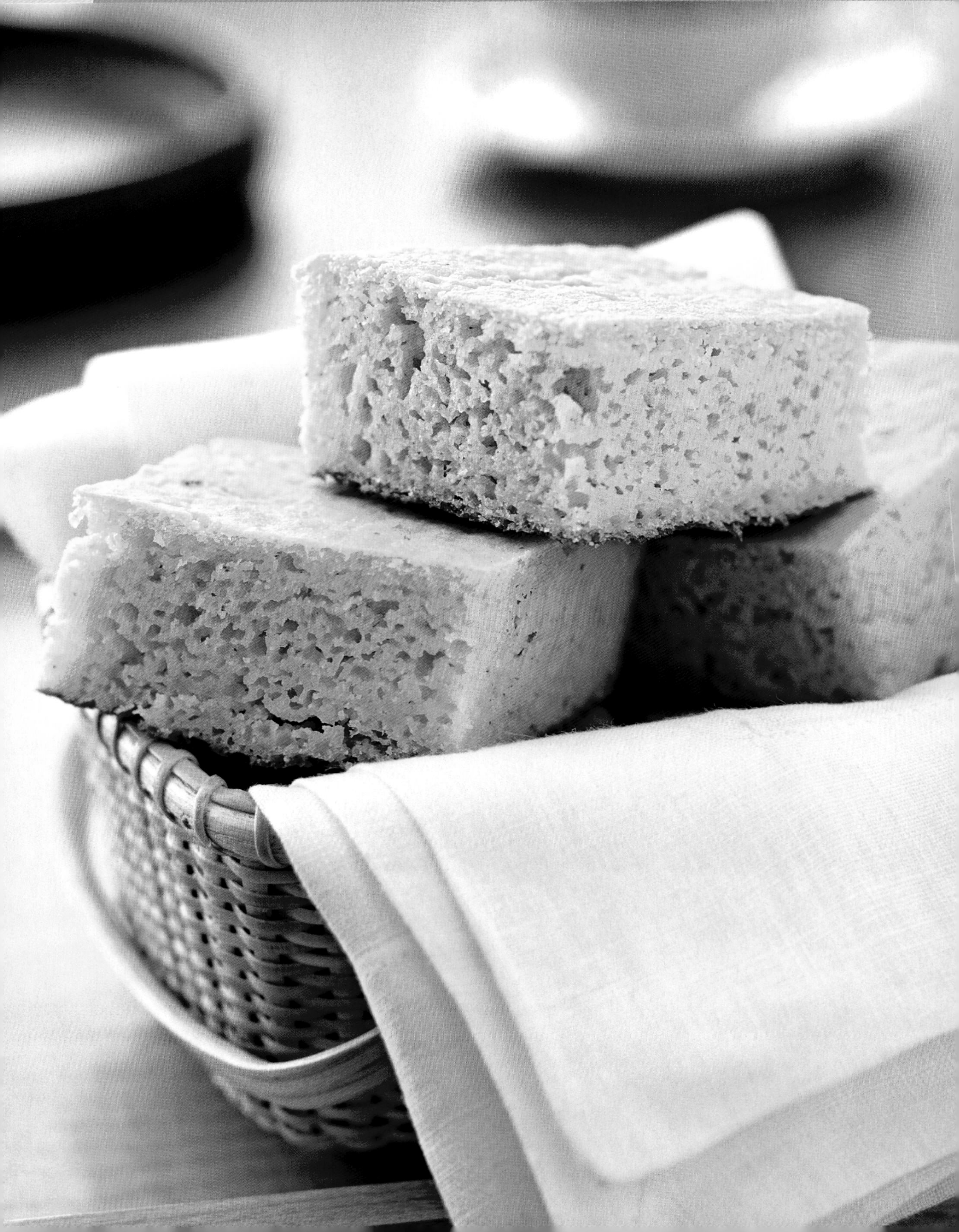

Carrot-Flecked Corn Bread

Grated carrots don't change the flavor, but they do transform an ordinary quick bread into a nutritious superfood.

9 SQUARES

Prep 10 min ◆ **Cook** 25 min

- 2 **tablespoons vegetable oil**
- 2 **cups white or yellow cornmeal**
- ⅓ **cup all-purpose flour**
- 2 **teaspoon baking powder**
- 1 **teaspoon baking soda**
- 2 **tablespoons sugar**
- 1 **teaspoon salt**
- 1¾ **cups low-fat buttermilk**
- 1 **large egg, lightly beaten**
- 2 **medium carrots, peeled and finely shredded**

1 Preheat oven to 400°F. Swirl oil in 8 x 8 x 2-inch-square baking pan. Place pan in oven for 5 minutes while preheating.

2 Meanwhile, in large bowl, combine cornmeal, flour, baking powder, baking soda, sugar, and salt. Stir in buttermilk, egg, and carrots. Carefully pour in oil from baking pan. Mix well. Pour batter into hot pan.

3 Bake until toothpick inserted in center comes out clean, 25 minutes. Let cool in pan 10 minutes. Turn out onto wire rack. Let cool slightly before cutting. Serve warm.

Per square: 202 calories, 6 g protein, 34 g carbohydrates, 5 g fat, 1 g saturated fat, 26 mg cholesterol, 3 g fiber, 550 mg sodium

DID YOU KNOW ● ● ●

. . . that corn bread made with cornmeal only, no flour, is a Southern tradition in the U.S.? And in the South, they are likely to add bacon fat or even pork cracklings (fried pork skin) to the batter for richer flavor and crispy texture. Northern corn bread is made with a mixture of cornmeal and flour, and has a texture that is more cakelike than its Southern cousin.

Red Pepper & Green Chile Spoon Bread

Whether it's fresh, frozen, or canned, corn contributes powerful antioxidants that help fight age-related blindness.

6 SERVINGS

Prep 20 min ◆ **Cook** 55 min

- 1 **cup yellow cornmeal**
- 1 **cup low-fat (1%) milk**
- 1 **teaspoon salt**
- 1 **tablespoon butter**
- 1 **can (4½ ounces) green chiles, rinsed and drained**
- 1 **red bell pepper, seeded and cut into small chunks**
- 1 **cup corn kernels, fresh, drained canned, or thawed frozen**
- 3 **large eggs, separated**

1 Preheat oven to 375°F. Coat 2-quart casserole with vegetable oil.

2 In small saucepan, bring 1½ cups water and cornmeal to a boil. Lower heat. Simmer, stirring frequently, 3 minutes. Transfer to medium bowl. Stir in milk, salt, butter, chiles, bell pepper, and corn until butter melts. When cool, stir in lightly beaten egg yolks.

3 In medium bowl, beat egg whites until stiff peaks form. Fold into cornmeal mixture. Pour into prepared casserole.

4 Bake until center is firm and top is browned, 50 minutes. Serve at once.

Per serving: 183 calories, 7 g protein, 27 g carbohydrates, 5 g fat, 2 g saturated fat, 113 mg cholesterol, 3 g fiber, 474 mg sodium

VEGETABLES FOR VITALITY

Whole-Wheat Winter Squash Loaf

This homey honey-sweetened bread is as nutritious as it sounds, and equally delicious.
The wheat germ and bran in whole-wheat flour supply significant amounts of fiber and vitamin E
that are lost in the processing of white flour.

2 LOAVES (ABOUT 12 SLICES EACH)

Prep 25 min + rising ◆ **Cook** 30 min

- 3½ **cups whole-wheat flour**
- 3 to 3¼ **cups all-purpose flour**
- 2 **tablespoons active dry yeast**
- ⅔ **cup low-fat (1%) milk**
- ½ **cup water**
- ½ **cup honey**
- 2 **teaspoons salt**
- 2 **large eggs, lightly beaten**
- 1½ **cups pureed winter squash**
- 2 **tablespoons olive oil**
- 2 **bunches scallions, coarsely chopped (about 2 cups)**
- 2 **tablespoons chopped fresh rosemary**
- 1 **cup unsalted, shelled sunflower seeds**

1 In large bowl, combine whole-wheat flour and 3 cups of the all-purpose flour. In another large bowl, combine 3 cups of flour mixture with yeast.

2 In medium saucepan, heat milk, water, and honey just until warm (105°F to 115°F). Stir into flour-yeast mixture. Add salt and eggs. Beat with mixer on low speed 30 seconds, scraping down side of bowl constantly. Beat on high speed 3 minutes.

3 Add squash, oil, scallions, rosemary, sunflower seeds, and remaining flour mixture, beating until well mixed.

4 Turn dough out onto lightly floured surface. Knead until smooth and elastic, 6 to 8 minutes, adding more all-purpose flour as needed to prevent sticking. Shape dough into ball. Place dough in lightly oiled bowl. Turn to coat. Cover loosely with plastic wrap. Let rise in warm place until doubled in volume, about 1 hour.

5 Punch dough down. Turn out onto lightly oiled surface. Divide in half. Let rest 10 minutes.

6 Lightly oil two 9 x 5-inch loaf pans. Shape each half of dough into loaf. Place each in loaf pan. Cover loosely with plastic wrap. Let rise in warm place until almost doubled in volume, about 50 minutes.

7 Preheat oven to 375°F.

8 Bake until loaves sound hollow when tapped, about 30 minutes. Turn out onto wire rack. Let cool.

Per slice: 150 calories, 5 g protein, 26 g carbohydrates, 4 g fat, 1 g saturated fat, 14 mg cholesterol, 3 g fiber, 155 mg sodium

HINT helpful HINT HINT HINT HINT HINT HINT HINT

Breads made with whole-wheat flour taste more like the grain itself than loaves that are prepared with white flour only. You can use regular all-purpose flour or bread flour to make yeast breads, but the best breads are made with higher-protein flour that contains 12 to 14 grams of protein per cup or with a combination of flours that averages 14 or more grams per cup. You can check the Nutrition Facts label on the bag to see how much protein your flour contains.

Store all-purpose or bread flour in a tightly covered container at a cool room temperature for up to six months. Whole-wheat and other whole-grain flours, which are slightly higher in fat and therefore can turn rancid more quickly, should be stored in the refrigerator for up to six months or in the freezer for up to a year. Bring chilled flours to room temperature before using in bread or any other recipes for baked goods.

VEGETABLES FOR VITALITY

Tomato-Rye Bread
with Rosemary & Garlic

The red pigment in tomato juice colors this bread and adds the cancer-fighting power of a phytochemical called lycopene. The tomatoes also supply plenty of vitamins A, C, and E.

1 LOAF (ABOUT 12 SLICES)

on the menu

Slice this tasty loaf and use it to make the best ham or ham and cheese sandwiches ever. For a party, add watercress to the sandwiches, cut each into four triangles, trim off the crust, if you like, and pass around as appetizers.

Prep 30 min + rising ◆ **Cook** 50 min

½ cup tomato juice
1 tablespoon olive oil
1 teaspoon salt
½ teaspoon dried rosemary, crumbled
2 cloves garlic, minced
1 envelope active dry yeast
½ cup warm water (105°F to 115°F)
¾ cup rye flour
2 to 2¼ cups all-purpose flour
⅓ cup finely chopped sun-dried tomatoes (not oil-packed)

1 In small saucepan, bring tomato juice, ½ cup water, oil, salt, rosemary, and garlic to simmer. Transfer to medium bowl. Let cool to lukewarm.

2 In small bowl, sprinkle yeast over warm water. Let stand until foamy, 5 minutes. Stir to dissolve.

3 Add yeast mixture to tomato juice mixture. Gradually stir in rye flour. Gradually knead in 2 cups of all-purpose flour until dough comes together and is workable (dough will be sticky). Knead in sun-dried tomatoes. Turn dough out onto floured surface. Knead for 1 minute. Let rest 10 minutes.

4 Knead dough on lightly floured surface until smooth and elastic, about 10 minutes, adding more all-purpose flour as needed if dough is very sticky (dough should be slightly sticky). Place dough in lightly oiled bowl. Turn to coat. Cover loosely with plastic wrap. Let rise in warm place until doubled in volume, about 1 hour.

5 Punch dough down. Lightly coat 8½ x 4½ x 2½-inch loaf pan with olive oil. Place dough in pan, patting into corners. Cover loosely with plastic wrap. Let rise in warm place until doubled in volume (loaf should rise above top of pan), about 1 hour.

6 Preheat oven to 375°F.

7 Bake until loaf sounds hollow when tapped, 40 to 50 minutes. Turn out onto wire rack. Let cool completely before slicing.

Per slice: 95 calories, 3 g protein, 18 g carbohydrates, 1 g fat, 0 g saturated fat, 0 mg cholesterol, 2 g fiber, 196 mg sodium

Potato Bread with Poppy Seeds

Potato bread recipes come from many different countries. The poppy seeds in this one give a nice finish to the crust, but it's the potato that gives you lots of potassium and vitamins C and B_6.

1 LOAF (12 SLICES)

Prep 25 min + rising ◆ **Cook** 45 min

- 3 tablespoons sugar
- ¼ cup warm water (105°F to 115°F)
- 1 envelope active dry yeast
- 1 cup mashed potato
- 1 cup low-fat (1%) milk
- 2 tablespoons butter
- 1½ teaspoons salt
- 4 to 4¼ cups all-purpose flour
- 1 large egg beaten with 1 tablespoon milk for glaze
- 2 teaspoons poppy seeds

1 In small bowl, stir 1 tablespoon of the sugar into warm water. Sprinkle yeast over top. Let stand until foamy, about 5 minutes. Stir to dissolve yeast.

2 Meanwhile, in small saucepan, stir together potato, milk, remaining 2 tablespoons sugar, butter, and salt. Heat just to warm mixture and melt butter. Force through strainer with rubber spatula into large bowl to remove any potato lumps. Stir in yeast mixture and 3 cups of the flour to form dough.

3 Sprinkle 1 cup of the flour on work surface. Turn dough out onto surface. Knead, working in flour, until smooth and elastic, about 10 minutes, adding more flour as needed to prevent sticking. Place dough in lightly oiled bowl. Turn to coat. Cover loosely with plastic wrap. Let rise in warm place until doubled in volume, about 1¼ hours.

4 Lightly oil 9 x 5-inch loaf pan. Punch dough down. Knead briefly. Press into loaf pan. Cover loosely with plastic wrap. Let rise in warm place until doubled in volume, about 45 minutes.

5 Heat oven to 350°F. Brush top of loaf with glaze. Sprinkle with poppy seeds. Using serrated knife, cut ½-inch-deep slit lengthwise down middle of loaf.

6 Bake until browned and loaf pulls away slightly from edges of pan, 40 to 45 minutes. Turn out onto wire rack. Let cool at least 1 hour before slicing.

Per slice: 164 calories, 5 g protein, 30 g carbohydrates, 3 g fat, 1 g saturated fat, 19 mg cholesterol, 1 g fiber, 265 mg sodium

FRESH ❧IDEAS

Add more seasonal flavor by substituting pure maple syrup for the honey.

helpful HINT

Use a serrated knife for easier, neater slicing, especially when bread is freshly baked. A wooden cutting board is best for slicing because it is easier on the knife edge than a hard plastic board.

VEGETABLES FOR VITALITY

Whole-Wheat Pumpkin Rolls with Honey & Pumpkin Seeds

The whole-wheat flour and the pumpkin puree add antioxidant vitamins and fiber to these delicious rolls; the pumpkin seeds add minerals and a tasty crunch to every bite.

24 ROLLS

Prep 30 min + 1½ hr rising ◆ **Cook** 12 min

- 1 envelope active dry yeast
- ½ cup warm water (105°F to 115°F)
- ¼ cup honey
- 1 can (15 ounces) solid-pack unsweetened pumpkin
- 2 tablespoons olive oil
- 4¼ to 4½ cups all-purpose flour
- 1 cup whole-wheat flour
- 2 teaspoons salt
- 1½ cups unsalted, shelled pumpkin seeds, lightly toasted

1 In large bowl, sprinkle yeast over warm water. Let stand until foamy, about 5 minutes. Stir in honey until dissolved. Stir in pumpkin and oil. Stir in 4 cups of the all-purpose flour, whole-wheat flour, and salt until dough forms.

2 Turn dough out onto floured surface. Knead until smooth and elastic, about 10 minutes, adding more flour as needed to prevent sticking. Work in pumpkin seeds. Place dough in lightly oiled bowl. Turn to coat. Cover loosely with plastic wrap. Let rise in warm place until doubled in volume, about 1½ hours.

3 Line 2 baking sheets with foil. Punch dough down. Form dough into 24 equal-size rolls. Place on prepared baking sheets. Cover loosely with plastic wrap. Let rise in warm place until doubled in volume, about 1 hour.

4 Preheat oven to 400°F. Uncover rolls.

5 Bake until puffed and golden and rolls sound hollow when tapped on bottom, about 12 minutes. Serve warm or at room temperature.

Per roll: 177 calories, 6 g protein, 27 g carbohydrates, 6 g fat, 1 g saturated fat, 0 mg cholesterol, 2 g fiber, 197 mg sodium

FRESH ✿ IDEAS

Save the seeds from your Halloween jack-o'-lantern. Let them dry a day, then clean off pumpkin fiber and spread them on a baking sheet. Spray with no-fat cooking spray and sprinkle with salt and pepper or a favorite herb. Bake in a 300°F oven until toasted—about 20 minutes—and enjoy a great fall munchie.

Focaccia with Tomatoes, Peppers & Parsley

Fresh parsley adds even more antioxidant power to the vitamin-rich veggie mix that tops this classic Italian yeast bread. Focaccia is flat like pizza, but more moist and thicker.

8 SERVINGS

Prep 25 min + rising ◆ **Cook** 40 min

- 2 teaspoons sugar
- 2 cups warm water (105°F to 115°F)
- 1 envelope active dry yeast
- ⅓ cup chopped parsley
- 3½ tablespoons olive oil
- 1½ teaspoons salt
- ½ teaspoon dried sage, crumbled
- 5½ to 5¾ cups all-purpose flour
- 2 cloves garlic, minced
- 3 medium tomatoes, thinly sliced
- 1 large yellow bell pepper, seeded and cut in thin strips
- 2 tablespoons grated Parmesan cheese

1 In large bowl, stir sugar into warm water. Sprinkle yeast over top. Let stand until foamy, about 5 minutes. Stir to dissolve yeast.

2 Reserve 2 tablespoons parsley for top of bread. Stir remaining parsley, 3 tablespoons of the oil, salt, and sage into yeast mixture. Add 2 cups of the flour, mixing vigorously. Stir in 3 more cups of the flour to make stiff dough.

3 Sprinkle ½ cup flour on work surface. Turn dough out onto surface. Knead until smooth and elastic, about 10 minutes, adding more flour as needed to prevent sticking. Place dough in lightly oiled bowl. Turn to coat. Cover loosely with plastic wrap. Let rise in warm place until doubled in volume, about 1¼ hours.

4 Lightly oil 15 x 11-inch jelly-roll pan. Punch dough down. Knead briefly. Roll or pat out into rectangle to fit into pan. Place in pan. Cover dough loosely with plastic wrap. Let rise in warm place until doubled in volume, about 40 minutes.

5 Preheat oven to 400°F. Place oven rack in lowest position.

6 Make small dimples in dough with fingertips. Brush top with remaining ½ tablespoon oil. Sprinkle top with garlic. Arrange tomato slices over top, slightly overlapping. Top with yellow pepper. Sprinkle with cheese.

7 Bake on bottom rack until browned around edges, 35 to 40 minutes. Transfer to wire rack. Sprinkle with reserved parsley. Let cool at least 20 minutes before serving.

Per serving: 395 calories, 11g protein, 71 g carbohydrates, 7 g fat, 1 g saturated fat, 1 mg cholesterol, 3 g fiber, 468 mg sodium

Onion Bread Sticks

Fresh sautéed onions add vegetable power and a zesty taste to frozen bread dough.

12 BREAD STICKS

Prep 20 min + 1 hr rising ◆ **Cook** 35 min

- 1 pound prepared pizza dough, thawed if frozen
- 2 tablespoons olive oil
- 2 medium onions, very thinly sliced
- ½ teaspoon coarse salt, such as sea salt or kosher salt

1 Lightly oil large baking sheet. On lightly floured surface, pat dough out to 12 x 6-inch rectangle. Cut into twelve 6-inch-long bread sticks. Gently twist each stick. Place on baking sheet. Cover loosely with plastic wrap. Let rise in warm place until doubled in volume, about 1 hour.

2 In large nonstick skillet, heat oil over medium heat. Add onions. Sauté until very soft and golden, about 12 minutes.

3 Preheat oven to 400°F. Place oven racks in lowest position and top position.

4 Just before baking, distribute sautéed onions over surface of each bread stick without deflating dough. Sprinkle each with pinch coarse salt.

5 Bake on bottom rack 15 minutes. Then move baking sheet to top rack. Bake until onions are crisp and golden, 5 to 8 minutes. Transfer to wire rack. Let cool.

Per bread stick: 110 calories, 3 g protein, 19 g carbohydrates, 3 g fat, 0 g saturated fat, 0 mg cholesterol, 1 g fiber, 258 mg sodium

Broccoli, Cheese & Walnut Bread

This fast-to-fix loaf is easy, fun, and an unusual way to add a power vegetable to your diet.

1 LOAF (ABOUT 16 SLICES)

Prep 20 min ◆ **Cook** 25 min

- ½ pound broccoli, cooked and coarsely chopped (about 1½ cups)
- 1 cup shredded part-skim mozzarella cheese
- ½ cup shredded provolone cheese
- ⅓ cup walnuts, coarsely chopped
- 2 cloves garlic, minced
- ½ teaspoon dried basil, crumbled
- 1 tube (10 ounces) refrigerated pizza dough
- 1 large egg whisked with 1 tablespoon milk for glaze
- 2 teaspoons sesame seeds

1 Preheat oven to 375°F. Lightly oil 15 x 11-inch jelly-roll pan.

2 In medium bowl, combine broccoli, mozzarella, provolone, walnuts, garlic, and basil.

3 Unroll dough. Pat out to 14 x 11-inch rectangle. Spread broccoli filling over dough, leaving ½-inch border along long sides. Starting from a long side, tightly roll up dough. Place roll, seam side down, on prepared pan. Brush top and sides of roll with glaze. Sprinkle with seeds. Insert fork in several places along top of roll to make vents.

4 Bake until well browned, 25 minutes. Transfer to wire rack. Let cool slightly. Slice and serve warm.

Per slice: 212 calories, 11 g protein, 20 g carbohydrates, 10 g fat, 3 g saturated fat, 42 mg cholesterol, 2 g fiber, 375 mg sodium

SWEET

dessert

TEMPTATIONS

Old-Fashioned Secret-Ingredient Chocolate Cake

Cocoa, flour, sugar, eggs, and oil are the old-fashioned ingredients.
The surprise is tomato juice, laden with the cancer-fighting antioxidant lycopene.

16 SLICES

Prep 20 min ◆ **Cook** 30 min

FOR CAKE

- ¾ **cup tomato juice**
- ¼ **cup water**
- ⅔ **cup unsweetened cocoa powder**
- 2¼ **cups all-purpose flour**
- 1 **teaspoon baking soda**
- ½ **teaspoon baking powder**
- ¼ **teaspoon salt**
- 1½ **cups sugar**
- ½ **cup vegetable oil**
- 3 **large eggs**
- 1½ **teaspoons vanilla extract**

FOR ICING

- 1 **ounce unsweetened chocolate**
- 2 **tablespoons low-fat (1%) milk**
- 1 **tablespoon unsweetened cocoa powder**
- 4 **ounces ⅓-less-fat cream cheese**
- 2½ **cups confectioners' sugar, sifted**
- ½ **cup seedless raspberry jam**

HINT helpful HINT HINT HINT HINT HINT HINT HINT

To make a square layer cake, substitute two 8 x 2-inch square pans for the two 9-inch rounds. To make a single layer sheet cake, substitute a 13 x 9 x 2-inch pan. Start checking for doneness about ten minutes before the recommended baking time. If you use glass pans instead of metal, reduce the baking temperature by 25°F.

For cakes with a lighter texture, separate the eggs before adding. Add the yolks to the creamed sugar and butter (or oil) mixture. Beat the whites separately until stiff peaks form and gently fold into the batter.

To prevent cake layers from sticking to cooling racks, spray the racks lightly with nonstick cooking spray before turning layers out.

1 Preheat oven to 350°F. Coat two 9-inch-round cake pans with nonstick cooking spray.

2 In small saucepan, bring tomato juice and water to a boil. Whisk in cocoa powder until smooth. Remove from heat.

3 In medium bowl, stir together flour, baking soda, baking powder, and salt.

4 In large bowl, beat together sugar, oil, eggs, and 1 teaspoon vanilla extract until combined. Beat in cocoa mixture. Beat in flour mixture just until evenly moistened. Divide batter between prepared pans.

5 Bake until toothpick inserted in centers of cakes comes out clean, 25 to 30 minutes. Transfer pans to wire rack. Let cool 10 minutes. Turn cakes out onto rack. Let cool completely.

6 Prepare icing: In medium microwave-safe bowl, microwave together chocolate and milk on high power 1 minute. Stir until smooth. Whisk in cocoa powder until smooth. Whisk in cream cheese and ½ teaspoon vanilla extract. Stir in confectioners' sugar until combined.

7 Place one cake layer on flat plate or platter. Spread top of this layer with jam. Place remaining layer over layer with jam on it. Spread icing over side and top of cake.

Per slice: 359 calories, 6 g protein, 56 g carbohydrates, 14 g fat, 4 g saturated fat, 56 mg cholesterol, 2 g fiber, 268 mg sodium

FRESH 🌿 IDEAS

Instead of a thick layer of frosting, top chocolate cake with a dollop of freshly whipped cream. If you like, sprinkle the cream with fresh raspberries, sliced strawberries, or a grating of semi-sweet chocolate.

Bourbon-Squash Cake

Thanks to the addition of acorn squash, this cake offers a well-rounded supply of essential nutrients, including B vitamins, beta-carotene, vitamin C, iron, and magnesium.

16 SERVINGS

Prep 15 min ◆ **Cook** 50 min

- 2 cups all-purpose flour
- 2 teaspoons baking powder
- 1 teaspoon baking soda
- 1 teaspoon salt
- 2 teaspoons cinnamon
- 1½ cups granulated sugar
- 1 cup vegetable oil
- 4 large eggs
- 1¾ cups mashed, cooked acorn squash
- ¼ cup bourbon
- Confectioners' sugar, for dusting *(optional)*

1 Preheat oven to 350°F. Coat 10-cup Bundt or tube pan with nonstick cooking spray.

2 In small bowl, stir together flour, baking powder, baking soda, salt, and cinnamon.

3 In large bowl, beat together sugar, oil, eggs, and squash until blended. Beat in flour mixture until evenly moistened. Beat in bourbon. Using rubber spatula, scrape batter into Bundt pan.

4 Bake until toothpick inserted into top comes out clean, 45 to 50 minutes. Transfer pan to wire rack. Let cool in pan 15 minutes. Run thin knife around edge and center tube of pan. Turn out cake onto rack. Let cool completely. Dust with confectioners' sugar, if desired.

Per serving: 282 calories, 3 g protein, 33 g carbohydrates, 15 g fat, 1 g saturated fat, 53 mg cholesterol, 1 g fiber, 289 mg sodium

Carrot-Pineapple Cake

There's no sweeter way to get so much vitamin A—80% of the daily requirement in every piece of cake!

16 SERVINGS

Prep 20 min ◆ **Cook** 50 min

FOR CAKE
- 2½ cups all-purpose flour
- 2 teaspoons cinnamon
- 1 teaspoon baking powder
- 1½ teaspoons baking soda
- ½ teaspoon salt
- 1½ cups sugar
- ½ cup vegetable oil
- 4 large eggs
- ½ cup unsweetened applesauce
- 1 pound carrots, peeled and grated (about 4½ cups)
- 1 can (8.5 ounces) crushed pineapple in juice
- ½ cup dark seedless raisins
- ½ cup walnuts, chopped

FOR ICING
- 2 packages (8 ounces) ⅓-less-fat cream cheese, softened
- 4½ cups confectioners' sugar, sifted
- 1 teaspoon vanilla extract

1 Preheat oven to 350°F. Coat two 9-inch round cake pans with nonstick cooking spray.

2 In medium bowl, stir together flour, cinnamon, baking powder, baking soda and salt.

3 In large bowl, beat together sugar, oil, eggs, and applesauce until blended. Beat in flour mixture just until evenly moistened. Stir in carrots, pineapple with juice, raisins, and walnuts. Divide batter between prepared pans.

4 Bake until toothpick inserted in centers of cakes comes out clean, 45 to 50 minutes. Transfer pans to wire rack. Let cool 30 minutes. Turn cakes out onto racks. Let cool completely.

5 To prepare icing: In large bowl of mixer, beat cream cheese on low speed 1 minute. Add confectioners' sugar and vanilla extract and beat just until smooth.

6 Place one cake layer on flat plate or platter. Spread about ¾ cup of the icing over top of this layer. Place remaining layer over iced layer. Spread remaining icing over side and top of cake.

Per serving: 479 calories, 8 g protein, 75 g carbohydrates, 18 g fat, 5 g saturated fat, 75 mg cholesterol, 2 g fiber, 357 mg sodium

Chocolate Marble Cake

Canned yams are the "magic" ingredient in this very moist and flavorful cake. Besides adding a good dose of fiber and beta-carotene to every slice, they sweeten the batter and provide the deep golden color that makes this a perfect cake for any fall occasion.

12 SERVINGS

Prep 15 min ◆ **Cook** 60 min

   3 cups all-purpose flour
1¼ cups sugar
   2 teaspoons baking powder
   2 teaspoons baking soda
   2 teaspoons cinnamon
   ¼ teaspoon ground cloves
   1 teaspoon salt
   2 cans (15¾ ounces each) yams in syrup, drained
1½ cups vegetable oil
   4 large eggs
   4 ounces semisweet chocolate, melted
   1 teaspoon vanilla extract
   1 cup confectioners' sugar
   1 tablespoon unsweetened cocoa powder
   ½ teaspoon vanilla extract
2 to 3 tablespoons boiling water

1 Preheat oven to 350°F. Coat 10-inch Bundt or tube pan with nonstick cooking spray. Dust with flour.

2 In medium bowl, stir together flour, sugar, baking powder, baking soda, cinnamon, cloves, and salt.

3 In large bowl, beat yams and vegetable oil until blended. Beat in eggs, one at a time. Beat in flour mixture until smooth. Spoon one-third of batter into small bowl. Stir in melted chocolate and vanilla.

4 Spoon batters alternately into pan and swirl together with a knife for marble effect.

5 Bake until toothpick inserted in center comes out clean and side of cake shrinks from side of pan, 50 to 60 minutes. Transfer pan to wire rack. Let cool in pan on rack 10 minutes. Turn cake out onto rack. Let cool completely.

6 To prepare glaze: In small bowl, whisk together confectioners' sugar and cocoa powder. Whisk in vanilla extract and 2 to 3 tablespoons boiling water until you get good glazing consistency. Drizzle glaze over cooled cake.

Per serving: 600 calories, 7 g protein, 71 g carbohydrates, 34 g fat, 5 g saturated fat, 71 mg cholesterol, 3 g fiber, 512 mg sodium

Fresh Pumpkin Tartlets

Nutritious pumpkin tarts are a new take on a fall favorite.

MAKES 8 TARTLETS

Prep 35 min ◆ **Cook** 20–25 min

   1 tablespoon vegetable oil
   1 tablespoon butter
   3 eggs
   8 ounces reduced-fat evaporated milk
   ¼ cup light-brown sugar
   ¼ cup shredded coconut
      Grated zest and juice of 1 orange
   ½ teaspoon each ground cinnamon, ground ginger, and grated nutmeg
   1 can (15 ounces) solid-pack pumpkin puree
   4 sheets phyllo pastry (20 x 11 inches each)
   ½ pint blackberries
      Confectioners' sugar for dusting

1 Preheat oven to 375°. In small saucepan, warm oil and butter together until butter melts. Remove from heat. Use a little of this mixture to lightly grease eight 3-inch individual pie or tart pans.

2 In large bowl, whisk together eggs, milk, brown sugar, coconut, orange zest and juice, and spices until well combined. Stir in pumpkin purée.

3 Cut 32 five-inch squares from phyllo pastry (8 from each sheet). Layer 4 phyllo squares in each prepared pan, brushing each with oil and butter mixture. Add squares at different angles for petal-edge effect. Spoon pumpkin filling into pastry-lined pans.

4 Bake tartlets until filling is set, 20 to 25 minutes. Transfer pans to wire rack to cool slightly. Just before serving, top tartlets with blackberries and dust lightly with confectioners' sugar.

Per tartlet: 170 calories, 5 g protein, 26 g carbohydrates, 6 g fat, 3 g saturated fat, 75 g cholesterol, 6 g fiber, 170 g sodium

Pumpkin Maple Cheesecake

If you're going to indulge in a slice of rich, creamy, cheesecake, choose this one and you'll also get a huge helping of beta-carotene, the antioxidant in pumpkin that helps fight cancer and other chronic diseases.

16 SERVINGS

Prep 15 min ◆ **Cook** 60 min

- 1 cup graham cracker crumbs
- 3 tablespoons vegetable oil
- 3 packages (8 ounces each) ⅓-less-fat cream cheese, softened
- ½ cup firmly packed light-brown sugar
- 1 can (15 ounces) solid-pack pumpkin puree
- ½ cup maple syrup
- 3 large eggs
- 2 tablespoons cornstarch
- 2 teaspoons pumpkin pie spice
- 1 teaspoon vanilla extract
- ½ teaspoon salt

1 Preheat oven to 350°F. Lightly coat 9-inch springform cake pan with nonstick cooking spray.

2 In small bowl, stir together cracker crumbs and oil. Press mixture over bottom and ½ inch up side of pan. Bake until crust just begins to color, about 10 minutes.

3 In large bowl, beat together cream cheese and brown sugar until well blended. Beat in pumpkin, maple syrup, eggs, cornstarch, pie spice, vanilla, and salt until smooth. Pour filling into crust.

4 Bake cheesecake until center is just set, 55 to 60 minutes. Transfer pan to wire rack. Let cool completely. Cover and refrigerate at least 4 hours before serving.

Per serving: 236 calories, 6 g protein, 22 g carbohydrates, 14 g fat, 7 g saturated fat, 72 mg cholesterol, 1 g fiber, 291 mg sodium

No-Bake Pumpkin Pie with Gingersnap Crust

Around the winter holidays, when the kitchen gets so busy, you'll really appreciate this recipe for a quick-fix dessert that's packed with beta-carotene and fiber.

8 SERVINGS

Prep 10 min ◆ **Refrigerate** 5 hr

- 2 cups fine gingersnap crumbs
- ¼ cup butter, melted
- 2 packages (3⅛ ounces each) instant vanilla pudding mix
- 1½ cups milk
- 1 can (15 ounces) solid-pack pumpkin puree
- 1¼ teaspoons cinnamon
- ¾ teaspoon ground ginger
- ¼ teaspoon ground nutmeg
  Pecan halves, for garnish (optional)

1 In small saucepan, stir together gingersnap crumbs and melted butter until crumbs are evenly coated. Pat over bottom and up sides of 9-inch pie pan.

2 In medium bowl, whisk together pudding mixes and milk until thick and blended. Stir in pumpkin puree, cinnamon, ginger, and nutmeg. Spread evenly over gingersnap crust. If desired, garnish with pecan halves. Cover and refrigerate at least 5 hours or overnight.

Per serving: 335 calories, 5 g protein, 51 g carbohydrates, 13 g fat, 6 g saturated fat, 22 mg cholesterol, 3 g fiber, 456 mg sodium

---

helpful HINT

Instead of a mixer, you can use a food processor or blender to combine the filling ingredients for a pudding-type pie. To make such a pie even easier—and quicker—to assemble, use a store-bought graham cracker or vanilla cookie crust.

VEGETABLES FOR VITALITY

Sweet Potato Pie with Cranberry-Pecan Marmalade

A fresh cranberry-nut layer lightens the texture of this classic Southern dessert and adds its own special blend of antioxidants, as well as flavors.

8 SERVINGS

Prep 20 min ◆ **Cook** 60 min

- 6 ounces whole cranberries, fresh or frozen
- ½ plus ⅔ cups sugar
- ½ cup water
- ¾ cup pecans, toasted and chopped
  Prepared pie pastry for single-crust pie
- 2 cups mashed cooked sweet potatoes (about 2 medium)
- 1 can (12 ounces) fat-free evaporated milk
- 1 large egg, lightly beaten
- 2 large egg whites, lightly beaten
- ½ teaspoon vanilla extract
- ½ teaspoon cinnamon
- ¼ teaspoon ground nutmeg
- ¼ teaspoon ground allspice
- ⅛ teaspoon salt

1 Prepare Cranberry-Pecan Marmalade: In small saucepan, combine cranberries, ½ cup sugar, and water. Bring to a boil. Reduce heat and gently boil until cranberries pop and are softened, about 10 minutes. Remove from heat. Stir in pecans. Let cool.

2 Preheat oven to 450°F. Roll out pastry to 12-inch circle. Fit into 10-inch pie plate. Crimp edges.

3 In large bowl, stir together mashed sweet potatoes, evaporated milk, ⅔ cup sugar, egg, egg whites, vanilla, cinnamon, nutmeg, allspice, and salt.

4 Spread cooled marmalade over bottom of pie shell. Pour in potato mixture.

5 Bake pie 10 minutes. Lower oven temperature to 350°F. Bake until center is set, 40 minutes. Transfer pie to wire rack. Let cool 30 minutes. Refrigerate to cool completely.

Per serving: 455 calories, 8 g protein, 72 g carbohydrates, 16 g fat, 4 g saturated fat, 33 mg cholesterol, 4 g fiber, 218 mg sodium

FRESH ❧ IDEAS

If whole cranberries are unavailable when you want to make this sweet potato pie, substitute 1½ cups (about 12 ounces) whole-berry cranberry sauce. Heat gently, just to soften. Stir in pecans and let cool before using.

Sweet & Spicy Carrot Pie with Nut Crust

Just like pumpkin, pureed carrots make a wonderful pie filling that's chock-full of beta-carotene, fiber, and great taste. Nuts add healthful fats and rich flavor to a crust in which most of the butter has been replaced by vegetable oil.

8 SERVINGS

Prep 20 min ◆ **Cook** 70 min

- ½ cup walnuts, lightly toasted
- ½ cup hazelnuts, lightly toasted
- 1 cup graham cracker crumbs
- ¼ cup packed light-brown sugar
- 1¼ teaspoons cinnamon
- 1¼ teaspoons ground ginger
- 3 tablespoons vegetable oil or "light" olive oil
- 2 tablespoons melted butter
- 1 pound carrots, peeled and cut into chunks
- 1 cup granulated sugar
- 1 tablespoon all-purpose flour
- ½ teaspoon salt
- ¼ teaspoon ground nutmeg
- ⅛ teaspoon cloves
- 4 large eggs, lightly beaten
- ¾ cup whole milk

1 Prepare Nut Crust: In food processor, combine walnuts and hazelnuts. Pulse until coarsely chopped. Add graham cracker crumbs, light-brown sugar, ¼ teaspoon cinnamon, and ¼ teaspoon ground ginger. Pulse two or three times to combine. Add vegetable oil and melted butter. Pulse until crumbs are evenly moistened. Press over bottom and up sides of 9-inch deep-dish pie plate.

2 In large pot of lightly salted boiling water to cover, cook carrots until tender, about 20 minutes. Drain well. Transfer to food processor. Whirl until pureed. Let cool slightly.

3 Meanwhile, preheat oven to 400°F.

4 In small bowl, stir together sugar, flour, remaining teaspoon ginger, remaining teaspoon cinnamon, salt, nutmeg, and cloves. Add to carrots in processor. Whirl to combine. Add eggs and milk. Whirl until smooth and well blended. Pour into crust.

5 Bake until toothpick inserted in center of pie comes out clean, about 45 minutes. Serve warm or let cool to room temperature. Refrigerate several hours to serve cold.

Per serving: 415 calories, 8 g protein, 51 g carbohydrates, 22 g fat, 4 g saturated fat, 117 mg cholesterol, 3 g fiber, 284 mg sodium

helpful HINT

Just like cheesecake, custard-type pies that are made with eggs and milk may develop a crack across the top during baking or cooling. This is often due to excessive moisture loss during baking and can sometimes be alleviated by placing a shallow pan of hot water on the bottom shelf of the oven. However, since cracking doesn't affect the flavor or texture of the pies, it's okay to ignore it.

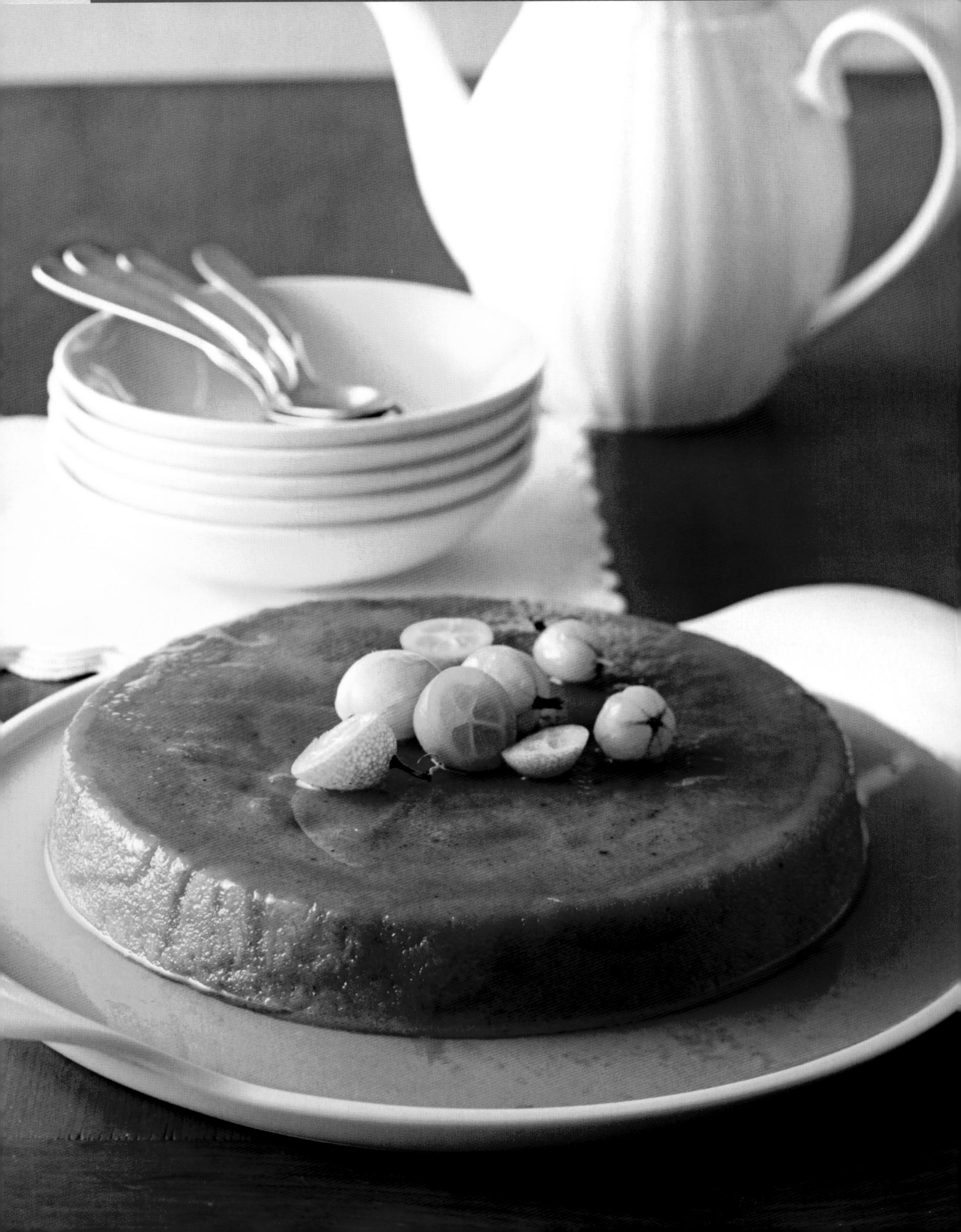

Winter Squash Flan with Caramel Sauce

Flan is always rich and creamy; this one—thanks to its vitamin-packed winter squash base—is good for you too!

12 SERVINGS

Prep 15 min ◆ **Cook** 40 min ◆ **Chill** 2 hr

- ⅓ **cup granulated sugar**
- ¼ **cup water**
- 2 **cups evaporated low-fat (2%) milk**
- 5 **large eggs**
- ¾ **cup packed light-brown sugar**
- 1 **cup frozen winter squash, thawed**
- 2 **tablespoons dark rum**
- 1 **teaspoon vanilla extract**
- ¼ **teaspoon ground allspice**

1 In small heavy saucepan, combine granulated sugar and water. Cook over medium heat until sugar turns amber color, about 5 minutes. Immediately pour caramel into 8-inch round cake pan and, using pot holders, turn and swirl pan until its bottom and sides are coated with caramel syrup. Let cool. Lightly oil any parts of pan that are not coated with caramel.

2 Preheat oven to 350°F.

3 In small saucepan, bring evaporated milk to a boil, stirring occasionally.

4 In medium bowl, whisk together eggs and brown sugar. Pour hot milk mixture into eggs, stirring constantly. Stir in squash, rum, vanilla, and allspice.

5 Place cake pan in small roasting pan. Pour egg mixture into cake pan. Fill roasting pan with enough boiling water to come halfway up sides of cake pan. Set in oven.

6 Bake until center is set, 30 to 35 minutes. Transfer cake pan from water bath to wire rack. Let cool. Then refrigerate at least 2 hours.

7 To serve, run knife around edge of pan. Place serving platter upside down on top of cake pan. Holding two firmly together, quickly invert and unmold flan, letting any caramel from pan drip over flan.

Per serving: 150 calories, 6 g protein, 26 g carbohydrates, 3 g fat, 1 g saturated fat, 92 mg cholesterol, 0 g fiber, 79 mg sodium

Coconut-Topped Sweet Potato Pudding

When a dessert provides as much beta-carotene as this one, it's worth serving just to celebrate!

10 SERVINGS

Prep 15 min ◆ **Cook** 1¾ hr

- 2 **medium sweet potatoes, peeled and grated**
- 1 **can (12 ounces) fat-free evaporated milk**
- 2 **tablespoons vegetable oil**
- ½ **cup packed light-brown sugar**
- 2 **tablespoons orange juice concentrate, thawed**
- ½ **teaspoon ground ginger**
- ½ **teaspoon ground cloves**
- ½ **teaspoon ground allspice**
- ½ **teaspoon salt**
- 1 **large egg, lightly beaten**
- 4 **large egg whites, lightly beaten**
- ½ **cup shredded coconut**

1 Preheat oven to 350°F. Coat 2-quart baking dish with nonstick cooking spray.

2 In large bowl, stir together sweet potatoes, evaporated milk, oil, brown sugar, orange juice concentrate, ginger, cloves, allspice, salt, egg, and egg whites. Pour into baking dish. Cover dish with foil.

3 Bake 1½ hours. Sprinkle top with coconut. Bake, uncovered, until center is set and coconut is golden, 30 minutes.

Per serving: 167 calories, 6 g protein, 24 g carbohydrates, 5 g fat, 3 g saturated fat, 72 mg cholesterol, 1 g fiber, 220 mg sodium

Carrot-Zucchini Sweet Bread with Orange Glaze

In every slice of this delicious tea bread, you'll get A, B, and C vitamins from the vegetables, omega-3 fatty acids from the walnuts, plus fiber from the wheat bran in the whole-wheat flour.

12 SLICES

on the menu

Sweet quick breads make great food gifts that are easy to carry along when you're invited to someone's home for dinner. They are also perfect for an afternoon tea break or an after-school snack for the kids.

Prep 15 min ◆ **Cook** 60 min

- 1½ **cups all-purpose flour**
- ½ **cup whole-wheat flour**
- 1¼ **teaspoons baking soda**
- 1 **teaspoon baking powder**
- 1 **teaspoon cinnamon**
- ½ **teaspoon salt**
- ¼ **teaspoon nutmeg**
- 1¼ **cups sugar**
- ¾ **cup vegetable oil**
- 3 **large eggs**
- 1 **teaspoon vanilla extract**
- 1 **cup grated carrots (about ½ pound carrots), blotted dry**
- 1 **cup grated zucchini (about ½ pound zucchini), blotted dry**
- ½ **cup walnuts, chopped** *(optional)*
- ½ **cup confectioners' sugar**
- 1½ **tablespoons orange juice**
- 1¼ **teaspoons grated orange zest**

1 Preheat oven to 350°F. Coat 9 x 5-inch loaf pan with nonstick cooking spray and dust with flour.

2 In medium bowl, stir together both flours, baking soda, baking powder, cinnamon, salt, and nutmeg.

3 In large bowl, beat together sugar, oil, eggs, and vanilla until blended. Stir in carrots and zucchini. Beat in flour mixture until evenly moistened. Stir in walnuts, if using. Spread batter in prepared pan.

4 Bake until toothpick inserted in top comes out clean, 55 to 60 minutes. Transfer pan to wire rack. Let cool 10 minutes. Loosen edges of loaf with thin-bladed knife. Turn bread out onto rack. Let cool completely, then glaze.

5 In small bowl, stir together confectioners' sugar, orange juice, and orange zest. Add another 1 to 2 teaspoons of orange juice to thin, if necessary. Pour half the glaze over cooled bread and spread evenly. Let set for 5 minutes. Then pour on remaining glaze.

Per slice: 325 calories, 4 g protein, 43 g carbohydrates, 16 g fat, 1 g saturated fat, 53 mg cholesterol, 2 g fiber, 280 mg sodium

Carrot-Flecked Potato Doughnuts

These are classic fried doughnuts with one big difference—thanks to the shreds of carrot, they're also a good source of the protective antioxidant beta-carotene.

18 DOUGHNUTS

Prep 15 min ◆ **Refrigerate** 1 hr ◆ **Cook** 25 min

- 2½ cups all-purpose flour
- 4 teaspoons baking powder
- ¾ teaspoon salt
- ½ teaspoon cinnamon
- ½ teaspoon ground nutmeg
- 2 large eggs
- 1 cup mashed potatoes, at room temperature
- ¾ cup finely shredded raw carrot
- ¼ cup low-fat (1%) milk
- 2 tablespoons vegetable oil
- ½ cup sugar
- 6 cups vegetable oil, for frying
  Confectioners' sugar or cinnamon-sugar, for dusting *(optional)*

1 In medium bowl, stir together flour, baking powder, salt, cinnamon, and nutmeg.

2 In large bowl, lightly beat eggs. Beat in potatoes, carrot, milk, oil, and sugar until well blended. Beat in flour mixture until well blended. The dough will be soft and sticky. Cover. Refrigerate until chilled, about 1 hour. The dough should be easy to handle.

3 Pour 6 cups of oil into large saucepan. Slowly heat until oil registers 375°F on deep-fat frying thermometer.

4 Meanwhile, lightly flour work surface. Roll out dough to ½-inch thickness. Cut out doughnuts with 3-inch doughnut cutter. Gather scraps together. Re-roll and cut out more doughnuts until all dough is used.

5 Drop 3 or 4 doughnuts into hot oil. Cook until medium brown, 3 to 4 minutes, frequently turning over with slotted spoon. Remove doughnuts to paper towel-lined tray to drain. Let oil return to 375°F before adding another batch of doughnuts. Dust cooked doughnuts with sugar, if you like. Serve warm.

Per doughnut: 292 calories, 3 g protein, 24 g carbohydrates, 20 g fat, 2 g saturated fat, 27 mg cholesterol, 1 g fiber, 250 mg sodium

HINT **helpful HINT** HINT HINT HINT HINT HINT HINT HINT

To boost the fiber content and healthfulness of any doughnut, including these potato ones, substitute one cup whole-wheat flour for one cup of the all-purpose flour called for in the recipe.

Soft Pumpkin Cookies

These cookies are loaded with beta-carotene and fiber.

2 DOZEN COOKIES

Prep 15 min ◆ **Cook** 15 min

- ½ **cup all-purpose flour**
- ½ **cup whole-wheat flour**
- ½ **teaspoon cinnamon**
- ¼ **teaspoon salt**
- ¼ **teaspoon baking soda**
- ¼ **teaspoon ground allspice**
- ¼ **cup packed light-brown sugar**
- 3 **tablespoons honey**
- ¼ **cup vegetable oil**
- 1 **large egg white**
- 1 **cup canned solid-pack pumpkin puree**
- ½ **cup dried sweetened cranberries or dark seedless raisins**
- ⅓ **cup walnuts, chopped** *(optional)*

1 Preheat oven to 350°F. Coat baking sheet with nonstick cooking spray.

2 In medium bowl, sift together flours, cinnamon, salt, baking soda, and allspice.

3 In large bowl, beat together brown sugar, honey, oil, and egg white. Stir in pumpkin. Stir in flour mixture just until evenly moistened. Fold in dried cranberries, and walnuts, if using.

4 For each cookie, drop 1 heaping teaspoon of dough onto baking sheet, spacing about 1 inch apart.

5 Bake until pick inserted in cookie comes out clean, about 15 minutes. Let cookies stand on sheets 1 minute. With metal spatula, transfer cookies to wire rack to cool. Store in airtight container up to a week.

Per cookie: 63 calories, 1 g protein, 11 g carbohydrates, 2 g fat, 0 g saturated fat, 0 mg cholesterol, 1 g fiber, 17 mg sodium

Carrot-Oatmeal-Raisin Cookies

Oats help protect your heart by lowering cholesterol.

4 DOZEN COOKIES

Prep 20 min ◆ **Cook** 10 to 12 min

- 1 **cup all-purpose flour**
- 2½ **teaspoons baking powder**
- ½ **teaspoon salt**
- ½ **teaspoon cinnamon**
- ¼ **teaspoon ground cloves**
- 1 **cup old-fashioned rolled oats**
- 1 **large egg**
- ½ **cup vegetable oil**
- 1 **teaspoon vanilla extract**
- 1 **cup packed light-brown sugar**
- 1 **cup shredded carrots (about ½ pound carrots)**
- ¾ **cup dark seedless raisins**

1 Preheat oven to 375°F. Coat baking sheets with nonstick cooking spray.

2 In medium bowl, stir together flour, baking powder, salt, cinnamon, and cloves. Stir in oats.

3 In large bowl, beat together egg, oil, and vanilla until blended. Beat in sugar. Beat in flour mixture in batches until evenly moistened. Fold in carrots and raisins. Dough will be stiff.

4 For each cookie, drop 1 heaping teaspoon dough on baking sheet, spacing about 2 inches apart.

5 Bake until golden brown and slightly darker around edges, 10 to 12 minutes. Let cookies stand on baking sheets 2 minutes. With metal spatula, transfer cookies to wire rack to cool. Store in airtight container for up to a week.

Per cookie: 64 calories, 1 g protein, 10 g carbohydrates, 3 g fat, 0 g saturated fat, 4 mg cholesterol, 1 g fiber, 49 mg sodium

helpful HINT

To freeze the dough for drop cookies, dispense dough as directed onto baking sheets and place sheets in freezer until dough is frozen solid. Then transfer the dough drops to a freezer bag or container. To bake, transfer frozen drops to prepared baking sheets. Thaw completely at room temperature before baking as directed in recipe.

on the menu

Soft, unfrosted cookies like these Carrot-Oatmeal-Raisin Cookies travel well, so they're great for mailing as gifts. To wrap, pair cooled cookies with their bottom (flat) sides together in a foil-lined tin or heavy-duty box, separating layers with wax paper. Place the tin or box in a slightly larger, outer mailing box, cushioned with crumpled paper, foam peanuts, or popcorn.

VEGETABLES FOR VITALITY

Homemade Pumpkin Spice Ice Cream

Unlike store-bought frozen desserts, this one supplies fiber and protective antioxidant vitamins along with lovely fresh flavor and creamy texture that can only come from doing it yourself.

6 SERVINGS (3 CUPS)

Prep 20 min

> 1¼ cups evaporated low-fat (2%) milk
> 1 large egg
> ½ cup packed light-brown sugar
> ⅔ cup canned solid-pack pumpkin puree
> 1 teaspoon vanilla extract
> ½ teaspoon ground ginger
> ½ teaspoon cinnamon
> Large pinch ground nutmeg
> Pinch salt

1 In medium saucepan, bring milk to a boil.

2 In large bowl, whisk together egg and sugar. Gradually whisk in boiling milk. Stir in pumpkin, vanilla, ginger, cinnamon, nutmeg, and salt. Refrigerate until thoroughly chilled.

3 Freeze in ice cream maker, following manufacturer's directions. Soften slightly before serving.

Per 1/2 cup: 141 calories, 5 g protein, 26 g carbohydrates, 2 g fat, 1 g saturated fat, 40 mg cholesterol, 1 g fiber, 102 mg sodium

HINT **helpful HINT** HINT HINT HINT HINT HINT HINT

To soften ice cream enough to scoop it out easily, transfer the container from the freezer to a plate in the refrigerator for 20 to 30 minutes before you plan to serve it. A minute in the microwave can also help.

FRESH IDEAS

Creative toppings and custom "stir-ins" are all the rage at ice cream parlors, and you can certainly follow suit at home. Some ideas for Homemade Pumpkin Spice Ice Cream add-ins: dried fruit such as raisins, cranberries, or chopped apricots; chopped toasted walnuts or pecans; maple syrup swirl or crushed gingersnaps.

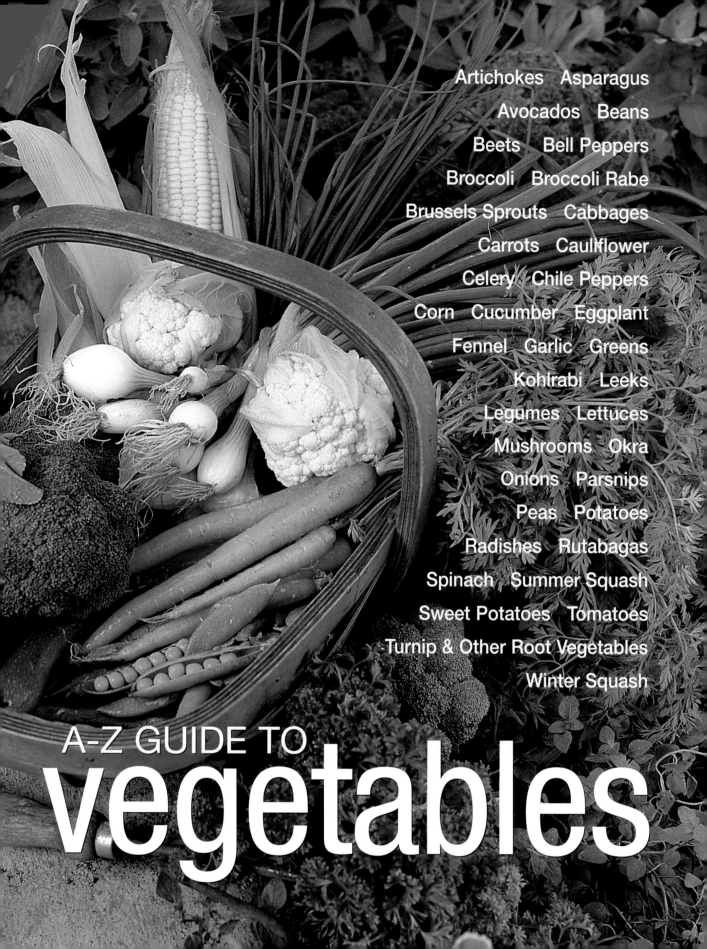

Artichokes   Asparagus
Avocados   Beans
Beets   Bell Peppers
Broccoli   Broccoli Rabe
Brussels Sprouts   Cabbages
Carrots   Cauliflower
Celery   Chile Peppers
Corn   Cucumber   Eggplant
Fennel   Garlic   Greens
Kohlrabi   Leeks
Legumes   Lettuces
Mushrooms   Okra
Onions   Parsnips
Peas   Potatoes
Radishes   Rutabagas
Spinach   Summer Squash
Sweet Potatoes   Tomatoes
Turnip & Other Root Vegetables
Winter Squash

A-Z GUIDE TO
vegetables

Artichokes

When you eat a green globe artichoke, you are actually feasting on a giant flower bud plucked from the stalk of a bushy thistle plant. Health-conscious cooks and gourmets alike prize this vegetable for its rich nutrients and earthy flavor.

PACKED INTO **ONE** STEAMED ARTICHOKE:

ABOUT **60** CALORIES • 20% OF THE DAILY REQUIREMENT FOR **vitamin C** • 15% OF THE DAILY REQUIREMENT FOR THE **B vitamin folate** • ESSENTIAL MINERALS SUCH AS **iron**, **copper**, AND **magnesium** • 6 GRAMS OF **fiber**

At the Market

SEASON Springtime is peak season for artichokes, but you'll also see them in the market at other times throughout the fall and winter.

WHAT TO LOOK FOR Spring artichokes should be a healthy green. Artichokes harvested in cooler weather are darker and may have bronze-tipped petals. Choose meaty-leafed globes that are heavy for their size.

In the Kitchen

STORING Store artichokes, unwashed, in a sealed plastic bag in the refrigerator for up to two weeks.

PREP To prepare artichokes for cooking, wash well under cold running water. Trimming techniques are shown at right.

BASIC COOKING To steam an artichoke, arrange washed and trimmed whole artichokes in a nonreactive steamer over boiling water. Cover and cook until an outer leaf easily pulls out, about 30 minutes. Drain artichokes upside down in a colander before serving. To serve, sprinkle with lemon juice and salt. You can also cook artichokes in a large pot of lightly salted boiling water for 30 to 40 minutes.

BEST USES IN RECIPES Artichokes are usually served with a dip as a first course. Hot artichokes are traditionally offered with melted butter or hollandaise sauce; cold ones with a vinaigrette or mayonnaise.

At the Table

It's proper to eat an artichoke with your fingers. Pluck a leaf from the side and dip the free end into sauce, put that end into your mouth, and bite down. Pull the leaf through your teeth, scraping off all the pulp.

Nestled at the base of the artichoke is the heart, prized for its buttery texture and nutty flavor. To get to the heart, remove the outer leaves, then pull out the pale center petals and scrape off the choke (the fuzzy layer that sits on top of the heart).

fresh ideas

● For a party, pluck leaves from a couple of hot cooked artichokes and arrange them on a platter with a small dip bowl in the center. A traditional dip is equal parts olive oil and melted butter with a few drops of fresh lemon juice.

● Try a new artichoke dip: Make a puree of mashed roasted garlic, freshly ground black pepper, soft silken tofu, and lemon juice.

● Tender baby Italian artichokes, available seasonally, can be trimmed, halved lengthwise, and added to a mixed vegetable sauté or cooked on a grill. They have no choke.

GETTING READY

With a chef's knife, cut stem at base of globe. You can cook the stem and eat it, if you like.

1

Snip off sharp tips from petals with a pair of scissors.

2

Rub raw surfaces with lemon to keep them from discoloring.

3

fresh ideas

● When it comes to flavor, asparagus can certainly stand on its own. But it also goes well with lemon or balsamic vinaigrette, mustard-mayonnaise dressing, ginger-flavored soy sauce, or a topping of shaved Parmesan cheese.

● A favorite party nibble for the low-carbohydrate crowd is low-fat ham slices rolled around short spears of cold cooked asparagus—with or without a dab of mayonnaise. Asparagus has a low glycogenic count.

● Leftover cooked green asparagus, pureed in a food processor or blender, can be heated up with a little milk and a pinch each of chopped parsley and chopped tarragon to make an almost instant cream of asparagus soup.

DID YOU KNOW . . .

. . . that the reason asparagus is so expensive—compared to other vegetables—is that it must be harvested by hand?

. . . that an asparagus stalk can grow 10 inches in a 24-hour period?

Asparagus

A member of the lily family, asparagus was considered a delicacy by the Greeks and Romans (as well as a cure for toothache and a bee-sting preventive). We, too, prize it for its great taste but also appreciate its high-power nutrients.

PACKED INTO **ONE CUP** OF ASPARAGUS:

LESS THAN **50** CALORIES ● TWO-THIRDS THE DAILY REQUIREMENT FOR THE B VITAMIN **folate**, WHICH HELPS NEW BLOOD CELLS FORM AND PREVENTS SERIOUS BIRTH DEFECTS ● **thiamine** AND OTHER B VITAMINS NECESSARY FOR ENERGY METABOLISM ● MORE THAN ONE-FOURTH THE DAILY REQUIREMENT FOR **vitamin C** ● 4 GRAMS OF **fiber** ● A PHYTOCHEMICAL CALLED **glutathione**, ONE OF THE MOST POTENT ANTIOXIDANTS FOR FIGHTING THE CELL DESTRUCTION THAT LEADS TO DISEASE

At the Market

SEASON Asparagus appears in Western markets as early as February with the first California crop (California, Washington, and Michigan are the prime producers in the United States). In the Midwest and East, the growing season lasts from May through July. Imported asparagus is sold in the fall and winter.

WHAT TO LOOK FOR Good fresh asparagus has firm round spears with tightly closed tips of deep green or purple. Spears at least a half-inch in diameter tend to be more tender than smaller ones. Pick spears of uniform size, if you can, so that they will cook evenly.

In the Kitchen

STORING Asparagus should be eaten as soon as possible after being picked. Stored at room temperature, it can, for example, lose half its vitamin C in two days. If you must keep it overnight, wrap the bottom ends in damp paper towels, cover it with plastic wrap, and put it in the refrigerator. Or you can stand the spears upright in a glass of water in the refrigerator, covered with a plastic bag, for up to two days.

PREP To ready asparagus for cooking, wash it carefully to rid it of any sand. Snap off and discard the tough ends *(facing page)*. If your asparagus has thick stalks, use a swivel-blade peeler to peel off the skin on the bottom of the remaining stem.

BASIC COOKING Asparagus can be cooked many different ways.
● Steaming or boiling are the traditional methods for cooking whole spears. It takes about 3 to 5 minutes to cook asparagus either way. Be careful not to overcook asparagus or it will become soggy and limp. In fact, you should remove asparagus from the heat when the spears are just tender-crisp because they will continue to cook as they cool.

VARIETIES

Green and purple asparagus are used interchangeably in most recipes. White asparagus has its own special following. And wild asparagus, still a forager's treat in the United States for those who know where to find it, is now cultivated in France and called baby green asparagus.

White asparagus has a milder flavor than green asparagus—and fewer nutrients.

Purple asparagus is a newcomer on the

asparagus scene. It has a dramatic burgundy-hued exterior and a cream-colored flesh. Purple spears are larger and less fibrous than green asparagus spears. Purple asparagus also has a higher sugar content and therefore can be eaten raw. Diagonally cut purple-edged slices with a cream center garnish salads quite handsomely and perk up stir-fries. Cooked purple asparagus has a mild nutty flavor. Cooking it too long, however, turns it dark green.

White asparagus has long been considered

a delicacy, particularly by Europeans, who developed it in the late 18th century by growing green asparagus underground. Spears that never saw the sun did not undergo the process of photosynthesis that makes green asparagus green. Today white asparagus commands a high price in the United States because there is a limited supply and it is a labor-intensive crop. Grown commercially under sandy-soil mounds or black plastic "polyhouses" to protect them from the sun, white asparagus spears are harvested by hand daily in season.

Wild asparagus

is green asparagus returned to nature by birds or other wildlife that dispurses seeds. On first sight, it seems a spindly step-child to cultivated asparagus, but it has avid followers, who head eagerly for their favorite foraging spots every spring.

● Microwaving is another easy way to cook asparagus spears: Place a pound of spears, tips to the center, in a shallow microwaveable dish, add ¼ cup water, cover tightly and cook at 100 percent power for 4 to 7 minutes.

NEW COOKING TECHNIQUES

● More recently, it has become popular to roast asparagus spears in the oven with a little olive oil and seasonings. Preheat the oven to 375°F. Lay the spears in a single layer in a shallow pan, spray with olive oil, and season with salt and pepper. Roast until spears are tender-crisp, about 20 minutes.

● To grill asparagus, brush the spears with olive oil, sprinkle with salt, and place crosswise on the grill rack over a medium fire. Grill, turning often, until tender, 4 to 6 minutes, depending on the thickness of the spears. Sprinkle with pepper and lemon juice before serving. To make grilling easier and quicker, you can first parboil asparagus in a large pot of rapidly boiling, lightly salted water for just 1 minute. Drain and spread spears out to cool quickly and prevent further cooking. Then grill for just 3 to 4 minutes.

BEST USES IN RECIPES Whole asparagus spears, served on their own, make an elegant first course or a special occasion side dish. The traditional sauce for hot asparagus spears is lemony, buttery hollandaise and for cold asparagus spears, vinaigrette or mayonnaise. Cut-up asparagus makes a good addition to stir-fries. Parboiled or stir-fried asparagus pieces are delicious in omelets, salads, soups, and stews.

TRIMMING ASPARAGUS

Feel along the lower stalk for a natural breaking place—a divide between tough and more tender parts.

You can snap off the end of the stalk at that point, readying the spear for cooking.

fresh ideas

● Use mashed avocado to bind a sandwich of sprouts and chopped vegetables, seasoned with salt and pepper, and tucked neatly into a whole-wheat pita pocket.

● For a creamy tart salad dressing, mash an avocado with plain nonfat yogurt, lime juice to taste, salt, and hot sauce.

● Try an avocado smoothie: In a blender puree fresh avocado with milk, a touch of honey, and a couple of ice cubes.

● Avocado for dessert? Puree fresh avocado with some sugar or honey and lemon juice for a quick and easy mousse. Top with a few toasted almonds.

THE TOOTHPICK TEST

You can feel an avocado to see if it's ripe, but if you don't trust your touch, use a toothpick. Stick a pick into the stem end, and if it moves in and out with ease, the avocado is ripe and ready to eat.

Avocados

Nicknamed "alligator pears," avocados are tropical fruits that are most often used like a vegetable in appetizers and salads. Healthful, unsaturated fats give the fruit its buttery texture and rich, nutty flavor.

PACKED INTO **ONE-FOURTH** OF AN AVOCADO:

81 CALORIES • A SIGNIFICANT AMOUNT OF **vitamin E**, WHICH SLOWS DOWN THE AGING PROCESS AND PROTECTS AGAINST CANCER • **monounsaturated fats**, WHICH HELP LOWER BLOOD LEVELS OF LDL (BAD) CHOLESTEROL • **glutathione**, AN ANTIOXIDANT THAT PROTECTS BODY CELLS FROM DAMAGE • **beta-sitosterol**, WHICH HELPS BLOCKS ABSORPTION OF CHOLESTEROL IN THE INTESTINE • **lutein**, WHICH PROTECTS AGAINST CANCER AND DISEASES OF THE EYE • **folate** TO HELP PROTECT AGAINST HEART DISEASE • **magnesium** TO HELP WITH ENERGY METABOLISM AND MUSCLE FUNCTION • **potassium** TO KEEP ELECTROLYTES IN BALANCE

At the Market

SEASON Avocados, originally cultivated in Central America, are grown mainly in California and Florida for the U.S. market. Because they don't start to ripen until they are cut from the tree, fresh avocados are available all year long. Farmers can wait for months to harvest an avocado crop so that they always have fresh ones to go to market That explains why you usually find unripe avocados in your grocery.

WHAT TO LOOK FOR Avocados vary in size, color, and skin texture, depending on the variety and where they are grown *(facing page)*. No matter what type of avocado you buy, however, look for heavy fruit and avoid those with bruised or sunken spots on their skin. A perfectly ripe avocado yields to gentle pressure from your hand.

In the Kitchen

STORING If you buy an unripe avocado, it will ripen at room temperature over the course of a few days. To speed up ripening, place the avocado in a brown paper bag. Store at warm room temperature for a day or two or until the avocado yields to gentle pressure from your hand. You can ripen a cut avocado this way too, but be sure to cover the cut surface closely with plastic wrap to prevent its turning brown. Ripe avocados can be stored in the refrigerator for four or five days. Don't store unripe avocados in the refrigerator; they will never ripen properly afterward. If you find yourself with too much ripe avocado, peel and pit the fruit and puree it with lemon or lime juice to prevent discoloration. Use about 2 teaspoons juice for each avocado. Pack the puree into a covered container, label with the date, and freeze for up to four months.

VARIETIES

Avocados were first grown in the United States in the mid-1800s in both California and Florida. These two states still have the world's largest avocado production. Between them the states raise twenty-odd varieties of avocado, which seem to depend on their specific growing conditions for their identities because the various species don't transplant well to other locations.

California avocados
Almost 90 percent of the U.S. crop of avocados is grown in California. The state's most abundant—and popular—variety is Hass, a medium-sized avocado that averages about half a pound in weight and has a pebbly skin that turns from green to a purplish black as it ripens. More smooth-skinned California varieties include Bacon, Fuerte, and Zutano.

Florida avocados
The Sunshine State raises larger and less expensive avocados than California that, ironically, contain about half the fat and two-thirds the calories. The texture of Florida avocados is, therefore, less creamy. Also, Florida avocados don't keep as well. Among the most popular Florida avocado varieties are Booth, Lula, and Waldin.

PREP To peel an avocado, first slice it into quarters *(right)* or halves lengthwise, cutting to the large center seed. You can twist the cut avocado to separate halves. Remove the seed with a paring knife if it doesn't lift right out. If the avocado is ripe, you can use your fingers to peel back the skin *(right)*. Otherwise, use a paring knife. Always rub or sprinkle cut avocado with lemon or lime juice to prevent discoloration. This inevitable browning doesn't affect the flavor or nutrition, but it does make the avocado flesh less appetizing to look at. Cover mashed or pureed avocado with a heavy-duty plastic wrap applied directly to the surface. The convenient idea—often repeated—that leaving the seed in with the mashed avocado will prevent browning is, unfortunately, not true.

BEST USES IN RECIPES Avocados are usually eaten raw. High heat causes them to turn bitter, so avocado pieces are added to hot dishes after cooking. Sliced or chopped avocado adds a rich note to salads or sandwiches. Avocado is the basis for many classic American dishes such as avocado stuffed with crab or shrimp salad and avocado and grapefruit salad with a honey-mustard dressing.

BEST RECIPE Mashed avocado is traditionally used to make the Mexican dip guacamole, now appreciated world wide. To make guacamole for a party, you will need 2 ripe Hass avocados, halved and pitted; 1 medium tomato, peeled, cored, seeded, and coarsely chopped; ½ cup finely chopped red onion; ⅓ cup chopped fresh cilantro (coriander); 3 tablespoons lime juice; ¾ teaspoon ground cumin; ¾ teaspoon salt; and ¾ teaspoon jalapeño pepper sauce. Scoop avocado flesh into a medium bowl and mash with a fork until not quite smooth. Add remaining ingredients and mix well. Cover with plastic wrap and keep in the refrigerator until ready to use. Guacamole is traditionally served with tortilla chips, but many health-conscious people enjoy it just as well with raw vegetables.

CUTTING UP AN AVOCADO

With a sharp knife, cut out a quarter of the avocado.

1

Pull off the skin with your fingers as shown here; it will come right off a ripe fruit.

2

Slice through the peeled flesh with a paring knife and sprinkle with lemon juice.

3

DID YOU KNOW . . .

. . . that avocados, unlike other fruits, lose their sugar content as they ripen?

fresh ideas

● Beans can be jazzed up with various finishing flavors. Before combining the just-cooked beans with other ingredients, be sure to toss them in a hot skillet to evaporate any moisture. This will ensure that the beans will better absorb the flavors.

● Garlic oil: Combine 2 tablespoons olive oil per pound of beans with 2 cloves finely chopped garlic; heat until just beginning to sizzle. Add beans and cook, tossing, until heated through. Season with salt and pepper.

● Lemon butter: Toss one pound of cooked beans with 1½ tablespoons melted butter in a hot skillet. Sprinkle lightly to taste with fresh lemon juice, salt, and pepper.

● Toasted almonds: Lightly brown slivered or sliced almonds in vegetable oil or butter; toss with cooked beans and season to taste.

● Prosciutto or ham: Thinly slice 3 ounces prosciutto or smoked ham. Heat 1½ tablespoons olive oil or butter in large skillet. Add beans and prosciutto and toss to mix.

● Parmesan cheese: Toss beans with melted butter and sprinkle with freshly grated Parmesan and freshly ground black pepper.

Beans

Depending on where you're from, the most familiar fresh bean is called a green bean, snap bean, or string bean. This category of edible pods also includes wax beans, Chinese yard-long beans, and France's famous *haricots verts,* among others.

PACKED INTO **ONE CUP** OF BEANS:

ABOUT **35** CALORIES ● 30% OF THE DAILY REQUIREMENT FOR **vitamin C** ● THE B VITAMIN **folate**, IMPORTANT IN PREGNANCY AND FOR NORMAL GROWTH ● PHYTOCHEMICALS CALLED **saponins**, BELIEVED TO STIMULATE THE IMMUNE SYSTEM ● **insoluble fiber**, WHICH SERVES AS A DIGESTIVE AID AND MAY HELP LOWER CHOLESTEROL

At the Market

SEASON Fresh green beans are a year-round staple in the supermarket produce section, but just-picked beans from a summer farm stand usually offer the very best flavor and texture. That's because fresh beans, like corn, will lose their crunchy sweetness during prolonged storage; the sooner they make it from field to table, the better.

WHAT TO LOOK FOR Regardless of which variety you are shopping for, choose beans that snap rather than bend when folded in half. The pods should be straight with a "peach fuzz" feel and no blemishes or brown spots. Limp beans as well as those with large seeds will be tough and bland. Pick slender beans of a uniform size for even cooking.

In the Kitchen

STORING Keep beans in the vegetable bin of your refrigerator, loosely wrapped in plastic, and use as soon as possible.

PREP To prepare fresh beans, simply snap or trim off the stem end of the vegetable; the fine point at the tip is appealing and edible so there's no reason to remove it. Beans can be left whole or cut to any length desired; they look better cut on the diagonal.

BASIC COOKING Steam or simmer beans for 3 to 10 minutes, depending on their thickness, until they're cooked but still retain a bit of crunch—it's best to take a test bite to determine this. Beans also cook well and retain their color in the microwave. Many cooks like to blanch beans for 1 or 2 minutes in a huge pot of lightly salted boiling water and then finish them later by sautéing them in butter or olive oil just before serving. However you cook them, drain beans immediately. If you are planning to finish the beans later or you are using them chilled for a salad recipe, plunge the tender-crisp cooked beans into ice water to stop the cooking process and retain their bright color; drain and pat completely dry before adding to other ingredients or refrigerating.

VARIETIES

The beans that we eat fresh are not different species from the dried beans that we cook for hours to make chili and Boston baked beans. Fresh beans are edible pods that are picked at a different time in the plant's growth cycle. Green beans and wax beans, for example, are the immature—and delicious—pods of kidney beans. There are, however, different varieties of edible pods:

Chinese long beans
These mild-tasting green beans that are slim and very long—usually up to 18 inches—came to the U.S. from the Orient and are also called yard-long and asparagus beans. They are related to black-eyed peas, but taste like other green beans when cooked. Often cut up for use in stir-fries, they are a staple of Chinese cooking. Although the beans can grow to as long as 30 inches, they are at their best and most tender when they are young and half that size.

Haricots verts
Developed by the French from varieties of standard green beans, these small, slender relatives are tasty miniatures that are now available in North American markets. They have a delicate flavor that is quite distinctive.

Italian green beans
Recognizable by their broad flat shape and deep green color, these beans, sometimes called Romano beans, are a specialty of Italian markets.

Purple wax beans
Exotic-looking at the market with their deep-colored pods, these smaller cousins of yellow wax beans lose their wonderful hue during cooking, turning green, and taste much like other wax beans.

Yellow or wax beans
Color and nutrition separate wax beans from green beans, which they resemble in both size and flavor. Green beans, however, have eight times as much beta-carotene as the paler yellow beans.

BEST USES IN RECIPES Fresh green beans, sautéed in butter and seasoned with salt and pepper, make a refreshing accompaniment to almost any main dish. Any fresh bean, cut to a manageable length, is a welcome addition to a stir-fry or hot pasta dish. Cold cooked green beans add depth and color to potato and pasta salads.

SHELL BEANS—lima, fava, and soybeans, or edamame—fall nutritionally between fresh green beans and dried beans that have developed high-protein and carbohydrate and low-vitamin counts. Used much like dried beans (except they don't need to be soaked), shell beans have protein, potassium, iron, and vitamin C in different degrees. Lima beans, which indeed do come from Lima, Peru, are the most popular shell bean in North America. They provide high amounts of iron and potassium. Fava beans, or broad beans, are similar to lima beans, just a little larger and richer in folate and vitamin C. Both are used cold in salads and hot as a side dish alone or in soups or stews. Soybeans are a staple of Asian food markets. Fresh soybeans are unique among beans in having high amounts of complete protein. They also contain unsaturated fat. Soybeans have a mild flavor. Keep refrigerated and shell them right before you cook them.

DID YOU KNOW . . .

. . . that string beans don't have strings anymore? The annoying fibers that used to be attached to either side of the pod were bred out almost 100 years ago, but the name "string bean" is still as common for this vegetable as snap bean or green bean.

fresh ideas

● Young beets up to an inch in diameter have tender, edible skin that doesn't require peeling. Baby beets also have the sweetest greens. Cook the leaves and roots separately and then serve them together: Steam the roots for about 15 minutes. Meanwhile, sauté the greens in a little olive oil and butter. Drain the beetroots, cut them in half, sprinkle with salt and pepper, and serve them warm on their own bed of sautéed greens.

● Sprinkle hot beets with lemon juice, butter, and salt and pepper.

● Serve hot or cold beets with a yogurt-horseradish sauce.

● Sliced chilled cooked beets, sliced purple onions, and segments of orange in a vinaigrette dressing on a bed of watercress make a lovely summer salad.

DID YOU KNOW . . .
. . . that beets are one of the few vegetables that most people agree taste almost as good out of the can as fresh?

Beets

Ruby-red beets are extra-sweet because they contain more natural sugar than any other vegetable that we eat. Beets are, however, still low in calories, very low in fat, and packed with important vitamins and minerals.

PACKED INTO A **HALF-CUP** OF COOKED BEETS:

37 CALORIES • A SIGNIFICANT AMOUNT OF **folate,** WHICH IS IMPORTANT FOR NORMAL GROWTH AND PROTEIN METABOLISM AND REDUCES THE RISK OF BIRTH DEFECTS SUCH AS SPINA BIFIDA PLUS **magnesium**, **potassium** , AND **vitamin C**

At the Market

SEASON Beets are available all year long, but are at their best during summer months, when baby beets are also available.

WHAT TO LOOK FOR Choose beets with their tops on (clipped-top beets have been in storage). The beet tops should look fresh and the beets themselves firm, smooth, and unbruised. Pick bunches of uniform-size beets up to 3 inches in diameter. If you shop at a specialty food market, you may also see golden yellow, pink, or near-white beets. These hybrids are cooked and used the same way as red beets, but their roots and greens are milder in flavor.

In the Kitchen

STORING To store beets, first cut off the leafy tops, leaving an inch or two of stem attached to the beets. Leave the long root intact. Store the greens and beets in separate plastic bags in the vegetable drawer of your refrigerator. You must use the greens within a couple of days, but the beets will keep up to a couple of weeks.

PREP To prepare beetroots, gently scrub under running water and dry on paper towels. Leave two inches of stem attached to unpeeled whole beets to prevent color (and nutrients) from "bleeding out" during cooking.

BASIC COOKING To preserve their color and nutrients, beets are never peeled or cut before cooking. Baking, steaming, and microwaving are the best ways to cook beets to retain their color and flavor. To bake beets, simply wrap them in foil, put them in a baking pan, and cook them in a 350° oven for 1½ to 2 hours. Let them cool enough to peel and then serve hot or cool and refrigerate for salads.

BEST USES IN RECIPES Beets are most commonly eaten cooked as a hot side dish, cooked but cold in appetizers or salads, and pickled as a condiment, but they can also be grated raw and added to salads. And, of course, beets are the key ingredient in the Russian and Central European peasant soup borscht, which is a great winter warmer-upper, but also a refreshing summer treat when served cold.

Bell Peppers

Like a string of multicolored lights, red, yellow, purple, orange, and green bell peppers brighten the produce section of almost every supermarket these days. This brilliant display starts with the humble green pepper.

PACKED INTO A **HALF-CUP** OF BELL PEPPER:

LESS THAN **14** CALORIES • MORE THAN 150% OF THE DAILY REQUIREMENT FOR **vitamin C** • MORE THAN 100% OF THE DAILY REQUIREMENT FOR VITAMIN A • THE ANTIOXIDANT **beta-carotene** TO FIGHT CHRONIC DISEASE • **folate** FOR NORMAL GROWTH • **vitamin B$_6$** FOR NORMAL BRAIN FUNCTION AND FORMATION OF RED BLOOD CELLS

At the Market

SEASON You can always find sweet bell peppers in your produce section, but they're most plentiful in summer.

WHAT TO LOOK FOR Choose nicely shaped globes with firm, glossy skin and no cuts, blisters, or bruises. Avoid peppers with moldy stems, which might be a sign of rot on the inside. Peppers should feel heavy for their size and look crisp, not limp.

In the Kitchen

STORING Store peppers, unwrapped, in the vegetable drawer of your refrigerator. Green bells keep for about a week. Yellow, orange, and red peppers keep up to five days.

PREP To clean a bell pepper before eating or cooking, cut it in half through the stem end. Remove the stem, seed pods, and white ribs. Cut the pepper into flat panels that can then be sliced or chopped. To peel a sweet pepper for recipes, you must first char it over a gas flame or charcoal fire or under a broiler, turning often for even blackening. Steam charred peppers in a paper bag for 15 minutes, and then scrape off the skin, cut out the stem, and core and discard the seeds.

BASIC COOKING You can grill whole peppers outdoors for 20 minutes, or slow roast them in a 375°F oven for 30 minutes. Save purple bell peppers for salads; they turn an ugly color when cooked. Whole bell peppers, tops cut through to make a lid, can be stuffed with meat or grain mixtures. Microwave shells alone for 2 minutes, then stuff and heat whole dish through.

BEST USES IN RECIPES Raw peppers, chopped or sliced, are good additions to all kinds of salsas and salads—pasta, potato, rice, or mixed green. Raw or cooked, red, yellow, and orange bell peppers are sweeter than green ones. Chopped and sautéed in oil, bell peppers enhance pilafs, pasta sauces, soups, stews, and stir-fries.

PEELING PEPPERS

Roast peppers on broiler pan lined with foil until skins are charred and blistered.
1

Put cooked peppers in paper bag and seal tightly. Let steam for 10 minutes.
2

Peel away skin, then remove stem and seeds.
3

Cut peppers into bite-size chunks.
4

DID YOU KNOW . . .
. . . that a red bell pepper has nearly 11 times as much beta-carotene as a green one? And three times as much vitamin C?

fresh ideas

● Broccoli stalks, which many people simply throw away, are actually tender and tasty parts of the plant that can be put to good use in the kitchen. Trim off the end, peel the stalk if you like, and cut into thin coins or small sticks. You can blanch, steam, or stir-fry broccoli stems, or shred and serve them raw in salad or slaw.

● Puree cooked broccoli with a little chicken broth, some milk or fat-free half-and-half, a pinch of marjoram, some salt and cayenne pepper to make a quick and nourishing cream soup.

DID YOU KNOW...

...that the first broccoli harvested for commercial use in the United States was grown in Brooklyn, New York, in the early 1920s.

...that cooked broccoli offers even more benefits than raw? Cooking ups the indole content by freeing a crucial enzyme.

Broccoli

A true guardian of good health, broccoli is well regarded as one of the most nutritious vegetables you can eat. It is super-high in vitamins, full of fiber and loaded with phytochemicals that help fight off disease.

PACKED INTO ONE CUP OF BROCCOLI:

LESS THAN **25** CALORIES • MORE THAN A DAY'S REQUIREMENT FOR **vitamin C** • ALMOST HALF A DAY'S REQUIREMENT FOR **vitamin A** • **folate** TO HELP FIGHT BIRTH DEFECTS • **fiber** TO HELP CONTROL BLOOD SUGAR • **calcium** TO HELP FIGHT BONE DISEASE • **sulforaphane**, A PHYTOCHEMICAL THAT HELPS FIGHT CANCER • **lutein** A CAROTENOID THAT HELPS FIGHT MACULAR DEGENERATION • **indoles** TO FIGHT CANCER.

At the Market

SEASON Broccoli is at its best and most abundant in mid-fall through the winter.

WHAT TO LOOK FOR When choosing broccoli, look for dark green heads and leaves and bright green stems. The stalks holding the florets should be slender and crisp and the florets themselves tightly closed and uniformly green. Yellowed, flowering buds are a sign of old age and a toughness that cannot be overcome with longer cooking.

In the Kitchen

STORING Keep broccoli in a plastic bag in the vegetable drawer of the refrigerator for three or four days.

PREP Wash broccoli well. Peel tough skin from stalks with a swivel-bladed peeler or sharp paring knife, if desired. If cooking long spears with florets attached, slice spears lengthwise as far up as the florets. Also wash and cook the leaves, which are full of vitamins and good flavor. Add them to soups or stir-fries.

BASIC COOKING Use broccoli florets raw or briefly blanched in a large pot of lightly salted boiling water for snacks and party trays with dip. As a side dish, blanch, steam, sauté or stir-fry florets and chopped-up stems and leaves with a little added liquid for just 3 to 5 minutes. Short cooking time brings out the best flavor and color and helps prevent broccoli's valuable vitamins from leaching out into the cooking water. It also prevents the breakdown of chemicals in broccoli that can release strong-smelling sulfur compounds that smell like rotten eggs. This may explain why you didn't like broccoli as a child, when vegetables were cooked much longer.

BEST USES IN RECIPES Raw broccoli is a favorite on raw vegetable platters or in salads. Broccoli florets can be sautéed with garlic and olive oil, added at the beginning of a vegetable stir-fry, or steamed and topped with

VARIETIES

Green broccoli, purple broccoli, broccolini, and broccoflower can all be used interchangeably in most recipes that call for some kind of broccoli.

Broccoflower is a cross between cauliflower and broccoli that ends up looking like green cauliflower and tasting more like cauliflower than broccoli. It is a vivid chartreuse. Choose broccoflower with a tightly closed rounded or pyramid-shaped head.

Broccolini is a cross between regular broccoli and Chinese broccoli that results in a baby-broccoli-like plant with small, thin stems and tiny heads. It is similar in flavor to broccoli, but a bit milder. Choose bright green, fresh-looking bunches.

Chinese broccoli With large dark green leaves, thin stems, and tiny, flowering buds, Chinese broccoli looks like large spinach leaves but tastes like a sweet, mild version of green broccoli. To cook Chinese broccoli, separate the leaves from the stems. Peel and blanch the stems, then combine with leaves in a quick stir-fry.

Purple broccoli Although it is a deeply colored variety of broccoli, it looks like purple cauliflower because of its tight heads. Purple broccoli nevertheless tastes like green broccoli and can add a lively color note to raw vegetable platters. The purple fades in cooking, however. Purple broccoli can also be used decoratively; several heads together make a dramatic centerpiece for a buffet table.

cheese sauce, white sauce, or a low-calorie squeeze of fresh lemon juice, salt, and pepper. Sautéed broccoli florets can be used as a healthy pizza topping and as a delicious addition to a cheese-based quiche or omelet. Broccoli stems and leaves can be cooked in chicken broth as the base for a cream of broccoli soup: Puree the cooked broccoli, add milk or cream, and season to taste with salt, pepper, and a little dried oregano.

HISTORY . . . Broccoli was first mentioned in writings during the Roman Empire, but its origins are not known. It was introduced into France by Catherine de Médicis when she came north to marry Henry II in 1533. Broccoli isn't mentioned in English texts until the early 1700s. The real late-comers to broccoli, however, are Americans, who only began to discover this superstar vegetable in the 1920s, which is when *The New Yorker* ran a cartoon showing a harassed mother trying to persuade her son to try a serving of the new vegetable on his dinner plate. The caption reads:

> *"It's broccoli, dear."*
> *"I say it's spinach, and I say the hell with it!"*

CUTTING UP BROCCOLI

Cut off but save the stem and side shoots, which are delicious and tender when cooked.

1

Remove individual florets of broccoli for a stir-fry or to put on a raw vegetable platter.

2

fresh ideas

● Use cooked broccoli rabe with a little sautéed onion and bacon and a touch of thyme to stuff mushroom caps for a hot hors d'oeuvre. Bake the stuffed mushroom for 5 minutes before serving.

● Broccoli rabe gives a pungent lift to white beans cooked with tomatoes. Add the cut-up vegetable for the last 15 minutes of cooking.

● Sauté blanched, cut-up broccoli rabe with sultana raisins and pine nuts for a Southern Italian side-dish treat.

● Cook pasta in the water that you have used to blanch broccoli rabe. Then make a simple sauce by sautéing the vegetable with garlic and other seasonings in olive oil. The broccoli rabe water will flavor the pasta and punch up the impact of the sauce.

DID YOU KNOW . . .

. . . that broccoli rabe is a best-selling vegetable in Hong Kong?

Broccoli Rabe

Not even a distant cousin to broccoli, broccoli rabe is actually a member of the turnip family. But its flavor, often called pleasantly bitter, is similar to that of strong broccoli and thereby comes its name.

PACKED INTO ONE CUP OF BROCCOLI RABE:

LESS THAN **20** CALORIES • MORE THAN A DAY'S REQUIREMENT FOR **vitamin C** • 7.6 MG OF **beta-catotene** • **sulforaphane**, A PHYTOCHEMICAL THAT HELPS FIGHT CANCER • **indoles** TO FIGHT CANCER

At the Market

SEASON Broccoli rabe, also known as broccoli rape, broccoli raab, or rapini, is a cool-weather plant that is at its best and most abundant from fall to midwinter. Popular in Southern Italy, where it grows wild as well as under cultivation, broccoli rabe—thanks to early Italian immigrants—was introduced to North America in the 19th century. More recently, Chinese immigrants have demanded this pungent vegetable at their markets too. It is a staple in Chinese home cooking. So broccoli rabe is now grown in the United States and Canada.

WHAT TO LOOK FOR Broccoli rabe resembles broccoli but with thinner stems, smaller florets, and more and bigger leaves. The stalks holding the florets should be crisp and the florets themselves tightly closed. Stalks, florets, and leaves should all be uniformly green and fresh-looking. Avoid limp stalks or discolored leaves.

In the Kitchen

STORING Keep broccoli rabe, unwashed, in a plastic bag in the vegetable drawer of the refrigerator for three or four days at most.

PREP Wash broccoli rabe well. Peel or remove tough lower stalks with a sharp paring knife. Stalks, florets, and leaves are all edible.

BASIC COOKING Many cooks prefer to blanch broccoli rabe in a large pot of lightly salted boiling water for 2 to 3 minutes before proceeding with any recipe. This slakes its bitterness. Put the cooked vegetable into ice-cold water to stop the cooking. Then drain well and chop the broccoli rabe into manageable pieces. You can sauté the pieces in olive oil with a little garlic until it is tender—2 or 3 minutes. Season with salt and pepper and a squeeze of lemon and serve as a side dish for meat or poultry. You can also braise broccoli rabe in wine with shallots and basil.

BEST USES IN RECIPES Broccoli rabe has been described as having stalks that taste like asparagus, florets that taste like broccoli, and leaves that taste like mustard greens. It offers a nice sharp note to many dishes such as pasta sauces, omelets, frittatas, and polentas. It also adds a distinctive note to soups and stew.

Brussels Sprouts

Thanks to generations of overcooking, Brussels sprouts may be the most maligned vegetable at the market. Savvy cooks know, however, that these mini cabbages have a delicious, earthy flavor if treated well in the kitchen.

PACKED INTO A **HALF-CUP** OF BRUSSELS SPROUTS:

---

30 CALORIES • 80% OF THE RECOMMENDED DAILY AMOUNT OF **vitamin C** • THE B VITAMIN **folate** • PLENTY OF **fiber** • PHYTOCHEMICALS CALLED **indoles** AND **isothiocyanates**, WHICH HELP PROTECT AGAINST CANCER

At the Market

SEASON Brussels sprouts are autumn vegetables, usually not seen in markets until September or October.

WHAT TO LOOK FOR When choosing Brussels sprouts, freshness is key. A strong off-flavor and aroma develops with prolonged storage, so look for bright green, tightly packed leaves, and fresh-looking stems indicating that the sprouts are newly harvested. Avoid any whose leaves have begun to yellow and unfurl or whose stem ends are browned and dry. If serving the sprouts whole, it's wise to look for ones that are approximately the same size so cooking time will be uniform. Keep in mind that smaller sprouts generally have a milder, sweeter taste than larger ones.

In the Kitchen

STORING Store Brussels sprouts, unwashed, in a paper bag in the refrigerator for up to 2 days.

PREP Before cooking Brussels sprouts, proceed as shown *(right)*. Of course, for halved or thinly sliced Brussels sprouts, scoring is not necessary. Sprouts that are more than 1 inch thick are best halved or quartered to make them easier to cook and eat.

BASIC COOKING Boil Brussels sprouts, uncovered, in lightly salted water for 5 to 10 minutes, depending on their thickness; they should be just tender enough to be pierced by a skewer. Avoid overcooking, which will render the sprouts mushy, pale, and strongly flavored. Brussels sprouts can also be steamed or cooked in the microwave oven to the same degree of doneness.

BEST USES IN RECIPES Thinly sliced sprouts work well in stir-fries and sautés, more easily absorbing savory sauces and dressings than whole sprouts. If you're inclined to grill regardless of the cool season, Brussels sprouts can be threaded on skewers, brushed with a little olive oil, and grilled until lightly charred and just tender.

fresh ideas

● Here are some common ingredients that pair deliciously with Brussels sprouts: Butter and lemon, mustard, caraway, curry spices, juniper, smoked ham, apples, Cheddar cheese, dill, thyme, balsamic vinegar, toasted walnuts, onion.

● Loose leaves from Brussels sprouts make a lovely, nutritious garnish for soups, stews, salads, or any dish that can use a little color. After trimming sprouts, peel off outer leaves and stem over boiling water for about 3 minutes—just long enough to soften leaves but still leave a little of their crunch.

BRUSSELS SPROUTS PREP

Trim stems and discard discolored or wilted outer leaves.

1

To bring heat to the center during cooking, score each bottom with an X.

2

fresh ideas

● Use cabbage leaves as edible steamer wrappers: Sprinkle thick fish fillets with herbs (chervil, tarragon, or dill), wrap in cabbage leaves, and steam over seasoned broth (use more of the same herbs in the broth).

● Steam cabbage or bok choy leaves and wrap around matchsticks of carrot and bell pepper. Serve the packets with a spicy dipping sauce.

● Stir-fry cut-up cabbage and onions, add to coarsely mashed potatoes, and use as a stuffing for roast chicken or turkey.

DID YOU KNOW...

...that the sauerkraut you eat with hot dogs at the ballpark is really just pickled cabbage?

Cabbages

Now that more is known about the health benefits of this once-humble vegetable, cabbage has become a nutritional superstar. Four basic types of cabbage—green, red, Savoy, and napa—are used often by health-conscious cooks the world over.

PACKED INTO **ONE CUP** OF RAW CABBAGE:

LESS THAN **25** CALORIES • ONE-THIRD OR MORE OF THE DAILY REQUIREMENT FOR **vitamin C** • 2 GRAMS OF **fiber** • PHYTOCHEMICALS CALLED **indoles**, WHICH HELP PROTECT AGAINST BREAST, PROSTATE, AND COLON CANCERS • **sulforaphane**, **isothiocyanates**, AND **dithiolethiones**, ALL PHYTOCHEMICALS WITH KNOWN DISEASE-FIGHTING CAPABILITIES • **anthocyanins** IN RED CABBAGE THAT FIGHT INFLAMMATION AND PROTECT BLOOD VESSELS

At the Market

SEASON Cabbages are available all year long, with peak season in midwinter. Savoy cabbage is available throughout the fall, winter, and early spring.

WHAT TO LOOK FOR When choosing red or green cabbages, choose firm heads that are quite heavy for their size. Looser-leafed, elongated varieties such as napa, or Chinese cabbage will also be heavy for their size. Choose heads with fresh-looking cores and no wilted leaves or signs of yellowing. A 2-pound head will serve four to six people for a side dish and will make about 10 cups of shredded cabbage.

In the Kitchen

STORING All varieties of cabbage should be stored, unwashed, in a plastic bag in the crisper section of the refrigerator. Green or red cabbages with tight heads will keep up to two weeks; loose-leaf Chinese, or napa, cabbage will keep up to one week.

PREP Remove and discard any damaged or wilted outer leaves and trim away any brown spots. Remove and discard tough outer leaves from larger heads of cabbage. Clean cabbage just before using by rinsing well with cold water. Use a knife, grater, or food processor to shred heads of green or red cabbage. First, cut the head into quarters with a large, heavy knife. Then remove the core by cutting out its wedge-shaped remainder from each quarter. You can then shred the cabbage several different ways:
● Put each wedge, a flat side down, on a cutting board and slice it vertically.
● Shred each wedge against the coarse side of a grater.
● Stuff each wedge into the food processor, using the grating disk.

BASIC COOKING One simple technique for cooking all types of cabbage is to first steam sliced or chopped cabbage over boiling water until just barely tender, about 5 minutes. Drain well. Just before serving, sauté the

VARIETIES

COMMON CABBAGES

Green cabbage is the most widely available and universally used cabbage. It has a tight head with smooth, pale- to medium-green leaves. An all-purpose vegetable, it is used in a remarkable variety of dishes—accompaniments, salads, wraps, stuffings, soups, and stews.

napa (Chinese) cabbage has elongated white ribs and tender, pale green leaves. It has a milder taste than its green cabbage cousin. napa, available at many supermarkets, is used raw in Asian salads and cooked in soups and stir-fries.

Red cabbage, a staple in Central Europe, is often combined with fruit and other sweet ingredients in soups, such as beet-based borscht, and side dishes like sweet-and-sour cabbage with apples.

Savoy cabbage has very tender, crinkled, pale green leaves and a gentler flavor than green cabbage, although it is used interchangeably. It is often featured in European dishes.

AN UNCOMMON CABBAGE

Bok choy is a variety of Chinese cabbage that has become increasingly available in markets throughout other parts of the world. It is a non-heading cabbage and, with its long, firm white ribs and deep green leaves, it looks more like chard and other leafy green vegetables than other cabbages. It is richer in beta-carotene and calcium than green cabbage. To prepare bok choy or baby bok choy, simply trim the stems and braise the vegetable whole or you can chop the leaves and slice the base along its ribs *(see below)* raw. Heat a little oil or butter in a deep skillet. Add a layer of bok choy and sauté 2 minutes. Add ¼ to ½ cup broth or water, cover, and simmer until tender.

cabbage in a little butter or olive oil to heat through. Sprinkle with salt and pepper and serve.

BEST USES IN RECIPES Grated raw cabbage is used to make salads and slaws. Crisp cabbage leaves can be cut up and substituted in any recipe that calls for lettuce, including sandwiches. Whole raw cabbage leaves, especially Savoy cabbage leaves, can be used in place of tortillas for a crunchy, flavorful, and low-calorie wrap for sandwich fillings. Cooked cabbage is often served as a side dish with meat, poultry, and sausages. It is also used to fill dumplings and other pastry cases, such as the Russian *peroshki*. Cabbage is a popular ingredient in a wide variety of soups, stews, salads, side dishes, and stir-fries.

BEST RECIPE One of the most popular recipes for cabbage in North America is coleslaw, a mixture of shredded cabbage, carrots, and an almost sweet creamy dressing, traditionally made from mayonnaise, but more frequently fashioned from sour cream and/or yogurt these days. A quick coleslaw dressing can be made in a medium bowl by whipping together 3 tablespoons plain, low-fat yogurt, 2 tablespoons sour cream, ¾ teaspoon prepared yellow mustard, ½ teaspoon sugar, ½ teaspoon cider vinegar, ¼ teaspoon celery seeds, ⅛ teaspoon salt, and ⅛ teaspoon black pepper. To make the salad, add 1¾ cups coarsely shredded cabbage and ¼ cup coarsely grated carrot, mix well, and refrigerate for 2 to 3 hours, tossing occasionally. This recipe will serve 4.

CUTTING UP BOK CHOY

First separate the leaves from the base with a sharp knife.

1

Chop the bundle of leaves into 2-inch pieces.

2

Finally, slice the base into slivers along the ribs, perpendicular to the base.

3

fresh ideas

● Use carrot juice instead of water in homemade bread or pizza dough to add extra nutrients to the finished product.

● Sauce grilled chicken with a carrot-based gravy: sauté sliced carrots with olive oil and garlic until very soft. Puree with carrot juice and a little lemon juice to taste and serve.

● Stir shredded carrots into cooled rice pudding to add some vitamin punch.

● Substitute carrot juice for broth in soups, stews, and sauces.

● Use grated carrot instead of coconut in cookies to cut calories and boost nutrition.

DID YOU KNOW . . .

. . . that cooking carrots with a little bit of fat makes beta-carotene more available for absorption by the body?

. . . that a USDA study suggests that calcium pectate, a type of soluble fiber found in carrots, has a cholesterol-lowering effect?

Carrots

If one vegetable gets top prize for both versatility and good nutrition, it's the humble carrot. Recipes that use raw and cooked carrots can be found in cookbooks from just about every country in the world.

PACKED INTO A **HALF-CUP** CARROTS:

35 CALORIES • ALMOST TWICE THE DAILY REQUIREMENT FOR **vitamin A**, IN THE DISEASE-FIGHTING FORM OF BETA-CAROTENE • A GOOD SUPPLY OF **vitamin B_6** TO MAINTAIN BRAIN FUNCTION • **fiber** TO KEEP YOUR DIGESTIVE TRACT HEALTHY

At the Market

SEASON Carrots are available throughout the year and most abundant during winter and early spring. They are among the five most-bought vegetables in the United States.

WHAT TO LOOK FOR Whether you buy them long and tapered or short and stubby, in bunches or in plastic bags, choose smooth, firm, evenly colored, and evenly shaped carrots. Avoid carrots that are soft, withered, oversized, or green around the shoulders. Look for bunched carrots with bright green, fresh-looking feathery tops. Small, slender carrots are usually the sweetest.

In the Kitchen

STORING The leafy green tops that remain on fresh bunches of carrots steal nutrients from the roots, so they should be cut off and discarded before storing carrots. (You can add them to the compost pile or feed them to a pet rabbit.) Keep carrots, loosely wrapped in a plastic bag, in the vegetable crisper of your refrigerator. Tiny, early carrots keep only a day or two, while large carrots keep at least a week. Small, bagged carrots are usually good for a couple of weeks.

PREP Many of the nutrients in a carrot are concentrated just below the surface of the skin. For this reason, it's best to simply scrub tender young carrots, rather than peel them, before eating or cooking. This isn't always practical, particularly with large not-so-young carrots. To julienne a carrot, trim off both ends of the carrot, then cut crosswise into 2-inch lengths *(facing page)*. Cut these lengths into thin broad slices. Cut the slices into matchsticks.

BASIC COOKING Carrots can be boiled, steamed, roasted, or grilled. Raw carrot sticks and raw baby carrots are a nutritious snack or a popular addition to a raw vegetable platter (even children seem to love them). Grated carrots are used to add color and nutrition to salads and sweets. Chunks of carrot are found in casseroles, soups, and stews for the same reason. Sliced carrots can be steamed, stir-fried, or roasted to serve on their own or with other vegetables as a simple side dish. Cooked carrots are often mashed

CARROTS OF MANY COLORS

Although we think of varieties of carrots as having to do with size and shape—long, skinny carrots vs. short, round carrots—that is not the only difference. In recent years, farmers have come up with some eye-catching variants.

Orange, yellow, red, purple, and white...these are now all carrot colors, but you may have to hunt some of them down in specialty food markets or plant hybrid seeds in your own garden if you want to try them.

There's more to these colorful carrots than good looks. Although they taste pretty much the same, each pigment provides different disease-fighting antioxidants.

Purple carrots contain a pigment called anthocyanin, which fights harmful free radicals that destroy healthy body cells.

Red carrots contain lycopene, the same super cancer-fighting phytochemical found in tomatoes and watermelon.

White carrots are mild and sweet and have no pigment at all, but they contain other types of phytochemicals that may protect your health.

Yellow carrots contain xanthophylls, which are similar to the beta-carotene in their orange cousins.

---

with turnips. Fresh-cooked carrots are delicious dressed with a little butter or olive oil, dill or parsley, salt, and pepper.

To braise carrots, add butter or oil, orange juice, a pinch of orange zest, sugar, salt, and pepper to a medium saucepan. Bring to a boil, cover, lower the heat and cook for 5 minutes. Then uncover, raise the heat, and stir until the liquid has evaporated and the carrots are tender.

To glaze carrots, in a small saucepan combine brown sugar, salt, ginger, and a little cornstarch. Add orange juice. Cook and stir until thickened, then stir in butter to taste and spoon over hot roasted carrots.

HISTORY . . . Carrots are not native to the New World. In fact, they are believed to have originated in Afghanistan and made their way East and West from there. They are, however, likely to have come to North America with the first settlers. Why? Because wild carrots are so pervasive here. Botanists say that it takes a long time for cultivated plants to return to the wild, and we have wild carrots growing along every back road and byway. You may know the plant by its popular name, Queen Anne's lace.

HEALTH BONUS—Our most abundant source of beta-carotene, carrots have long been considered to be good for your eyes. Now we know that while carrots can't correct vision problems such as myopia or farsightedness, they can help prevent night blindness, an inability of the eye to adjust to dim lighting or darkness. Vitamin A combines with the protein opsin in the retina's rod cells to form the substance (rhodopsin) that the eye needs for good night vision. Consuming just one carrot every few days will provide enough vitamin A to prevent or overcome night blindness.

MAKING MATCHSTICKS

Section peeled carrots into 2-inch lengths; then cut these into broad slices.

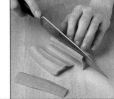

1

Putting several broad slices in a pile, you can cut off matchstick slices in bunches.

2

DID YOU KNOW . . .

. . . that eating too many carrots can turn your hands orange? It's a harmless phenomenon that goes away when you cut back.

fresh ideas

Cauliflower's mild flavor allows it to marry well with many different sauces and seasonings. Here are a few ideas for topping (or dipping) cooked or raw cauliflower:

- Cheese sauce
- Vinaigrette dressing
- Mustard-mayonnaise sauce
- Curry sauce
- Yogurt (plain) with fresh or dried herbs

DID YOU KNOW . . .

. . . that purple cauliflower is a cross between broccoli and cauliflower and hard to distinguish from purple broccoli? When cooked, purple cauliflower turns white and tastes like white cauliflower.

. . . that chartreuse cauliflower stays bright green when it is cooked? It has a mild and delightful flavor.

Cauliflower

Creamy white, purple, or brilliant chartreuse—these are the colors of today's cauliflower. This vegetable with a tightly closed, round head is a close relative of broccoli, every bit as nutritious as its cousin, but much milder in flavor.

PACKED INTO ONE CUP OF CAULIFLOWER:

29 CALORIES • 100% OF THE DAILY REQUIREMENT FOR **vitamin C** • LOTS OF **folate** TO PROTECT YOUR HEART • **fiber** TO MAINTAIN GOOD DIGESTION • **indoles** AND **isothiocyanates**, CANCER-FIGHTING PHYTOCHEMICALS

At the Market

SEASON Peak season for cauliflower is in the fall, but it is plentiful throughout most of the year.

WHAT TO LOOK FOR When buying white cauliflower, be sure to choose a head with fresh, crisp, creamy-white curd. The size of the head has no effect on quality. Avoid cauliflower that is turning brown or with curd that appears to have been trimmed. This is an indication of old age, and old cauliflower gives off an unpleasant odor when it is cooked. It will also have a strong taste. Try to buy cauliflower with some or all of its leaves intact, as they protect the curd from damage and help keep it fresh longer.

In the Kitchen

STORING Cauliflower is generally not a good keeper, especially if it has been trimmed of its leaves. If you can't use a head of cauliflower the day you buy it, place the unwashed head in a perforated or open plastic bag and refrigerate for no more than a day or two. The same goes for leftover cooked cauliflower. Rather than reheat it as a side dish or serve it cold as a salad vegetable, it's best to puree leftover cauliflower with a little broth and use it for soup the next day.

PREP Wash cauliflower just before cooking or eating raw. Use a small, sharp knife to separate the florets into bite-size pieces, leaving on a bit of stem. To serve cauliflower raw as a snack or dipper, cut it into bite-size florets. To keep the florets crisp and white until serving, place in a bowl of ice water, stir in a squeeze of fresh lemon juice, and refrigerate. Drain and pat dry just before serving.

BASIC COOKING Cook cauliflower carefully and check often during cooking, because it goes from undercooked to overcooked in the blink of an eye. Florets are done as soon as the stem end is tender.

BEST USES IN RECIPES Raw cauliflower is a staple of raw vegetable platters. Cooked cauliflower is served with a sauce, made into soup, or added to vegetable curry mixtures.

Celery

Although celery will never be famous for its nutrition, it is an excellent seasoning and snacking vegetable. It's not really true that celery has fewer calories than you need to chew up a stalk of it; its low calorie count comes from its water content.

PACKED INTO ONE CUP OF CELERY:

ONLY **10** CALORIES • **vitamin C** FOR HEALTHY GUMS AND TEETH • **potassium** TO MAINTAIN BLOOD PRESSURE • A MEDICINAL SUBSTANCE CALLED **polyacetylene** THAT HELPS REDUCE INFLAMMATION

At the Market

SEASON Celery has no peak season—it is available all year long.

WHAT TO LOOK FOR Choose celery with firm stalks that are pale to medium green in color with crisp, fresh-looking leaves. The greener the stalk, the more intense the celery flavor. Celery can be sweet or bitter and it's hard to tell just by looking. Scratch the bottom of a bunch with your fingernail. If it smells bitter, it will taste bitter.

In the Kitchen

STORING Wrap celery in several layers of damp paper towels and store it in the crisper section of the refrigerator for up to two weeks. Keep celery away from the coldest parts of the refrigerator—the back and side walls—because it freezes easily and then becomes limp and unusable.

PREP To peel a celery stalk really means to remove its fibrous strings. After trimming celery, cut into either end of the stalk with a small, sharp knife and pull down and out to remove stringy fibers.

BASIC COOKING To cook celery for a side dish, slice the stalks and sauté them in vegetable oil or cut the stalks into 2-inch lengths and simmer in a bit of broth. If you like, sprinkle cooked celery with grated cheese and run under the broiler until lightly browned.

BEST USES IN RECIPES Every part of the celery plant is usable. You can add the strongly flavored leaves to soups and stews for seasoning. You can cut up the outer ribs and sauté, braise, or stir-fry them with other vegetables. Many cooks use the tender inner stalks on raw vegetable platters or for snacking out of hand. Along with onions, chopped celery is an essential seasoning ingredient in many traditional soups, stews, casseroles, and other mixed dishes, such as the stuffing for poultry.

HISTORY . . . The Romans believed that wearing wreaths of celery would protect them from hangovers when they imbibed too much wine. They also used celery as a seasoning in soups and stews, as well as the principal ingredient in a sweet dessert that featured honey, pepper, and celery.

fresh ideas

When you need a fast idea for finger food, fill two-inch lengths of celery stalk with:

● Cream cheese with onions and chives or cream cheese with chopped peppers

● Curried egg salad

● Chicken salad combined with dill mayonnaise

● A blend of cottage cheese and blue cheese

● Peanut butter

JULIENNING CELERY

First trim off top and bottom of stalks.

1

Cut stalks into 2-inch sections, lining up cut pieces as guides.

2

Then sliver each 2-inch piece of stalk into matchstick-size slices.

3

fresh ideas

● Add diced chile peppers to corn bread or corn muffins.

● Make a hot and sweet pepper salsa: Mince red, green, and orange bell peppers along with jalapeño and chipotle peppers. Add minced red onion, vinegar, and chopped fresh cilantro. Serve with meat or poultry.

● Add both bell and chile pepper pieces to mashed potatoes for a spicy side dish.

● A sprinkling of chopped chile peppers will add zip to tomato sauce, meat loaf, or a bland cheese sauce.

DID YOU KNOW . . .

. . . that red chiles contain more than 10 times the amount of beta-carotene as green chiles?

. . . that in Latin America hot peppers are called chiles, but mild peppers are called pimientos? Pimientos in the U.S. are a variety of red bell pepper.

Chile Peppers

These are the hot peppers that spice up the cuisines of many countries around the world, particularly tropical ones, from Mexico to Thailand. The North American romance with this ethnic cooking ingredient knows no limits.

PACKED INTO A **QUARTER-CUP** OF CHILE PEPPERS:

LESS THAN **20** CALORIES • MORE THAN 150% OF THE DAILY REQUIREMENT FOR **vitamin C** • MORE THAN 100% OF THE DAILY REQUIREMENT FOR **vitamin A** • THE ANTIOXIDANT **beta-carotene** TO FIGHT CHRONIC DISEASE • **folate** FOR NORMAL GROWTH • **vitamin B$_6$** FOR NORMAL BRAIN FUNCTION AND FORMATION OF RED BLOOD CELLS • THE ANTIOXIDANT **capsaicin** TO FIGHT CANCER AND ULCERS

At the Market

SEASON Most supermarkets carry some fresh chile peppers, which are generally available all year. Some groceries stock a wider variety than others. Latin and Asian markets are usually the best sources for chiles.

WHAT TO LOOK FOR Fresh chile peppers should be well shaped, firm, and glossy, with no wrinkles and fresh-looking green stems. Dried hot peppers should also be glossy and unbroken.

In the Kitchen

STORING Unwashed chile peppers should be wrapped in paper towels rather than plastic bags because moisture causes them to decompose. Keep fresh chiles in the crisper drawer of the refrigerator for up to three weeks. Dried chile peppers should be stored in an airtight container at room temperature; they will last as long as four months. In the refrigerator, they will last even longer

PREP Capsaicin is the substance that makes chile peppers hot. Contained in the membranes and seeds of chile peppers, capsaicin can irritate your skin badly and is particularly painful if it gets in your eyes. So you must be careful in handling chile peppers. If you have sensitive skin, you might want to wear rubber or latex gloves for protection while you work with hot peppers. Wash the chile peppers, cut them open, and remove the ribs and seeds if you want a milder flavor in your dish. After chopping the chile pepper, wash the cutting board and utensils as well as your gloves. When grinding dried chiles to use as chile powder, be careful not to inhale fumes or let fumes get near your eyes. You can first heat the dried chiles on an ungreased griddle to soften them. Or you can soak them in hot water for half an hour, puree them with the soaking liquid, and proceed with your recipe.

BASIC COOKING Just a sprinkling of chopped chile pepper adds zing to all kinds of dishes from hamburgers to salad dressings. You can roast and peel

VARIETIES

Most chile peppers have a predictable heat level, depending on what kind they are. A chile pepper's pungency, however, is determined not only by its variety, but also by its growing conditions. That's why some common hot peppers, such as jalapeños, can be mild enough to eat out of hand or so explosive they set your mouth on fire.

Anaheim peppers are among the most popular chile peppers used in the United States. Eaten both young and green and red and mature, they range from mild to medium hot. The Mexican dish chiles rellenos, or stuffed chiles, uses these flavorful peppers.

Cascabel peppers are usually available dried; their seeds rattle inside the brownish red pepper covering, giving rise to the name, which means "jingle bell" in Spanish. They are moderately hot.

Cayenne peppers have long, thin red pods that come to a point. They grow as long as 10 inches and are fiery hot. Dried ground cayenne is a staple seasoning in North American homes.

Cherry peppers, which you can buy fresh, are round and red, as you would expect, and range in intensity from mild to moderately hot.

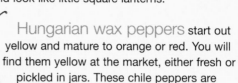

Habanero peppers are the hottest of all the cooking peppers. Sometimes called Scotch bonnets, they are yellow-orange, yellow, orange, or red in color and look like little square lanterns.

Hungarian wax peppers start out yellow and mature to orange or red. You will find them yellow at the market, either fresh or pickled in jars. These chile peppers are medium hot.

Jalapeño peppers, like the Anaheims, are very popular chile peppers, sold fresh and canned, sliced and pickled. About 2 inches long and tapered, they have tiny cracks at the stem end. They usually are found in their mature green stage, not the fully ripe red stage. They are very hot fresh, a little less so canned.

Poblano/ancho peppers (poblano refers to the fresh pepper, ancho to dried pepper) are mild to medium hot and are used to flavor sauces.

Serrano peppers are a favorite in Tex-Mex cooking. Torpedo-shaped chile peppers that are extremely hot, serranos are usually sold green and are used fresh in salsas.

large mild chiles like Anaheims, just as you do bell peppers *(page 295)*, then stuff them with cheese or meat and deep-fry them. Be sure, however, to remove the ribs and seeds when you peel them.

PUTTING OUT THE FIRE

Although they're all called capsaicin, several different substances give a chile pepper its characteristic "heat" and have different effects when they reach your mouth. Some peppers give the back of your throat a quick burn; others seem to explode on your tongue and linger on the roof of your mouth. If you bite into an unbearably hot pepper, the best way to extinguish the flames is with a food that's high in fat, such as whole milk, ice cream, avocado, peanut butter, or buttered bread. Water won't do it!

SEEDING CHILE PEPPERS

Wear plastic gloves for protection. Remove seeds and ribs from peppers with melon baller.

 1

fresh ideas

● Add fresh corn to pancake or waffle batter.

● Add fresh corn to corn bread or corn muffin batter.

● Add fresh corn to tomato salsa, along with finely chopped cilantro.

● Combine fresh corn with cherry tomatoes, avocado, cubes of cheese, and chopped fresh basil or cilantro to make a hearty main-dish salad.

● Combine fresh corn with leftover chicken, other leftover vegetables such as carrots and sweet peppers, and chicken broth for a quick soup.

● Combine fresh corn with left-over pasta, sliced cherry tomatoes, and smoked mozzarella to make a hearty pasta salad.

DID YOU KNOW ...

... that the word "corn" in England means wheat, and that in Scotland and Ireland it means oats? The vegetable that Americans refer to as corn is called maize in other countries.

Corn

No other food says, "Summer is here!" like fresh, sweet corn-on-the-cob. When those first plump ears appear at the market or roadside stand, it's time to fire up the grill or put a pot of water on to boil and head outdoors for dinner.

PACKED INTO AN **EAR** OF CORN:

ABOUT **75** CALORIES • PLENTY OF **fiber** • A MIX OF **B vitamins** THAT AID IN ENERGY METABOLISM • **magnesium** TO HELP MAINTAIN NERVES AND MUSCLES • **phosphorus** TO HELP GENERATE ENERGY • **ferulic acid**, AN ANTIOXIDANT THAT DESTROYS NATURALLY OCCURRING TOXINS IN THE BODY KNOWN AS FREE RADICALS, REDUCING THE RISK OF HEART DISEASE AND CANCER

At the Market

SEASON Corn is at its sweetest and most abundant during the summer months. However, supersweet corn varieties from Florida and California have extended the season considerably.

VARIETIES There are more than 200 varieties of the vegetable that we call corn or sweet corn. They are all actually a grass, and the kernels on the ears are the grain. Sweet corn has been developed to have a high sugar content—up to 6 percent of its weight—and it is picked at an immature stage to be eaten on the cob. Field corn is picked at a more mature, starchier stage and is used as livestock feed and, after refining, for a number of products from whiskey to plastics. Sweet corns have all yellow kernels, all white kernels, or a bi-colored mix of white and yellow.

WHAT TO LOOK FOR For the loveliest flavor, try to buy local corn that was picked earlier the same day. Choose ears with bright green husks. Pull back the husk to inspect the ear. It should be evenly formed with straight rows of plump, smooth, shiny kernels. Check the silky end to be sure there's no decay or worm holes. Avoid ears with dry, shriveled husks or dull, odd-sized or oversized kernels.

WHERE TO BUY THE BEST Beyond your own garden, the best place to look for just-picked corn is at local farm stands or greenmarkets, where it is probably freshest.

In the Kitchen

STORING The naturally occurring sugars that sweeten local corn quickly turn to starch once the ear is plucked from its stem, so the sooner you use it, the sweeter it will be. Although supersweet varieties don't turn to starch quite so quickly, they have spent a day or two in transit, so they, too, should be eaten as soon as possible. If you must store corn, place ears in a plastic bag and keep in the vegetable crisper in your refrigerator for a day or two.

POPCORN

Christopher Columbus observed in 1492 that the West Indians wore popcorn corsages and decorated their ceremonial headdresses with strings of popped corn. His sailors bought popcorn from the natives. Cortés described his first encounter with popcorn in 1519 when he made contact with the Aztecs in Mexico. Popcorn graced ceremonial headdresses, popcorn necklaces adorned statues of their gods, and young Aztec women danced with garlands of popcorn around their heads.

Popping, in fact, may have been the first use of the wild corn native to the New World. Tiny popcorn ears more than 5,600 years old were found in a cave in New Mexico in 1948. Corn thrived throughout North and South America. In fact, the brother of Chief Massasoit of the Wampanoag tribe brought popcorn to the first

Thanksgiving dinner at Plymouth, Massachusetts. The colonists loved popcorn and would serve it for breakfast with sugar and cream long before the first puffed wheat or puffed rice was invented.

In the late 19th century, popcorn carts with steam or gas poppers used to follow the crowds through parks, fairs, carnivals, and expositions, selling bags of hot popped corn. During the second World War, when sugar was rationed and candy scarce, popcorn came into its own as a popular snack.

Perry Spencer, inventor of the microwave oven, started experimenting with popcorn in 1945. Micro-wave popcorn is now a $250 billion-a-year business.

Air-popped popcorn (with no butter) is still considered a very healthy—if somewhat historic—snack food, filling and full of fiber but not full of extra calories.

PREP Remove the husk and silk from corn just before cooking. For grilling or roasting, you may want to keep the husks attached *(right)* to protect the kernels during cooking.

BASIC COOKING Corn-on-the-cob can be steamed, boiled, grilled, roasted in the oven, or cooked in the microwave oven. The important thing to remember about cooking fresh corn is that it needn't cook for a long time. Steamed or boiled corn cooks in just two or three minutes; grilling and roasting in a hot oven takes about 20 minutes. Cooking time for corn in a microwave oven is 90 seconds per ear. You can grill corn on the grill rack or nestled in the coals. Either way, pull back the husks and brush the kernels with vegetable oil or melted butter and a seasoning, if you like. Refit the husks back over the ears and put the ears in ice water until you are ready to cook them. Grill over medium-hot coals for 10 to 20 minutes, turning often. Sprinkle with salt before serving.

SEASONING SWEET CORN

Flavored butters are excellent for brushing on fresh corn-on-the-cob and can be used to dress up a simple side dish of canned or frozen kernels. Heat a half-and-half combination of butter and olive oil in a small saucepan to melt the butter. Add a pinch of salt, then add any of the following to taste and heat 1 minute longer before serving: finely chopped fresh or dried basil, finely chopped cilantro, finely minced onion, curry powder, fresh lime juice, or chili powder.

PREPPING FOR THE GRILL

First shuck corn from its tip to the stem without removing the husk all the way.

1

Remove the corn silk by hand as shown or with a dry vegetable brush.

2

Pull husks back up over the corn kernels. Soak the ears in ice water until you grill.

 3

fresh ideas

● Add crisp slices of cucumber to almost any sandwich for some crunchy coolness.

● Shred a cucumber and combine with a small amount of plain yogurt, chopped fresh cilantro or mint, ground cumin, and pepper to make the Indian condiment called raita that is a cooling accompaniment hot curries.

● Slice a cucumber lengthwise, scoop out seeds, poach in water to cover for 5 minutes, and fill with hot seasoned rice.

● Sauté cucumber slices in butter or oil and sprinkle with dill as a hot side dish.

● Puree in a blender or food processor peeled cucumber chunks with plain yogurt, a peeled garlic clove, fresh dill, lemon juice, salt, and pepper for a cold summer soup.

DID YOU KNOW ...

...that scoring the skin of a cucumber gives slices a decorative green and white edge? Trim both ends, stand the cucumber on one of them, and run the tines of a fork down the length of the cucumber, pressing gently. Repeat, moving around the cucumber.

Cucumber

Being called "cool as a cucumber" is a high compliment. For, indeed, cucumbers are cool to the tongue and refreshing to the mouth. They go well with hot foods like curries. They also add a bit of crunch and a bit of fiber to salads and salsas.

PACKED INTO **ONE CUP** OF SLICED CUCUMBER:

ONLY **14** CALORIES • PLENTY OF **water** TO HELP MAINTAIN NORMAL BODY TEMPERATURE • **vitamin C** TO HELP YOUR BODY ABSORB IRON FROM OTHER FOODS

At the Market

SEASON You can always find a cucumber at the supermarket, but they're at their best during summer months. Pickling cucumbers, such as Kirbys and gherkins, are also at their peak in warm weather. Kirbys are crisp and delicious to eat by themselves without being pickled. Hydroponic cucumbers are hothouse grown in water and available all year. They are long and straight and tightly packaged in plastic wrap.

WHAT TO LOOK FOR Select firm, dark green cucumbers that are heavy for their size, with no soft spots or shriveled skin. Cucumbers that have very glossy skin have been waxed to protect against spoilage and should be peeled or well washed before eating.

In the Kitchen

STORING Cucumbers that are waxed or plastic wrapped will keep up to a week in the crisper of the refrigerator. Cut or unwaxed cucumbers should be tightly wrapped and checked every day for signs of decay—soft spots can develop very quickly.

PREP Some people prefer to remove the seeds from cucumbers before eating. Peel the cucumber, if you wish, then cut lengthwise in half. Use the tip of a spoon to scoop out the center row of seeds from each half. Discard seeds. Chop, slice, or fill the cucumber as directed in a recipe. Hothouse cucumbers are almost seedless and have a very thin skin, so they can be sliced and used as is.

BASIC COOKING Sliced cucumbers can be steamed, sautéed, or stir-fried in a little cooking oil, sprinkled with salt and chopped fresh dill, and served warm as a side dish.

BEST USES IN RECIPES Cucumbers are most commonly eaten raw, in salads and mixed vegetable platters, as snacks, and as part of cold, uncooked soups such as gazpacho. They are also the base for many types of pickles. Short of pickling, you can make a sweet-and-sour cucumber salad by marinating thin slices of cucumber and onion in a dressing of vinegar, sugar, salt, and pepper for several hours in the refrigerator. Serve cold with meat or fish.

Eggplant

Like tomatoes and avocados, eggplant is actually a fruit that is treated like a vegetable. Long a mainstay of European cooking, eggplant is also a key ingredient in Middle Eastern and Asian recipes that are now enjoyed all over the world.

PACKED INTO **ONE CUP** OF EGGPLANT:

ONLY **25** CALORIES • MORE THAN 2 GRAMS OF **fiber** TO HELP PREVENT CONSTIPATION AND FORMATION OF HEMORRHOIDS • **B vitamins** FOR ENERGY PRODUCTION

At the Market

SEASON Eggplant is available all year long, but is at its best in summer months, when you can buy it locally grown.

WHAT TO LOOK FOR Different varieties of eggplant come in different sizes, shapes, and colors. Whether it's purple, white, or lavender, long and narrow or short and plump, look for eggplant with firm, glossy, unblemished skin and a healthy-looking crown. There's no test to determine whether or not the eggplant you choose will be bitter, but most experts agree that age and size make a difference. Eggplants that are approximately 3 to 6 inches in length tend to be less bitter than larger varieties. Overripe eggplants, evidenced by soft spots, brown flesh, and overdeveloped seeds on the interior, can also be bitter.

In the Kitchen

STORING Try to use eggplant the same day you buy it. If you must store eggplant, keep it in a cool place but preferably not in the refrigerator, where it is likely to soften and become bitter very quickly.

PREP It's not necessary to peel an eggplant before cooking, unless the skin is especially thick or you simply prefer your vegetables peeled.

BASIC COOKING Most recipes call for frying or sautéing eggplant and even baked, broiled, or grilled dishes use a substantial amount of oil. That is why it is prudent to salt slices of eggplant (right) and let them drain before cooking. Wipe off the salt and dry the slices before beginning a recipe. The salting removes moisture, which compresses the vegetable and makes it less oil-absorbent. When eggplant is used as the base of a dip, such as Middle Eastern baba ghanoush, however, it is often baked whole or boiled until the flesh is soft enough to mash, avoiding the oil issue altogether.

To grill or broil eggplant for a simple side dish, cut crosswise into half-inch-thick slices. Brush with oil and cook, with oiled side facing the heat source, until browned on both sides, brushing with oil and turning a couple of times during cooking. Sprinkle with salt, pepper, and chopped fresh parsley or basil before serving.

fresh ideas

● Bread slices of small eggplants and bake in a hot oven until tender to make crisp hors d'oeuvres that you can top with chopped fresh basil or oregano leaves.

● Roasting gives eggplant a rich meaty flavor. Halve an eggplant lengthwise and prick the skin. Place cut-side down on a broiler pan and broil until skin is blistered and blackened. Enclose in a paper bag for a few minutes to loosen the skin, then peel off the skin. Chop or mash the flesh, drizzle with oil, and season with salt and pepper for a side dish.

SALTING EGGPLANT

First slice the eggplant into uniform pieces with a sharp knife.

 1

Lay slices on paper towels and sprinkle with salt. Let stand 30 minutes to release moisture.

 2

fresh ideas

- Sprinkle chopped fresh fennel leaves on cooked shrimp or clams.

- Use fennel stalks as "boats," similar to celery sticks, for carrying fillings such as chicken salad or tuna salad.

- Add fennel stalks along with other "soup greens" to flavor poultry and fish broths.

- Add chopped fennel stalks to the other seasoning vegetables (onion, garlic, and carrot) when making tomato sauce.

- Use chopped fennel leaves to season potato home fries and "hash" mixtures.

PREPARING FENNEL

Cut feathery fronds from fennel.

1

Peel fennel bulb with a vegetable peeler.

2

Cut bulb vertically, letting the slices fall away.

3

Fennel

From seed to stem, the entire fennel plant is edible and used in many different ways to impart mild, anise-like flavor to foods. Fennel's unusual licorice taste goes especially well with tomato and fish dishes.

PACKED INTO ONE CUP OF FENNEL:

ABOUT **25** CALORIES • THREE TIMES THE DAILY REQUIREMENT FOR **vitamin C** TO HELP KEEP SKIN HEALTHY • 10% OF THE DAILY REQUIREMENT FOR **fiber** TO HELP MAINTAIN INTESTINAL HEALTH • ONE-THIRD OF A DAY'S SUPPLY OF VITAMIN A

At the Market

SEASON Fennel is widely available in fall and winter months.

WHAT TO LOOK FOR Choose stalks with smooth whitish-green bulbs and stems with no cracks and fresh-looking, feathery fronds.

WHERE TO BUY THE BEST Fennel is available in most well-stocked supermarkets, and it is always found in Italian food markets.

In the Kitchen

STORING Separate fennel stems from the bulb before storing. Wrap stalks and bulb separately in plastic bags and put in the crisper section of the refrigerator for up to three or four days. Use the stalks first, because they don't keep as well. Fennel becomes less flavorful with longer storage; it dries out and starts to turn brown.

PREP To prepare fennel for cooking or eating raw, trim the base and remove any tough outer ribs. Trim off stalks with feathery leaves. Halve, core, and slice the bulb. Raw fennel will turn brown soon after slicing. To prevent discoloring, drop sliced fennel into a bowl of water with a little lemon juice and refrigerate until ready to cook or serve.

BASIC COOKING Fennel can be steamed, boiled, braised, or eaten raw. To braise fennel, combine 2 sliced fennel bulbs and ½ cup chicken broth, vegetable broth, or white wine in a large skillet. Bring broth to a boil over medium heat. Reduce heat, cover, and simmer until fennel is tender when pierced with a fork, about 20 minutes. Sprinkle with salt and pepper. Makes 4 servings. The stalks and feathery leaves can be used as a seasoning or garnish for soups, salads, and seafood. You can cut up fennel stalks and use the pieces as you would celery: on a vegetable platter, in a stuffing, or in a tuna fish salad.

BEST USES IN RECIPES Fennel has an affinity for fish. In France, for example, fish is often baked in a bed of sliced fennel bulb. You can grill fish over fennel stalks or add fennel leaves to the poaching broth for a large salmon.

Garlic

In addition to adding incomparable flavor to foods, garlic has a long history of healing, curing, and warding off evil spirits. This cousin of an onion has antibacterial and antifungal qualities that help keep your immune system up to par.

PACKED INTO **ONE CLOVE** OF GARLIC:

5 CALORIES • A PHYTOCHEMICAL KNOWN AS **allicin** THAT MAY HELP LOWER CHOLES-TEROL AND REDUCE THE RISK OF CANCER• CALCIUM, POTASSIUM, AND PHOSPHORUS

At the Market

SEASON Garlic is available throughout the year.

WHAT TO LOOK FOR Look for firm, plump bulbs of garlic with dry, tight-fitting skin. Garlic should feel heavy and firm in your hand and the cloves appear plump and well-formed. Garlic can be creamy colored throughout or tinged with pink. Extra-large varieties, such as elephant garlic, are actually a form of leek and have a mild garlic flavor.

In the Kitchen

STORING Depending on how fresh it is when you buy it, garlic will keep in a cool, dark, dry place for up to three months. Vented and lidded garlic jars made of a porous material, such as terra cotta, make ideal storage containers.

PREP To peel a garlic clove, lay it under the flat side of a large knife and then hit the side of the knife with your fist, hard enough to split the clove so the skin can easily be removed.

BASIC COOKING Garlic is a basic seasoning in all types of dishes. You can rub a wooden salad bowl with a cut clove of raw garlic to season a salad. For hot dishes, be aware that the longer garlic cooks, the mellower its flavor becomes. When sautéing or stir-frying garlic, however, be careful not to burn it. Burned garlic has a bitter flavor.

Garlic cloves can be roasted to a soft paste that makes an excellent low-fat spread for bread and grilled meats. Roasted garlic can also be sliced and added to cooked dishes such as soups, stews, and pasta sauces.

To roast a whole bulb of garlic, preheat oven to 375°F. Cut across the top of the bulb with a sharp knife to expose all of the cloves. Brush the tops of the cloves with olive oil and season with salt. Wrap the bulb in aluminum foil and bake until very soft, 30 minutes to 1 hour. When cool enough to handle, push the softened garlic cloves from their skins. To roast individual cloves, separate them from a bulb of garlic and toss, unpeeled, with 1 tablespoon olive oil in a small baking pan. Roast in oven until tender when pierced with a knife, about 15 minutes.

fresh ideas

● For a rich garlic flavor, mince fresh garlic into tiny pieces; the finer the chopping, the more flavor is imparted to the dish.

● Because garlic burns so easily, you may want to cook it slowly in olive oil over a low heat, then discard the garlic and use the oil to impart mild garlic flavor to foods.

● It is not just lamb roasts that benefit from slivers of raw garlic tucked into slits in the meat. Try it with beef or veal as well.

● Make garlic bread with olive oil instead of butter for a different flavor as well as better health (no saturated fats).

ROASTED GARLIC PASTE

Cut ½ inch off top of garlic head.

 1

Roast as directed (left). Push out the roasted cloves, one by one.

 2

Mash garlic with fork until smooth.

 3

fresh ideas

Some simple seasonings for cooked greens are:

- Balsamic vinegar
- Fresh lemon juice
- Oriental sesame oil and soy sauce
- Finely chopped fresh dill
- Toasted sesame seed

CUTTING UP GREENS

To quickly chop up greens, roll a bundle of leaves together into a cigar shape.

1

Then slice across the cigar to reduce the greens to shreds for fast cooking or soups.

2

Greens

Leafy green vegetables meant for cooking—rather than salad making—are a large and diverse group. Next time you go shopping, be adventurous—there's more for the palate to discover within the leafy realm of "greens" than you might imagine.

PACKED INTO ONE CUP OF COOKED MIXED GREENS:

ABOUT **33** CALORIES • **beta-carotene** THAT IS CONVERTED INTO VITAMIN A IN THE BODY • HALF THE DAILY REQUIREMENT FOR **vitamin C** • ANTIOXIDANT **vitamin E** TO PROTECT YOUR HEART • PHYTONUTRIENTS KNOWN AS **organosulfur compounds** THAT DETOXIFY POTENTIAL CARCINOGENS • **carotenoids** TO REDUCE THE RISK OF AGE-RELATED EYE DISEASE AND CERTAIN KINDS OF CANCER

At the Market

SEASON Greens are among the most widely available fresh vegetables. Even in the most remote markets you're likely to find at least half a dozen greens to choose from—kale, spinach, escarole, mustard greens, collards, beet greens, to name a few. Because they grow best in moderately cool conditions, greens are harvested year-round in one part or another of our hemisphere, so their price and availability are fairly constant.

WHAT TO LOOK FOR It's easy to choose good greens. Regardless of the variety, pick brightly colored, crisp leaves. Size is not so much an indication of flavor quality as the condition of the plant. Avoid bruised or excessively dirty leaves as well as any limp or yellowing specimens—sure signs of age. The exception is beet greens, which turn red and ragged at the edges when they age. Collard greens, kale, and mustard greens show other signs of being too mature: Woody stems and coarse veins in the leaves practically guarantee that the vegetable will be tough and bitter.

WHERE TO BUY THE BEST At a local farmers' market, greens will be newly picked. In a supermarket, greens that are displayed in a refrigerated section of the produce department are likely to stay fresh, since cool temperatures discourage decay and bacteria.

In the Kitchen

STORING Do not wash greens before storing them—too much moisture encourages the leaves to rot. Use perforated plastic storage bags, which allow air to circulate around the leaves and maintain just enough moisture to preserve their crispness.

PREP Soak in cold water and then rinse thoroughly immediately before cooking to release any dirt trapped in stems or crinkly leaves. Trim any bruised outer leaves and cut off tough stems. Stems are generally inedible and should be discarded, except for the colorful yellow or red chard stems, which are delicious cooked separately from their leaves.

VARIETIES

Beet greens Like fresh spinach leaves, beet greens are tender and cook quickly. They are mild-tasting. Cook beet greens in a covered skillet using just the water that clings to their rinsed leaves and a little butter or olive oil. Possible seasonings include garlic, shallots, ground cumin, or hot pepper sauce.

Chard Often called Swiss chard (for no apparent reason), this large-leafed variety is mostly interchangeable with spinach and beet greens but has an "earthier" taste. Chard leaves can be sautéed, steamed, or blanched; The stem, or rib, which comes in vivid red, yellow, or a bright white color, can be chopped and sautéed separately in oil or butter. The stem takes longer to cook.

Collards These large, round, smooth leaves have a cabbage-like quality. They take longer to cook than most greens—about 25 minutes if simmered, although Southern cooks simmer collards for hours until meltingly tender. Bacon, ham hocks, or another smoked meat is traditionally added to the cooking liquid. Collard stems are inedible; discard them.

Escarole A member of the chicory family (which includes endive, curly endive, and radicchio), escarole resembles a sturdy loose-leaf lettuce. The inner tender leaves of escarole should be almost white; these are suitable for salads. The outer leaves need braising—about 15 minutes—to intensify both their faint sweetness and pleasant bitterness. Escarole's big flavor can stand up to rich, creamy sauces or hot, spicy seasonings. Wilted escarole—sautéed about 5 minutes—makes a wonderful base for warm winter salads. Surround it with roasted pears, gorgonzola, and walnuts for a delicious cold-weather first course.

Kale This green comes in several varieties with leaves that are very crinkly, serrated, or feathery and tones of blue-green, reddish purple, gray-green, or light green. All but the first tender kale leaves of the season are quite tough—they need braising for 12 to 15 minutes. Kale is especially good chopped and added to hearty soups near the end of cooking.

Mustard greens These light green, crinkly leaves pack a hot punch, especially if simmered for no more than 15 minutes. Longer cooking mellows the flavor. Many cooks blanch the leaves to cut the sharp taste, then drain and sauté with various seasonings. Asian flavorings such as fresh ginger, soy sauce, and toasted sesame seeds are an interesting match for mustard greens.

Spinach *(See page 331.)*
Probably the best-known green, spinach comes with dark green, crisp crinkly leaves or softer pale green flat leaves. Cook trimmed spinach leaves in a saucepan with just the water clinging to its leaves from rinsing it. Cover and steam for 1 or 2 minutes.

Turnip greens These have an assertive flavor. Southern Americans cook their turnip greens for hours to give them a silky texture and soften their bite. Other cooks may prefer to keep the vegetable's color, crunch, and sharp flavor with shorter cooking, about 20 minutes.

BASIC COOKING Greens are frequently the victim of overcooking, which leaves them soggy, bland, and grayish in color. Brief and gentle cooking, however, brings out subtle flavors without ruining the delicate texture of the leaves. More specific cooking recommendations for each variety are listed above. But one general rule applies to all greens: Remember that greens cook down to about one-third of their original volume.

fresh ideas

● Add small amounts of shredded raw kohlrabi to salads as a pungent sweet accent.

● To pickle kohlrabi, slice kohlrabi and onion and then soak the slices for several hours in a quart of ice water and 4 tablespoons pickling salt. Drain the vegetables and place in a medium bowl. In a saucepan, boil 2 cups vinegar, ¾ cup sugar, 1 tablespoon mustard seed, 1½ teaspoons celery seed, and ¼ teaspoon turmeric for several minutes, stirring to make sure sugar is dissolved. Pour over vegetables, let cool, cover, and refrigerate for 3 days.

● Stuff hollowed-out kohlrabi bulbs with your favorite stuffing plus the sautéed extra kohlrabi meat. Bake in an open pan for 30 minutes in a 350°F oven, basting the kohlrabi several times with stock or white wine.

DID YOU KNOW . . .

. . . that more than 40,000 tons of kohlrabi are harvested each year in Germany?

. . . the Pennsylvania Dutch used to dry kohlrabi peelings to use in soup in the winter?

Kohlrabi

Sometimes called cabbage turnip, kohlrabi has a bulblike stem that tastes like a mild sweet turnip with traces of its cruciferous cousins, cabbage and Brussels sprouts, and a bit of radish. It has edible greens that are rich in iron.

PACKED INTO A **HALF-CUP** OF COOKED KOHLRABI:

ABOUT **29** CALORIES • HALF THE DAILY REQUIREMENT FOR **vitamin C** • VITAMIN A PRECURSOR **beta-carotene** TO PROTECT YOUR EYES AND AID IN NORMAL CELL DIVISION AND GROWTH • ANITOXIDANT **bioflavonoids** TO PREVENT CELL DAMAGE BY FREE RADICALS • **antioxidants** TO PREVENT CANCER • PLENTY OF **fiber** • 200 MG OF **potassium** TO MAINTAIN FLUID BALANCE AND PROMOTE PROPER METABOLISM AND MUSCLE FUNCTION

At the Market

SEASON Fresh kohlrabi, because it is a cool-weather plant, is available from mid-spring to mid-fall.

WHAT TO LOOK FOR Choose fresh-looking deep-colored green leaves with no yellowing and firm bulbs with smooth skin and no soft spots that are heavy for their size. Kohlrabi bulbs less than 3 inches in diameter are the most tender; larger bulbs tend to be tough and woody. Kohlrabi bulb and stem color can run from white to pale green and from red to deep purple, depending on the variety, but the flesh beneath the skin is always white and the flavor is essentially the same.

In the Kitchen

STORING You can keep fresh kohlrabi in a ventilated plastic bag in the crisper drawer of the refrigerator for up to 2 weeks.

PREP Kohlrabi leaves are even more nutritious than the bulb, which is an argument for cutting them up and cooking them with the bulb. Discard the leaf stalks. The bulb can be easily peeled with a small, sharp knife, but some cooks think the flavor is better if the vegetable is cooked with its peel still in place. Once cut, kohlrabi flesh is quick to discolor, so you may want to put slices or cut-up pieces in a bowl of water with a little lemon juice until ready to cook.

BASIC COOKING Kohlrabi is usually peeled, sliced or chopped, and steamed until tender, then buttered and seasoned with salt and pepper. It is also delicious braised in a beef or chicken broth, seasoned with onions and herbs. Many cooks steam or microwave kohlrabi pieces and then mash them with butter and seasonings. Sliced kohlrabi is often used in Asian stir-fries as a substitute for water chestnuts—it has the same crispness with a bit more flavor.

Leeks

With a milder, sweeter flavor than onions and a crunchy bite when cooked, leeks are a great vegetable for a savory, nutritious side dish. Too often, however, these healthy taste treats are used only to add an oniony note to soups and stews.

PACKED INTO **ONE CUP** OF COOKED LEEKS:

ABOUT 61 CALORIES • 20% OF THE DAILY REQUIREMENT FOR **vitamin C** TO FIGHT INFECTION • 34% OF THE DAILY REQUIREMENT FOR **folate** TO REGULATE GROWTH • A PHYTOCHEMICAL KNOWN AS **diallyl sulfide** THAT IS THOUGHT TO LOWER THE RISK OF STOMACH CANCER • **kaempferol**, AN ANTICANCER SUBSTANCE THAT MAY BLOCK CANCER-CAUSING COMPOUNDS • **quercetin**, ANOTHER PHYTO-CHEMICAL THAT FIGHTS CANCER AND HEART DISEASE • **fiber** FOR PROTECTION AGAINST HIGH CHOLESTEROL

At the Market

SEASON Available all year round, leeks are most abundant from fall to early spring. California, Florida, and New Jersey are the big suppliers.

WHAT TO LOOK FOR Fresh leeks look like giant scallions with straight root ends. Check both ends—the tops should be a healthy-looking dark green and the root end, white for several inches with unblemished skin that gives a little when you press it. The root end shouldn't be bigger than 1½ inches in diameter with a bush of small roots still attached.

In the Kitchen

STORING Loosely wrap unwashed, untrimmed leeks in plastic and store in the crisper drawer of the refrigerator for up to a week.

PREP Leeks need careful cleaning (they are grown in furrows that are filled in with dirt as they grow to keep the bottoms white). First trim off any tough outer leaves and the roots at the base. Slit a leek lengthwise from the base to the top and fan out the leaves under water, checking every layer for grit.

BASIC COOKING Whole leeks are often braised in stock or wine (2 to 3 cups of liquid for eight medium leeks) for 20 minutes or more. Be careful not to overcook them or they will lose their crispness and get slimy. Cut-up leeks cook more quickly: You can steam or microwave them in 5 to 8 minutes. Sliced leeks add interest to soups and stews. Vichyssoise is the classic cold leek-and-potato soup: In a medium saucepan, sauté two sliced leeks and one chopped onion in butter until tender, about 5 minutes. Add two pota-toes, peeled and sliced, and 2½ cups chicken stock. Simmer until potatoes are tender, 10 to 20 minutes. Let cool and then puree in batches in a food processor. Stir in a cup of no-fat half-and-half and salt and pepper to taste. Chill before serving and garnish with chopped fresh chives.

fresh ideas

● Brush cleaned and trimmed leeks lightly with olive oil and grill over charcoal as an accompani-ment for steak.

● Stir sautéed leeks into mashed potatoes for a comfort food treat.

● Raw young leeks add flavor and crunch to salads. Slice thinly as you would a scallion.

● Braise leeks and fresh carrots together in stock. Sprinkle the ten-der vegetables with dill and serve as a side dish for fish.

● Bundle baby leeks, cook them as you would asparagus, and serve them with lemon juice, salt, and pepper.

DID YOU KNOW . . .

. . . that Welsh people still wear leeks on St. David's Day in memory of King Cadwallader's victory over the Saxons in 640, a battle in which the Welsh prevented friendly fire by identifying themselves to each other with leeks in their caps?

fresh ideas

● Combine mashed white beans with tuna fish, minced onion, and dill to make a sandwich spread or dip.

● Mash chickpeas with garlic, parsley, lemon juice, salt, and pepper for a low-calorie, low-fat hummus. Serve with small triangles of pita bread.

● Mix types of beans (black, red, pinto, for example) in a vegetarian chili for a more complex flavor.

● Dress warm lentils with a light vinaigrette dressing and toss with chopped onion, cherry tomatoes, arugula, and shredded romaine for a room-temperature salad.

DID YOU KNOW ...

...that peanuts are actually legumes, the shell-enclosed seeds of a leguminous plant, and not true nuts?

Legumes

Black, white, pink, green, and many colors in-between, dried beans play an important role in cuisines around the world. In this age of fusion cooking, beans jump from cuisine to cuisine, mixed and matched into a variety of intriguing dishes.

PACKED INTO **ONE CUP** OF BLACK BEANS:

ABOUT **225** CALORIES • MORE THAN 30% OF A DAY'S REQUIREMENT FOR **protein** • MORE THAN HALF THE DAILY REQUIREMENT OF **folate** TO HELP FIGHT BIRTH DEFECTS AND **fiber** TO MAINTAIN A HEALTHY DIGESTIVE SYSTEM • **iron** TO PREVENT ANEMIA • **magnesium** TO KEEP BONES HEALTHY, ESPECIALLY AFTER MENOPAUSE • **phosphorus** TO MAINTAIN STRONG TEETH • **zinc** TO FIGHT OFF INFECTION

At the Market

SEASON Legumes have no peak season; dried, canned, and frozen varieties are available throughout the year.

WHAT TO LOOK FOR Name-brand products are usually better quality than generic or store-brand products, but the nutritional value is the same. Generically labeled packages and cans may or may not contain more broken or squashed beans. When buying dried beans in bags or bulk, look for clean, smooth, evenly shaped beans with little or no debris.

WHERE TO BUY THE BEST If you have a good health food store or natural foods market nearby, this may be your best bet for buying dried legumes in bulk. Health food stores are also the best source for dried and canned organic beans and lentils. All supermarkets carry packaged dried beans and canned beans; some carry organic brands.

In the Kitchen

STORING Dried and canned beans keep indefinitely. Store dried beans in a sealed package or covered container to keep out debris and insects.

PREP Dried legumes should be well rinsed before using and picked over to remove any foreign particles such as pebbles or clumps of dirt that may have slipped through. With the exception of lentils, all dried beans should be soaked before cooking. Place in a large bowl with plenty of cold water to cover. Let stand at room temperature for eight hours or overnight. Or, combine beans with water to cover in a large saucepan. Heat to boiling; boil 2 minutes. Remove from heat, cover, and let stand for 1 hour. With either presoaking method, replace water before cooking.

BASIC COOKING After presoaking, all legumes can be cooked using a ratio of 1 part beans to 3 parts water. Combine beans and water in a saucepan. Heat to boiling over medium-high heat. Boil 10 minutes. Reduce heat to low, cover, and simmer until tender, about 1½ to 2 hours for most beans. (For black beans and lima beans, check after 1 hour.)

THE BEAN SCENE

Adzuki These small reddish-brown beans with a white stripe have a sweet flavor and are particularly popular in Japanese cooking.

Black (turtle) These earthy beans are used in Mexican and Southwestern American dishes, as well as in a soup served in the U.S. Senate dining room.

Black-eyed peas (cowpeas) These medium-sized, creamy white beans with a black spot play a key role in Southern U.S. and Caribbean cuisines.

Cannellini Large white Italian kidney beans, available canned and dry, cannellinis are used in salads and soups.

Chickpeas (garbanzo beans) Medium-sized, tan, and acorn-shaped, these beans are featured in Mediterranean and Middle Eastern dishes.

Cranberry beans Medium-sized and oval, cranberry beans are pink and beige in color and nutty in flavor—an addition to soups and stews.

Fava beans Large and brown when dried, fava beans are staples in Middle Eastern and Mediterranean cooking and are often used in soups.

Flageolets These pale green kidney beans are traditionally served with lamb, but can also be used with other meats, in soups, stews, and salads.

Great Northern Kidney-shaped and mild, these are the largest white beans.

Kidney beans Large pink or red kidney-shaped legumes, kidney beans are a mainstay of Mexican and Southwestern American dishes, like chili con carne and red beans and rice.

Lentils Very small brown, green, orange, or yellow legumes, lentils are featured in Middle Eastern and Central European cuisines in soups, stews, salads, and side dishes.

Lima beans Starchy and filling, limas come in two sizes: large Fordhooks and smaller butter beans or baby limas. They are very popular in succotashes, casseroles, and soups.

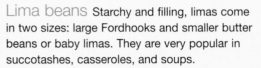
Mung beans Small greenish-brown, yellow, or black legumes, mungs cook quickly and have a sweet, fresh flavor. They are available at Asian markets or health food stores.

Navy beans Also called Yankee beans, these small, white rounded legumes are used in traditional American dishes, such as Boston baked beans.

Pigeon peas These small, creamy white beans with orange mottling are used in Caribbean, African, and Indian cooking and are also popular in U.S. Southern dishes.

Pinto beans Medium-sized, mottled pinkish-tan, kidney-shaped beans, pinto beans are used in Latin American, Mexican, and Southwestern American cooking.

Soybeans Medium-sized, round, and green when fresh, soybeans are black or yellow when dried. They are valued for their high nutrition.

Split peas: Made from fresh green peas, these favorite soup legumes split when dried.

BEST USES IN RECIPES Soups, stews, rice dishes, and simple side dishes, such as succotash and baked beans, are the most common use for dried beans and lentils. Traditionally, you'll find black beans in Latin American and Caribbean soups and stews, cranberry and cannellini beans in Italian minestrone, red beans in Southern American rice dishes, pinto beans in Mexican frijoles, and soybeans in Asian appetizers and snack mixtures. Beans can be mixed to taste.

fresh ideas

● Shred a mix of sturdy, spicy lettuces, such as watercress or arugula, to serve as a bed for a grilled lamb chop or slices of flank steak.

● Use individual leaves of Belgian endive to hold a savory dip—spiced Smithfield ham or herbed goat cheese—as an hors d'oeuvre.

● Wrap sandwich fillings, such as egg or tuna salad, in lettuce leaves instead of bread to cut down on calories and carbohydrates.

● Grill fish in a covering of lettuce to keep it moist over the hot fire; spicier lettuces will add some flavor too.

DID YOU KNOW . . .

. . . that Americans eat about 30 pounds of lettuce a year? That is a great increase from the past and probably due to the availability of fresh salad greens all year round. Improved shipping and storing methods make that possible.

Lettuces

Tossed green salads are always more interesting, more flavorful, and more nutritious when you combine the shapes, textures, colors, and flavors of several different kinds of lettuce in the bowl. Three lettuces should be the minimum.

PACKED INTO ONE CUP OF ROMAINE LETTUCE:

9 CALORIES • 22% OF THE DAILY REQUIREMENT FOR **vitamin C** • THE B VITAMIN **folic acid**, FOR PROTEIN METABOLISM • PHYTOCHEMICALS CALLED **carotenoids**, WHICH HELP PREVENT AGE-RELATED BLINDNESS DUE TO MACULAR DEGENERATION

At the Market

SEASON Lettuce of many varieties is available in food markets throughout the year. Farmers' markets have especially fresh lettuce in summer.

WHAT TO LOOK FOR Regardless of the variety, lettuce should always look clean and fresh, with no wilted leaves or rust-colored spots. Avoid large heads of lettuce with tough outer leaves and ribs.

In the Kitchen

STORING Wash lettuce before storing and dry well. Discard any wilted or discolored outer leaves. Wrap loosely in paper towels, then overwrap in plastic. Store in the crisper section of the refrigerator. Tender leaf lettuces will keep for a day or two; sturdier lettuces, such as romaine and iceberg, will keep well for up to four days.

PREP you can tear small, tender lettuce leaves by hand. To shred large lettuce leaves, stack several leaves on a cutting board. Roll the leaves up tightly from one long end. Cut the roll crosswise into slices. Shredded lettuce makes an attractive, edible bed for grilled seafood and marinated meats.

SERVING Never toss a green salad with dressing until it's time to eat or you'll end up with soggy lettuce. To be well prepared ahead of time and to save on clean-up, mix salad dressing in the bottom of the salad bowl, top with salad greens, then refrigerate up to two hours ahead of time. Toss greens and dressing together just before serving. Be careful not to drown the greens in dressing—a little goes a long way.

DRESSING The classic vinaigrette blends one part vinegar to three parts olive oil. Beating them together with a fork or a whisk will emulsify them. A vinaigrette can be seasoned with salt and pepper, garlic, herbs, mustard, or poppy seeds—whatever you like. Lemon, lime, or orange juice can be substituted for all or part of the vinegar, and walnut or dark sesame oil for the olive oil. Vinaigrettes are very personal: You should experiment until you find a combination that you like. Nowadays people tend to use a smaller pro-portion of oil to vinegar.

A GLOSSARY OF SALAD GREENS

Arugula, or rocket, has several rounded and spiked tender leaves jutting from slender stems. Its flavor is peppery and it becomes more pungent with age.

Belgian endive Smooth and pale, this bullet-shaped, tightly closed head of greens is a member of the chicory family. Kept from the sun so that it can develop pale white or creamy leaves, Belgian endive has a distinctive tangy taste.

Butterhead is a category of lettuces that includes Boston and Bibb. These are small head lettuces with soft, tender leaves and a mild flavor.

Curly endive is a head lettuce with curly leaves tapering to sharp points along its stems. Outer leaves are lacy and green-rimmed; inner leaves are pale yellow and form a compact heart. Curly endive has a slightly bitter flavor.

Escarole is a head lettuce with a scalloped pattern on its leaves. It has a bitter flavor and is often cooked into soups and stews as well as mixed into green salads.

Iceberg, or crisphead, is a tight head lettuce that looks like a cabbage with pale green leaves and a mild flavor.

Leaf lettuce is a category of loose head lettuces with tender dark green, deep red, or green with red-tipped leaves. Its flavor is mild but can become bitter with age.

Oak leaf is a loose lettuce with tender reddish-brown or green scalloped leaves. It has a mild, nutty flavor.

Mache, or field salad, is a bunching lettuce, high in beta-carotene, with very tender, rounded leaves and mild flavor. Often sold with roots attached, it is quite perishable and should be used right away.

Radicchio is a tight head lettuce with crisp vibrant red or reddish-purple leaves with white veining. It is very bitter in flavor.

Romaine, or cos, is a loose head lettuce with long, sturdy, dark green outer leaves, pale green inner leaves, and crispy ribs. It has a mild, tangy flavor.

WATERCRESS—Although watercress is a popular salad vegetable, it's not actually a lettuce, but rather a member of the high-nutrition cruciferous vegetable family. It has dark green leaves and a pungent mustard-like flavor. It grows in streambeds and is sold in bunches. The best watercress has small leaves and thin stems and can be found in the spring and the fall. Avoid watercress with flowering stems. Watercress has a distinctly spicy flavor. The best watercress has small leaves and thin stems and can be found in the spring and the fall.

Mushrooms

Thousands of varieties of fungi, including edible mushrooms, cover the planet. Many wild mushrooms are toxic, even deadly, so unless you're an expert, it's best to pick your exotic mushrooms at a supermarket or specialty food store.

PACKED INTO **ONE CUP** OF COMMON MUSHROOMS:

LESS THAN **20** CALORIES • A VARIETY OF **B vitamins** FOR ENERGY METABOLISM • **copper** TO SUPPORT THYROID ACTIVITY • **potassium** TO REGULATE BLOOD PRESSURE

At the Market

SEASON All but the most exotic mushrooms on the market are farm-raised and available year-round.

WHAT TO LOOK FOR Regardless of variety, choose mushrooms with smooth, dry skin and stems and no bruises. Buy only as many mushrooms as you will use within a day or two. A pound of mushrooms yields about 5 cups sliced, which cooks down to about 1½ to 2 cups.

In the Kitchen

STORING Keep mushrooms in a paper bag, or layered between sheets of paper towel, in the refrigerator for up to a two days.

PREP Clean mushrooms just before using with a damp paper towel or a soft vegetable brush to remove dirt. If the mushrooms will be added directly to liquid, such as a soup, stew, or sauce, you can clean them by rinsing in a colander under cold running water. Trim stems as desired.

BASIC COOKING The best way to cook mushrooms is to sauté slices in olive oil. Add chopped onion and season with soy sauce, parsley, thyme, and/or balsamic vinegar. Use to fill omelets, top meats, or as a side dish.

fresh ideas

● When you can't find exotic mushrooms at your market, use reconstituted dried mushrooms, along with button mushrooms. The dried mushrooms will add the rich flavor you want, while the buttons will give the dish the texture that you expect from mushrooms.

● To flavor soups, stews, and sauces, use the liquid from the reconstituted dried mushrooms, strained through cheesecloth.

● Brush portobello mushrooms with oil, salt, and pepper and broil or grill as you would hamburgers. They make meaty-tasting low-fat, low-calorie sandwiches.

DID YOU KNOW . . .

. . . that fresh cooked mushrooms have 3 times the niacin and potassium, twice the iron, and 15 times the riboflavin as the same amount of canned mushrooms?

VARIETIES

Common Button mushrooms are white or off-white with round caps and very subtle flavor.

Criminis are brown with round-caps similar to button mushrooms but with a slightly richer, meatier flavor and more texture.

Enokis are unique among edible mushrooms in having a crunchy texture and are best eaten raw. Creamy-colored enokis have long, thin stems with a tiny button cap.

Oysters are creamy white to gray with a very delicate texture. They actually have an oysterlike flavor that intensifies with cooking.

Portobellos come in a variety of sizes from average to extra-large and have a rich flavor.

Shiitakes, often featured in Asian cooking, are strongly flavored, with a meaty texture. The tough stems are usually discarded.

Many varieties of mushrooms, including shiitake, porcini, and morels, are available in dried form for long storage.

Okra

It used to be that finding okra on the menu nearly guaranteed you were eating in the American South. But nowadays this ribbed, pointy, hairy pod with the slippery juice is making its way into kitchens all around the country.

PACKED INTO ONE CUP OF OKRA:

ABOUT **65** CALORIES • ONE-THIRD THE DAILY REQUIREMENT FOR **vitamin C** • MORE THAN HALF THE DAILY REQUIREMENT FOR **folate**, WHICH PREVENTS BIRTH DEFECTS AND PROMOTES NORMAL GROWTH • FIBROUS **pectin**, WHICH REDUCES CHOLESTEROL IN THE BLOOD AND PROTECTS AGAINST STOMACH ULCERS AND OTHER INTESTINAL DISORDERS • **lutein** AND **carotenoids**, PHYTOCHEMICALS THAT HELP PREVENT BLINDNESS DUE TO MACULAR DEGENERATION AND CATARACTS AND HELP LOWER THE RISK OF CANCER

At the Market

SEASON Fresh okra's prime season is summer, but it can sometimes be found among fall produce as well. Florida, Georgia, and Texas are the major producers in North America.

WHAT TO LOOK FOR Choose bright green pods no more than 3 inches long, avoiding any oversized okra, which will be fibrous and tough. Pods should be firm with no browning or discoloration at the tips.

In the Kitchen

STORING Okra is quite perishable; if you must store it, spread the unwashed pods in a single layer in a perforated plastic bag and refrigerate for a day or two. If kept longer, the okra will lose its texture and color.

PREP Wash okra just before using it. Some cooks prefer to gently scrub the pods with a soft brush or towel to remove the fine fuzz on the surface, while others contend that this is not necessary, because the fuzz is imperceptible after cooking. In any case, do cut off and discard the stem end. Avoid cutting into the okra's interior flesh—except when chopping the okra for stews or sautés—or its slippery juice will be released.

BASIC COOKING Okra can be steamed, stewed, cooked in the microwave, or fried. One of the most popular ways to cook okra as a side dish is to fry it: For one pound of trimmed whole okra, you'll need flour and cornmeal for dredging, two eggs lightly beaten in a bowl, plus vegetable oil for deep-frying. Once the oil is good and hot (about 365°F), toss the okra in the flour, dip it in the eggs, and then roll it in cornmeal. Fry the okra in batches, without overcrowding, until well browned—about 3 minutes. Drain on paper towels, sprinkle with salt, and serve.

BEST USES IN RECIPES Okra is an essential ingredient in Southern gumbo recipes. It is often stewed with tomatoes and lamb.

fresh ideas

● Try okra on the grill. The trick is to thread four or five pods onto two parallel skewers, creating a vegetable "ladder." Brush the pods with olive oil and sprinkle with salt. Grill on both sides until lightly charred. Sprinkle with a little vinegar or lemon juice and serve hot.

● Serve raw okra on a vegetable platter with a dip.

● Add okra to stewed tomatoes: The okra keeps the tomatoes from becoming too watery, and the acid in the tomatoes keeps the okra from becoming too gelatinous.

● Add slices of raw okra to a salad for extra crunch.

DID YOU KNOW . . .
. . . that while okra cooks, it releases sticky juices that thicken whatever liquid it is in? That's why it is such an important ingredient in gumbos and other Creole dishes that don't use a roux of flour and fat for thickening.

fresh ideas

● Cook sliced red or sweet white onions in olive oil over low heat until they are very tender and golden brown. Serve them with meat, fish, or poultry, or as a sandwich relish.

● You can stuff big sweet onions that have been cored with a seasoned rice mixture and bake as you would stuffed peppers.

● Add sautéed onions or scallions, along with chopped fresh dill, to bread doughs.

● Stuff cored apples with sautéed red onions and bake until tender. Serve with sausage and scrambled eggs for brunch.

DID YOU KNOW . . .
. . . that in the area of Georgia where Vidalia onions are grown, the stomach cancer mortality rate is far lower than the national level?

Onions

There are very few kitchens in the world where onions are not a staple food. White, yellow, and red storage onions are used almost daily. Fresh onions, such as shallots and scallions, are brought in for special recipes.

PACKED INTO A **HALF-CUP** OF CHOPPED ONION:

30 CALORIES • **vitamin C** TO FIGHT INFECTION AND HELP HEALING • A PHYTO-CHEMICAL KNOWN AS **diallyl sulfide** THAT IS THOUGHT TO LOWER THE RISK OF DEVELOPING STOMACH CANCER • **quercetin**, ANOTHER PHYTOCHEMICAL THAT FIGHTS CANCER AND HEART DISEASE

At the Market

SEASON Onions fall into two basic categories: Storage onions, which are grown in the northern parts of the United States and harvested in late summer and early fall, and spring/summer onions, which are grown in Texas, Georgia, and Arizona, and are harvested and shipped from late spring to fall. The storage onions are "cured" for several months before they are shipped to market, so they are available from late fall to early spring. Spring/summer onions, which include scallions, tend to be juicy and mild enough to eat raw. Shallots, which are available year-round, are grown in New Jersey and New York or imported from France.

WHAT TO LOOK FOR Look for dry, firm, evenly shaped onions and shallots with smooth, brittle, papery skin. Avoid onions with soft spots or wet, discolored skin. Scallions should be bright white, with deeply colored green leaves and fresh-looking roots.

In the Kitchen

STORING Store onions in a mesh bag in a cool, dry open space away from bright light. Don't store them with potatoes; the potatoes give off moisture and a gas that causes onions to spoil more quickly. They should keep up to a month. Milder, sweeter onions such as Vidalia onions and shallots often don't keep as long as sharper-tasting onions. In fact, you might put sweet onions, uncovered, in the crisper drawer of your refrigerator. Scallions are not meant to be stored for long periods. They should be wrapped in plastic and refrigerated for use within a few days of purchase.

PREP Onions contain a substance called a lachrymator, which is released into the air when the vegetable is peeled or cut. When these vapors combine with moisture from your eyes, sulfuric acid is formed, resulting in a painful burning sensation and tears. There are several ways to prevent "onion tears." You can cook pearl onions whole, before peeling, for example. When this technique isn't practical, try peeling the onion while holding it under cold running water. Generally, if you use a sharp knife and make quick work of

VEGETABLES FOR VITALITY

VARIETIES

Pearl onions are small, white or red, oval-shaped onions that are often pickled and also used whole in stews and braised dishes.

Red onions are mild enough to eat raw in salads and sandwiches, but they are often added to cooked dishes as well.

Scallions, also known as green onions, spring onions, and bunching onions, can be thinly sliced and served raw in salads or as a garnish to hot foods. But they are also good cooked and are often added to stir-fries and other Asian dishes.

Shallots grow in bunches, similar to large cloves of garlic. They have light brown skin and white or pur-plish flesh. Shallots have a delicate but distinctive and delicious flavor that defines many French sauces and braised dishes.

Spanish onions are large, sweet, white or yellow-skinned onions that are usually eaten raw. They can be used in cooking, but they are so mild they don't contribute enough onion flavor for most tastes.

Sweet onions such as Vidalia, Walla Walla, Maui Sweets, and Texas 1015 have white or tan skin and are generally larger and sometimes flatter than regular yellow onions. They are eaten raw in salads and sandwiches and are also good on the grill.

Yellow onions are the most popular onions for cooking. Their flavor ranges from pungent to almost sweet, but they can hold up to the long cooking sometimes required for soups and stews.

chopping onions (right), tears won't be a problem. And, indeed, soft vegetables like onions are best chopped by hand. If you use a food processor, pulse gently off and on to avoid mashing the onion.

BASIC COOKING Onions can be steamed, microwaved, battered and deep-fried, roasted, broiled or grilled all on their own to be served with meat, poultry, or fish as a side dish. But onions are most often used—raw or sautéed—to season soups, stews, sauces, cooked vegetable dishes, casseroles, pilafs, bean dishes, stir-fries, and stocks. Many cooks use yellow onions, skin and all, for stock because they produce a lovely chestnut color. Caramelizing is a popular way to cook onions to accompany meat. To serve four, thinly slice three yellow onions. In a heavy skillet over medium heat, heat 1 tablespoon olive oil. Add onions and cook, covered, for 10 minutes, stirring often. Remove cover and cook for 10 more minutes, stirring occasionally. A pinch of sugar speeds the caramelizing process, which gives you beautifully browned, soft, aromatic onions to complement any dish.

BEST RECIPE Classic onion soup makes cold weather bearable. To make enough for four people, preheat the oven to 400°F. In a 5-quart Dutch oven over moderately high heat, melt 2 tablespoons butter. Add five thinly sliced yellow onions and sauté until onions are lightly golden, about 10 minutes. Reduce heat to moderately low and sauté 10 more minutes, stirring occasionally. Add 3½ cups beef broth and 5 cups water and bring to a boil over high heat. Reduce heat to low and simmer, uncovered, for 20 minutes. Add salt and pepper to taste and return to a boil. Ladle soup into four 8-ounce ramekins and place on a heavy-duty baking sheet. Top each portion with a toasted ½-inch slice of French bread and 1 tablespoon grated Gruyère cheese. Baked uncovered until cheese melts—about 5 minutes— and serve.

CUTTING UP AN ONION

Halve onion lengthwise. Make several horizontal cuts, stopping about ¼" from root.

1

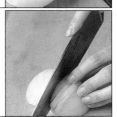

Make vertical cuts from top to bottom, keeping root intact.

2

Hold onion by root end, slice crosswise, letting onion fall apart into small, even pieces.

3

fresh ideas

● Grate tender young parsnips raw into salads or slaws to add flavor and vitamin C.

● Pureed parsnips can be made into delicious pancakes with the addition of a shredded carrot, two cut-up scallions, an egg, a table-spoon of flour, and some salt. Cook pancakes in batches in a nonstick skillet with a little oil. Serve pancakes warm with apple-sauce or sour cream.

● Substitute chunks of cooked parsnips and carrots for the pota-toes in your favorite potato salad recipe for a refreshing change.

CUTTING UP PARSNIPS

Trim top and bottom from parsnips. Then use a vegetable peeler to trim away a thin layer of peel.
1

To dice, cut parsnip in two along its length and remove any woody core. Then cut across each piece.
2

Parsnips

Related to carrots but lacking the orange color (and the beta-carotene), parsnips look like pale, top-heavy imitations of their cousins. They do, however, have a distinct flavor of their own and are high in fiber and nutrients.

PACKED INTO ONE CUP OF COOKED PARSNIPS:

LESS THAN **126** CALORIES • A THIRD OF THE RECOMMENDED DAILY AMOUNT OF **vitamin C** FOR HEART HEALTH • **folate** FOR MAKING RED BLOOD CELLS • **magnesium** FOR BONE GROWTH AND METABOLISM

At the Market

SEASON Parsnips are in greatest supply from fall through early spring, but many markets carry them year-round. They are grown mainly in northern California and Michigan, but you can find them at local farmers' markets too. Growers place parsnips in cold storage for a couple of weeks before ship-ping them to market to allow their starch to convert to sugar, making them much sweeter. That is why many farmers and home gardeners in northern climates allow parsnips to winter over in the ground, enjoying a natural cold storage.

WHAT TO LOOK FOR Choose firm, medium-sized roots that are uniformly shaped and free from bruises or soft spots. Parsnips more than 8 inches long can have a woody core.

In the Kitchen

STORING Keep parsnips—without their greens—in a perforated plastic bag in the crisper drawer of the refrigerator for up to four weeks.

PREP For most uses, trim the tops and bottoms of parsnips and peel with a vegetable peeler (left). If you are going to puree parsnips, however, you can cook them first, and easily peel afterward by hand.

BASIC COOKING Parsnips are best when they are not overcooked, but just tender. Steaming is a good method to use, as is microwaving. You can also braise parsnips in stock and season them with herbs or bake them as you would sweet potatoes with fruit juice, spices like cinnamon and ginger, and brown sugar. You can puree cooked parsnips in a blender or food processor and serve with butter and salt and pepper. Or you can combine pureed parsnips with pureed winter squash or sweet potatoes. Chunks of parsnip enrich the flavor and nutrition of soups and stews; just be careful not to put them in too soon or they will get mushy.

HISTORY . . . Until the 1800s, parsnips were a kitchen staple and the princi-pal source of starch on both European and North American tables. During the 19th century, they were gradually replaced by potatoes on both sides of the Atlantic.

Peas

Thanks to the popularity of snow peas and the introduction of sugar snaps in the 1970s—both peas with edible pods that require little preparation—more people are eating fresh peas today than ever before.

PACKED INTO A **HALF-CUP** OF COOKED PEAS:

ABOUT **65** CALORIES • **B vitamins** FOR ENERGY PRODUCTION • **vitamin C** FOR RESISTANCE TO INFECTION • **folate** TO PROMOTE NORMAL GROWTH • **iron** TO CARRY OXYGEN THROUGH YOUR BODY • PLENTY OF **fiber** TO MAINTAIN DIGESTIVE HEALTH

At the Market

SEASON Fresh sweet peas are available late spring and early summer. The season for fresh sugar snap peas and snow peas extends throughout the summer. Crops from California, Florida, and Central America extend the season into winter months.

WHAT TO LOOK FOR The freshest pea pods at the market will look shiny and firm; if rubbed together they squeak a little. Avoid any pale green or yellow pods, for that indicates that their sugars have begun to turn to starch. If possible, take a nibble of one to test. The sweetest green shell peas are best small to medium size. They should fit snugly in their pods without looking swollen or crowded. Large, heavy shell pea pods usually signal that the peas will be tough and starchy. On the other hand, light, thin pods indicate immature, bland peas.

WHERE TO BUY THE BEST The best fresh sweet peas are usually found at local farm stands or in your backyard garden.

In the Kitchen

STORING Like sweet corn, time is of the essence when it comes to serving fresh peas, so storage is not recommended. If you must, store peas briefly in plastic in the coldest part of the refrigerator.

PREP To shell green peas, snap off the top of the pod and pull the string down the side, opening the pod in the process. The peas will pop right out. Sugar snap pods are edible, but you may encounter some varieties that need stringing. To string sugar snaps, bend the stem tip toward the flat side of the pod to snap it, then gently pull downward, removing the string with the stem. Snow peas need only the stem tip trimmed.

BASIC COOKING Nothing could be simpler than cooking fresh peas. Just boil water, add a bit of salt, and stir in the peas. Sugar snap peas and snow peas will be tender-crisp in 1 to 2 minutes; shell peas will cook in 2 to 4 minutes depending on their size and freshness. A pinch of sugar in the cooking water will boost the flavor of peas that are not perfectly sweet.

fresh ideas

● Toss some blanched peas into fresh salads.

● Pluck a handful of fresh shell peas from their pods and eat them out of hand to enjoy a sweet, nutritious snack.

● Add raw shelled peas to stews, soups, and vegetable sautés during the last minutes of cooking.

● Add peas to plain grains such as rice, couscous, and pasta.

● Garnish a platter of sliced roasted meat with a handful of blanched shell peas.

● For a smoky taste that complements their sweetness, sauté sugar snap peas with a little crumbled bacon.

● Cut blanched snow peas into small pieces and add them to creamy mixtures such as egg salad or tuna salad to provide an interesting texture.

DID YOU KNOW . . .

. . . that a three-quarter-cup serving of fresh green peas has more protein than a whole egg?

. . . that snow peas, so closely associated with Chinese stir-fries, are thought to have been developed in Holland in the 1500s?

fresh ideas

● Add potatoes to soups and, once cooked, mash some of them to thicken the soup without adding extra flour.

● Make a festive potato salad with unpeeled red, white, blue, and yellow potatoes.

● Substitute mashed potatoes for some of the oil in a salad dressing. Then add chopped garlic and lemon juice or vinegar and whisk until smooth. The dressing will have a creamy texture.

● Bind meat loaf or hamburger with small cubes of cooked potato instead of using bread crumbs or oatmeal.

● Top a baked potato healthfully with no-fat half-and-half and your favorite fresh herbs, such as dill, parsley, or chives, as well as salt and pepper.

DID YOU KNOW . . .

. . . that potato skins are richer in B vitamins, fiber, iron, calcium, phosphorus, potassium, and zinc than potato flesh?

Potatoes

It's hard to believe the ever popular and highly nutritious potato was once thought to be poisonous. Today, many different varieties of red, white, blue, and yellow potatoes regularly compete for space on grocery and market shelves.

PACKED INTO A **SIX-OUNCE** BAKED POTATO:

LESS THAN **200** CALORIES • PLENTY OF **potassium** TO HELP MAINTAIN NORMAL BLOOD PRESSURE • MORE THAN ONE-THIRD THE DAILY REQUIREMENT FOR **vitamin C** • INSOLUBLE **fiber** FOR BETTER DIGESTION • FLAVONOIDS AND OTHER PROTECTIVE **phytochemicals**, ESPECIALLY IN ITS SKIN

At the Market

SEASON Since most mature potatoes store well, they are available all year long. New potatoes are only harvested from spring through fall.

WHAT TO LOOK FOR Choose potatoes that are firm, dry, and well formed, with no bruises, cuts, cracks, or sprouted eyes. Avoid potatoes with green spots, which indicates the presence of a toxin that develops when potatoes are exposed to light.

In the Kitchen

STORING Keep potatoes loosely wrapped in paper, netting, or ventilated plastic bags in a cool, dry place with good air circulation. Under the best conditions, potatoes will keep for several months.

PREP Scrub potatoes well before cooking. Cut off and discard any sprouted areas.

BASIC COOKING depends on the variety. **All-purpose (chef's)** potatoes — round, with smooth, pale skin and waxy flesh—are best when steamed, boiled, or roasted. **Bliss** potatoes, red-skinned and no larger than 1½ inches in diameter, are excellent for roasting and steaming. Early summer is their peak-season. **Blue (purple)** potatoes with their deep bluish-purple skin and flesh are used to make potato salads, home fries, and sautés. Summer is peak-season for blue potatoes. **Idaho (russet)** are long potatoes with russet brown skin. They are best for baking and frying and also excellent for mashing. **New potatoes** are young potatoes, no more than 1½ inches in diameter, with thin, tan, or red skin. They are usually boiled, steamed, or cut up and roasted. It's not necessary to peel new potatoes. Unlike more mature potatoes, new potatoes don't store well and should be kept in the refrigerator for use within a week of purchase. **Yukon golds** are tan-skinned potatoes with golden yellow flesh and a buttery flavor. They can be baked, boiled, and mashed as a side dish, or sliced and incorporated into salads or casserole-style dishes. They can also be fried.

Radishes

A bunch of crisp round red radishes or tapered white radishes can go a long way toward livening up a salad or a plate of appetizers in the winter, when fresh vegetable pickings are slim. Radishes add a zip to dishes without really burning.

PACKED INTO A **HALF-CUP** OF RADISHES:

ABOUT **6** CALORIES • 14% OF THE DAILY REQUIREMENT FOR **vitamin C** • CANCER-FIGHTING PHYTOCHEMICALS KNOWN AS **flavonoids**

At the Market

SEASON Radishes from California and Florida are available throughout the year but are most abundant in early spring.

VARIETIES Although red radishes are the best known, in most vegetable markets, you can now find long, tapered white radishes, which are milder than red ones, and daikons, which are large white carrot-shaped radishes, native to Asia, that have a sharper flavor than red radishes. In Polish or Russian markets, you will find black radishes, which are shaped like turnips but have dull black or brown skins and pungent white flesh. Horseradish is a cousin that is long and tapered with a brown skin.

WHAT TO LOOK FOR Choose firm red radishes with taught, brightly colored skin and fresh-looking leaves. White radishes, daikons, and horseradish should be firm, unblemished, and smooth. Black radishes should be heavy for their size and crack-free.

In the Kitchen

STORING Remove and discard any leaves before storing. Wrap red and white radishes, daikons, and horseradish in plastic and store in the refrigerator for up to one week. Store black radishes in perforated plastic bags in the refrigerator for up to a month.

PREP Scrub radishes and trim ends. Peel daikons, horseradish, and thick-skinned black radishes. If your radishes have started to wither, revive them by soaking in ice water for an hour or two before serving.

BASIC COOKING Though red radishes are most often eaten raw in salads, they can also be steamed or sautéed until tender and served as a side dish. The flavor of all radishes mellows with cooking, and many people who don't care for raw radishes often enjoy eating them cooked. Steam whole, trimmed red or white radishes for about 10 minutes; sauté sliced radishes for 2 to 4 minutes. The simplest seasoning is a sprinkling of salt and a bit of butter. Shred daikon radishes with carrots and steam for five minutes, then season with a vinaigrette. Black radishes can be boiled or steamed and served hot. They can also be parboiled and sliced to serve cold with dip. Horseradish is peeled and shredded into yogurt or vinegar to make a relish for meat.

fresh ideas

● For an easy, flavorful side dish salad, toss together any of these combinations with a simple vinaigrette dressing:
oranges and radishes
cucumbers and radishes
snow peas and radishes

● If you like a little spiciness in your food but can't take the heat of a chile pepper, try garnishing dips, salads, slaws, hot or cold soups, stir-fries, and other dishes with slivered or grated radishes.

● Simmer daikon slices in stock and then glaze with orange juice, just as you do carrots (page 303).

MATCHSTICK RADISHES

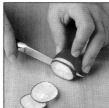

With a paring knife, cut radishes into ⅛-inch-thick coins.

1

Stack 3 or 4 coins and cut crosswise into ⅛-inch sticks.

2

DID YOU KNOW . . .

. . . that a radish's hot taste comes from a mustard oil that forms in its skin. Peeling the skin removes most of the vegetable's spicy heat.

fresh ideas

● Serve mashed rutabagas with roast duck; their strong flavors complement each other.

● Combine mashed rutabagas with mashed carrots and mashed potatoes for a richer-tasting accompaniment to pork loin roasts or grilled steaks.

● Try using rosemary to season roasted rutabagas, along with oil, salt, and pepper.

● Like sweet potatoes, rutabagas go well with ground ginger, cloves, and honey or brown sugar. Glaze microwaved rutabaga chunks with this combination.

DID YOU KNOW . . .

. . . that rutabaga comes from the Swedish word for "round root" and that sometimes rutabagas are called swedes?

Rutabagas

Larger and rounder than turnips, with which they are often confused, rutabagas are a separate species that might be a cross between a turnip and a wild cabbage. They are large round roots with yellow flesh that has a strong, sweet flavor.

PACKED INTO **THREE-QUARTER CUP** OF CUBED RUTABAGA:

LESS THAN **36** CALORIES • 25 MG OF **vitamin C** FOR CONTROLLING CHOLESTEROL • **folate** FOR RED BLOOD CELLS • **beta-carotene** FOR HEALTHY SKIN AND GUMS • **potassium** TO REGULATE BLOOD PRESSURE • **insoluble fiber** TO LOWER LEVELS OF CHOLESTEROL

At the Market

SEASON Rutabagas are available all year, mainly because they store well. A cool-weather crop, they are grown principally in Canada for the North American market.

WHAT TO LOOK FOR Rutabagas are sold with their greens trimmed off, and they are often coated in clear wax to prevent moisture loss. They should feel firm and solid and be free of bruises or scars. Check that the wax has no mold on it. Try to find rutabagas that are four inches or less in diameter; these smaller ones tend to be sweeter.

In the Kitchen

STORING Rutabagas can be stored uncovered in the refrigerator for two weeks or more.

PREP Use a sharp paring knife to peel the coating of wax and the skin from a rutabaga. It is easier if you quarter them first.

BASIC COOKING Rutabagas can be sliced or quartered and baked on their own in a covered baking pan or roasted with meat or poultry for about an hour. Sliced or cubed rutabagas can be braised in seasoned stock for 15 or 20 minutes and served with the reduced cooking liquid as sauce. Microwaved or steamed rutabagas can be mashed by themselves or mixed half and half with mashed potatoes and seasoned with scallions, dill, and chives.

Spinach

When it comes to dark leafy vegetables, spinach is the powerhouse choice. Delicious raw in salads, it is also cooked and served as a side dish. Spinach puree bases sauces and pesto; other spinach mixtures stuff pasta shells and meat rolls.

PACKED INTO **TWO CUPS** OF RAW SPINACH:

ABOUT **13** CALORIES • **beta-carotene** TO PROTECT AGAINST CANCER AND MACULAR DEGENERATION • **folate** TO PROTECT AGAINST ANEMIA AND BIRTH DEFECTS • **lutein** AND **zeaxanthin** TO PREVENT MACULAR DEGENERATION AND COLON CANCER • ANTIOXIDANT **vitamin C** TO HELP PREVENT OSTEOARTHRITIS AND STROKE

At the Market

SEASON Curly-leaf, or Savoy, spinach, grown mainly in California and Texas, is available in bags year-round. Loose stems of flat-leaf and curly-leaf spinach appear in early spring both in local stores and at farmers' markets. New Zealand spinach, which grows in warm weather and may appear in markets in the summer, is actually a different botanical family; it has a milder flavor but can be used in place of regular spinach.

WHAT TO LOOK FOR Select from loose piles of spinach, if you can, and choose small leaves with crisp, springy texture and a clear green color. Avoid leaves with insect damage, wilt, bruises, or yellow spots. Choose thin stems over thick stems (a sign of younger leaves). Finally, use your nose: Fresh spinach should smell sweet and fresh, not musty. If you must choose from packages, check that the spinach feels resilient when you squeeze the package.

In the Kitchen

STORING Store bagged spinach in the crisper drawer of the refrigerator. Also store loose spinach leaves in plastic bags in the crisper. Both kinds can keep for up to four days.

PREP Spinach, particularly the curly-leaf kind, needs careful washing to get rid of the sand and grit in which it is grown. Trim off the stems and place leaves in a bowl or sink of cool water. Stir the leaves about with your hands and remove them; the sand and grit should settle to the bottom. Empty the sink or bowl and repeat the process until leaves are free of particles. If you are using the spinach for a salad, dry the clean leaves in a salad spinner or on kitchen towels. If you will be cooking the spinach, leave water clinging to the leaves; you can use it for cooking water.

BASIC COOKING Whole spinach leaves can be blanched or microwaved briefly (2 minutes) before stir-frying or sautéing in a little bit of oil and stock (5 minutes). Chopped spinach *(see Cutting Up Greens, page 314)* cooks more quickly.

fresh ideas

● Puree steamed spinach with some fresh garlic and plain yogurt, top with scallions, and serve cold as a summer soup.

● For a quick pasta sauce, puree steamed spinach with parsley and lemon juice.

● Make a salad dressing in a blender with pureed steamed spinach, parsley, basil, garlic, salt, and pepper. Slowly add olive oil and lemon juice.

DID YOU KNOW . . .
. . . that Popeye was wrong and spinach is not a great source of iron? Although it contains good supplies of iron, it also contains oxalic acid, which limits how much iron the body can absorb.

fresh ideas

● Thick sticks of zucchini, resembling fat French fries, can be briefly roasted, then used for dipping into savory sauces.

● Stuff blanched pattypan squash with crumbled feta and top with fresh garlic bread crumbs.

● Add small cubes of cooked summer squash to pasta sauces.

● Make zucchini ribbons to garnish salads by running a cheese planer lengthwise down the sides of a raw zucchini.

● Overgrown, tough squash can be used as serving containers, in the same way watermelon is carved and cored for filling. Cut out a handle from the top of squash, core and scrape out the interior, and brush with lemon juice. Fill with crudités or salads.

● Add cooked squash along with tomato, herbs, and onion to omelets for a Mediterranean-style brunch.

DID YOU KNOW . . .

. . . that squash blossoms can be stuffed as an appetizer? Male flowers, those without tiny squash attached, are best. Fill blossoms with herbed goat cheese, for example, then pinch shut and sauté briefly in hot oil. Drain on paper towels and serve.

Summer Squash

Summer squash are wonderfully versatile and quick to cook. When you buy fresh ones, you know that they will be good any number of ways—sautéed, roasted, stir-fried, grilled, steamed, or even mixed into a muffin batter.

PACKED INTO **ONE CUP** OF ZUCCHINI:

25 CALORIES ● ALMOST ONE-FOURTH THE DAILY REQUIREMENT FOR **vitamin C** ● SEVERAL **B vitamins** USED IN ENERGY PRODUCTION ● **magnesium** TO HELP REGULATE NERVES AND MUSCLES

At the Market

SEASON Despite their name, summer squash—which include green and yellow zucchini, round scalloped yellow or green pattypan squash, and pale yellow crookneck squash, familia—are available throughout much of the year. But in summer you usually find the freshest, tastiest examples of these easy-to-grow vegetables. Another bonus of the summer harvest is the availability of squash blossoms—a true garden delicacy.

WHAT TO LOOK FOR Zucchini and summer squash are best when young and small—no bigger than about 7 inches. They are capable of growing to enormous sizes as the season progresses, but these giant squash will be seedy, watery, and tough. Choose small squash with bright, shiny skins and a firm texture. Don't be bothered by a few surface scratches; they're practically unavoidable, since the skins of summer squash are so tender.

In the Kitchen

STORING Store zucchini and other summer squash in a perforated plastic bag in the refrigerator, where they should keep for 3 to 4 days.

PREP Give squash a good rinse and trim their ends. Small and moderate-sized squash have edible skin. With oversized summer squash, it's best to peel the tough skin and scoop out the seeds. Discard any dry, pulpy parts. Squash can be precut for later use, covered with a damp towel, and refrigerated for several hours. To use squash in baking breads and muffins, grate the raw vegetable and blot it with paper towels to remove some of the excess liquid.

BASIC COOKING Summer squash can be steamed, sautéed, stir-fried, or grilled. An easy way to prepare summer squash is to cut green and yellow varieties into julienne sticks or thin slices, and sauté in a little olive oil until they just begin to soften and brown. Add chopped garlic, fresh herbs, salt, and pepper and cook another minute or two. Drizzle with fresh lemon juice and serve. To grill, cut small squash in half lengthwise, lightly oil the cut surface, and put on the grate just until lightly charred and tender.

Sweet Potatoes

Gardeners know by their purple, heart-shaped leaves that sweet potatoes belong to the morning glory family. Health experts know by analysis that these orange tubers belong to a select group of power vegetables loaded with important nutrients.

PACKED INTO A **HALF-CUP** OF SWEET POTATOES:

---

170 CALORIES • MORE THAN FIVE TIMES THE DAILY REQUIREMENT FOR **vitamin A** • ALMOST HALF THE DAILY REQUIREMENT FOR **vitamin C** • MORE THAN 10% OF THE DAILY REQUIREMENT FOR **fiber**

At the Market

SEASON Sweet potatoes, products of California, Louisiana, and New Jersey, are most abundant and at their best from early fall through the winter months. Some, however, are available all year.

WHAT TO LOOK FOR Choose firm sweet potatoes with smooth, dry skin and no cracks or blemishes. Check the tips of the potatoes, which is where decay usually begins.

In the Kitchen

STORING Keep sweet potatoes in a cool, preferably 55°F, dark place for up to a month. At normal room temperature, they will last up to a week. Don't put raw sweet potatoes in the refrigerator; they tend to harden and develop an "off" taste. You can freeze cooked sweet potatoes for longer storage.

PREP Scrub unpeeled whole potatoes well before baking. Potatoes to be cut up can be peeled with a swivel-blade peeler.

BASIC COOKING To bake whole sweet potatoes, preheat oven to 425°F. Pierce each potato in several places with a fork or knife tip. Arrange potatoes in a foil-lined baking pan. Bake until very tender, about 1 hour.

BEST USES IN RECIPES Baked sweet potatoes are served split and mashed with butter as a side dish. Their sweetness can be enhanced with a drizzle of maple syrup or by cooking sweet potatoes with pear, apple, or orange juice. For a different taste, sweet potatoes can be seasoned with lime juice and cilantro or mashed with roasted garlic, salt, and pepper. Baked or boiled sweet potatoes can be mashed to use as a side dish or to make desserts such as sweet potato puddings and pies.

VARIETIES In the United States, two kinds of sweet potatoes are grown. One has moist, deeply colored orange flesh, and the other has drier yellow flesh. The moist orange-fleshed sweet potatoes are usually plumper in shape and sweeter, but both varieties can be used interchangeably in recipes.

fresh ideas

● Mash sweet potatoes with maple syrup and serve as a pudding for dessert.

● Make sweet potato salad with chunks of cooked sweet potatoes. Dress with lime juice, olive oil, minced scallions, curry powder, and salt.

● Mash cooked sweet potatoes with grated Parmesan cheese and use in place of half the cheese in your favorite lasagna recipe.

● Make sweet potato chips: Thinly slice sweet potatoes, drizzle with olive oil, and bake in a 400°F oven until tender and crisp.

DID YOU KNOW . . .
. . . that a true yam is a large (up to 100 pounds) root vegetable native to Africa and rarely seen in North America? Sweet potato growers in the United States tried to distinguish between two sweet potato varieties by calling one a yam. It isn't.

fresh ideas

● Cook fresh tomatoes with sugar, cinnamon, and orange zest to make a savory jam.

● Combine tomato juice with an equal amount of carrot juice and chill. Garnished with chopped fresh tomato and a dollop of yogurt, the mixture serves as a refreshing summer soup.

● To give a nutritional boost to savory soups, replace half of the water with tomato juice.

● Make a quick sauce for pasta salad by combining tomato paste, tomato juice, olive oil, balsamic vinegar, and chopped fresh basil.

DID YOU KNOW . . .

. . . that lycopene-rich food may protect against prostate cancer? In a six-year study of 48,000 men who consumed 10 or more servings per week of tomato products, participants experienced a 45 percent reduction in prostate cancer.

Tomatoes

Although Italy and other Mediterranean countries are probably best known for dishes that feature tomatoes, they are actually native to Central America.

PACKED INTO ONE MEDIUM TOMATO:

ABOUT **25** CALORIES • MORE THAN ONE-THIRD THE DAILY REQUIREMENT FOR **vitamin C** • AN ANTIOXIDANT CALLED **beta-carotene** THAT IS CONVERTED TO VITAMIN A IN THE BODY • A PHYTOCHEMICAL CALLED **lycopene** THAT HELPS FIGHT PROSTATE CANCER • ANTICANCER CHEMICALS **caffeic, ferulic, and chlorogenic acids** • SIGHT-PROTECTIVE **lutein and zeaxanthin** THAT HELP STAVE OFF VISION LOSS

At the Market

SEASON There are tomatoes in the market throughout the year, but summer is the only time to get mouthwatering fresh tomatoes from local growers— or your own backyard (tomatoes are the first pick of home gardeners). Throughout the rest of the year, tomatoes are shipped from Florida, California, or Mexico. Or they are grown in greenhouses in soil or water (hydroponically); tomatoes are the most popular greenhouse vegetable. The term "vine-ripened" doesn't tell you anything significant; tomatoes that are picked green can color as well and taste as good as ones picked red. Many cooks, however, feel that outside of summer and early fall, canned tomatoes are the best buy.

WHAT TO LOOK FOR Choose firm-ripe, evenly shaped, deeply colored tomatoes with no tears or bruises in the skin. Ripe tomatoes give off a lovely tomato fragrance.

WHERE TO BUY THE BEST Farm stands and greenmarkets that sell local, fresh-picked produce are most likely to have the sweetest, juiciest, vine-ripened tomatoes.

In the Kitchen

STORING Always store tomatoes at room temperature. Store slightly under-ripe tomatoes in a brown paper bag to ripen and improve flavor. Refrigeration destroys a tomato's taste and texture.

PREP Use a sharp, serrated knife to slice tomatoes. To remove seeds, cut the tomato in half and gently squeeze out seeds and liquid. To peel toma-toes, follow instructions and photographs *(facing page)*.

BASIC COOKING Tomatoes can be halved and broiled, grilled, or roasted in a hot oven until they begin to shrivel, ten to fifteen minutes. Be careful not to overcook or tomatoes will collapse.

VARIETIES

Beefsteaks are very large, deeply ridged, dark red tomatoes that are wonderful for salads and sandwiches.

Cherry tomatoes are small red or yellow tomatoes that are often sweeter and lower in acid than regular slicing tomatoes.

Grape tomatoes are also called pear tomatoes. They are small, red or yellow, grape-shaped, and, like cherry tomatoes, can be eaten out of hand.

Green tomatoes are merely tomatoes that were picked from the vine prior to ripening. If wrapped in paper and left at room temperature, they will slowly ripen and turn red, though don't expect them to be sweet. Firm and tart, green tomatoes are commonly used for pickling or frying.

Plum tomatoes are red, egg-shaped, fleshy tomatoes that are especially good for sauces, soups, and other cooked dishes. Plum tomatoes can also be eaten raw in salads and can be used to make dried tomatoes.

Tomatillos are small, round, green tomatoes encased in a brown, papery husk. They are very tart and usually cooked before eating. Tomatillos are most often used in Mexican and Southwest American-style sauces.

Yellow slicing tomatoes are medium to large in size, round in shape, and deep, bright yellow in color. Yellow tomatoes are generally eaten raw in salads or on sandwiches as a substitute for red slicing tomatoes. You can also find yellow tomatoes in cherry-size variations, as well as plum and heart-shaped versions.

BEST USE IN RECIPES Most tomatoes are used to make sauce. They are also used in soups, stews, casseroles, and sautés and eaten raw in salads. Cherry and pear tomatoes are served on vegetable appetizer platters and eaten out of hand as snacks.

HEIRLOOM TOMATOES—With global mass marketing of food, many ancient varieties of fruits and vegetables can no longer be found. What's available instead are hybrid varieties preferred by farmers, marketers, and many consumers for their uniform good looks and hardiness to travel. Unfortunately, many of today's hybrid vegetables aren't as flavorful as the originals. But thanks to a few devotees who, years ago, began saving nonhybrid seeds, "heirloom" tomatoes with unusual coloration and interesting shapes can still be found in specialty food markets, farmers' markets, and the home gardens of anyone who buys seeds descended from the originals. Several varieties of heirloom tomatoes are considered among the best-tasting. These include Black Plum, Carbon, Sweet Olive, Sungold, Green Zebra, Red Robin, and Goose Creek.

Black Plum

PEELING A TOMATO

Cut a shallow X in bottom of each tomato.

1

Blanch in boiling water just until skin begins to shrivel, about 1 minute.

2

Remove skin with paring knife or your fingers.

3

fresh ideas

● Steam sliced turnips, carrots, and potatoes together and mash them; the combination is smoky and delicious.

● Sauté cubes of turnip in olive oil with garlic and shredded turnip greens as a side dish.

● Add shredded turnips and dill to the shredded potatoes you are using to make potato pancakes, for a fresh new taste.

● Make a slaw of shredded turnips and shredded apples; dress with a combination of apple cider, apple cider vinegar, and Dijon mustard.

DID YOU KNOW ...

... that some turnips grow to massive sizes and weigh as much as 30 pounds? Gardeners used to vie with each other to produce these behemoths, but only for show. Smaller turnips are sweeter and more delicious.

Turnips & Other Root Vegetables

A member of the cabbage family, turnips are prized for their roots as well as their greens. A staple vegetable since early Roman times, turnips were brought to North America by both French and British settlers.

PACKED INTO **THREE-QUARTER CUP** OF TURNIPS:

LESS THAN **28** CALORIES • MORE THAN A THIRD OF THE DAILY RECOMMENDATION FOR **vitamin C** TO CONTROL BLOOD CHOLESTEROL• **indoles** TO FIGHT CANCER • **lysine** TO PREVENT COLD SORES • **soluble and insoluble fiber** TO LOWER CHOLESTEROL AND PREVENT CONSTIPATION

At the Market

SEASON Turnips, raised mainly in California, Colorado, and Indiana, are winter vegetables, but because they store well, you can find them in most markets year-round.

WHAT TO LOOK FOR Choose smooth, heavy, firm turnips on the small side—closer to golf ball size than baseball size—with a minimum of fibrous root hairs at the bottom. Large turnips can develop a strong flavor that is too assertive for most tastes. If greens are attached, they should be crisp and a good green color.

In the Kitchen

STORING Keep turnip roots in a plastic bag in the crisper drawer of the refrigerator for up to a week. Detach and store turnip greens separately and use sooner.

PREP Trim a slice from the top and bottom of each turnip and peel as thinly as possible with a swivel vegetable peeler to save nutrients.

BASIC COOKING To avoid darkening the flesh, cook turnips in nonreactive pans and save cut turnip pieces in cold water with lemon or vinegar added. To preserve their mild, peppery flavor, try not to cook turnips beyond the crisp-tender stage. Overcooking intensifies the flavor.

Turnip chunks can be roasted with meat or poultry or in a shallow roasting pan by themselves (30 to 45 minutes at 350°F). Turnips can also be boiled, steamed, microwaved, or braised, whole or in pieces. Cooking turnips whole takes longer—up to 30 minutes. Sliced or matchstick turnips can be successfully stir-fried or sautéed. Turnip chunks add a sweet, peppery note to soups and stews. Mashing boiled or microwaved turnips with butter,

OTHER ROOT VEGETABLES

Celeriac, or celery root
A knobby root that tastes like celery and has a crisp texture, celeriac is low in calories and rich in vitamin C, potassium, and phosphorus. It can be grated fresh for salads,

cut up and braised as a side dish, or diced and added to soups and stews as a flavoring. Scrub the root well and peel before cutting it up for cooking or raw vegetable platters. Roast celeriac in its skin for easy peeling afterward.

Jicamas
A Mexican tuber with white flesh and a thin brown skin, a jicama has a bland flavor and a juicy crispness more like an apple than a potato or turnip. This makes fresh jicama slices—sprinkled with lime or lemon juice to keep them from browning—a welcome addition to salads or raw vegetable platters. Jicama slices add a lovely crunch to stir-fries. Although jicama can be boiled or baked like a potato, it has fewer calories—about 50 in a cup of sliced jicama. Jicamas have lots of vitamin C and some potassium, iron, and calcium. A jicama can weigh anywhere from a half-pound to five pounds. Pick unblemished roots that feel heavy for their size. You can peel the papery skin with a knife. Store peeled jicama in a container of water in the refrigerator.

Jerusalem artichokes, or sunchokes
Another native American tuber is this gnarled little root, full of vitamin C, calcium, iron and fiber, that has a nutty taste and a crisp texture. Grated or thinly sliced fresh sunchoke adds a bright flavor and crunch to salads and slaws. Dunk cut-up or peeled sunchokes in cold water with lemon or lime juice to keep the flesh from turning brown, and use nonreactive cookware. Prepare sunchokes as if they were potatoes: Bake them for 30 to 60 minutes or boil them 10 to 20 minutes and mash or puree them with parsley and other fresh herbs and a little butter or oil. Braise sunchokes

with potatoes, carrots, and celery in beef or chicken stock for a side dish with roasts or chops. Use slices of sunchoke in place of water chestnuts in stir-fries for both flavor and texture.

Lotus root
The rhizome of the water lily, this sausage-shaped delicacy is available in Asian markets from midsummer to the middle of winter. Slices of lotus root are lacy-looking because the rhizome is riddled with air tunnels. Slightly sweet-tasting, lotus root is used raw in salads and cooked in stir-fries and soups.

Salsify, or oyster plant
With tan skin and white flesh, salsify looks like a parsnip and is treated like parsnips in cooking. Its flavor is more like an oyster, however, and a serving (about ⅔ cup) has 80 calories, vitamin C, and potassium. Salsify is available in fall and winter.

salt, and pepper is a classic way to serve the vegetable. But mashed turnip also goes well with other mashed vegetables, such as potatoes or peas, spiced with some onion or roasted cloves of garlic and fresh herbs like chives or parsley.

Pureed turnips on their own are deliciously sweet, but their bulk and texture tends to be a little on the thin side. Adding one medium potato for every three turnips makes a creamier, richer puree.

DID YOU KNOW . . .
. . . that turnips are one of the only vegetables that you can plant near potatoes, because potatoes tend to need lots of space to spread and grow and are poor garden companions?

fresh ideas

● A little olive oil or butter will enhance the flavor of cooked squash. You can also add any of these seasonings:

  Brown sugar
  Curry powder
  Honey and sage
  Honey, ginger, and cinnamon
  Maple syrup, cinnamon,
    and nutmeg
  Jalapeño pepper and cilantro

● Add some peeled and diced butternut squash to chili, soups, and stews.

● Add peeled, shredded winter squash to pancake batter.

● Make a sauce of pureed winter squash and grated Parmesan cheese to serve with pasta.

● Cook chunks of winter squash with sugar, raisins, red pepper, and spices until tender. Serve as a chutney with meats or poultry.

DID YOU KNOW . . .

. . . that pumpkins are heavy consumers of nutrients in the garden, so it's best to grow a different vegetable, like lettuce or cabbage, in that spot the next year.

Winter Squash

There are many colorful types of winter squash—each with a different shape, size, marking, and flavor—but they all are powerhouses of good nutrition, the kind that fights heart disease, cancer, vision loss, and depression.

PACKED INTO **ONE CUP** OF BUTTERNUT SQUASH CUBES:

82 CALORIES • MORE THAN 100% OF THE DAILY REQUIREMENT FOR VITAMIN A IN THE FORM OF THE CANCER-FIGHTING ANTIOXIDANT **beta-carotene** • MORE THAN HALF THE DAILY REQUIREMENT FOR **vitamin C** • **B vitamins** TO HELP WITH ENERGY PRODUCTION • 6 GRAMS OF **fiber** TO HELP MAINTAIN DIGESTIVE HEALTH • EYE-PROTECTIVE **lutein** • HEART-HELPING **magnesium** AND **potassium**

At the Market

SEASON Although some varieties are available all year long, winter squash are at their peak from late fall through the winter months. Fresh pumpkins are only available in the fall and early winter, but canned pumpkin, which is wonderful for making desserts and other baked goods, is always available in the supermarket.

WHAT TO LOOK FOR When choosing any variety of winter squash, look for dry, hard, tough-looking skin with no soft spots or bruises. When choosing a fresh pumpkin for cooking, pick smaller pumpkins, approximately five to eight pounds, for their sweeter flavor and more tender flesh. A five-pound pumpkin yields about 4½ cups of mashed or pureed cooked pumpkin. A one-pound can of pumpkin yields about 2 cups.

In the Kitchen

STORING At home, store winter squash in a paper bag in the refrigerator for up to a week. Some squash, such as hubbard and butternut, will keep for several weeks stored in a cool, dry place. Pumpkins can be stored in the refrigerator or at cool room temperature for up to three months. Once a pumpkin is cut open, however, it should be used immediately.

PREP To prepare winter squash, use a large chef's knife or cleaver to split the vegetable in half. You can use a paring knife or heavy-duty vegetable peeler to remove the skin on smooth squash, if necessary. It's nearly impossible to peel acorn squash and other ridged squash. Remove seeds and fibrous pulp. Cut flesh into small pieces. Use a sharp paring knife to peel.

BASIC COOKING Winter squash can be baked, steamed, boiled, stewed, or cooked in a microwave oven. A quick way to prepare any type of winter squash for a simple side dish is to bake it. Halve the squash lengthwise, scoop out and discard the seeds, and place, flesh-side down, in a lightly greased baking pan. Bake at 400°F degrees until very tender (a fork or

VARIETIES

Acorn squash is small- to medium-sized, acorn-shaped, with dark green, orange, green and orange, or white, deeply ridged skin. Its yellow flesh is sweet and moist. Acorn squash are best baked.

Banana squash is large and long, with yellow skin and orange flesh. Blue- and pink-skinned bananas are also grown in home gardens.

Buttercup squash is small to medium in size, drum-shaped, with dark green skin marked with gray. Its orange flesh is dense, dry, and sweet.

Butternut squash is medium-sized and shaped like a big peanut. It has smooth tan or yellow-orange skin. Its bright orange flesh is mildly sweet.

Delicata squash is small to medium, elongated, and has cream-colored skin striped with orange or green. Unlike other winter squash, its skin is edible, its flesh is creamy, and its sweet corn-like flavor is very delicate.

Hubbard squash is large with dusty blue-green, warty, faintly ridged skin. Its yellow-orange flesh is dry and slightly bland in flavor.

Golden hubbards have dark orange skin and slightly sweeter flesh.

Kabocha squash is a medium-sized Japanese hybrid, shaped like a flattened globe, with dark green, bumpy skin. Its orange flesh is dense, dry, and very sweet.

Pumpkins for eating are round, ridged, and have dark orange skin. Their flesh is not as sweet as that of some other winter squash.

Spaghetti squash is medium-sized, oblong, with smooth yellow skin. After boiling or baking the squash whole, it is halved, and the flesh is pulled out with a fork into spaghetti-like strands that are crunchy and rather bland.

Sweet dumpling squash are very small— each squash is an individual serving. Their skin is yellow with dark green strips, and their flesh is yellow-orange, sweet, and moist. Sweet dumplings are best baked.

Turban squash has bright orange-red skin and a decorative, turbanlike topknot. It is a relative of the buttercup squash, with dry, mildly sweet flesh.

---

toothpick inserted into the flesh through the skin moves easily in and out), about 45 minutes to 1 hour, depending on the size of the squash. Slice or cut into smaller pieces to serve.

To steam winter squash, place cut pieces on a steamer in a large covered pot. Cover and cook over boiling water until tender, 45 to 50 minutes. To boil, place squash pieces in lightly salted water to cover. Bring to a boil and cook until tender, 20 to 25 minutes. Let cool. Use a blender, food processor, food mill, or potato masher to puree the squash. Fresh squash puree can be used in any recipe calling for pumpkin puree. Or simply season it with butter, salt, and pepper, and serve it as a vegetable side dish.

Use smaller pumpkins, called sugar pumpkins, for eating. These pumpkins can be used to make pies, breads, muffins, griddle cakes, and soups, as well as savory side dishes.

PREPARING WINTER SQUASH

With a knife, cut off stem and halve lengthwise. With a spoon, scoop out all the seeds.
1

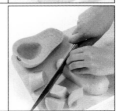
Cut the halves lengthwise into quarters and then cut the flesh into chunks.
2

A Glossary of Good Nutrition

Refer to this mini-dictionary when you come across diet and nutrition terms in this book that you don't understand.

ANTIOXIDANT: This term refers to certain vitamins and other substances in plant foods that help prevent disease by fighting off toxic substances in the body known as free radicals, and repairing the cell damage they cause.

BETA-CAROTENE: A member of a family of substances known as carotenoids, beta-carotene is the pigment that gives orange color to carrots, sweet potatoes, winter squash, and other fruits and vegetables. It is also found in dark green vegetables, but its color is obscured by the green color of chlorophyll found in those vegetables. Beta-carotene is converted to vitamin A in your body and also functions as an antioxidant to help the body fight cancer and other chronic disease.

CAPSAICIN: This phytochemical is found in all peppers but is most heavily concentrated in hot (chile) peppers. Capsaicin may protect against chronic diseases such as cancer and prevent blood clots.

CARBOHYDRATES: The major components of foods are carbohydrates, protein, and fat. Carbohydrates are either starches or sugars and are found in all plant foods—vegetables, grains, legumes, and fruits. Foods that are high in carbohydrates are our main source of energy and, when carefully selected, can also be our best source of certain essential vitamins and minerals.

CARCINOGEN: A substance that causes the growth of cancer cells.

CAROTENOIDS: This is a family of more than 600 phytochemicals responsible for the yellow, orange, and red pigments found in vegetables and fruits. Some carotenoids, such as lutein and lycopene, function as antioxidants or have other disease-fighting properties. The antioxidant beta-carotene is the best-known member of the carotenoid family.

CHOLESTEROL: This is a waxy, fatlike substance present in every cell in animals, including humans. Cholesterol is essential to many body functions, including the production of vitamin D, essential skin oils, and hormones. Excess cholesterol in the blood can adhere to artery walls, forming a substance called plaque that contributes to hardening of the arteries and, ultimately, heart disease.

CRUCIFEROUS VEGETABLES: This family of vegetables, including cabbage, broccoli, Brussels sprouts, cauliflower, and leafy greens, contains phytochemicals known as indoles that help protect against cancer.

FLAVONOIDS: These phytochemicals are found in broccoli, carrots, onions, soybeans, and other foods. They are the same phytochemicals that are thought to give red wine and tea their antioxidant potential to help reduce the risk of heart disease.

FREE RADICALS: These unstable compounds form in the body during normal metabolism and also result from other factors such as environmental pollution, radiation, smoking cigarettes, and drinking alcohol. Free radicals set up a chain reaction of events that lead to cell destruction and potentially cause cancer. Antioxidants found in vegetables and fruit help the body repair damage done by free radicals.

HOMOCYSTEINE: People with elevated levels of this amino acid in their blood are at increased risk of developing heart disease. Vitamins B_6, B_{12}, and folate help convert homocysteine into a nondestructive form.

INDOLES: Cruciferous vegetables such as cabbage, cauliflower, and Brussels sprouts contain this phytochemical, which is thought to be protective against hormone-sensitive diseases such as breast cancer.

ISOFLAVONES: These are phytochemicals in soybeans and other legumes that are called phytoestrogens—plant substances that mimic estrogen's action in the body and may protect against heart disease and hormone-sensitive cancers.

ISOTHIOCYANATES: These are phytochemicals found in cruciferous vegetables such as broccoli and cauliflower that stimulate cancer-fighting enzymes in the body.

LEGUMES: All beans, peas, lentils, and peanuts are in the legume family. That makes them good plant sources of protein and iron, nutrients more often associated with animal foods. They are also good sources of B vitamins and fiber.

LUTEIN: This carotenoid is found in avocado, kale, spinach, parsley, red peppers, and other vegetables and fruit. Lutein is thought to protect against age-related blindness resulting from macular degeneration.

LYCOPENE: This carotenoid is found in tomatoes, tomato products such as paste and sauce, watermelon, pink grapefruit, and other fruits and vegetables. Studies have found that lycopene may be protective against prostate cancer and other chronic diseases.

PECTIN: This soluble fiber, found in many fruits, vegetables, and legumes, helps lower cholesterol and regulate intestinal function.

PHYTOCHEMICALS: These plant substances help boost immunity and fight chronic disease such as cancer and heart disease.

PHYTOESTROGENS: These phytochemicals, found in soybeans and other legumes, mimic the action of the estrogen produced by the human body. Because of this action, phytoestrogens may help protect against heart disease and hormone-sensitive cancers such as breast cancer.

PHYTONUTRIENTS: These phytochemicals have nutritional value in addition to disease-fighting capabilities.

RESVERATROL: This phytochemical helps lower cholesterol and protect against heart disease.

SULFORAPHANE: Broccoli, cabbage, and Brussels sprouts contain this phytochemical, which stimulates the production of anticancer enzymes.

ZEAXANTHIN: This carotenoid, found in broccoli and kale, helps prevent age-related blindness due to macular degeneration.

Vegetable Freezing Chart

Vegetables that are to be frozen are always thoroughly cleaned and trimmed, and most are precooked by blanching in boiling water. Not all vegetables freeze successfully. Asparagus, for instance, breaks down and becomes limp and watery when thawed. Other vegetables that freeze poorly include beets, whole or cut-up carrots, cauliflower, cucumber, eggplant, fennel, salad greens, leeks, potatoes, radishes, zucchini, and other summer squash. Following are instructions for handling those vegetables that freeze well.

BEANS, GREEN	Blanch trimmed beans 3 minutes per pound. Cool completely in ice water. Drain well and place in freezer container.	Use within 12 months
BROCCOLI	Blanch bite-size pieces of broccoli for 3 minutes. Cool completely in ice water. Drain well and place in freezer container.	Use within 12 months
BRUSSELS SPROUTS	Blanch trimmed sprouts for 3 to 5 minutes, depending on the size of the head. Cool completely in ice water. Drain well and pack into freezer container.	Use within 12 months
CARROTS	Cook carrots completely and puree before freezing. (Whole and cut-up carrots do not freeze well.) Cool completely before packing into freezer container.	Use within 6 months
CORN	Blanch whole ears for 4 to 8 minutes, depending on the size of the ear. Cool completely in ice water. Cut off kernels or leave ears whole and pack into freezer container.	Use within 6 months
GREENS, COOKING	Blanch whole leaves for 2 minutes. Cool completely in ice water. Drain well and pack into freezer container.	Use within 6 months
OKRA	Blanch trimmed, whole okra pods for 4 minutes. Cool completely in ice water. Drain well and pack into freezer container.	Use within 6 months
ONIONS	Pack raw, finely chopped onions, scallions, or chives loosely in freezer container.	Use within 6 months
PARSNIPS	Cook parsnips completely and puree before freezing. (Whole and cut-up parsnips do not freeze well.) Cool completely before packing into freezer container.	Use within 6 months
PEAS	Blanch shelled peas for 2 minutes. Cool completely in ice water. Drain well and loosely pack in freezer container.	Use within 12 months
	Blanch sugar snap peas for 2 minutes. Cool completely in ice water. Drain well. Place in single layer on a baking sheet or tray. Freeze, then pack frozen peas into freezer container.	Use within 9 months
PEPPERS	Pack finely chopped, raw peppers in freezer container.	Use within 12 months
PUMPKIN	Cook pumpkin completely and puree before freezing. Cool completely before packing into freezer container.	Use within 6 months
SPINACH	Blanch whole leaves for 2 minutes. Cool completely in ice water. Drain well and pack in freezer container.	Use within 6 months
SQUASH, WINTER	Cook squash completely and puree before freezing. Cool completely before packing into freezer container.	Use within 6 months
SWEET POTATOES	Cook sweet potatoes completely and puree before freezing. Cool completely before packing into freezer container.	Use within 6 months
TOMATOES	Blanch whole tomatoes for 2 minutes. Cool completely in ice water. Drain well and freeze for later use in cooking. Tomato sauce also freezes well.	Use within 12 months
TURNIPS and RUTABAGAS	Cook turnips or rutabagas completely and mash or puree before freezing. Cool completely before packing into freezer container.	Use within 6 months

Index

Note: Page numbers in *italic* indicate photographs; those in **boldface** indicate tables.

VEGETABLES FOR VITALITY

VEGETABLES FOR VITALITY

VEGETABLES FOR VITALITY

conversion CHARTS

Baking Pan Sizes

U.S.	Metric
8 x 1 1/2-inch round baking pan	20 x 4 cm-cake tin
9 x 1 1/2-inch round baking pan	23 x 3.5-cm cake tin
11 x 7 x 1 1/2-inch baking pan	28 x 18 x 4-cm baking tin
13 x 9 x 2-inch baking pan	30 x 20 x 3-cm baking tin
2-quart rectangular baking dish	30 x 20 x 3-cm baking tin
15 x 10 x 1-inch baking pan	30 x 25 x 2-cm baking tin (Swiss roll tin)
9-inch pie plate	22 x 4- or 23 x 4-cm pie plate
7- or 8-inch springform pan	18- or 20-cm springform or loose-bottom tin
9 x 5 x 3-inch loaf pan	23 x13-7-cm or 2-pound narrow loaf tin
1 1/2-quart casserole	1.5-liter casserole
2-quart casserole	2-liter casserole

Metric Abbreviations

mm = millimeter

cm = centimeter

m = meter

in = inch

ft = foot

ml = milliliter

l = liter

tsp = teaspoon

tbsp = tablespoon

oz = ounce

fl oz = fluid ounce

qt = quart

gal = gallon

g = gram

kg = kilogram

lb = pound

C = Celsius

F = Fahrenheit

Temperature

Fahrenheit	Celsius	
0°F =	-18°C	(freezer temperature)
32°F =	0°C	(water freezes)
180°F =	82°C	(water simmers)
212°F =	100°C	(water boils)
250°F =	120°C	(low oven)
350°F =	175°C	(moderate oven)
425°F =	220°C	(hot oven)
500°F =	260°C	(very hot oven)

Length

U.S.	U.K./Australia
1/2 inch	=1.3 centimeters
1 inch	= 2.5 centimeters
12 inches =1 foot	= 30 centimeters
39 inches	=1 meter

USEFUL INGREDIENT SUBSTITUTIONS

Instead of: 1 teaspoon lemon juice
  Use: 1/4 teaspoon vinegar

Instead of: 2 cups tomato sauce
  Use: 3/4 cup tomato paste plus 1 cup water

Instead of: 1 square unsweetened chocolate
  Use: 3 tablespoons unsweeteened cocoa plus one tablespoon butter

Instead of: 1 cup sifted cake flour
  Use: 7/8 cup all-purpose flour (1 cup minus 2 tablespoons)

Instead of: 1 cup packed brown sugar
  Use: 1 cup granulated sugar plus 2 tablespoons molasses

Instead of: 1 cup honey
  Use: 1 1/4 cups sugar plus 1/4 cup of liquid from recipe

Instead of: 1 cup buttermilk
  Use: 1 tablespoon vinegar plus enough milk to make 1 cup